Andreas Schertzinger

Creating Value in Insurance Mergers and Acquisitions

GABLER EDITION WISSENSCHAFT

Andreas Schertzinger

Creating Value in Insurance Mergers and Acquisitions

With a foreword by Prof. Dr. Dirk Schiereck

GABLER EDITION WISSENSCHAFT

Bibliographic information published by the Deutsche Nationalbibliothek
The Deutsche Nationalbibliothek lists this publication in the Deutsche Nationalbibliografie; detailed bibliographic data are available in the Internet at http://dnb.d-nb.de.

Dissertation European Business School Oestrich-Winkel, 2008

D 1540

1st Edition 2009

Editorial Office: Frauke Schindler / Britta Göhrisch-Radmacher

Gabler is part of the specialist publishing group Springer Science+Business Media.
www.gabler.de

Cover design: Regine Zimmer, Dipl.-Designerin, Frankfurt/Main
Printed on acid-free paper
Printed in Germany

ISBN 978-3-8349-1454-5

Foreword

This thesis takes up a very acutely relevant topic: „Do M&A transactions in the European insurance sector create value in the short- and long-term?" After national consolidation of the European banking and insurance markets had progressed in the 2nd half of the 1990s, the recent years showed an increasing amount of cross-border M&A especially in the banking sector. This development is surprising in light of the M&A paradox, according to which the rate of successful bank transactions is very low, yet the number of size of completed transactions constantly increases.

The current empirical evidence gives reason to devote a comprehensive academic analysis to M&A in the European insurance industry. Furthermore, research to this topic area shows a significant industry-specific gap and largely an absence of respective empirical studies. Research concerned with the overall success of European M&A transactions are extremely rare to date, and the state of knowledge on the success of cross-border transactions in the European insurance industry are very limited.

The primary objective of this thesis was therefore to determine the success of European insurance transactions not only on a short-term basis on market data, but also to analyze the success in the mid- and long-term based on market-oriented performance studies. This cross-sectional analysis is deepened by case studies of insurance transactions, which allow for a detailed analysis of value creation and of the underlying success factors. Only this integrated perspective through a combination of methodologies could answer the question of the actual value creation through M&A transactions in the European insurance industry and derive profound recommendations for action for the insurance practices.

Mr. Schertzinger exceeds the high aimed aspirations in this thesis. His thesis contains a plenitude of highly interesting results and is written so that readers will enjoy reading it. I wish the thesis a wide distribution.

Prof. Dr. Dirk Schiereck

Overview of Contents

Table of Contents

List of Figures

List of Tables

List of Abbreviations

AR	American Re
BAHR	Buy-and-hold abnormal return
bn	Billion
bp	Basis points
CAR	Cumulative abnormal return
CEA	Comité européen des assurances
CER	Combined entity return
CGNU	Commercial and General Norwich Union
CGU	Commercial and General Union
CTAR	Calendar time abnormal return
EC	European Commission
EEA	European Economic Area
EMU	European Monetary Union
EU	European Union
EUR	Euro
GBP	British Pound
M&A	Merger & Acquisitions
mn	Million
MR	Munich Re
n/a	Not available
No.	Number
NU	Norwich Union
OECD	Organisation for Economic Co-operation and Development
OLS	Ordinary least squares
P&C	Property & Casualty
p.a.	Per annum
SIC	Standard Industry Classification
USD	United States Dollar

1 Introduction

The European insurance sector went through a radical transformation, which began in the 1990s and is still continuing. Deregulation, implementation of the EMU, progress in information and communication technology, and economic forces such as favorable financial markets, highlighted solvency concerns and soft insurance markets drove the transformation process.[1] Regulatory harmonization took a quantum leap with the introduction of the Third Generation Insurance Directives for life and non-life insurance in 1992, which for example eliminated price and product regulations, ensured cross-recognition of licenses and restrictted host country control to solvency requirements.[2]

European insurers reacted promptly. Dealogic reports 779 completed insurance M&A transactions with European acquirers in the years 1995 to 2005. While the number of insurance companies operating in the EU-25 decreased only slightly from 5,083 in 1993 to 4.933 in 2004, the market share of the 10 largest life and non-life insurers increased remarkably from 49.5% to 75.1%, and 59.0% to 80.6% respectively.[3]

M&A activity of European insurers reached its peak in 1999 with 102 transactions and a total disclosed transaction volume of USD 38 bn,[4] but was continuously declining thereafter. Beginning in 2005, the M&A market gained momentum again. Although the number of transactions increased only slightly compared to the previous year, the average transaction volume per deal rose from USD 0.3 bn to USD 0.8 bn. But is this pickup in activity merely a blip in

1 Swiss Re (1999a and 2000), and OECD (2000a).

2 OECD (2000b). Later directives brought European operating environment further into line, e.g. the Insurance Group Directive in 1998 (OECD, 1998), and the Reinsurance Directive in 2005 (European Commission, 2005). Reformation of EU regulation affected Switzerland and Norway as well, since both adopted elements (OECD 2001a, p. 126 and 172).

3 CEA (2006).

4 Transaction volume available only for 51 out of 102 transactions.

the market, or does it mark the entry into the next cycle of transactions? In order to answer this question, chapter 2 identifies drivers and hurdles of further consolidation in the European insurance industry, and builds hypotheses on the direction of future M&A activity. The analyses show that although concentration especially in the European primary insurance sector is already high, again M&A is likely to catalyze investors' pressure on management to create value.

This finding confronts with a paradox: Empirical studies of M&A in the financial services industry frequently doubt value creation, in particular in the banking industry.[5] Despite the current relevancy for the European insurance sector, little empirical research addressed the question of value creation by M&A in this industry. Firstly, prior research on short-term cumulative abnormal returns (CARs) of investors in acquirers or targets indicates that value creation by U.S. and European insurance M&A differs substantially.[6] Thus, findings of U.S.-focused event studies with respect to abnormal returns of combined entities (CERs)[7] may not hold for European markets. Unfortunately, the only studies on the European insurance market either do not analyze CERs at all[8] or cover Europe only as one of many regions with insufficient observations for detailed market-specific analyses.[9] Secondly, these studies limit their analysis on determinants of value creation on few univariate comparisons of cross-sections, and do not carry out a multivariate analysis, which is necessary to properly separate effects of several determinants on abnormal returns. Thirdly, further on, long-term value creation for European insurers has – to the best of the author's knowledge – never been investigated before.

For the industry, investors but also regulators, this gap in empirical evidence reinforces the pressing question: Does M&A in the European insurance industry create value, and what are major determinants of success? Chapter 4 answers this question by analyzing short- and long-term capital market reactions

5 See overviews in Beitel and Schiereck (2003), and Pilloff and Santomero (1998).

6 Cummins and Weiss (2004) obtain significantly negative acquirer CARs on their European sample, whereas all other studies on the U.S. or global market report significantly positive acquirer CARs.

7 Akhigbe and Madura (2001) and Cummins and Xie (2005) observe significantly positive CERs.

8 Cummins and Weiss (2004) only present evidence on acquirer and target CARs.

9 Floreani and Rigamonti (2001) include N = 16 transactions of European bidders in their analysis of CERs and thus do not analyze the European market in detail.

and their determinants to announcements of M&A by European insurance companies between 1990 and 2005. Chapter 3 reviews the required event study methodology.

For the industry, it is of additional relevance to understand whether the influence of determinants of value creation depends on the time horizon of the analysis. If this is the case, management needs to either choose a strategy according to its strategic time horizon, or invest further into adequate capital market communication. For investors, it is of further importance to understand whether long-term value creation depends on short-term capital market reactions. If this is the case, investors could derive insights for their mid-term investment strategy from announcement effects.[10] Chapter 4 concludes with an investigation of these questions.

A comparison of the outcome of the above analyses on determinants of value creation by M&A with previous studies points out that further research is indispensable. Previous research mostly examines different sets of determinants, and often obtains contradictory results for those determinants included in several studies. For example, Floreani and Rigamonti (2001) find on their U.S.-dominated sample that in the short-term, fully diversifying transaction strategies pay off for investors in the combined entity, but Cummins and Xie (2005) find on their U.S. sample that any geographical or industry diversification is significantly worse than full geographical and industry focus.

Therefore, recent studies on value creation in M&A turned from analyzing large samples to studying individual cases[11] in search for a rationale. The case study methodology enhances event study approaches by attaching greater importance to a "process perspective".[12] The term "process" refers to the transaction parties' conduct during transaction and post-acquisition integration, which is thought to influence realization of value potential.[13] However, previous research on value creation by insurance M&A does not apply case study methodology to transactions.

10 Further on, inference on adequacy or stickiness of investors' initial assessment of M&A announcement can be drawn.

11 Calomiris and Karceski (1998), Pilloff and Santomero (1998), Calomiris (1999) employ case study techniques to analyze efficiency gains of and value creation from bank mergers.

12 See Jemison and Sitkin (1986).

13 See Pablo et al. (1996).

Chapter 5 fills this gap by examining the question: How do motives for M&A manifest in individual transactions, and how does the conduct of these transactions influence realization of associated benefits? Two prominent cases, Munich Re's acquisition of American Re (1996), and CGU's merger with Norwich Union to form Aviva (2000), are selected due to their focus on long-tail business, exceeding the time horizon even of long-term event studies, and diametrically opposed value creation. The case studies test hypotheses for sources of value creation, identify process-related determinants of value creation and discuss these in light of determinants isolated in the event study.

In summary, this study analyzes value creation by European Insurance M&A. Chapter 2 provides evidence for the relevancy of this subject. The Industry is about to enter a new M&A cycle. Chapter 3 reviews event study methodologies for analysis of capital market reactions to M&A announcement. Chapter 4 utilizes selected methodologies to analyze value creation by M&A and its determinants based on the previous M&A cycle between 1990 and 2005. The association between short- and long-term value creation is examined from an industry and an investor perspective. Chapter 5 studies two transactions to test occurrence of motives of M&A and analyze determinants of success in greater detail from a process perspective. Chapter 6 summarizes the findings on value creation by European insurance M&A, and proposes subjects for further research on an industry and a firm level.

2 Overview of M&A in the European Insurance Industry

2.1 Objectives

M&A activity in the European insurance sector increased sharply in the early 1990s. Dealogic reports 49 completed insurance M&A transactions with European acquirers for the year 1995, with a total disclosed deal volume of USD 7.4 bn.[14] For the next four years, the number and disclosed volume of transactions rose by 20% and 50%, respectively. Regulatory harmonization, particularly the introduction of the Third Generation Insurance Directives for life and non-life insurance in 1992[15] was the major driver[16] behind this pickup in M&A momentum.

After reaching its peak in 1999, the European insurance M&A market entered a phase of depression. In 2004, number and volume of transactions had returned to 1995 level.[17] However, momentum was building up again in 2005, indicated by a strong increase of average transaction volume from USD 0.3 bn in the two previous years to USD 0.8 bn. The objective of this chapter is to investigate whether this pickup in activity should be considered a blip, or whether it marks the entry into the next cycle of transactions in the European insurance industry. The chapter is structured as follows.

---

14 Transaction volume available only for 20 out of 49 transactions.

15 These directives for example eliminated price and product regulations, ensured cross-recognition of licenses and restricted host country control to solvency requirements, see OECD (2000b).

16 Other factors include implementation of the EMU, progress in information and communication technology, and economic forces such as favorable financial markets, highlighted solvency concerns and soft insurance markets, see Swiss Re (1999a and 2000), and OECD (2000a).

17 Dealogic records 56 transactions and a disclosed transaction volume of USD 6.5 bn (based on 22 transactions).

Section 2.2 provides a brief summary on types of M&A and the typical transaction process. The discussion shall familiarize the interested reader with basic aspects of M&A. Further on, the presented frameworks provide the basis for the analysis of the transaction structure and the transaction process in the case studies in chapter 5. Section 2.3 gives an overview of the M&A market in the European insurance industry. Further on, evidence on current market consolidation is presented, and drivers and hurdles for European insurance M&A are systematized. Section 2.4 employs this framework to develop hypotheses on sources and direction of further M&A activity. Section 2.5 summarizes the above findings to conclude on the question whether the observed upswing indicates a new wave of transactions.

2.2 Overview of M&A

2.2.1 Definition

This section provides a brief introduction on the topic of M&A in general; readers familiar with the topic may continue with section 2.3. The term M&A refers to transactions in the market for companies, portfolios of companies' assets, shares in companies and participations, and to the business segment of professsional services firms or banks who consult transaction parties.[18] Academic literature provides a variety of definitions in the context of the former notion.

Khemani and Shapiro compiled definitions in OECD (1993) and characterize a merger as "an amalgamation or joining of two or more firms into an existing firm or to form a new firm", and an acquisition as "obtaining ownership and control by one firm, in whole or in part, of another firm or business entity". Thus, an acquisition does not necessarily entail combining operations of the target with the operations of the acquirer. The European Union Merger Regulation[19] picks up Khemani and Shapiro's notion that acquisition refers only to increasing

18 Achleitner (1999, p. 141).
19 European Council (2004, Art. 3 (1)).

control, whereas merger emphasizes additionally the combination of operations.[20]

In the context of this study, M&A is interpreted in a narrower sense.[21] The data sample underlying the empirical analyses of value creation in chapter 4 includes only those M&A transactions which lead to a change of control, i.e. the initial stake of the acquirer in the target before the transaction was smaller than 50%, and the final stake after the transaction is higher than 50%. Further on, portfolio transactions[22] are excluded from the analyses. Both definitions of M&A give rise to the question on how individual transactions can be systematized along few, most relevant dimensions. The following section discusses typical categorizations of transactions.

2.2.2 Types of transactions

Prior academic literature discusses a variety of systematizations for types of M&A. Figure 1 summarizes typical dimensions for classification of transactions. It shall be noted, that some of the dimensions are not mutually exclusive. For example, direction and industry focus are interdependent.

The most relevant dimensions for this study are *direction*, *geographic focus*, *industry focus*, and *instruments* of transactions. With respect to *direction*, transactions can be classified into horizontal, vertical and lateral (or conglomerate) deals.[23] If the acquirer and the target operate in the same industry and production stage, a transaction involving both parties is considered horizontal. An example from the insurance industry is an acquisition of a life-insurer by another life-insurer.

---

20 The corresponding U.S. horizontal merger guidelines (U.S. Department of Justice and the Federal Trade Commission, 1997) do not provide a definition.

21 Picot (2002, p. 19) even extends the definition of M&A by further corporate events such as IPOs, Joint Ventures and Cooperations. Beitel (2002, p. 8) provides an overview of typical definitions.

22 Section 2.2.2 defines and discusses portfolio transactions in detail.

23 See e.g., Achleitner (1999, p. 142).

Dimension	Characteristics
Competitive impact	Beneficial, neutral, limiting
Direction	Horizontal, vertical, lateral
Duration	Temporary, indefinite
Geographic focus	Within-country, cross-border, transcontinental
Industry focus	Within-industry, cross-industry
Institutionalization	Without own operations, with own operations
Instruments	Contract, linkage of personnel, equity deal, asset deal
Intensity	Limited independence, eliminated independence
Mode	Friendly, hostile
Payment	Cash, shares, other
Range	Sub-function related, function related, company related
Relation of partners	Co-ordinated, subordinated
Status	Announced, pending, completed, withdrawn

Source: Pausenberger (1993, Sp. 4438), own research.

Figure 1: Typical dimensions for classification of M&A

Transactions across industries but in the same production stage are referred to as lateral or conglomerate transactions.[24] Settnik (2006, p. 37) emphasizes that certain insurance sectors may only operate in independent legal entities, so that conglomerate M&A transactions in these sectors are only indirectly feasible through a holding company acquiring insurers operating in different industries.

If the acquirer and the target conduct business in the same industry but operate in directly succeeding (forward-integration) or preceding (backward-integration) production stages, a transaction between both parties is named vertical. An example for forward-integration from a primary insurer's perspective is

24 Issues with respect to exact demarcation of these transactions exist especially with respect to the distinction between horizontal and conglomerate mergers, since classification heavily depends on the precise definition of the industry classes, see e.g., Paprottka (1996, p. 11).

its acquisition of a reinsurer. Besides economies of scale for the reinsurer, this transaction internalizes margins of reinsurance coverage bought by the direct insurer. An example for backward-integration is the acquisition of a distribution channel by a direct insurer in order to secure and better steer product distribution.

The direction of a transaction is relevant for this study, since it is an important indicator for transaction motives: Horizontal transactions are a potential source of economies of scale, and lateral transactions may give rise to economies of scope. Vertical transactions are typically conducted for strategic reasons. Section 2.3.2 discusses drivers of transactions in detail.

Besides direction of a transaction, the *geographic focus* and *industry focus* are important dimensions for empirical analyses of value creation by M&A, since they are closely linked with the direction of a transaction. Thus, previous research on value creation frequently analyzes these dimensions: Four out of five short-term event studies on insurance M&A analyze geographical strategies, three out of five short-term studies examine industry strategies, and the only long-term study discusses both dimensions. This study implements a cross-sectional analyses on both dimensions as well, see chapter 4.

The dimension *instrument* captures how control is acquired. Transactions where the acquirer buys shares of the target are referred to as equity deals. Transactions where assets of the target are transferred are called asset deals.[25] The third type of instrument, "portfolio transaction",[26] is specific for the insurance industry. Koch and Weiss (1994) define a portfolio transaction as a contract under which the entire or part of the in-force business is transferred from an insurance company to another insurance company. In-force business in this context is understood as all underwritten and still running policies, i.e. including related technical provisions, provisions for unearned premiums, and investments allocated to these policies. Settnik (2006, pp. 61) discusses general conditions, such as regulatory aspects of portfolio transactions in the German jurisdiction in de-

25 See Berens (1998, p. 23), and Picot (1995, p. 10).
26 Other common terms are e.g., closed-book or run-off portfolio acquisition.

tail. Motives for carrying out portfolio transactions differ from motives for other transactions,[27] therefore these deals are excluded from the empirical analyses.

Beyond these structural properties of M&A, recent empirical research on the success of such transactions attach ever greater importance to aspects regarding the M&A process.[28] For this reason, this study explicitly includes case study research into the range of utilized empirical analysis approaches, see chapter 5. The following chapter lays out a basic framework to systematize transaction processes into their typical elements.

2.2.3 The transaction process

The M&A transaction process can be subdivided into three phases: Planning, transaction, and integration, whereas transaction may be further separated into first round bid, second round bid, and closing. Figure 2 presents major buy-side activities in the individual stages of this process, based on discussions by Toole and Herget (2005, pp. 27) and Achleitner (1999, p. 153).

In the planning phase, an insurance firm firstly determines its growth strategy based on geographical, industry or product growth targets. Secondly, it decides whether to grow organically or through M&A. In the latter case, the potential acquirer identifies preliminary targets and assembles a deal team comprised of financial advisors, legal counsel on corporate law and taxation, accountants and actuaries. Based on outside-in information, it carries out a rough valuation of the stand-alone target and synergy effects from a possible combination of the target's with its own operations.

The transaction phase begins with the first round bid. The potential acquirer contacts its potential targets[29] and the involved parties agree on the modus operandi, establish operative working arrangements, and sign confidentiality agree-

27 Acquirers seek to maximize run-off profits by efficiently managing the remaining book of business. The choice between equity and asset deal however should not influence value creation of a transaction, see Beitel (2002, p. 13).

28 See Jemison and Sitkin (1986).

29 In case of an active selling strategy, targets or their divesting parent companies would identify and contact potential acquirers.

Planning	Transaction			Integration
	First round bid	Second round bid	Closing	
• Decide on growth strategy • Decide on M&A strategy • Identify targets • Assemble deal team • First (outside-in) valuation	• Contact target, establish working arrangements • Agree on confidentiality and prepare contingency plan • Develop non-binding offer including synergy valuation and assessment of benefits and risks • Initiate dialogue with regulators • Prepare non-binding offer including questions regarding due-diligence	• Conduct due-diligence (request list, data room) • Revise estimates in non-binding offer • Prepare deal structure, financing alternatives and assess core aspects of post-merger integration • Develop binding offer	• Prepare negotiation process • Set-up negotiation team and prepare negotiation tactics • Start post-merger integration preparation • Closing of transaction including regulatory agreement and public announcement	• Launch integration project • Closely monitor progress and achievement of planned impact/ synergies

Source: Own research

Figure 2: Overview of the transaction process

ments. For acquirer and target it is equally important to prepare contingency plans in case information is leaked. Afterwards, the seller provides the potential acquirer with a confidential information memorandum, a rather fact based, detailed report on the seller and the industry it operates in. Financial advisors of the target prepare an accompanying bid process letter, laying out the general bidding process (e.g., mode and timeline) and preliminary aspects of the deal structure. Afterwards, the acquirer develops a non-binding offer, containing a more detailed valuation of the stand-alone target entity, estimate of synergy potentials, and assessment of restructuring costs. The acquirer then conducts a first review of financing options, and develops core aspects of the deal structure, e.g., governance after transaction, acquiring vehicle, legal, taxation, and accounting issues. Already at this point in time, involved parties may initiate a dialogue with regulators, especially if concerns regarding antitrust or insurance regulation exist. This phase is concluded with the preparation of the non-binding offer, including the proposed deal structure, indicative valuation, underlying assumptions, and core questions to be resolved through due diligence in the second round bid. Simultaneously, the seller begins to build a data room for the due diligence and, especially in case of long-tail business, involves independent actuaries for appraisal and reserve review.

Due diligence is the first step of the second round bid.[30] Based on the more detailed information available in the data room, the acquirer's deal team revises first round estimates and proposals, especially their assessment of value and risk. After board approval of the revised offer, the deal financing is detailed, and core aspects of post-merger integration, e.g., organization, compensation and other personnel topics, are outlined. The second round bid phase concludes with the creation of the binding offer, comprising a bid letter, financing letter, and a sale and purchase agreement.

In the last step of the transaction phase, the closing, involved parties firstly setup negotiation teams, prepare the negotiation content (e.g., value of strategic options for involved parties, sensitivity of valuation to assumptions), and negotiation tactics. At the same time, sell and buy-side start to setup the governance and the timeline for the post-merger management. If negotiations are closed successfully, the transactions partners discuss the transaction and specific conditions with regulators, e.g., the responsible insurance supervisory authorities, anti-trust authorities, and exchange supervisory authorities. As a result, the transaction may be accepted as proposed, may be subject to further obligations or conditions, or may be rejected entirely. After acceptance of regulators, the deal is announced to the public, detailed information is provided to employees, and agreement of shareholders is advertised.

As a final step, the post-merger management process is initiated. Strict controlling of achievement of milestones and realization of benefits, and early identification and management of integration risks are of particular importance. After this brief conceptual overview on M&A transactions in general, the following section shall now begin the analysis of the European insurance M&A market by examining current consolidation levels in the insurance industry, systematizing rationale for insurance M&A and developing hypotheses on further transactions in the European insurance market.

---

30 See e.g., Pack (2002) for a detailed discussion of due diligence.

2.3 M&A in the European insurance industry

2.3.1 *Status of consolidation*

Consolidation of an industry may be analyzed from different perspectives. A review of related literature in the insurance industry shows that consolidation and the related terms integration and concentration can be defined as a process or a status

- *Process:* OECD (1993) state that consolidation generally refers to the process of combination or merging. The European Council (2004, Article 3) defines concentration as mergers of previously independent undertakings or acquisitions of indirect or direct control, where control changes on a lasting basis.
- *Status:* OECD (1993) defines concentration as "the extent to which a small number of firms or enterprises account for a large portion of economic activity such as total sales, assets or employment." They distinguish aggregate, market (seller), buyer and ownership concentration. With respect to integration, the European Commission (2007b) mentions "level of penetration of the EU insurance markets by foreign (EU) insurers and the corresponding possibility for consumers to access foreign insurers" as one important indicator. CEA (2006, p. 21) discusses integration based on concentration measures.

This section focuses on the status of consolidation and its development in recent years, and presents evidence on concentration and integration of the European insurance industry. Both are equally relevant to gain insights on current and future M&A activity in the market: Transparency on market concentration allows assessing general potential for further M&A within or across markets, possibly limited by antitrust concerns. Analysis of market integration provides insights on the particular importance of M&A across markets.

A clear definition of the relevant market, measurement methodology and underlying measure is crucial for adequately capturing market concentration and integration. The U.S. Department of Justice and the Federal Trade Commission

(1997) emphasize the importance of the geographical and product dimension to demarcate markets for the analysis of concentration in the context of antitrust regulation. In the insurance industry, both dimensions are interdependent: Primary insurance shows a strong national tendency, whereas reinsurance is a global business. The European Commission (2007b, pp. 39) in their recent sector inquiry[31] on primary business insurance[32] discusses prominence of primary insurers on the country level, despite the emergence of "European insurers".[33] In contrast, Cummins and Weiss (2000) and Swiss Re (2003) analyze consolidation of reinsurance providers in the "global reinsurance market", and Standard & Poor's annually publishes a report on the "global reinsurance sector". This study follows these market definitions for the analysis of concentration and integration.

For the measurement of market concentration, industrial organization economics provides a multitude of approaches, which can be classified into distribution curves, quantile measures, indices and other measures. Distribution curves are a widely used visual instrument to analyze concentration, and the most important type is the Lorenz curve.[34] The Lorenz curve shows the proportion of a given total amount (e.g., total market output) assumed by the smallest x% of the values. Quantiles of the Lorenz curves are frequently used to further aggregate information. A prominent example is the concentration ratio, which OECD (1993) define as "the percentage of total industry output [...] which a given number of large firms account for". Thus, the concentration ratio is equal to 1 minus the respective upper quantile of the distribution function. A prominent index measure is the Herfindahl-Hirschmann-Index (*HHI*), which, in contrast to quantile measures, accounts for the total number of firms on the market. It is defined as $HHI = \sum_{i=1}^{n} s_i^2$, where s_i is the output proportion of the i-th firm. Other index measures, such as the Gini-Coefficient,[35] are less relevant in the context of

31 The European Commission may start sector inquiries if "circumstances suggest that competition may be restricted or distorted within the common market", see http://ec.europa.eu/comm/competition/antitrust/sector_inquiries.html; accessed May 5, 2007.

32 European Commission (2007b, p. 7) defines "business insurance" for the purpose of the inquiry as "provision of insurance products and services to any type of business, irrespective of its size, form of organization or legal structure."

33 Swiss Re (2000).

34 Bosch (1998, p. 36).

35 E.g., Bosch (1998, p. 40).

economic theory.[36] Other measures such as number of firms operating in one market are typically only used either as preliminary indicators or if more granular data is unavailable.

Application of concentration measures varies amongst regulators and Industry organizations. The U.S. Department of Justice and the Federal Trade Commission (1997) assesses post-merger market concentration based on the post-merger HHI of all transaction participants. The European Council (2004) does not introduce explicit measures to assess concentration in the EC Merger Regulation. However, in their recent sector inquiry on primary business insurance, the Directorate General for Competition (DG Competition) of the European Commission reverted to concentration ratios for the 5, 10 and 15 largest insurance groups and development of number of firms to assess prevailing market concentration, following the approach of CEA (2006). For the reinsurance market, Standard & Poor's (2006) also uses concentration ratios. With respect to the underlying measure, OECD (1993) suggest to use "output" in general, and total premiums specifically for the insurance industry. CEA (2006) and European Commission (2007b) use turnover.[37]

Similar to market concentration, several approaches to measure market integration are discussed in literature. Chen and Knez (1995) and Kiranand (2004) review frequently utilized measurement methodologies, but agree that more recent definitions share the notion that markets are integrated if the law of one price holds across them. However, European Commission (2007b) and OECD (2007) revert to simpler measures of integration: They utilize cross-border sales in percent of total premiums written, market share of branches/agencies of foreign undertakings in total domestic non-life business, and overall non-life market share of foreign companies as proxies to assess market integration in the insurance industry within Europe.

This study follows the approaches utilized by the CEA, the European Commission, Standard & Poor's and the OECD for concentration and integration. Firstly, these sources provide the most granular data available for the European

36 See OECD (1993, p. 25) for detailed references to literature discussing mathematical and economic properties of these and further indices.

37 CEA does not provide a definition of the term turnover.

insurance industry. Secondly, their measurements and derived conclusions are major determinants for regulatory actions and changes to jurisdictions.

Concentration and integration of the European primary insurance industry

Figure 3 illustrates the development of number of insurance firms operating in the Euro-12 zone and the EU-25 as a first indicator for concentration. The overall effect indicates a slight concentration by 3% (–150 firms) between 1993 and 2004. In comparison to the insurance sector, the European banking sector underwent a much stronger concentration in the recent years: The number of credit institutions decreased from 9,363 firms in 2001 to 8,613 firms in 2004,[38] corresponding to an annual concentration of 3.7% compared to 0.3% in the insurance sector.

The indicated concentration was driven by Euro-12 zone countries. The number of firms operating within this region decreased by 15% (–495 firms) between 1993 and 2004, where the number of firms increased by 20% (+345 firms) in other EU-25 countries.[39]

Figure 4 presents concentration ratios for non-life insurance groups in Europe.[40] In 2004, the 5 largest insurance groups held a market share of 69% in the average, up from 52% in 1993. Except for Hungary, Switzerland and Greece, concentration increased in all markets (where data is available), especially in Italy, where the market share of the 5 largest insurance groups increased by 35 percentage points.[41] At the same time, concentration across European markets balanced: The standard deviation of concentration decreased from 22% points in 1993 to 16% points in 2004. Slovenia, Finland, Sweden and Slovakia were the most concentrated markets: The 5 largest insurance groups held a turnover mar-

38 See ECB (2005, p. 48).

39 Considering the growth of total direct premium income in the same time frame, concentration also increased in other EU-25 countries: Premium income per insurance firm increased by 149% in the Euro-12 zone, but only by 84% in these other EU-25 countries.

40 EU-25, Norway, and Switzerland.

41 The merger between Fondiaria Assicurazioni SpA and Societa Assicuratrice Industriale SpA, and Assicurazioni Generali SpA and Istituto Nazionale delle Assicurazioni, as well as acquisitions by Istituto Nazionale delle Assicurazioni may have contributed significantly to the concentration of the Italian market.

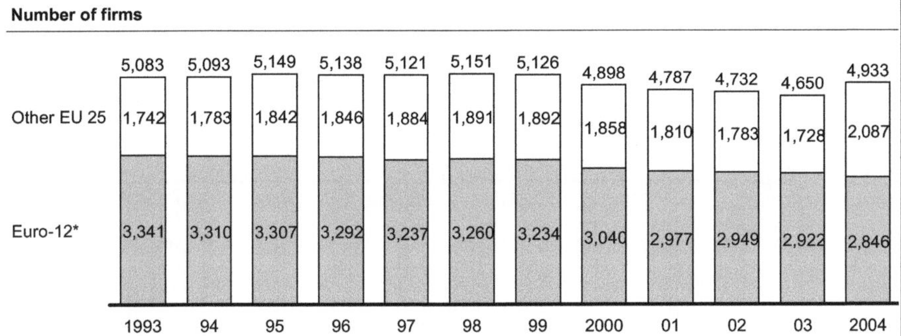

Total direct premium income (EUR trillion)

Total	**404**	**432**	**456**	**491**	**542**	**576**	**652**	**755**	**771**	**807**	**821**	**867**
Other EU 25	123	118	114	131	163	187	221	296	273	278	263	271
Euro 12*	281	314	342	361	379	390	432	458	499	530	558	596

*Austria, Belgium, The Netherlands, Denmark, France, Germany, Ireland, Italy, Luxembourg, Portugal, Spain, Greece
Source: CEA (2006)

Figure 3: Development of number of primary insurers and their total direct premium income in Europe

ket share of above 90%. The most fragmented markets were Greece and Spain, where the 5 largest insurance groups only accounted for 39% of the total market turnover.

Concentration ratios for life insurance groups in Europe are illustrated in Figure 5. The average concentration in 2004 is comparable to non-life insurance groups: The largest 5 life insurers covered 71% of the market (up from 62% in 1993), compared to 69% of the largest 5 non-life insurers. Diversity of concentration measured as standard deviation of market share of 5 largest groups is also similar for life and non-life, with 16% points and 13% points (20% and 16% in 1993), respectively.

However, the development of concentration across time differs notably between non-life and life markets. Whereas most countries in the former industry concentrated between 1993 and 2004, in the latter industry deconcentration occurred almost as frequently (7 out of 16 countries) and severely (average of –9 percentage points compared to +12 percentage points) as concentration. This fact may be explained by a stronger tendency of deconcentration in the life industry

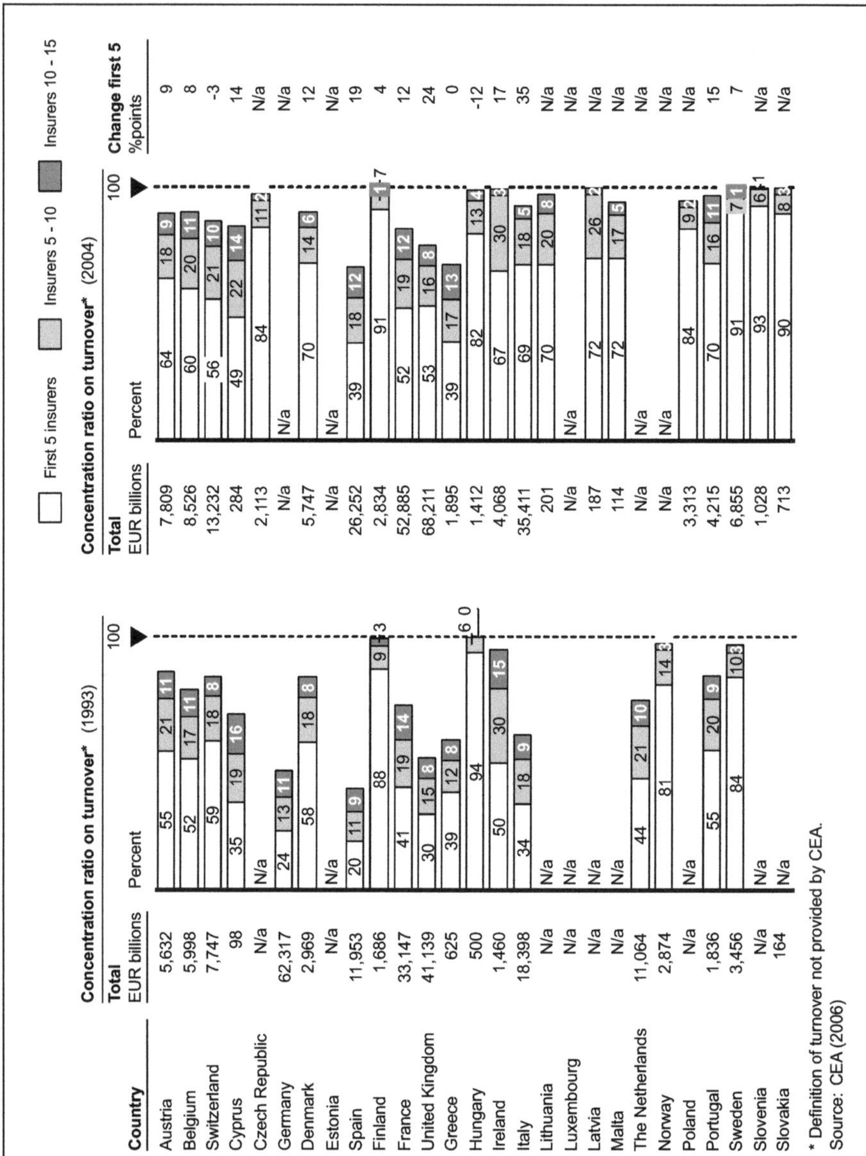

Figure 4: Development of concentration in the European primary non-life insurance industry

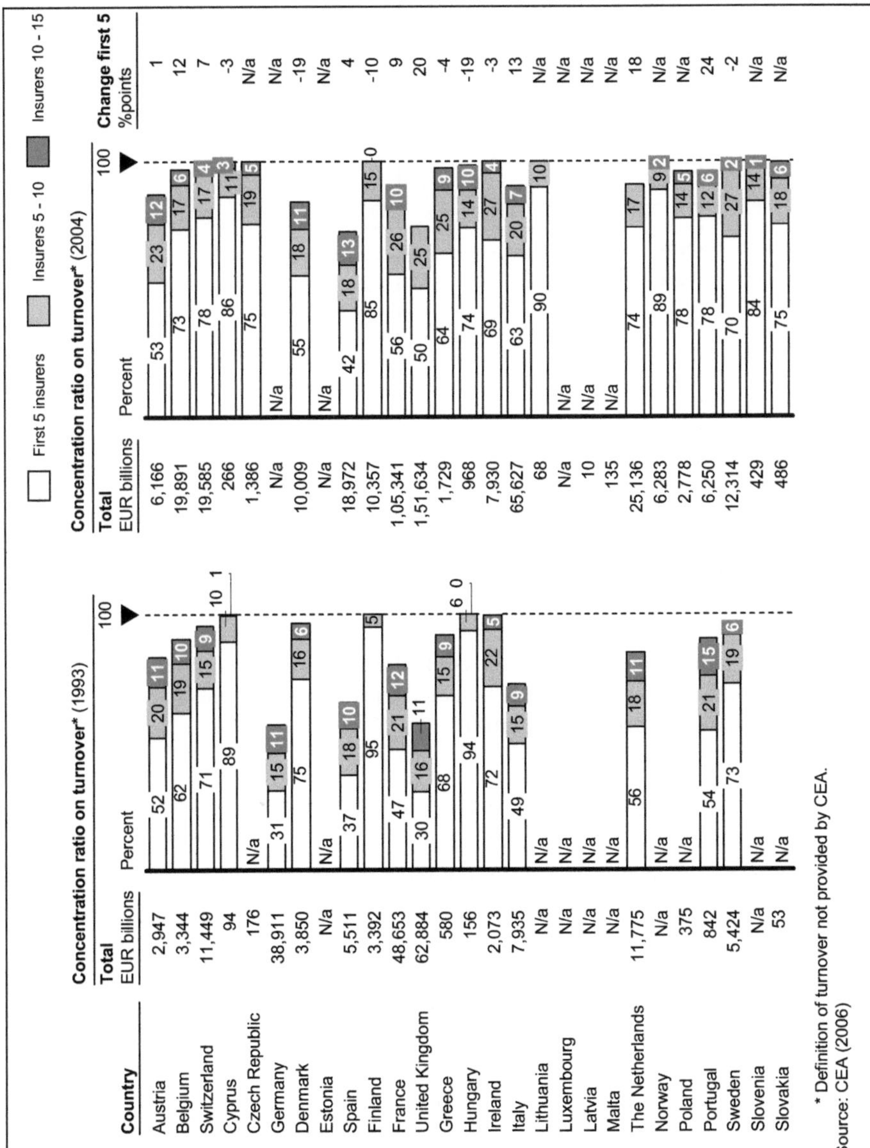

Figure 5: Development of concentration in the European primary life insurance industry

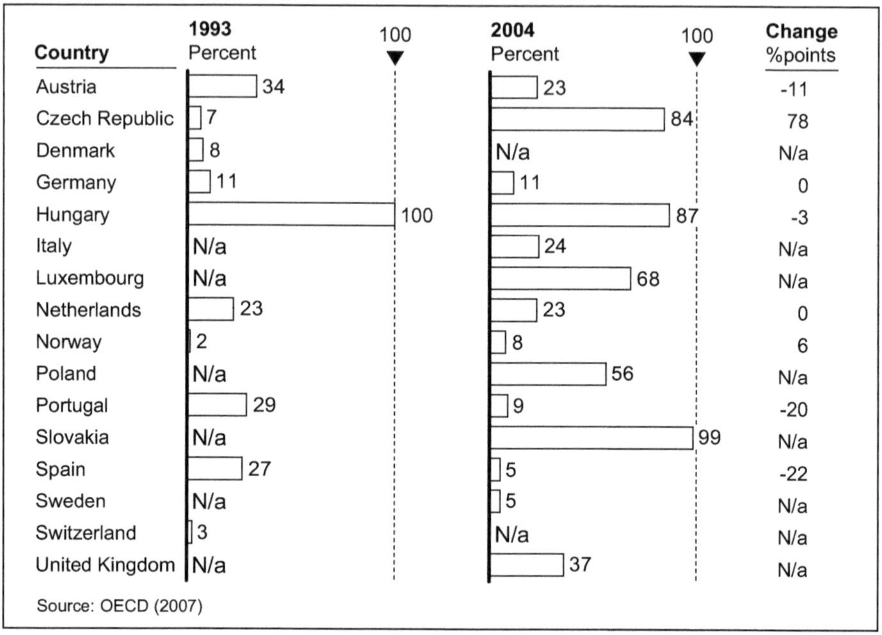

Figure 6: Market share of foreign controlled insurance companies and their branches or agencies in selected European countries (percent of total domestic gross premiums)

compared to the non-life industry, unless insurers invest in expansion of their market share: The most attractive markets[42] concentrated both in the life and the non-life industry, probably due to dominant players seeking further growth. In less attractive markets, where insurers are less incentivized to invest in market share expansions, only the non-life industry concentrated weakly, whereas the life-industry deconcentrated. A possible explanation for the deconcentration tendency in the life industry may be the fact that new business in non-life insurance is largely driven by renewals of existing policies, whereas life premium turnover is mostly determined by new acquisitions.

In contrast to concentration, integration of markets is more difficult to assess due to lack of data. Figure 6 depicts the market share of foreign controlled

42 Fastest growing national markets in terms of absolute turnover between 1993 and 2004.

insurance companies and their branches or agencies in total domestic gross premiums for all European countries where OECD (2007) provides data. In 2004, foreign undertakings accounted for 39% of total gross premiums in the average, up from 22% in 1993. Foreign companies especially dominated the markets Slovakia, Hungary, Czech Republic, Luxembourg and Poland. However, their influence decreased in all of these countries except for the Czech Republic.

Concentration of the global reinsurance industry

The global reinsurance market is less concentrated than European primary insurance markets. In 2005, the 5 largest reinsurance providers achieved a market share of 47% in terms of net reinsurance premiums written compared to about 70% in the life and non-life primary insurance sectors. Still, a notable concentration is recorded between 1994 and 2005, where the market share of the 5 largest reinsurance providers increased by 15%.

Summary

Compared to the European banking sector, the European primary insurance market is rather concentrated. The 5 largest non-life and life insurers accounted for 69% and 71% of revenues in 2004, respectively. However, the 5 largest credit institutions only carried 59% of total assets in 2004, down from 60% in 2001.[43] The reinsurance market is less concentrated with 47%.[44] The integration of European primary insurance is also higher than integration in the EU banking industry. Foreign primary insurance undertakings accounted for 39% of total gross premiums, whereas ECB (2005, pp. 58) presents evidence that foreign credit institutions from EEA countries only accounted for 17% of total assets in 2004, up from 16% in 2001.[45]

In contrast with these findings, the European anti-trust authority never ruled a requirement to dissolve concentration,[46] a refusal of concentration[47] or a condi-

43 Average across EU-25 member states (ECB, 2005, p. 50).
44 2005 figure.
45 Data on integration of the reinsurance market is not available.
46 According to European Council (2004), Art. 8(4) (Powers of decision of the Commission; Decision to require the undertakings concerned to dissolve concentration).
47 According to European Council (2004), Art. 8(3) (Powers of decision of the Commission; Decision that concentration is incompatible with the common market).

tional acceptance of concentration[48] against merged entities or filed transactions with respect to insurance M&A between 1990 and 2006.[49] Still, the DG Competition initiated a sector inquiry on primary business insurance in June 2005, accounting for "indications that in certain areas of insurance to businesses, distortive forms of cooperation may take place between insurers and that certain arrangements for distribution of insurance products and services to businesses may give rise to competition concerns."[50] From interim results published in January 2007 they conclude that the EU non-life markets, which are dominated by multi-domestic competition by cross-border entities,[51] become more concentrated. However, concrete issues confirming previous competition concerns[52] were not detected.

In summary, further consolidation of primary insurance markets may be restricted by already high concentration of national markets and related antitrust concerns, and could therefore again involve either cross-border transactions in the primary insurance sector, possibly after disengagement of acquirers in their home markets, or transactions in the reinsurance industry. However, examination of the consolidation status of the industry only gives a first indication why European insurers could or would choose to pursue further M&A transactions. The following section thus analyzes transaction momentum in greater depth by systematizing hurdles and drivers for future M&A in the European insurance industry.

48 According to European Council (2004), Art. 8(2) with (conditions & obligations) (Powers of decision of the Commission; Decision that concentration is compatible with the common market with conditions and obligations).

49 Data provided by European Commission on European Commission (2007a).

50 European Commission (2007b, p. 7).

51 European Commission (2007b, p. 39 and p. 45).

52 European Commission (2004) notes that "average market share of the 5 largest institutions in EU15 countries comes close to 60% in both banking and insurance sectors", raising concerns of the responsible competition authorities.

2.3.2 Drivers and hurdles for further consolidation

2.3.2.1 Overview drivers and hurdles

Recent academic work discusses a variety of frameworks to classify motives for M&A transactions, e.g.,

- Beitel (2002, p. 17) draws a distinction between economic and strategic motives for M&A, and subdivides economic motives further into value maximizing[53] and non-value maximizing motives.
- Achleitner (1999, pp. 142) introduces a classification into strategic, financial and personal motives. Lorenz (2006, pp. 17) adopts this classification.
- Settnik (2006, pp. 73) discusses drivers for M&A from the perspective of neoclassical theory and institutional economics, and develops an integrating model based on socio-economic exchange theory.[54]
- BIS (2001) extensively discusses "causes of consolidation", i.e. motives that lead to either cost reduction or revenue increase, and "forces of change",[55] understood as changing external factors that encourage consolidation.

In contrast to these possible systematizations of drivers, reviewed academic work does not introduce a classification for hurdles of M&A transactions. Figure 7 presents a possible integrated systematization for drivers and hurdles, whereas Figure 8 provides further details. Drivers are structured following the approach of Beitel (2002), further separating economic drivers by their source into production and financing according to Settnik (2006). With respect to hurdles of M&A, factors indicated in recent academic work are separated into legal, financial,

53 Beitel (2002) argues that strategic motives are also value maximizing in their core, but that their impact is more difficult to quantify than the one of economic motives.

54 In the model, actors (acquirer insurance companies) are interested in resources (material or immaterial production factors) to satisfy their needs. Other actors (target insurance companies) control these resources, see Settnik (2006, p. 198).

55 Examples are technological progress, deregulation and harmonization of European supervisory standards, increased expectations of shareholders with respect to increase of performance and shareholder value, implementation of Euro, progressing globalization, and increase of competition. These factors are included in the discussion of specific drivers and hurdles later in this section, and in section 2.3.2.2.

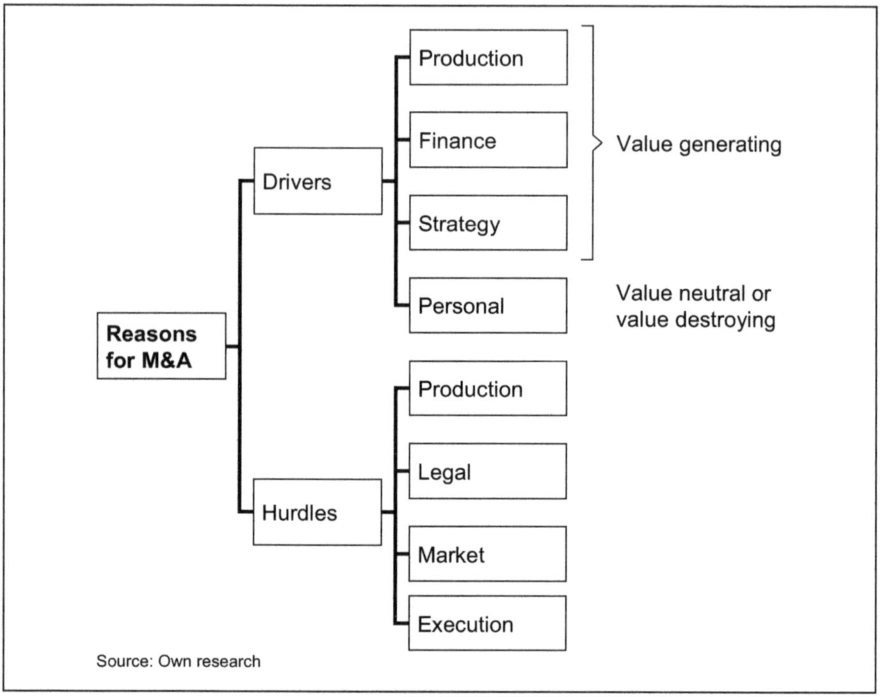

Figure 7: Possible systematization of reasons for M&A

market, and execution hurdles. The framework integrates the elements of "forces of change".[56]

The following subsections provide detailed, but general (i.e., not insurance industry-specific) descriptions of the individual drivers and hurdles. The reader familiar with the cited reasons for M&A may skip these subsection and continue with section 2.3.2.2, which discusses the identified drivers and hurdles specifically in the context of the European insurance industry.

56 See BIS (2001). For example, the force of change "deregulation" is discussed under the hurdle "regulation".

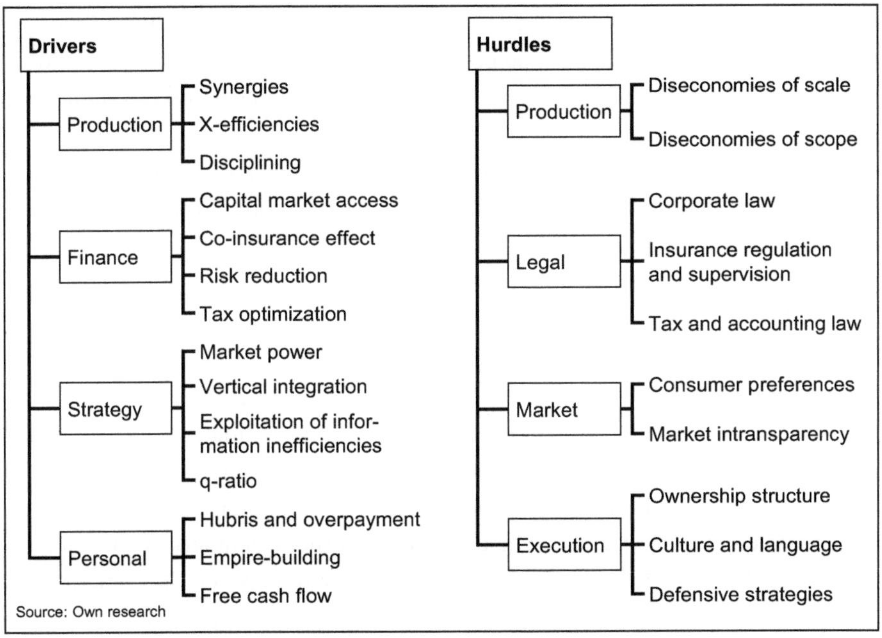

Figure 8: Details on possible systematization of reasons for M&A

2.3.2.1.1 Drivers

Synergies

Jensen and Ruback (1983) define synergies as potential savings, which can only be achieved through M&A, but not by stand-alone entities themselves. Synergies are the most frequently cited reason for M&A.[57] There are two types of synergies. Firstly, economies of scale[58] exist, if a transaction leads to a reduction of unit cost. Settnik (2006, pp. 85) further distinguishes economies of scale by their sources production, procurement, distribution, research and development and administration. Secondly, economies of scope exist, if the cost of merged entities is lower than the sum of the cost of the individual entities.[59] Beitel (2002, p. 19)

57 E.g., Paprottka (1996, p. 39), and Ebert (1998, p. 5).
58 E.g., Chandler (1990).
59 E.g., Panzar and Willig (1981).

distinguishes procurement, production, distribution, and financial diversification. The definitions for scale and scope economies are not mutually exclusive. However, cost degression of economies of scope is generally understood to stem from increasing diversity (e.g., geographies, products), not from increasing size. For example, Achleitner (1999, p. 144) argues that economies of scale are realized through horizontal transactions, and economies of scope from lateral transactions.

X-efficiencies

Efficiency measures output relative to required inputs for an individual firm. Efficiency is assessed against an analogously measured benchmark ("best practice"). In recent academic work, several approaches to estimate efficiency exist, e.g., financial ratio analysis, and frontier efficiency methodologies.[60] The latter defines the efficient frontier as all combinations of minimum inputs required to produce given outputs, i.e. the efficient frontier is the benchmark. Efficiency of an individual firm is defined as some distance measure between the combination of actual input and output of an individual firm and the efficient frontier. Berger et al. (2000b) discuss five types of efficiencies from consolidation, which are partly overlapping with synergy effects: Scale efficiency (economies of scale from increased cost or revenue efficiency), scope efficiency (economies of scope), X-efficiency of geographic diversification (improved cost or revenue efficiency from diversification of risks), X-efficiency of managing from distance (negative efficiency effects due to difficulties of monitoring and conducting business from a distance), and X-efficiency of the M&A process (efficiency improvement of the target company, if the acquirer is more efficient than the target and achieves to bring the target up to its own level of efficiency).

Disciplining

The disciplining hypothesis postulates that M&A is an effective instrument of corporate control.[61] Through aligning incentives or replacement of management, it corrects failure of current management of the target company caused by lack of

60 E.g., Klumpes (2006).
61 Easterbrook and Fischel (1991, p. 171).

skills or maximization of personal motives. Settnik (2006, p. 125) notes that the disciplining hypothesis requires an information efficient capital market, where valuation of the target suffers from ineffectiveness of current management.

Capital market access

Sautter (1989, p. 137) argues that M&A may improve access to external capital markets due to cost degression of fixed fees for capital market transactions. In addition, given a sufficiently large volume after M&A transactions, external capital markets may partially be substituted by an internal capital market, e.g. for liquidity and capital pooling, so that the cost differential between the external and internal capital market are earned.[62]

Co-insurance effect

Seth (1994, p. 432) defines the co-insurance effect as an increased debt capacity of merged entities (or reduced probability of insolvency given same financing structure). Levy and Sarnat (1970, p. 801) mention diversification of firm returns as the major source. In this respect, the co-insurance effect may be understood as a source for economies of scope. The co-insurance effect assumes, that capital markets measure solvency and price capital according to the entire risk (specific and market risk) of a company, and not only un-diversifiable market risk.[63]

Risk reduction

Related to co-insurance is the effect of risk reduction. It assumes that conglomeration leads to diversification of specific risk.[64] Besides increased debt financing capacity (comparable to the co-insurance effect), Paprottka (1996, p. 63) argues that higher precision of liquidity planning due to lower return volatility may be a source of additional value.

62 E.g., Perin (1996, p. 36).

63 The combination of two correctly priced companies under CAPM still lie on the security market line, and thus do not increase value for shareholders compared to the standalone entities. See e.g., Copeland/Weston (1988, pp 193).

64 See e.g., Jennings (1971, p. 131).

Tax optimization

Jensen and Ruback (1983, p. 24) define tax optimization as the increase in shareholder profit through a decrease of tax load or a more effective utilization of tax shields. Tax optimization is thus not necessarily value generating from a global perspective, since value is redistributed from tax authorities to transaction partners. Tax optimization as a source of value is discussed controversially in literature. BIS (2001) even refers to taxation as a "force discouraging consolidation", arguing that proper estimation of tax impacts in an M&A transactions is a very complex issue, and potential benefits may not outweigh related direct and indirect costs.

Market power

Achleitner (1999, p. 143) argues that merged entities in horizontal transactions have greater market power through reduction of competition. The increased market power is utilized to achieve higher prices for products and services, thus transferring wealth from customers to shareholders. Thus, the market power hypothesis is – similar to tax optimization – a redistribution hypothesis, because value is generated from the shareholder perspective, but not necessarily from a global market perspective.

Vertical integration

Achleitner (1999, p. 143) defines vertical integration benefits as synergy effects from combining entities in the same industry and successive steps in the value chain. She identifies two sources of value. Firstly, economies of integration can be derived from reduced communication cost across the value chain. Secondly, safeguarding supply with inputs and distribution of outputs reduces risk.

Exploitation of information inefficiencies

Preuschl (1997, p. 102) assumes that temporary market inefficiencies exist, i.e. not all information relevant for valuation are reflected instantaneously in share prices. However, if few market participants have access to this kind of information, they can take advantage of resulting misvaluation and extract value through M&A. Examples for such relevant, but publicly not available information may be unrealized gains[65] and possibility for strategy improvements or synergies.[66] In contrast to these temporary inefficiencies, the market-myopia-hypothesis is based on the assumption of systematic (i.e. persisting) market inefficiencies as a result of short-term profit focus of shareholders. Romano (1991, p. 26) finds that companies heavily invested in costly long-term projects, e.g., research and development with high upfront investments, are systematically undervalued and thus become takeover targets.

q-ratio

The q-ratio is defined as the ratio of the market value of equity of a firm divided by the replacement value of its assets.[67] Weston et al. (1990) argue that companies with a q-ratio higher than 1 can create value from buying companies with a q-ratio multiplied with acquisition premiums of smaller than one. In this case, organic growth would be more expensive for the acquirer than a direct purchase of the assets of the target.

Hubris and overpayment

Roll (1986, p. 213) defines Hubris as an excess payment for targets, even in an information efficient market environment, due to the believe of the acquirer's management, that they can add value through their superior capabilities compared to the target's management. Hubris is mostly driven by previous performance of managers, appraisal by public opinion and media, and experience and self-assessment of managers.[68] Black (1989, pp. 624) defines overpayment more broadly as the result of intransparency on the true value of the target, competition with several bidders, overly optimistic acquirer management, and agency conflicts between managers and shareholders of acquirers.

Empire-building

Preuschl (1997) argues that M&A produces agency costs, in that management pursues personal interests such as increase in personal income, power, prestige,

65 See Halpern (1983, p. 300).
66 See Bradley et al. (1983, p. 184).
67 E.g., Beitel (2002, p. 20).
68 E.g., Gaughan (1999, p. 160).

and job security. Expansion strategies are one possibility for managers to realize these benefits, especially in the context of M&A as a defensive strategy for hostile takeovers of the own company.[69] Swiss Re (1999a) argues analogously for the existence of a "bandwagon effect": If there is lots of activity on the M&A market, management is more likely to carry out M&A transactions itself, even in case of doubtful rationale, because it seeks to maintain its relative market power.

Free cash flow

Jensen (1986) observes that managers with high free cash flow[70] at their discretion are more likely to carry out M&A transactions than returning accumulated capital to shareholders. This bias towards M&A as one of several strategic options can be explained by management's desire to maintain power and may lead to value destroying transactions.

2.3.2.1.2 Hurdles

Production

Positive synergies are believed to be a major driver for M&A. Analogous, negative synergy effects are assumed to present an obstacle to consolidation. Diseconomies of scale may arise when institutions become too large and complex, leading to a dilution of control.[71] Diseconomies of scope may result from managing from distance[72] or customer preferences for specialized service providers instead of large conglomerates.[73] OECD (1999a) adds that consolidation across currency regimes results in currency risk which may offset positive diversification effects in other risk drivers.[74]

69 E.g., Marris (1963, pp. 186).
70 Jensen (1986, p. 323) defines free cash flow as "cash flow in excess of that required to fund all projects that have positive net present values when discounted at the relevant cost of capital".
71 E.g., Amel et al. (2003) and BIS (2001).
72 Berger et al. (2000b).
73 Berger et al. (2000a).
74 OECD (1999a) argues that the implementation of the Euro reduced currency risk for companies, and thus drove consolidation in the late 1990s.

Legal

Differences and discrimination across jurisdictions, especially in heavily regulated industries such as financial services, are discussed extensively in literature. Corporate law, supervisory rules and regulation, and tax and accounting law are cited as reasons. Berger et al. (2000b) note that corporate law may implicitly or explicitly impose constraints on competition, and thus present a deal breaker for M&A transactions. BIS (2001) additionally observes existence of new entry conditions for financial service providers which plan to extend their outreach into foreign markets, paired with case-by-case court rulings on cross-border M&A transactions.

Amongst other authors, Beckmann (2002), and BIS (2001) discuss local regulation of financial services as a major obstacle for cross-border consolidation. On the other hand, deregulation is often seen as a major catalyst to drive M&A.[75] Taxation may also pose difficulties to M&A. BIS (2001) refers to taxation as a "force discouraging consolidation" due to complexity of tax regimes, an argument which proves valid also for accounting rules given the manifold local accounting standards.

Market

Market entry hurdles are highly industry specific, and thus discussed specifically for the European insurance industry in section 2.3.2.2.

Execution

BIS (2001) mentions that the target's capital structure may present an obstacle, e.g., if few large investors or bondholders exert their influence on management or supervisory board in transaction negotiations. In extreme cases, especially if target is largely held privately, owners may even have implemented defensive strategies in manager contracts or ownership structure. Additionally, Berger et al. (2000b) and BIS (2001) mention cultural barriers between companies, and language barriers between companies and between countries as important obstacles to successful execution of M&A transactions.

75 E.g., BIS (2001) and Cummins et al. (2006).

2.3.2.2 Identification of drivers and hurdles for further consolidation in the European insurance industry

2.3.2.2.1 Drivers

Synergies – Economies of scale

Economies of scale in insurance can result from a variety of sources. Swiss Re (1999a) assumes that M&A transactions will increase efficiency of information technology, distribution, asset management, insurance portfolio management, and research and innovation. Further on, they argue that a "flight to quality" increases revenue scales, since especially corporate clients may favor large insurance groups. BIS (2001) emphasizes the importance of technological advances as a major force encouraging consolidation. Their survey[76] results indicate that especially IT and communications are very important for domestic consolidation within a certain industry (62% of respondents), but less relevant for diversifying transactions. Key examples for technology driven benefits are

- Entering new markets through electronic distribution channels prior to physical pre-existence. However, Beckmann (2002) argues that insurance is a trust-based and thus naturally local business. Nevertheless, few examples exist in the recent past, e.g., Standard Life's direct-only presence in Germany.
- Increased distribution capacity through direct channels or direct insurers. The marginal cost of required technology platforms decreases strongly with the number of customers. M&A is an opportunity to acquire necessary technological know how or to scale the customer base.
- Product differentiation or tailoring through data mining. Pricing sophistication, e.g., inclusion of further risk factors[77] or application of modern nonlinear statistical models (GNLMM) can be increased. M&A allows to

76 Exact specification of the survey, e.g., number of respondents, is not documented in the published report.

77 E.g., pricing motor insurance based on place of residence, pricing life annuity insurance based on health characteristics.

quickly acquire relevant knowledge and data. Settnik (2006, p. 177) emphasizes the importance of information for insurance M&A.

- Creation of new financial products through tailored products, e.g., fund wrappers on life insurance contracts, life insurance wrappers on funds, and securitization of insurance portfolios. Financial engineering and risk management capabilities are required in combination with respective data processing technology to provide these services.

However, Katrishen and Scordis (1998) hypothesize that especially large international groups may suffer from diseconomies of scale due to their organizational complexity.

Empirical evidence on the existence of economies of scale in the insurance industry is moderate and mixed. A significant amount of studies find scale economies only for small U.S. and European insurers.[78] Swiss Re (1999a) do not find empirical evidence to support the hypothesis of economies of scale in UK and U.S. life insurance industry at all. Cummins et al. (1998) provide evidence for fix cost degression effects at U.S. life insurers, probably resulting from centralization of services such as information systems, investment operations, and policyholder services. It shall be noted that major factors, such as recent technological advances, may not be adequately represented in the rather old samples of the above mentioned research. This hypothesis is underlined by findings of Amel et al. (2003, p. 21), who observe on their more recent global data sample that large insurers show a better ratio of management cost to net premiums, indicating existence of economies of scale.

Synergies – Economies of scope

Swiss Re (1999a) assumes that M&A lets insurers reap scope benefits from entering foreign markets, utilizing different distribution channels, taking higher or more complex risks, and expanding their product portfolio. Cummins et al. (1998) assume that extending the scope of operations leads to diversified earnings and thus increased predictability and reduced volatility of results. BIS

78 For the U.S. market, see e.g., Cummins and Weiss (1993), Hanweck and Hogan (1996), Yuengert (1993), and Cummins and Zi (1998). For the European market, see e.g., Focarelli (1992), Fecher et al. (1991), Mahlberg and Url (2000), and Kaye (1991).

(2001) points out that technological advances and deregulation encouraged lateral M&A, allowing financial institutions of all types to offer products which were typically only offered by other types of institutions ("blurring of distinctions"). This type of conglomeration is referred to as Bancassurance or Assurbanking. Examples for assimilation of products are life-cycle funds offered by banks, and unit-linked life insurance products offered by insurers. Examples for cross-selling of products are property insurance offered to mortgage customers, and motor insurance to car financing customers.

Cummins and Weiss (2000) find in their empirical study that global consolidation increases reinsurance capacity due to diversification. For the U.S. market, Berger et al. (2000a) document that significant profit scope economies only exist for some types of firms, especially large, efficient, vertically integrated and personal line oriented insurers. They attribute these benefits to cost economies of scale from shared production. Revenue diseconomies of scope only partially offset these benefits, and Berger et al. (2000b) assume that these diseconomies result from greater ability of specialists to tailor products to their customers' needs, thus invalidating the hypothesis of large benefits from one-stop shopping. Cummins et al. (2006) detect significant positive value creation for banks pursuing a bancassurance strategy.

X-efficiencies

Klumpes (2006) reviews literature on efficiency measurement in the insurance industry and provides an overview of insurance-specific definitions for inputs and outputs. He agrees with the arguments put forward by Cummins and Weiss (2000) to define efficiency for insurers following the value added approach,[79] either before cost of financial capital (gross value added) or after cost of financial capital (net value added), and suggests concrete measures for inputs[80] and

79 For the banking industry, Berger and Humphrey (1992) discuss two additional approaches, the asset approach, and the user cost approach. Cummins and Weiss (2000) argue that both approaches are not suitable for the insurance industry, because especially P&C insurers many services beyond financial intermediation (asset approach not suitable), and product revenues and opportunity costs are typically not available in the insurance industry due to product bundling (user cost approach not suitable).

80 Klumpes (2006) uses labor, business services, debt and equity capital as major inputs.

outputs.[81] Cummins and Weiss (2000) categorize outputs into risk-pooling and risk-bearing, financial services related to insurance, and financial intermediation, and choose different measures than Klumpes (2006).

Recent literature gives only few examples for specific sources of efficiency gains in the insurance industry. Amel et al. (2003, p. 21) assume that consolidation may lead to rationalization of the agency distribution system, thus increasing efficiency. Further on, they argue that regulation protected European markets[82] to outside investors, so that further efficiency potential may be left untapped. Donni and Fecher (1997) refer to technical progress as a possible source of efficiency gains. Beitel (2002, p. 51) argues that technical progress may increase M&A activity, because some players may have missed the optimal point in time to invest in new technology, and thus decide to acquire capabilities from outside. Concrete examples of technical advances are given above in the paragraph "Synergies – Economies of scale".

Cummins, Tennyson and Weiss (1998) find that M&A improves the efficiency of target insurance firms in the U.S. life insurance industry. Cummins and Xie (2005) observe on their U.S. P&C sample that more cost or revenue efficient acquirers create more value around announcement than other acquirers. Both results support the benchmarking hypothesis, i.e. that efficiency level of targets is raised through acquisition by more efficient acquirers. In contrast, Klumpes (2006) finds that acquiring European life insurers are more likely to benefit from efficiency gains associated with takeover activity than their target firms. For the Spanish insurance industry, Cummins and Rubio-Misas (2006) argue that M&A increased efficiency because inefficient firms exited the market, acquirers sought out more efficient target firms, and total factor productivity increased.

Finance

Swiss Re (1999a) states that life insurers can reduce earnings volatility and thus cost of capital, and improve their capital market access through consolidation. Reviewed empirical research on the insurance industry has not yet directly exam-

81 Klumpes (2006) chooses "actual premiums earned in the period plus income from the investment of the insurance technical reserves less claims which become due for payment during the accounting period less changes in actuarial reserves and provisions for with profits insurance".

82 Amel et al. (2003) give Belgium, France, Germany, and UK as examples.

ined these or other financial drivers. Nevertheless, several of these studies confirm the general importance of solvency aspects for M&A which are closely related to the co-insurance effect and risk reduction. Chamberlain and Tennyson (1998) find financial synergies (only) after industry capital shocks on their P&C sample. BarNiv and Hathorn (1997) present evidence that U.S. P&C insurers more frequently acquire distressed targets compared to acquirers from other industries. However, although acquirers carefully select[83] distressed targets, they show inferior capital market performance compared to insurers that are not involved in distressed acquisitions.

Strategy

Berger et al. (1999) conclude from their literature review that market power is – besides efficiency improvements – a major reason for M&A in the financial service industry. With respect to vertical integration, Cummins et al. (2006) argue that insurers may improve revenue and cost control by acquiring agencies or brokerages. Their empirical analysis for the U.S. market however does not yield significant abnormal returns for those insurers that pursued a vertical integration strategy[84] through M&A.

Personal

Two studies discuss empire building as a motive for insurance M&A. Berger et al. (2000b) assume that empire building may occur in case of weak corporate control, encouraged through healthy financial condition.[85] Settnik (2006, pp. 180) argues that such issues of control exist for mutual insurers. Firstly, principals of mutual insurers are policyholders, and exercise direct control only on their invested money. However, part of the invested funds stem from previous

83 BarNiv and Hathorn (1997) find significantly different characteristics between acquired distressed targets and insolvent insurers. The former are smaller, carry more invested assets and more cash relative to liabilities, are less but more successfully invested in equity, generate less premiums, carry fewer liabilities, and have a higher net income and surplus.

84 They define vertical integration as "M&A transactions between insurance carriers and insurance agency, broker or service firms".

85 See also Free Cash Flow hypothesis.

policyholder generations, and management exerts sole control on these funds.[86] Secondly, policyholders of mutual insurers cannot withdraw their money as easy as shareholders of public companies, thus weakening their influence. Besides issues of control, Settnik discusses issues of conflict of interest. Management of mutual insurers is less disincentivized to carry out non-value generating actions than exchange listed companies. They can neither participate in share price development, nor do they seek to avoid share price drops and thus the danger of becoming a takeover target. Additionally, in some jurisdictions the management board of mutuals may assert influence on the composition of the supervisory board.

The free cash flow hypothesis is taken up by Swiss Re (1999a). They argue that excess capital, built up through previous capital market upswing, and cheap financing conditions drive M&A transactions in the insurance industry.[87] ING (2006) see capital cushions ("corporate firepower") as a major driver for a new wave of insurance market consolidation in Western Europe. Again, mutual insurers may be more prone to pursue this personal motive: Wells et al. (1995) find that mutual insurers have more free cash flow at their discretion than other insurers.

2.3.2.2.2 Hurdles

Production

The implementation of the Euro in 1999 harmonized the currency regime in EMU countries, and may have reduced currency risk of insurers.[88] BIS (2001) assumes existence of further benefits especially for large insurers, such as an integrated money market (e.g., one interest rate), and integrated capital markets (e.g., only large groups may have the required knowledge to act on a European market).

---

86 In contrast, funds of non-mutual companies are entirely controlled by either shareholders or policyholders.

87 Their study is concerned primarily with the life insurance industry, however their argumentation in this case is unspecific to the insurance industry.

88 Assets backing European policyholders reserves for long-tail business (e.g., life insurance) are typically invested in Euro to match currency and thus interest rate environment.

Legal

Berger et al. (2000b) note that implicit or explicit constraints on competition exist in corporate law in some jurisdictions, which may especially prevent cross-border M&A transactions. BIS (2001) observes case-by-case court rulings against cross-border transactions, and notices new entry hurdles for geographically expanding financial service providers.

Besides corporate law, regulation is considered to be a major hurdle for insurance M&A transactions. Amel et al. (2003, p. 20) assume that differences in regulation make it more difficult for insurers to realize potential synergies by discouraging in particular cross-border deals. Berger et al. (2000b) agree that the difference in the supervisory structure in Europe is a barrier for consolidation. Inversely, prior research mostly agrees that deregulation drove M&A activity in the recent past:

- For the U.S. market, Cummins et al. (1998) give the implementation of a nationwide solvency regulation, especially the risk based capital (RBC) requirements, as an example. Firstly, RBC unified state-specific NAIC requirements, and thus contributed to the harmonization of U.S. insurance market regulation. Secondly, these RBC rules put insurers under pressure to strengthen their capital base or restructure their asset portfolio to reduce investment risk. As a result, some insurers were left with reduced solvency. Cummins et al. (1998) find evidence that the latter effect of RBC implementation drove M&A as well, since financially vulnerable insurers are more likely to be acquired.

- In the European market, regulatory harmonization took a quantum leap with the introduction of the Third Generation Insurance Directives for life and non-life insurance in 1992, which for example eliminated price and product regulations, ensured cross-recognition of licenses and restricted host country control to solvency requirements.[89] Later directives brought European operating environment further into line, e.g. the Insurance Group Directive in 1998,[90] and the Reinsurance Directive in 2005.[91] European insurers reac-

89 See e.g., OECD (2000b).
90 See e.g., OECD (1998).

ted promptly with increasing M&A activity, in particular in cross-border transactions.

- However, despite these observations, BIS' (2001) survey in the general financial services industry yields the result that deregulation is considered a very important factor for domestic within-segment and cross-segment consolidation for roughly 36% of respondents, but less so for cross-border consolidation. Still, roughly 60% of respondents state that legal and regulatory impediments are very important discouraging factors for cross-border transactions.

Despite recent deregulation efforts, regulatory obstacles for further cross-border consolidation within Europe remain. Beckmann et al. (2002) observe that consumer protection regulation still differs substantially across Europe, imposing country-specific product design criteria on insurance contracts. Further on, public reporting of accounts[92] and policyholder profit allocation are dominated by local accounting standards.

Besides regulatory barriers, taxation may be a "force discouraging consolidation" according to BIS (2001) since it induces difficulties to properly estimate tax impacts of M&A transactions. Beyond these issues of intransparency, Beckmann et al. (2002) document discriminatory taxation in Europe: In 1999, fiscal tax advantages prevailed in ten European countries,[93] and the European Commission observes that "taxation remains an obstacle to the insurance Single Market".[94]

Market

Consumer preferences may present an obstacle to cross-border insurance M&A. Beckmann et al. (2002) argue that insurance is a trust-based business, and thus especially retail customers show a strong preference for local providers. Further on, customers in European countries are likely to have deviating preferences due

91 See e.g., European Commission (2005).
92 E.g., building and taxation of equalization reserves.
93 OECD (1999a, p. 40).
94 Beckmann et al. (2002) quote the internet link "http://europa.eu.int/comm/internal_market/en/finances/ insur/87.htm#11"; this link has been removed in the meanwhile.

to differences in social security systems[95] (e.g., retirement age, funding model) and personal taxation.[96]

BIS (2001) discusses market intransparency ("information inefficiencies") as another market entry hurdle for financial service providers, and gives lack of comparability of accounting reports, difficulties in appraisal of asset and liabilities, and lack of transparency as sources of inefficiencies as examples. Beckmann et al. (2002) further on argue that information asymmetries may occur due to geographical and cultural distance and result in pricing difficulties for insurance contracts. However, this qualitative reasoning is only moderately reflected in the survey results of BIS (2001): Most respondents do not view information inefficiency as an important factor discouraging consolidation.

Execution

The ownership form "mutual company" of an insurance company poses difficulties for M&A[97] due to diversity and complexity of regulations. Firstly, AISAM (2006a) reports that three different models for mutual societies exist in Europe, ranging from openness with respect to industry, restriction to some industries such as insurance, and entire prohibition. Further on, AISAM (2006b) finds that governance of mutual insurers may also be determined by law applicable to joint-stock companies, insurers or specifically mutual insurers, but specific regulations differ across Europe.

Secondly, Barry and Walsh (2000) illustrate actuarial complexities involved for life insurers, e.g., determination of surplus, determination of the initial funding level of segregated funds for with-profit policies, and determination and justification of an appropriate share allocation formula. Viswanathan and Cummins (2003, p. 403) argue for the U.S. market that "given the actuarial, accounting, and regulatory considerations involved, demutualization [of an insurance company is] a significant endeavor". Swiss Re (1999b) gives the demutualization of Old Mutual, a British life insurer, as an example. Old Mutual had to collect

95 Amel et al. (2003, p. 20).

96 E.g., Swiss Re (1999a), Beckmann et al. (2002).

97 Mutual insurers may be involved into M&A through sponsored demutualization (direct acquisition by public insurer), mutual holding company conversion (acquisition of portfolio of mutual insurer by public insurer) or merger between mutual insurers, see Swiss Re (1999b).

votes from more than 3 mn policyholders in 42 countries before applying for demutualization to courts and other authorities. These hurdles are vitally important for European insurance M&A, since 68% of insurers in the EU-25 are mutual insurers, representing 27% of gross direct domestic premiums written.[98]

Besides execution hurdles related to the ownership structure, Berger et al. (2000b) argue that large differences in language and culture may be a barrier for cross-border transactions in Europe. BIS' (2001) survey identifies cultural differences between countries and between corporations, with over two third of respondents agreeing that cross-border consolidation is discouraged by cultural constraints.

2.4 Momentum in the European insurance M&A market

The starting point of the analyses presented in this chapter is the overarching question, whether the observed pickup in M&A activity beginning in 2005 should be considered merely a blip in the market, or whether it marks the entry into the next cycle of M&A transactions in the European insurance industry. Based on the systematization of drivers and hurdles of M&A transactions, this section identifies concrete sources of further consolidation along the developed framework and builds hypotheses on the direction of consolidation.

Sources of further consolidation

Swiss Re (1999 and 2000) and OECD (2000a) identify several sources for the wave of M&A transactions during the 1990s, which can be interpreted in the context of drivers and hurdles of M&A as systematized in section 2.3. Progress in information and communication technology may have promised insurers to realize *economies of scale* at lower *diseconomies of scope* from managing from the distance. Favorable financial markets increased the *free cash flow* of insurers especially from their investment management activities. Highlighted solvency concerns may have urged insurers to seek improvement of their capital basis by

98 AISAM (2007), 2004 figures.

reaping diversification benefits according to the *co-insurance effect* or *risk reduction hypothesis*. Soft insurance markets could have been countered by insurers through increasing their *market power*. Regulatory harmonization, particularly through the introduction of the Third Generation Insurance Directives for life and non-life insurance in 1992[99] was considered a major reason for the pickup in M&A momentum, since it considerately lowered *legal hurdles*.

Today, M&A is again likely to catalyze increased shareholder pressure for insurers to create value,[100] and major drivers and lowered hurdles identified as most relevant forces behind the M&A cycle between 1990 and 2005 prevail. ING (2006) assumes that margins are likely to decline again: The reinsurance market continues to be firm, but especially the non-life cycle is expected to soften again, i.e. insurers may need to reduce rates and thus suffer from reduced earnings. Consequently, PWC (2006) argues that revenue and margin enhancement is likely to be a motive for future transactions. Insurers may withstand this margin pressure by increasing their *market power*, but also by reaping further *economies of scale*. ING (2006) notes that insurers nowadays are more likely to realize especially technical synergies due to "shared service centers initiatives and more flexible operating systems". Further on, large acquirers could focus on smaller targets in order to reap economies of scale by transferring capabilities, and possibly by saving Solvency II capital due to roll-out of an internal model approach. This view is supported by PWC's (2006) hypothesis, that bolt-on acquisitions will dominate transformational deals due to execution risk and market skepticism inherent in the latter.

Although future profitability of European insurers is under pressure, increasing earnings, recovering equity markets, and rising interest rates[101] led to a currently rather comfortable capitalization of major European insurance compa-

99 These directives for example eliminated price and product regulations, ensured cross-recognition of licenses and restricted host country control to solvency requirements, see OECD (2000b).

100 BIS (2001) notes that shareholder pressure increases through wider application of professional investments (e.g., ROE driven allocation decisions), driven by institutionalization of pension savings of retail investors into hands of professional large-scale fund managers.

101 Especially life insurers invest with asset liability mismatch. Increasing interest rates thus leads to stronger devaluation of policyholder liabilities compared to investments. Additionally, reinvested bonds yield higher coupons, increasing the likelihood to cover contractual guaranteed interest rates.

nies[102]. According to the *free cash flow* hypothesis, insurers are more likely to invest this excess capital in growth rather than to return it to shareholders. Insurers' desire for quick growth[103] makes M&A the more likely strategy than inorganic growth.

In addition, further harmonization of jurisdictions are likely to reduce prevailing *legal hurdles* in the insurance industry. Firstly, the EU and the EMU are continuously extending their outreach especially to Central and Eastern Europe, thus further spreading harmonized regulation. Secondly, further changes of regulation and legislation are approaching: Solvency II is expected to be implemented between 2009 and 2012.[104] Although precise effects on the industry are yet unclear, analogies to earlier changes of regulation can be drawn. Solvency II explicitly accounts for investment risk. This very circumstance is assumed to have driven consolidation in the U.S. market after introduction of RBC.[105] In addition, insurers may be incentivized to use internal risk models instead of standard risk formulae and parameters in order to reduce capital requirements. Small insurers could merge to exploit scale economies for developing and implementing required know how and technology, or large insurers could buy small insurers to transfer know how and technology.

Further on, implementation of IFRS 4 at around 2020[106] will not only abolish intransparencies and complexities resulting from the diversity of local accounting standards, but bring along major methodological and technical difficulties such as fair valuation of policyholder liabilities. Both effects may drive M&A, following the argumentation in the previous paragraph. In addition, ING (2006) mentions that introduction of the legal form of European public companies (European Societas, SE) simplifies cross-border mergers between local public companies, and simplify further restructuring as soon as SE is built. Recent

102 ING (2006) estimates "corporate firepower", i.e. funds available for M&A without recourse to the equity market, at EUR 74 bn for the 13 covered insurance companies.

103 ING (2006) reports that large European insurance companies state growth ambitions especially in Central and Eastern Europe, Asia and Latin America. Management will probably desire quick growth to increase value soon.

104 E.g., ING (2006) assumes 2012, Towers Perrins Tillinghast (2006) assumes at the beginning of 2010, and CEA (2007) assumes during 2009.

105 See section 2.3.2.2.2.

106 ING (2006).

positive reports of converted insurers[107] may support this direction. Lastly, AISAM (2006a) advocate that a European Mutual Society Regulation, harmonizing country-specific laws that affect mutual insurers, should be central part of the European Commissions' Action Plan on the Modernization of Company Law and Corporate Governance. Few European countries already seek reforms of corporate law affecting governance of mutual companies.[108] Harmonized legislation could abolish complexities of demutualization through M&A or merger between mutuals.

Direction of further consolidation

From the above discussions, it may be concluded that cross-border transactions are again[109] likely to constitute a major part of future M&A transactions in the European insurance industry. Harmonization of jurisdictions already drove cross-border consolidation in the 1990s,[110] and expected further alignment of regulation may have the same effect. In addition, already high average national primary insurance market concentration and cross-border integration lead to increased alertness of antitrust authorities[111] and may thus even require insurers to seek inorganic growth across national or even European borders. ING (2006) supports this view by quoting senior management of major European insurers stating their desire to expand geographically.

Further hypothesis on the direction of consolidation can established with respect to the transaction instrument, method of payment and transaction intensity:

- Prominence of portfolio acquisitions may rise further due to acquirers' desire to further leverage their business model,[112] and sellers seeking to free up underwriting capacity for growth, immediately stop a long-tailed business

107 Allianz SE reports that conversion saved the insurer up to EUR 1 bn in the minority buyout of RAS Holding (Dow Jones International News, 23 April 2007).

108 AISAM (2006b).

109 Between 1990 and 2005, two thirds of the transactions in the long-term deal sample are either cross-border EU or cross-border world deals, see section 4.2.2.

110 Third Generation Insurance Directives were implemented by the EU in 1992. The volume share of cross-border M&A in the long-term deal sample increased from 37% in 1991 to 96% in 1993.

111 See discussion in section 2.3.1.

112 E.g., their ability to achieve higher investment returns or cutting costs through economies of scale, see discussions above.

line, or separate continuing business and run-off due to changes in market strategy or desired re-branding.[113]

- Minority buy-outs are more likely to occur in the near future for two reasons. Firstly, the introduction of European Societas simplifies buy-outs and comes with significant financial benefits.[114] Secondly, majority stakeholders are incentivized to buy-out minorities before required margin improvements increase the value of minority stakes and thus make the buy-out effort more expensive. Demutualization through M&A, and mergers between mutual insurers could gain importance, if either individual countries simplify or harmonize their regulations, or if a European Mutual Society Regulation is indeed introduced in the near future.

- Due to estimated high excess capitalization of insurers, the proportion of cash deals in the next wave of M&A transactions is likely to increase. However, especially large international insurance groups may find it difficult to pool and liquidate the necessary funds across legal entities in the holding company.

Taking all the different aspects into consideration, there are clear indications for a next wave of M&A transactions. These transactions are likely to be driven by motives that already triggered M&A in the 1990s. Again, cross-border transactions may constitute a major share of future deals due to already high concentration of primary insurance markets and related antitrust concerns.

113 E.g., Major (2005).
114 See case example of Allianz' minority buy-out of RAS above.

2.5 Summary

Especially the national primary insurance markets in Europe are relatively concentrated and integrated:

- The number of insurance firms decreased by 3% (–150 firms) between 1993 and 2004, mostly driven by firms operating in the Euro-12 zone (–15% equivalent to –495 firms). This corresponds to an annual concentration of 0.3%, compared to 3.7% in the EU banking sector.
- However, absolute concentration in the insurance markets is high compared to the banking sector. The 5 largest insurance groups accounted for roughly 70% of market turnover (2004 figures, life and non-Life), whereas the 5 largest credit institutions only held 60% of total assets. Although concentration increased especially in the non-life market (+15 percentage points non-life, +9 percentage points life) between 1993 and 2004, some markets are still fragmented, e.g., the Spanish life and non-life, and the Greek non-life market.
- Similarly, the European insurance market is more integrated than the European banking sector. The market share of foreign controlled insurance companies is at roughly 39% in 2004 (22% in 1993), whereas foreign EEA-based credit institutions only account 17% of assets in 2004.
- Still, the European Commission did not detect concrete issues with respect to market concentration, and no actions against market concentration were taken between 1990 and 2006.

However, the global reinsurance market is less concentrated than the European primary insurance markets. The 5 largest reinsurance firms only accounted for 47% of total net reinsurance premiums written in 2005, up from 32% in 1994. Although especially primary insurance markets already seem moderately concentrated, evidence is found that the current rise in M&A activity is likely to continue, thus marking the entry into a new cycle of transaction in the European insurance industry. The fundamental drivers for further consolidation resemble those motives identified for the M&A cycle between 1990 and 2005. Insurers may withstand increased margin pressure by increasing their *market power* and by reaping *economies of scale*. *Free cash flow* from advantageous financial markets may serve as a convenient source of funding of transactions. Further harmonization of jurisdictions is likely to further reduce existing *legal hurdles*. However, further M&A transactions may raise antitrust concerns of the European Commission. Especially national primary insurance markets are already closely observed by the DG Competition. Thus, further M&A may again strongly involve cross-border activities, possibly even in combination with prior disengagement of acquirers in their local markets.

In conclusion, the observed increase in M&A activity should not only be considered a short-term development, but could indeed mark the beginning of the next cycle of transactions in the European insurance sector. This finding confronts with a paradox: Empirical studies of M&A in the financial services industry frequently doubt value creation, in particular in the banking industry.[115] As only little empirical research addressed the question of value creation by M&A in the insurance industry in general, and specifically transactions of European insurers are only insufficiently examined,[116] chapter 4 analyzes short- and long-term capital market reactions and their determinants to announcements of M&A by European insurance companies between 1990 and 2005. The following chapter 3 reviews the required event study methodology.

115 See overviews in Beitel and Schiereck (2003), and Pilloff and Santomero (1998).

116 A detailed description of the identified gap in previous research is given in chapter 1 and the first paragraphs of chapter 4.

3 Recent Studies on the Success of Insurance Transactions

3.1 Objectives

This chapter reviews and selects event study methodologies for application in chapter 4. Section 3.2 provides an overview of recent success studies on the insurance industry. Section 3.3 reviews event study methodologies for analysis of short- and long-term value creation after announcement of M&A. Section 3.4 discusses and selects methodologies in the context of previous research.

3.2 Overview of recent studies on the success of M&A in the insurance industry

Twelve recent studies on the success of insurance M&A are identified, about half of which are event studies on the announcement effects of insurance M&A. The latter studies focus almost entirely on the U.S. insurance industry and P&C acquirers. Only three studies deal with either worldwide or European insurers. Four out of the five event studies on the insurance industry conduct short-term analyses (Akhigbe and Madura, 2001, Floreani and Rigamonti, 2001, Cummins and Weiss, 2004, and Cummins and Xie, 2005), and the only long-term analysis is focused on the U.S. market and P&C acquirers (Boubakri et al., 2006). Cummins and Xie (2005) utilize the most recent data sample of prior research, including transactions until 2003 for the U.S. P&C market. The only data sample with purely European focus for either acquirer or target, assembled by Cummins and

Weiss (2004), spans the years from 1990 to 2002.[117] Figure 9 provides an overview of these recent studies on the success of insurance M&A.

The reviewed prior research on short-term cumulative abnormal returns (CARs) of acquirers or targets indicates that value creation by U.S. and European insurance M&A differs substantially. Cummins and Weiss (2004) obtain an acquirer CAR of -0.61% and a target CAR of 7.50% (both significant at 1% level) on their European sample, whereas all other studies on the U.S. market report significantly positive acquirer CARs and notably higher target CARs. Akhigbe and Madura (2001) observe an acquirer CAR of 2.21%, and a target CAR of 20.78% (both significant at 5% level). Cummins and Xie (2005) detect acquirer and target CARs of 0.94% and 24.33%, respectively, both significant at 1% level. Thus, findings of U.S.-focused event studies may not apply for European markets.[118]

However, only Cummins and Weiss (2004) focus on the European market, but neither study combined entity returns (CERs) short-term around the announcement of transactions, nor do they analyze long-term value creation after announcement. Further on, they restrict their analyses of determinants of value creation to two univariate cross-sections,[119] and omit multivariate analyses entirely. Floreani and Rigamonti (2001) cover Europe only as one of many regions with insufficient observations for detailed, market-specific analyses.[120]

Further on, long-term value creation for European insurers has – to the best of the author's knowledge – never been investigated before. Only Boubakri et al. (2006) analyze long-term abnormal returns, but restrict their analyses to the U.S. insurance market and P&C acquirers. Thus, the objective of this study is to fill

117 Floreani and Rigamonti's (2001) global sample contains only 16 transactions of European bidders in their analysis of combined entity returns.

118 Possible reasons may be structural differences in the insurance markets leading to lower value creation potentials (e.g. already higher level of efficiency) and higher hurdles for realization of these potentials (e.g. stricter labor legislation), or disparities in capital markets (e.g., information efficiency, investor preferences and behavior).

119 Geographical focus (domestic vs. cross-border), and change of control (no change of control vs. change of control).

120 They examine the U.S., Australian and European market. However, their data sample contains only N = 16 transactions of European bidders, and they consequently do not analyze the European market in detail.

Author	Year	Type of study	Sample focus: Industry	Sample focus: Geography	Time span: From	Time span: To
• Akhigbe and Madura	2001	• Event (CAR)	• Acquirer and target is insurance	• US	1985	1995
• Boubakri et al.	2006	• Event (BAHR)	• Acquirer is P&C insurer, target is insurer	• Acquirer US, Targets world-wide	1995	2000
• Cummins and Weiss	2004	• Event (CAR)	• Acquirer or target is insurance company	• Western EU	1990	2002
• Cummins and Xie	2005	• Event (CAR), Efficiency	• Acquirer or target is P&C insurance company	• US	1997	2003
• Floreani and Rigamonti	2001	• Event (CAR)	• Insurance	• US, Europe, and Australia	1996	2000
• BarNiv and Hathorn	1997	• Event (CAR distress study)	• P&C insurance	• US	1985	1992
• Cummins and Rubio-Misas	2003	• Efficiency	• Acquirer and target is insurance	• Spain	1989	1998
• Cummins and Weiss	1998	• Efficiency	• Acquirer and target is Life insurance company	• US	1998	1995
• Cummins and Weiss	2000	• Efficiency (non M&A)	• Reinsurance	• Global	1991	1998
• Cummins et al.	2000	• Efficiency	• Insurance	• US	1993	1997
• Klumpes	2006	• Efficiency	• Acquirer and target is insurance	• Major EU insurance markets	1997	2001
• Chamberlain and Tennyson	1998	• Performance	• Target P&C insurance company	• Target US	1980	1990
• McCullough and Hoyt	2002	• Other	• Target P&C insurance company	• US (tbd)	1993	1997

* Standard market model on local Datastream General Market Index
** Weighted average of Datastream Life Insurance World and Datastream Insurance World
*** Based on CRSP equally weighted TRS index
Source: Own research

Figure 9: Overview of recent studies on the success of insurance M&A

this gap by analyzing short- and long-term value creation and its determinants for European insurers in depth. The following sections review and select relevant methodology.

3.3 Event studies on value creation

Throughout the history of event study research, a variety of methodologies have been developed. Figure 10 provides an overview of common methodologies and categorizes them along three dimensions:

- Time horizon of analyses.
- Abnormal return model: Measurement of abnormal returns, and benchmark construction.
- Tests for significance of abnormal returns.

Dependencies and thus general practice exists across these dimensions. Specifically, analyses shortly around announcement of transactions are usually conducted based on the cumulative abnormal return model.[121] Long-term analyses typically assess value creation based on buy-and-hold abnormal returns or calendar time portfolio abnormal returns.[122] Other, less common approaches such as econometric,[123] Bayesian[124] or nonparametric models[125] are generally universally applicable.

Benchmarks, against which cumulative returns and buy-and-hold returns are evaluated, range from single firms (or indices), reference portfolios to market regression models.[126] Returns of calendar time portfolios are typically compared to multi-factor market regression models, such as the Fama-French-Three-Factor model or the Carhart-Four-Factor model.[127] Besides specification of the bench-

121 E.g., Dodd and Warner (1983).
122 E.g., Lyon et al. (1999).
123 E.g., Acharya (1993), Cyree and DeGennaro (2002), and Solibakke (2002).
124 E.g., Anderson et. al. (2004).
125 E.g., Dombrow (2000).
126 E.g., Barber and Lyon (1997).
127 E.g., Loughran and Ritter (1995), Brav and Gompers (1997), and Brav et al. (1995).

Time	Abnormal return model*: Measurement of abnormal returns	Abnormal return model*: Benchmark construction		Tests for significance
Short term	Cumulative Abnormal Returns (CAR)	Single firm	• One firm/ entire index	**Significance of abnormal returns** • Parametric – (Conventional) t-statistic – Dodd-Warner t-statistic – Boehmer t-statistic • Non-parametric – Bootstrapped t-statistic – Bootstrapped skewness-adjusted t-statistic – Rank tests – Sign tests – Empirical p-value **Significance of difference between abnormal returns** • Parametric – (Conventional) t-statistic • Non-Parametric – Wilcoxon two-sample rank sum test
		Reference portfolio*	• Size (S) • Book-to-market (BM) • SBM	
		Market model	• Specification, e.g., CAPM standard market model • Estimation, e.g., OLS, ML, GMM	
Long term	Buy-and-hold abnormal returns (BAHR)	Other		
	Calendar-Time Portfolio Approach (CTR)	• Model specification, e.g., – Fama-French 3-Factor – Carhart 4-Factor • Model estimation, e.g., OLS, WLS		
Univer-sal	E.g., econometric models, bayesian models			

* Further distinction between equal or value weighting across firms
** Further distinction between rebalanced (average then compound) and buy-and-hold (compound then average), equal and value-weighted portfolio
Source: Own research

Figure 10: Landscape of event study methodologies

mark model itself, the estimation method for regression models may differ as well. However, simple ordinary least squares regression dominates recent academic work.[128]

Finally, the significance of these returns needs to be assessed. Two hypotheses are tested: Firstly, abnormal returns in one sample are different from zero. Secondly. abnormal returns in one sample differ from returns in another sample. Nonparametric tests gained popularity since they rely on fewer assumptions than parametric tests. However, several adjustments to parametric tests have been developed[129] in order to align these assumptions with biases of event study data samples. The following sections present specifications of typical methodologies of short- and long-term event study.

3.3.1 Short-term value creation

3.3.1.1 Measurement of abnormal returns

In short-term event studies, abnormal returns are typically measured as cumulative abnormal returns (CARs).[130] The abnormal return $AR_{i,t}$ of an individual firm *i* (acquirer or target) at time t is defined as the difference between the daily total return to shareholder $R_{i,t}$ of this firm *i* and a benchmark return $E(R_{i,t})$ for this firm i as a proxy for the expected return of firm *i* in the absence of the event at that point in time

$$AR_{i,t} = R_{i,t} - E(R_{i,t}) \tag{1}$$

With $AR_{i,t}$ Abnormal return of firm *i* at time *t*

$R_{i,t}$ Simple daily return of firm *i* at time *t*

$E(R_{i,t})$ Benchmark return for firm *i* at time *t*

---

128 Regression methods applied in recent event studies on insurance M&A are summarized in Figure 12.

129 E.g., Dodd and Warner (1983), Boehmer et al. (1991), and Lyon et al. (1999).

130 E.g, Brown and Warner (1985).

The abnormal return of the combined entity of an acquirer and its target is defined as the market value weighted average of the acquirer abnormal return $AR_{acquirer;i,t}$ and the target abnormal return $AR_{target;i,t}$

$$AR_{transaction;i,t} = \frac{AR_{acquirer;i,t} \cdot MV_{acquirer;i,t} + AR_{target;i,t} \cdot MV_{target;i,t}}{MV_{acquirer;i,t} + MV_{target;i,t}} \quad (2)$$

With $AR_{transaction;i,t}$	Abnormal return of transaction i
$AR_{acquirer;i,t}$	Abnormal return of acquirer i at time t
$MV_{acquirer;i,t}$	Market value of common stock of acquirer i at time t
$AR_{target;i,t}$	Abnormal return of target i at time t
$MV_{target;i,t}$	Market value of common stock of target i at time t

The cumulative abnormal return for firm i (CAR_i) across a specified event window from time t_{e1} to time t_{e2} is defined as

$$CAR_i = \sum_{t=t_{e1}}^{t_{e2}} AR_{i,t} \quad (3)$$

With CAR_i	Cumulative abnormal return for firm i
t_{e1}	Beginning of event window
t_{e2}	End of event window

Cumulative abnormal returns for the combined entity of acquirer and its target (CER) are computed analogously from abnormal returns of the transaction $AR_{transaction;i,t}$. These cumulative abnormal returns of individual firms are aggregated across all firms in a sample in order to test for significance of the observed abnormal returns. The aggregation method needs be chosen in accordance with the type of test applied. Parametric test statistics check for significance of the mean, i.e. an equally-weighted average of CARs is computed, and nonparametric tests for significance of the median, i.e., the 50% quantile of CARs is calculated.

3.3.1.2 Benchmark construction

Specification of benchmark model

Short-term event studies typically rely on simple specifications of the benchmark return $E(R_{i,t})$ such as an ordinary least squares fitted market regression model.[131] Within this class of models, the standard market regression model is commonly applied[132]

$$R_{i,t} = \alpha_i + \beta_i \cdot R_{M,t} + \varepsilon_{i,t} \tag{4}$$

$$E(R_{i,t}) = \hat{\alpha}_i + \hat{\beta}_i \cdot R_{M,t}$$

With $R_{M,t}$ Simple daily return of market portfolio at time t

$\varepsilon_{i,t}$ Regression residuals

$\alpha_i, \hat{\alpha}_i, \beta_i, \hat{\beta}_i$ (Estimated) regression coefficients

Examples for other market models are:

- Market-adjusted model: The benchmark return is defined[133] as $E(R_{i,t}) = R_{M,t}$. Beitel (2002, pp. 76) discusses further simple non-regression models, such as the mean adjusted return model. In this model, the benchmark return is defined as the average stock price return of the firm under investigation during the estimation period.

- CAPM: The benchmark return is defined as $E(R_{i,t}) = R_{ft} + \hat{\beta}_i \left(R_{M,t} - R_{ft}\right)$, with $\hat{\beta}_i = \dfrac{cov\left(R_{i,t}; R_{M,t}\right)}{var(R_{M,t})}$, and R_{ft} the risk-free return. Kothari and Warner (1997) discuss properties of this model.

131 E.g., Cable and Holland (1999b).

132 The standard market regression model is applied by half of recent event studies on insurance M&A, see Figure 12.

133 See e.g., Kothari and Warner (1997).

Cable and Holland (1999b) conduct a simulation study regarding the explanatory power of these and further market models and find that the standard market model is well suited for these types of studies. They add that finally the data sample at hand determines which model will give the best fit.

Besides these single-factor models, multi-factor models such as the Fama-French Three-Factor model or Carhart's Four-Factor model are utilized in the context of event studies. However, these models are typically used for medium and long-term analyses, since analyses on longer time horizons require a better benchmark model and thus justify a higher model complexity. These models are specified in section 3.3.2.1.2. A detailed discussion of advantages and disadvantages of market model is provided by Coutts (1994), and Beitel (2002). Other modeling approaches are less common in the context of event studies. Few authors utilize econometric time-series models such as ARMA-GARCH models,[134] or Bayesian models.[135]

Estimation of the benchmark model

Selection of an estimation method depends heavily on the model specification. For simple linear regression models, such as the standard market model, the benchmark approach for model estimation remains ordinary least squares[136] (OLS). OLS finds the set of parameters, which minimizes squared deviations between model predictions and actual data. Normality of regression residuals is a major prerequisite for the application of OLS. Although Cable and Holland (2000) find pronounced skewness and kurtosis in the course of their analysis. However, they argue that aggregation over time (i.e. computation of firm cumulative abnormal returns) and averaging across firms (i.e. computation of sample cumulative abnormal returns) restores normality for portfolios with sixty or more observations.

134 ARMA and GARCH models are extensions of simpler regression models. ARMA models adjust for conditional means, GARCH models for conditional volatility in the time series; see e.g., Acharya (1993), Cyree and Deegnnaro (2002), and Solibakke (2002).

135 E.g., Anderson et. al. (2004).

136 Greene (2003), p. 19.

Other, less frequently applied methods for estimation of simple linear regression models include general least squares,[137] maximum likelihood, or generalized method of moments.[138]

3.3.1.3 Tests for significance of abnormal returns

After computation of cumulative abnormal returns, two hypothesis need to be tested:

- Cumulative abnormal return of a data sample is significantly different from zero.
- Cumulative abnormal return of one data sample is significantly different from cumulative abnormal return of a second data sample.

Several parametric tests and nonparametric tests are available to test these hypotheses. A major difference between these two classes of tests is that the former test for significance of mean returns, the latter for significance of median returns. Further on, parametric tests require more assumptions to hold than nonparametric tests, e.g., normal distribution of the data sample under examination. Thus, especially for small samples, several authors suggest adjustments to the conventional test statistics in order to correct for biases in the data sample.

Tests for significance of abnormal returns in one sample

In order to test for significance of abnormal returns in one sample, Dodd and Warner (1983) suggest to standardize abnormal returns

$$
\begin{aligned}
Z_{DW,t} &= \frac{1}{\sqrt{n_t}} \cdot \sum_{i=1}^{n} SAR_{i,t} \\
Z_{DW} &= \frac{1}{\sqrt{t_{e2} - t_{e1} + 1}} \sum_{t=t_{e1}}^{t_{e2}} Z_{DW,t}
\end{aligned}
\qquad (5)
$$

137 See e.g., Backhaus et a.l. (2006), pp 368.
138 See e.g., Greene (2003).

With $Z_{DW,t}$ Dodd-Warner two-sided Z-statistic at event time t with $Z_{DW,t} \sim N(0,1)$

Z_{DW} Dodd-Warner two-sided Z-statistic for cumulative abnormal returns with $Z_{DW} \sim N(0,1)$ if SAR standard normal independent identically distributed

n_t Number of firms in sample at event time t

t_e Beginning of event window

t_{e2} End of event window

$SAR_{i,t}$ Standardized abnormal return of firm at time t

The null hypothesis that the observations have mean zero is rejected if $|Z_{DW}| > N(0,1;1-\frac{\alpha}{2})$. Standardized abnormal returns are defined as

$$SAR_{i,t} = \frac{AR_{i,t}}{\hat{\sigma}_{i,t}} \tag{6}$$

$$\hat{\sigma}_{i,t} = \sqrt{\sigma^2_{S,i} \cdot \left(1 + \frac{1}{T_S} + \frac{(R_{M,t} - \overline{R}_M)^2}{\sum_{s=t_{S1}}^{t_{S2}} \left(R_{M,s} - \overline{R}_M\right)^2}\right)}$$

With $\hat{\sigma}_{i,t}$ Estimated standard deviation of firm i at time t

$\sigma_{S,t}$ Sample standard deviation of returns of firm i during estimation period

T_S Days in estimation period, i.e. $t_{S2} - t_{S1} + 1$

t_{S1}, t_{S2} Beginning and end of estimation period

$R_{M,t}$ Simple daily return of market portfolio at time t in event window

$R_{M,s}$ Simple daily return of market portfolio at time s in estimation window

$\overline{R}_M$ Average simple daily return of market portfolio across estimation window

When analyzing cumulative abnormal returns of combined entities, the estimated standard deviation is computed as follows

$$\hat{\sigma}_{transaction,t} = \left[\begin{array}{l} \left(\frac{MV_{acquirer,t}}{MV_{acquirer,t} + MV_{target,t}} \right)^2 \cdot \hat{\sigma}^2_{acquirer,t} + \\ \left(\frac{MV_{target,t}}{MV_{acquirer,t} + MV_{target,t}} \right)^2 \cdot \hat{\sigma}^2_{target,t} + \\ 2 \cdot \left(\frac{MV_{acquirer,t}}{MV_{acquirer,t} + MV_{target,t}} \right)^2 \left(\frac{MV_{target,t}}{MV_{acquirer,t} + MV_{target,t}} \right)^2 \cdot \\ \rho_{acquiror,target} \cdot \\ \hat{\sigma}_{acquirer,t} \cdot \hat{\sigma}_{target,t} \end{array} \right]^{\frac{1}{2}} \tag{7}$$

With $\rho_{acquiror,target}$ Estimated correlation coefficient between acquirer and target abnormal returns in estimation period

Boehmer et al. (1991) introduce further modifications to the conventional *t*-statistic in order to adjust for skewness of abnormal returns

$$Z_B = \frac{1}{\sqrt{t_{e2,i} - t_{e1,i} + 1}} \sum_{t=t_{e1,i}}^{t_{e2,1}} Z_{B,t} \tag{8}$$

$$Z_{B,t} = \frac{\frac{1}{n_t}\sum_{i=1}^{n_t} SAR_{i,t}}{\sqrt{\frac{1}{n_t(n_t-1)}\sum_{i}^{n_t}\left(SAR_{i,t} - \sum_{i=1}^{n_t}\frac{SAR_{i,t}}{n_t}\right)^2}}$$

With $Z_{B,t}$ Boehmer two-sided Z-statistic for event-date t $Z_{B,t} \sim N(0,1)$

Z_B Boehmer two-sided Z-statistic for cumulative abnormal returns with $Z_B \sim N(0,1)$

n_t Number of firms in sample

The null hypothesis that the observations have mean zero is rejected if $|Z_B| > N(0,1;1-\frac{\alpha}{2})$.

Nonparametric tests evaluate whether the hypothesis of zero median abnormal returns can be rejected. Typical tests are the Generalized sign test, and the Wilcoxon signed rank test.[139] The Generalized Sign Test is defined as follows[140]

$$Z_{GST} = \frac{w - n\hat{p}}{\sqrt{n\hat{p}(1-\hat{p})}} \; ; \; \hat{p} = \frac{1}{n}\sum_{i=1}^{n}\frac{1}{T_S}\sum_{t=t_{S1}}^{t_{S2}} S_{i,t} \tag{9}$$

With Z_{GST} Generalized one-sample two-sided Sign Test statistic Z_{GST} approximately $\sim N(0,1)$

T_S Days in estimation period, i.e. $t_{S2} - t_{S1} + 1$

t_{S1}, t_{S2} Beginning and end of estimation period

n Number of firms in sample

w Number of firms with positive CAR in the event window

$S_{i,t}$ $S_{i,t} = \begin{cases} 1 & \text{if } AR_{i,t} > 0 \\ 0 & \text{otherwise} \end{cases}$

139 See e.g., Lorenz (2006).
140 Cowan (1992).

The null hypothesis that the observations are symmetrically distributed around zero is rejected if $\left|Z_{GST}\right| > N(0{,}1;1-\frac{\alpha}{2})$.

The Wilcoxon signed rank test is carried out as follows[141]: Firstly, sort observations ascending by their absolute value and assign ascending ranks R_i, beginning with rank 1. Secondly, apply the sign of the observation to the rank figures to obtain $\widetilde{R}_i$.

Then, compute the test statistic T^*

$$T^* = \frac{T^+ - \frac{1}{4}n\cdot(n+1)}{\sqrt{\frac{1}{24}n\cdot(n+1)(2n+1)}}; \; T^+ = \sum_{1}^{n} c_i \cdot R_i \qquad (10)$$

With T^* Asymptotic Wilcoxon one-sample two-sided signed rank test statistic; $T^* \sim N(0,1)$ for n > 20

c_i 1, if $\widetilde{R}_i > 0$; otherwise 0

The null hypothesis that the observations are symmetrically distributed around zero is rejected if $\left|T^*\right| > N(0{,}1;1-\frac{\alpha}{2})$.

Corrado (1989) suggests to apply a traditional t-test on the ranks of abnormal returns. To implement the test, firstly transform abnormal returns of each firm into ranks $K_{i,t}$.[142] Secondly, compute the average rank for each firm as $\overline{K}_i = 0.5 + 0.5\cdot(T_S + T_E)$ with T_S and T_E the number of days in the estimation and event period, respectively. Then, compute the Corrado rank statistic C as follows

141 Bosch (1998), pp. 695 and pp. 703.

142 The ranks are computed for each firm individually and across the abnormal returns in the estimation and event window.

$$C = \frac{\sum_{t=t_{S1}}^{t_{e2}} \frac{1}{T_S + T_E} \sum_{i=1}^{n} \left(K_{i,t} - \overline{K}_i\right)}{\sqrt{\sum_{t=t_{S1}}^{t_{e2}} S^2}} \tag{11}$$

$$S^2 = \sqrt{\frac{1}{T_E} \sum_{t=t_{e1}}^{t_{e2}} \frac{1}{n^2} \sum_{i=1}^{n} \left(K_{i,t} - \overline{K}_i\right)^2}$$

With C Corrado one-sample two-sided rank test statistic; C asymptotically $\sim N(0,1)$

n Number of firms in sample

T_S Days in estimation period

t_{S1} Beginning of estimation period

t_E Days in event window

t_{e2} End of event window

The null hypothesis that the observations are symmetrically distributed around zero is rejected if $|C| > N(0,1;1-\frac{\alpha}{2})$.

Mußhoff (2007) discusses advantages and disadvantages of parametric and nonparametric test statistics except for the Corrado rank test. For the latter test, Cowan and Sergeant (1996) detect a misspecification if abnormal return variance is increasing. In this case, the Boehmer test and Generalized Sign Test are superior. Higgins and Peterson (1998) confirm in their simulation study that the Boehmer test is superior to the Corrado rank test.

Tests for significance of difference between abnormal returns in two samples

The conventional t-statistic provides a simple test for significance of difference of abnormal returns in two samples

$$CAR_1 = CAR_2 \tag{12}$$

$$t = \frac{\frac{1}{n_1}CAR_1 - \frac{1}{n_2}CAR_2}{\sqrt{\frac{\left(n_1 \cdot \sigma_1^2 + n_2 \cdot \sigma_2^2\right)}{n_1 + n_2 - 2} \cdot \frac{n_1 + n_2}{n_1 \cdot n_2}}}$$

With t Two-sided t-statistic for equal average abnormal returns; $t \sim$ student-$t(n_1 + n_2 - 2)$ assuming equal variance of samples

n_1, n_2 Number of firms in the two samples

σ_1^2, σ_2^2 Sample variance $\sigma_i^2 = \frac{\sum_{j=1}^{n_j}\left(CAR_{ij} - \overline{CAR}_i\right)}{n_i - 1}$

The null hypothesis that $CAR_1 = CAR_2$ is rejected if $|t| > t\left(n_1 + n_2 - 2; 1 - \frac{\alpha}{2}\right)$.

Adjustments for biases in the data sample are not common in the context of event studies.

The nonparametric counterpart is the Wilcoxon two-sample rank sum test.[143] For testing the null hypotheses, that observations of two independent samples are identically distributed with unknown distribution, firstly combine the observations of the two samples, sort the combined sample ascendingly, and assign ranks ascendingly starting with 1. Afterwards, compute the sum of ranks $T_{n1,n2}$ of all observations from either the first sample or the second sample. Then, the define the test statistic T*

143 Bosch (1998), pp. 711.

$$T^* = \frac{T_{n_1;n_2} - \frac{n_1(n_1+n_2+1)}{2}}{\sqrt{\frac{n_1 n_2(n_1+n_2+1)}{12}}} \; ; \; T_{n_1;n_2} = \sum_{i=1}^{n_{12}} r(x_{12,i}) \qquad (13)$$

With T^* Asymptotic Wilcoxon two-sample two-sided rank sum test statistic; $T^* \sim N(0,1)$ for $n_{1,2} \geq 4$ and $n_1 + n_2 \geq 30$

The null hypothesis that the two samples have identical medians is rejected if $T^* < N(0{,}1;\frac{\alpha}{2})$ or $T^* > n_1(n_1+n_2+1) - N(0{,}1;\frac{\alpha}{2})$.

3.3.2 Medium- and long-term value creation

3.3.2.1 Event time

3.3.2.1.1 Measurement of abnormal returns

Barber and Lyon (1997) advocate buy-and-hold abnormal returns (BAHRs) for evaluating abnormal performance in event time over a long time horizon rather than CARs. $BAHR_i$ for acquirer i is computed from monthly acquirer TRS $R_{i,t}$ and the expected TRS of a benchmark $E(R_{i,t})$ based on the model

$$BAHR_i = \prod_{t=1}^{t_{e2}} \left(1 + R_{i,t}\right) - \prod_{t=1}^{t_{e2}} \left(1 + E(R_{i,t})\right) \qquad (14)$$

With $BAHR_i$ Buy-and-hold abnormal return of firm i across entire event window

$R_{i,t}$ Simple daily return of firm i at time t

$E(R_{i,t})$ Benchmark return for firm i at time t

t_{e2} End date of event window

Lyon et al. (1999) discuss properties of BAHRs in detail. Major advantages of this measure are that it reflects investor experience[144], and that it is not prone to the "hot market"[145] issue of calendar time approaches. Major disadvantages of BAHRs are their right-skewness as well as sampling biases[146] and cross-sectional correlation of returns[147] in non-random samples of firms. The right-skewness is eliminated by applying bootstrapped test statistics. The selection biases are mitigated by using a control firm benchmark with size and book-to-market ratios as control firm selection criteria, and by controlling for size and pre-event return performance in multivariate analyses of BAHRs.

3.3.2.1.2 Benchmark construction

Due to the long time horizon of these analyses, benchmark construction is of higher importance than for short-term analyses. Consequently, a wider variety of benchmark models was developed, ranging from control firm models, reference portfolios to multi-factor market regression models.

Barber and Lyon (1997) and Lyon et al. (1999) argue that the control firm approach with successive selection of control firms by firms size, then by book-to-market ratio shows the most favorable statistical properties[148]. Firm size is defined as market value of common equity in June of year t for the period $1.7.t - 30.6.t + 1$. Book-to-market ratio is defined as book value of common equity in year $t - 1$, divided by market value of common equity end of year $t - 1$ for the period $1.7.t - 30.6.t + 1$. The selection proceeds as follows:

144 BAHRs can be interpreted as the total performance of an investor's stock portfolio with a long position in the acquirer's stock and a short position in the benchmark portfolio.

145 Abnormal returns in periods of high M&A activity are probably higher than abnormal returns in other periods. However, abnormal returns in both periods are equally weighted for derivation of calendar time abnormal returns, see discussion by Mußhoff (2007, pp. 149).

146 E.g., driven by firm size, market-to-book ratio, pre-event return performance, and industry clustering, see Lyon et al. (1999, pp. 181).

147 E.g., due to calendar clustering of events or overlapping return calculations, see Lyon et al. (1999, pp. 188).

148 Using control firms as benchmarks eliminates the new listing bias (i.e., firms added to the index after an event, thus biasing index development), the rebalancing bias (i.e., portfolio returns typically assume some form of portfolio rebalancing), and size and book-to-market biases due to non-random samples of firms, see Barber and Lyon (1997) and Lyon et al. (1999). The issue that tests for abnormal returns jointly test for actual abnormal returns and correct specification of the benchmark ("bad-model problem") remains, see discussion in Mußhoff (2007, pp. 150).

- For each acquirer and each period in the event window, a short list of index constituents with firm size between 70% and 130% of the acquirer is created.
- For each acquirer and each period in the event window, a single control firm from this short list based on the lowest difference in book-to-market ratio between the firms contained in the short list and the acquirer is selected.

3.3.2.1.3 Tests for significance of abnormal returns

As for short-term analyses, two hypotheses need to be tested:

- Buy-and-hold abnormal return of a data sample is significantly different from zero.
- Buy-and-hold abnormal return of one data sample is significantly different from buy-and-hold abnormal return of a second data sample.

Lyon et al. (1999) firstly utilize the conventional two-sided *t*-statistic to test for the former hypothesis

$$t_{conv} = \sqrt{n} \cdot \frac{\overline{BAHR}}{\sigma(BAHR)} \tag{15}$$

With	t_{conv}	Conventional t-statistic
	t_{conv}	$\sim t(n-1)$[149]
	n	Number of firms in sample
	$\overline{BAHR}$	Sample mean of $BAHR_i$
	$\sigma(BAHR)$	Sample standard deviation of $BAHR_i$

The null hypothesis of that the observations are symmetrically distributed around zero is rejected if $|t_{conv}| > t\left(n-1;1-\frac{\alpha}{2}\right)$. However, Lyon et al. (1999) recommend to adjust for skewness of *BAHR*s

149 Bosch (1998), p. 411.

$$t_{sa} = \sqrt{n} \cdot \left(\frac{t_{conv}}{\sqrt{n}} + \frac{\hat{\gamma} \cdot t_{conv}^2}{3n} + \frac{\hat{\gamma}}{6n} \right) \tag{16}$$

With t_{sa} Skewness-adjusted two-sided t-statistic

t_{sa} $\sim t(n-1)$ according to Johnson[150]

n Number of firms in sample

$\hat{\gamma}$ Estimated coefficient of skewness with $\hat{\gamma} = \frac{\sum_{i=1}^{n} \left(BAHR_i - \overline{BAHR} \right)^3}{n \cdot \sigma(BAHR)^3}$

The null hypothesis that the observations are symmetrically distributed around zero is rejected if $|t_{sa}| > t\left(n-1;1-\frac{\alpha}{2}\right)$. Additionally, Lyon et al. (1999) argue that bootstrapping almost eliminates the skewness bias in the data sample. They devise the following bootstrapping procedure

- From the original sample, draw 1,000 bootstrapped resamples with size $n_b = n/4$ and recompute t_{sa}^b in each of these resamples.
- Compute lower critical value x_l^* and the upper critical value x_u^* as the lower and upper $\alpha/2$ quantile of the distribution of t_{sa}^b, where α is the level of significance.
- Reject the null hypothesis that the observations are symmetrically distributed around zero if either $t_{sa} < x_l^*$ or $t_{sa} > x_u^*$.

Tests for significance of difference between abnormal returns in two samples are defined as for short-term analyses in section 3.3.1.3.

150 Johnson (1978).

3.3.2.2 Calendar time

3.3.2.2.1 Measurement of abnormal returns and benchmark construction

The calendar time approach differs from the event time approach, in that it examines whether a portfolio of firms, which recorded an event in a specified period in the past, shows abnormal returns compared to a benchmark portfolio. Thus, it does not mirror investor experience, is prone to the "hot market" issue, and vulnerable to biases from non-random sampling of firms.[151] However, Lyon et al. (1999) identify favorable statistical properties, such as elimination of cross-sectional dependence, mitigation of the bad-model problem, and more robust test statistics.

Fama and French (1993) suggest a three-factor regression model (Fama-French-Three-Factor model) to measure abnormal returns. Total returns of acquirers show abnormal performance, if the following regression of the market portfolio excess return $R_{m,t} - R_{f,t}$, the return differential between small stocks and big stocks SMB_t, and the return differential between high and low book-to-market stocks HML_t against the calendar time portfolio excess return $R_{p,t} - R_{f,t}$ yields an intercept which is significantly different from zero

$$R_{p,t} - R_{f,t} = \alpha + \beta \cdot \left(R_{m,t} - R_{f,t}\right) + s \cdot SMB_t + h \cdot HML_t + \varepsilon_t \qquad (17)$$

With
$R_{p,t}$ Simple monthly return of calendar time portfolio at time t
$R_{f,t}$ Risk-free rate
$R_{m,t}$ Simple monthly return of market portfolio
α Regression intercept
β, s, h Regression slopes
SMB_t Difference of simple monthly returns of value-weighted portfolio of small stocks and big stocks at time t

151 See section 3.3.2.1.1 for a brief explanation, and Lyon et al. (1999) for a detailed discussion of these effects.

HML_t	Difference of simple monthly returns of value-weighted portfolio of high book-to-market stocks and low book-to-market stocks at time t
ε_t	Error term

The regression intercept is interpreted as a monthly abnormal return which can not be reached by neither holding the market portfolio, a risk-free portfolio, a SMB portfolio nor an HML portfolio. Thus, the regression intercept defines the monthly abnormal return. Fama and French construct the SMB and HML portfolios as follows:

- The constituents of an index are partitioned into small stocks and big stocks at the size median.
- The constituents are partitioned into stocks with low, medium, and high book-to-market ratio at the 30% and 70% quantile of the book-to-market distribution.
- The value-weighted returns for the six intersecting portfolios are computed.
- The equally-weighted average returns on the small stock, big stock, high book-to-market ratio, and low book-to-market ratio portfolios are computed.
- SMB is calculated as the difference between the average small stock and big stock portfolio returns.
- HML is calculated as the difference between the average high book-to-market ratio and low book-to-market ratio portfolio returns.

Other major multi-factor models include the CAPM, and Carhart's (1997) Four Factor model, which – in addition to the Fama-French-Three-Factor model – introduces the return differential between stocks with high and low past returns as a fourth regression factor. Mußhoff (2007, pp. 119) elaborates on the properties of these models.

3.3.2.2.2 Tests for significance of abnormal returns

The two hypotheses of significant abnormality or significant difference of abnormality need to be tested:

- The calendar time abnormal return (i.e. regression intercept) is significantly different from zero.
- The calendar time abnormal return of one data sample is significantly different from the calendar time return in a second data sample.

The conventional t-statistic tests for the first hypothesis[152]

$$t_0 = \frac{b_0}{s \cdot \sqrt{c_{00}}} \tag{18}$$

With t_0 Two-sided t-statistic with $t_0 \sim t(n-p-1)$ for n observations, and p independent variables

b_0 Regression intercept

s Estimated variance with $s = \frac{1}{n-p-1}\sum_{i=1}^{n}(y_i - \hat{y}_i)^2$ with y_i the dependent variables and $\hat{y}_i$ the expected dependent variables

c_{00} (1,1)-element of $C = \left(X^T X\right)^{-1}$ with $X = \begin{pmatrix} 1 & x_{11} & \cdots & x_{1p} \\ 1 & x_{21} & \cdots & x_{2p} \\ \vdots & \vdots & \vdots & \vdots \\ 1 & x_{n1} & \cdots & x_{np} \end{pmatrix}$

The null hypothesis that the regression intercept is zero is rejected if $|t_0| > t\left(n-p-1; 1-\frac{\alpha}{2}\right)$.

In order to test the second hypothesis of equality of intercepts of two multiple regressions, an indicator variable model[153] can be utilized

152 Bosch (1998), pp 627.

153 E.g., Larsen (2006), pp. 6.

$$y = \alpha_1 + \beta_1 \cdot x + \alpha_2 \cdot z + \beta_2 \cdot x \times z + \varepsilon \qquad (19)$$

With z the indicator variable (0 for the first sample, 1 for the second sample)

The intercepts are significantly different, if the null hypothesis $a_2 = 0$ can be rejected according to the standard t-statistic.

3.4 Summary

Previous event studies develop, refine and apply numerous methodologies for assessing abnormality of returns over a short- and long time horizon. Most of the studies with a focus on the insurance industry carry out short-term analyses (see section 3.2). All of these studies utilize cumulative abnormal returns to measure abnormal performance, see Figure 12. Half of these studies draw on the standard market model as the benchmark, whereas the other half reverts to a simple index as the benchmark. Cable and Holland (1999b) advocate to use a standard market regression model. With respect to tests for significance, three studies utilize non-parametric tests. Furthermore, only Cummins and Xie (2005) use bias-adjusting parametric tests, although Dodd and Warner (1983) and Boehmer et al. (1991) discuss the importance of bias correction, especially for inference on few observations.

This study pursues the objective to obtain meaningful results even on small data samples, but yet to ensure comparability of results with prior academic work. Thus, for short-term analyses, abnormality of returns is assessed based on cumulative abnormal returns. Following the approach of half of prior event studies on insurance M&A and the argument of Cable and Holland (1999b), the standard market regression model defines the benchmark. Significance of abnormal returns is evaluated with parametric and nonparametric tests. The rank test according to Corrado (1989) is not implemented due to its inferiority compared to the Boehmer test. Two sample bias adjustments for the former types of tests are implemented to improve their properties on samples with few observations.

○ No issue ● Severe issue

Root cause	Issue	BAHR (event time)		CTAR (calendar time)	
Non-random samples	• Sampling biases	• Mitigated by benchmark specification and multivariate analysis*	◑	• Yes	●
	• Cross-correlation	• Yes	●	• No	○
Inadequate benchmark	• Bad-model problem	• Yes	●	• Mitigated by benchmark specification***	◑
	• New listing bias	• Mitigated by benchmark specification**	◑	• No	○
	• Rebalancing bias	• Mitigated by benchmark specification**	◑	• No	○
	• Heteroskedasticity	• No	○	• Minor issue	◑
Definition of abnormal returns	• No investor experience	• No	○	• Yes	●
	• Hot market issue	• No	○	• Yes	●
	• Right-skewness	• Mitigated by boot-strapped test statistics	◑	• No	○

* Control firm approach reduces bias from size and market-to-book. Size and pre-event return performance are controlled for through multivariate analyses of BAHRs. An industry bias is inherent (if not intended) in this study since it focuses on the insurance industry

** Biases eliminated through control firm approach even when applying standard t-statistics

*** Market model controls for three factors

Source: Own research

Figure 11: Comparison of statistical properties of BAHR and CTAR approaches

Only Boubakri et al. (2006) analyze long-term value creation. They measure 3-year BAHRs relative to the S&P 500 index, but do not mention which particular test statistic they employ to assess significance of abnormal returns or significance of difference between abnormal returns. Barber and Lyon (1997) agree that BAHRs, especially when based on a control firm benchmark, are the preferable abnormal return model for long-term studies compared to CARs. However, a clear recommendation with respect to application of either BAHRs or calendar time abnormal returns (CTARs) cannot be given. Lyon et al. (1999, p. 198) conclude from their extensive simulation study that "though both [abnormal return measures] offer advantages and disadvantages, a pragmatic solution for a researcher who is analyzing long run abnormal returns would be to use both." Figure 11 summarizes their discussions of comparative advantages and disadvan-

	Akhigbe and Madura, 2001	Boubakri et al., 2006	Cummins and Weiss, 2004	Cummins and Xie, 2005	Floreani and Rigamonti, 2001	BarNiv and Hathorn, 1997
Abnormal return model						
• Measurement of abnormal returns	• CAR, CER	• BAHR	• CAR	• CAR, CER	• CAR, CER, BAHR	• CAR
• Benchmark construction	• Standard market model; estimation pe-riod [-220; -20]	• S&P 500 BAH 3-year	• Standard market model (log re-turns); estimation period [-250; -30]	• CRSP equally-weighted total index return; estimation peri-od [-150; -31]	• Daily value-weighed average of Datastream life insurance world and Data-stream insurance world	• Standard market model; estimation period [-500; -251]
Test for significance	• t-statistic	• (not explicitly stated)	• t-statistic on standardized CARs • Cowan generalized sign statistic	• Patell Z-statistic • Boehmer et. al. SCS Z-statistic • t-statistic • Cowan generalized sign statistic	• t-statistic • Wilcoxon sign statistic	• t-statistic
Time horizons (event window)	• Various in [-11; +10]	• 3 years	• Various in [-15; +15]	• Various in [-10; +15]	• Various in [-40; +40]	• [-250; +250]

Source: Own research

Figure 12: Methodology applied in recent event studies

tages of both approaches and illustrates that neither approach is clearly dominant by its fundamental statistical properties.

Thus, this study analyses both buy-and-hold abnormal returns, and calendar time abnormal returns. BAHRs are implemented as suggested by Boubakri et al. (2006). However, the benchmark and tests for significance are defined following the control firm approach and skewness-adjusted bootstrapped t-statistics favoured by Barber and Lyon (1997), and Lyon et al. (1999) in order to mitigate sampling, new listing, and rebalancing biases. Following discussions in the latter article, the CTARs are computed based on Fama and French's (1993) Three Factor market model as the benchmark. Figure 13 summarizes the BAHR and CTAR approaches applied in this study.

Although neither approach is to be favored by its basic statistical properties, this study shall rather draw on BAHRs for the analysis of determinants of value

		Long term analyses	
	Short term analysis	**Event time**	**Calendar time**
Abnormal return model			
• Measurement of abnormal returns	• CAR, CER, value generation	• BAHR, value generation	• CTA (equally-weighted, value-weighted)
• Benchmark construction	• Standard market model; estimation period [-270; -21]	• Control firm approach	• Fama-French-Three-Factor model
Test for significance	**Significance of abnormal returns** • Parametric – Conventional t-statistic – Dodd-Warner t-statistic – Boehmer t-statistis • Non-parametric – Generalized sign test – Wilcoxon signed rank test **Significance of difference between abnormal returns** • Parametric – (Conventional) t-statistic • Non-Parametric – Wilcoxon two-sample rank sum test	**Significance of abnormal returns** • Parametric – Conventional t-statistic – Skewness-adjusted t-statistic – Bootstrapped skewness-adjusted t-statistic **Significance of difference between abnormal returns** • Parametric – (Conventional) t-statistic	**Significance of abnormal returns** • Parametric – Conventional t-statistic **Significance of difference between abnormal returns** • Parametric – (Conventional) t-statistic on indicator variable regression model
Time horizons (event window)	• Various in [-20; +20]	• [0; +1 years] • [0; +2 years] • [0; +3 years]	• [0; +3 years]

* Value generated is defined as the relative cumulative abnormal return in the event window
Source: Own research

Figure 13: Methodology applied in this event study

creation: Only the BAHR approach allows for a multivariate analysis of abnormal returns, which is necessary to accurately separate simultaneous influence of several determinants. A multivariate analysis is not applicable to the CTAR approach since it adopts a portfolio perspective on all firms that record an event in a certain month; thus, differentiation of firms and their abnormal returns by control factors is not feasible. For the examination of overall value creation on the entire data sample, this study shall assign equal relevance to results of either methodology in the final assessment. The following chapter applies the presented approaches to assess short- and long-term value creation and its determinants.

4 Value Creation by M&A in the European Insurance Industry – an Empirical Investigation

4.1 Objectives

M&A activity in the European insurance sector increased sharply in the early 1990s. After reaching its peak in 1999, several years of depression followed. However, in 2005, momentum built up again. Analyses in chapter 2 provide evidence that this pickup in M&A activity should not only be considered a blip, but that it marks the entry into the next cycle of transactions in the sector. Besides upcoming reformation of legal, accounting and supervisory regimes, investors' pressure on management to create value is identified as major motive for further consolidation of the European insurance industry. This finding confronts with a paradox: Empirical studies of M&A in the financial services industry frequently doubt value creation, in particular in the banking industry.[154]

Despite the current relevancy for the European insurance sector, little empirical research addressed the question of value creation by M&A in this industry. Firstly, prior research on short-term cumulative abnormal returns (CARs) of investors in acquirers or targets indicates that value creation by U.S. and European insurance M&A differs substantially.[155] Thus, findings of U.S.-focused event studies with respect to abnormal returns of combined entities (CERs)[156] may not hold for European markets. Unfortunately, the only studies on the Euro-

154 See overviews in Beitel and Schiereck (2003), and Pilloff and Santomero (1998).

155 Cummins and Weiss (2004) obtain significantly negative acquirer CARs on their European sample, whereas all other studies on the U.S. or global market report significantly positive acquirer CARs.

156 Akhigbe and Madura (2001) and Cummins and Xie (2005) observe significantly positive CERs.

pean insurance market either do not analyze CERs at all[157] or cover Europe only as one of many regions with insufficient observations for detailed market-specific analyses.[158] Secondly, these studies limit their analysis on determinants of value creation to few univariate comparisons of cross-sections, and do not carry out multivariate analyses at all, which is necessary to properly separate effects of several determinants on abnormal returns. Thirdly, long-term value creation for European insurers has – to the best of the author's knowledge – never been investigated before. For the industry, investors but also regulators, this gap in empirical evidence reinforces the pressing question: Does M&A in the European insurance industry create value, and what are major determinants of success? The purpose of this chapter is to fill this gap and examine short- and long-term value creation by M&A in the European insurance industry.

This chapter is structured as follows. Section 4.2 describes the generation of the data sample and presents descriptive statistics on its characteristics. Sections 4.3 and 4.4 examine short- and long-term value creation and its determinants. The short-term study analyses capital market reactions shortly before and after announcement of the transactions using the cumulative abnormal return (CAR) methodology. Long-term value creation up to 3 years after announcement is examined according to the buy-and-hold-abnormal return (BAHR) and calendar-time abnormal return (CTAR) measures. Both approaches are applied since a clear recommendation for either one cannot be given based on their fundamental statistical properties.[159] Sections 4.3 and 4.4 firstly discuss overall value generation in the entire transaction data sample. Secondly, a multivariate analysis on determinants of abnormal returns is conducted. Thirdly, the multivariate analysis is complemented by further examination of major cross-sections in univariate analyses. The final assessment with regard to determinants of value creation shall draw on the multivariate analysis since it accurately separates simultaneous influence of several factors.[160]

157 Cummins and Weiss (2004) only present evidence on acquirer and target CARs.

158 Floreani and Rigamonti (2001) include only N = 16 transactions of European bidders in their analysis of CERs and thus do not analyze the European market in detail.

159 See section 3.3.2 for a detailed discussion, and section 3.4 for a brief summary of the rationale.

160 A multivariate analysis of long-term abnormal returns is only applicable to the BAHR approach, but not to the CTAR approach, see argumentation in section 3.4. Thus, conclusions

Section 4.5 reviews these findings in the context of prior research. Further on, the interdependence of short- and long-term value creation is examined from an industry and an investor perspective. Relevant for the industry is the question whether the influence of determinants on value creation depends on the time horizon of the analysis. This section examines which factors historically lead to value creation in the short run, and how these factors compare to those driving value creation in the long run. The results may support management in choosing the appropriate strategy depending on its strategic time horizon or in enriching its capital market communication. Relevant for investors is the question whether long-term value creation depends on short-term capital market reactions. If this is the case, investors could leverage information from short-term capital market reactions for their mid-term investment strategy. Further on, one could either infer that investors' initial assessment of announced M&A is adequate, or that their originally established opinion is "sticky".

4.2 Data sample

4.2.1 Generation of the data sample

European insurance M&A transactions between 1990 and 2005 are identified based on two primary data sources, Thomson Financial SDC Platinum, and Dealogic Merger & Acquisition database. The Dealogic database only covers transactions from 1995 onwards. Both deal lists are integrated, verified and amended through extensive press research. Capital market data and company account data is obtained primarily from Datastream, and complemented by Bloomberg and annual report data for early transactions. Figure 14 presents an overview of required data fields and respective data sources.

with respect to determinants of value creation on the long-term horizon are only drawn on results of the BAHR analysis.

	Data field	Sources of data: Primary	Sources of data: Secondary
Deal data	• Announcement date • Deal status • Deal value • Change of control* • Acquirer and target – Name – ISIN** – Country	SDC, Dealogic, own press research	Bloomberg, Datastream
	– Industry classification		S&P Global Reinsurance Highlights
Market and other company data	• Total return to shareholders index	Datastream	–
	• Market value of equity		Bloomberg
	• Book value of equity		Bloomberg, annual reports, other databases
Bench-mark data	• Total return to shareholders index	Datastream	–
	• Market value of equity		Bloomberg
	• Book value of equity		Bloomberg, annual reports, other databases
	• T-bills	Bloomberg	–

* Initial stake before transaction < 50%, final stake after transaction > 50%
** Alternatively, Datastream code or SEDOL
Source: <___>

Figure 14: Overview required data fields and data sources for the event studies

The following filter criteria are employed to identify the relevant M&A transactions:

- The transaction was announced between 1.1.1990 and 31.12.2005.
- The transaction has been closed (i.e., the transaction status is indicated as "completed").
- The transaction volume was equal to or larger than USD 100 mn.[161]

161 Transactions with missing transaction volumes are included in the downloads and accepted or rejected based on the volume obtained through press research; transactions with undisclosed financial terms are excluded.

- A change of control occurred through the transaction, i.e. the initial stake of the acquirer in the target before the transaction was smaller than 50%, and the final stake after the transaction is higher than 50%.
- The acquirer was member of EU-25 or Switzerland or Norway. The location of the target country is not restricted.
- The acquirer SIC and the target SIC were 63* (Insurance Carriers). Additionally, targets include SICs 6282 (Investment Advice), 6411 (Insurance Agents, Brokers, and Service), 6719 (Offices of Holding Companies, Not Elsewhere Classified), 6722 (Management Investment Offices, Open-End), and 6726 (Unit Investment Trusts, Face-Amount Certificate Offices, and Closed-End Management Investment Offices).
- The acquirer was a listed company.
- The acquisition object were the shares, not only the assets or policyholder liabilities of a target company.

Transactions with multiple bidder activity are not dropped from the sample, following the proposal of Pilloff and Santomero (1998). Further on, the industry classification “Reinsurance” is introduced, which is not distinguished by SIC, based on the Top-150 reinsurance provider lists published by Standard & Poor’s in their Global Reinsurance Highlights reports.

4.2.2 Characteristics of transactions

Figure 15 presents an overview of the N = 176 transactions between 1990 and 2005 that satisfy the set of criteria. Clearly, implementation of the Third Generation Insurance Directives in 1992 set the starting point for steadily increasing transaction numbers and volumes, culminating in 1999, when the stock market boomed and the EMU was implemented, with 27 transactions (15% of all transactions between 1990 and 2005) worth USD 51.6 bn. Cummins and Weiss (2004) observe a similar pattern in their data. The strongest pickup of deal volumes is observed in 1996 (USD 26.7 bn up from USD 5.3 bn in 1995), and 2005

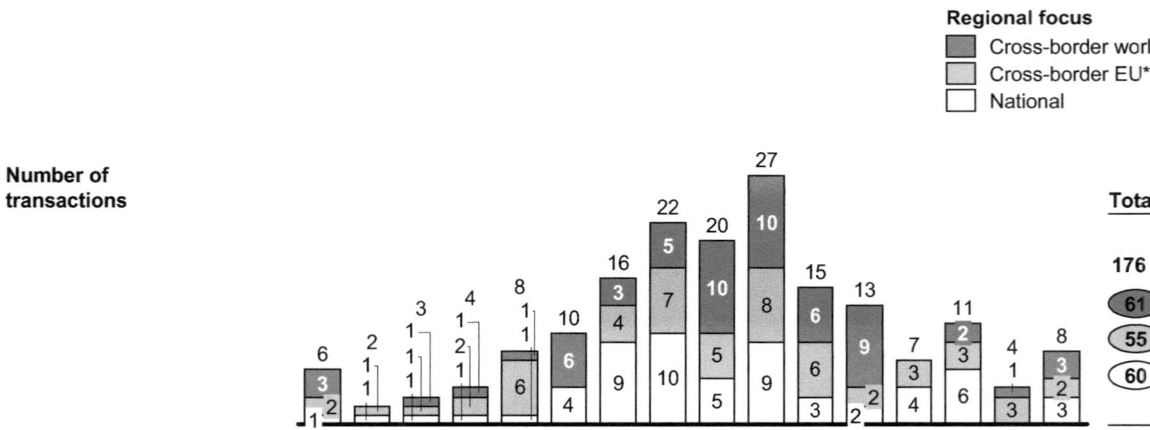

		1990	91	92	93	94	95	96	97	98	99	2000	01	02	03	04	2005	Total
Transaction volume USD billions	Cross-border world	4.0	0.0	0.1	0.1	0.1	4.0	6.4	4.9	5.4	20.0	7.8	6.1	0.0	1.6	0.3	8.1	**69.0**
	Cross-border EU*	0.5	0.2	0.4	2.7	4.6	0.0	3.3	28.5	5.1	9.0	21.5	1.6	2.3	0.9	2.1	7.3	**90.0**
	National	0.5	0.4	0.4	0.1	0.2	1.3	16.9	12.3	15.4	22.5	12.3	1.3	3.8	2.9	0.0	3.9	**94.3**
	Total	**5.0**	**0.6**	**0.9**	**2.9**	**4.9**	**5.3**	**26.7**	**45.7**	**25.9**	**51.6**	**41.6**	**9.0**	**6.2**	**5.4**	**2.3**	**19.3**	**253.3**
Average transaction volume USD billions	Cross-border world	1.3	n/a	0.1	0.1	0.1	0.7	2.1	1.0	0.5	2.0	1.3	0.7	n/a	0.8	0.3	2.7	**1.1**
	Cross-border EU*	0.2	0.2	0.4	1.3	0.8	n/a	0.8	4.1	1.0	1.1	3.6	0.8	0.8	0.3	0.7	3.6	**1.6**
	National	0.5	0.4	0.4	0.1	0.2	0.3	1.9	1.2	2.8	2.5	4.1	0.6	1.0	0.5	n/a	1.3	**1.6**
	Total	**0.8**	**0.3**	**0.3**	**0.7**	**0.6**	**0.5**	**1.7**	**2.1**	**1.3**	**1.9**	**2.8**	**0.7**	**0.9**	**0.5**	**0.6**	**2.4**	**1.4**

* EU-25, Norway, Switzerland

Source: Thomson Financial SDC platinum, Dealogic M&A database, press research

Figure 15: Development of transactions 1990–2005

(USD 19.3 bn up from USD 2.3 bn in 2004), both driven by significantly increased average deal volume, and risen number of deals. There are only slight, but insignificant linear trends[162] eminent in the data sample with respect to number of transactions (0.4 more transactions p.a., p-value of 35%[163]), volume of transactions (USD 0.9 bn more volume p.a., p-value of 38%), and average transaction volume (USD 61.9 mn more p.a. and transaction, p-value of 15%).

The aforementioned events clearly drove the geographical distribution of M&A activities. Between 1990 and 2005, national, cross-border within and outside of Europe[164] transactions accounted each for about a third of the total transaction numbers and volumes. After the implementation of the Third Generation Insurance Directives however, volume share of cross-border transactions within Europe rose from 43% in 1992 to 94% in 1994. The introduction of the Euro produced a less pronounced effect: Volume shares of cross-border transactions rose from 17% in 1999 to 52% in 2000. A linear trend with respect to geographical distribution of transaction numbers or volumes is not detected (p-values above 85%).

With respect to industry activity, Figure 16 illustrates that life insurers were the most frequent acquirers (131 transactions worth USD 203.9 bn), accounting for 80% of the total transaction volume between 1990 and 2005.[165] Further on, life insurers were the preferred target (103 transactions worth USD 177.0 bn). Consequently, life-life transactions dominated M&A activities in general (85 transactions worth USD 162.5 bn, 63% of total volume).

The regional focus of the transactions for the long-term analyses is documented in Figure 17. The majority of the transactions were carried out by EU-15 based acquirers (141 deals or 80% of deals; deal volume USD 185.9 bn or 73% of the total deal volume). However in average, largest transactions were completed by Swiss acquirers with an average deal size of USD 2.0 bn. Likewise, insurance companies from EU-15 countries were the most popular targets

162 The linear trend test is based on a linear univariate OLS regression model.
163 p-value of two-sided t-test of null hypothesis that slope of linear regression line is zero.
164 Europe is defined as member states of EU-25, Norway, and Switzerland.
165 The utilized industry classification is an aggregation of SICs.

Number of deals
Deal volume (USD bn)
Average deal volume (USD bn)

Acquirer \ Target	Life	P&C	Reinsurance	Agents/ brokers	Investment management	Other	Total
Life	85	18	2	9	11	6	**131**
	160.7	6.9	1.7	23.3	10.0	1.4	**203.9**
	1.9	0.4	0.8	2.6	0.9	0.2	**1.6**
P&C	7	7	1	0	1	0	**16**
	12.0	7.8	0.5	0.0	3.3	0.0	**23.6**
	1.7	1.1	0.5	n/a	3.3	n/a	**1.5**
Reinsurance	11	8	9	0	0	0	**28**
	4.2	9.5	11.8	0.0	0.0	0.0	**25.5**
	0.4	1.2	1.3	n/a	n/a	n/a	**0.9**
Agents/ brokers	0	0	0	0	0	1	**1**
	0.0	0.0	0.0	0.0	0.0	0.2	**0.2**
	n/a	n/a	n/a	n/a	n/a	0.2	**0.2**
Other	0	0	0	0	0	0	**0**
	0	0	0	0	0	0	**0**
	n/a	n/a	n/a	n/a	n/a	n/a	n/a
Total	**103**	**33**	**12**	**9**	**12**	**7**	**176**
	177.0	**24.2**	**14.0**	**23.3**	**13.3**	**1.6**	**253.3**
	1.7	**0.7**	**1.2**	**2.6**	**1.1**	**0.2**	**1.4**

Source: Thomson Financial SDC platinum, Dealogic M&A database, press research

Figure 16: Industry focus of transactions

(106 deals or 60% of deals; deal volume USD 174.1 bn or 69% of the total deal volume). Norwegian insurers were the largest in average to be acquired, with average deal size of USD 2.2 bn. Altogether, transactions within the EU-15 member states built the largest portion of all transactions (90 deals or 51% of deals; deal volume USD 129.7 bn or 51% of the total deal volume).

Figure 18 documents the distribution of transactions by country. British insurers were most active acquirers (49 transactions worth USD 70.4 bn), and the second most popular targets (34 transactions worth USD 93.8 bn). Only U.S. insurers were acquired more frequently (39 transactions), however with a notably smaller volume (USD 61.0 bn). Swiss acquirers were almost as active as British

Legend: Number of deals / Deal volume (USD bn) / Average deal volume (USD bn)

Acquirer \ Target		EU-15	Other EU-25	Norway	Switzerland	World	Total
EU-15	Number of deals	90	3	1	2	45	**141**
	Deal volume (USD bn)	129.7	2.0	3.8	1.4	49.0	**185.9**
	Average deal volume (USD bn)	1.4	0.7	3.8	0.7	1.1	**1.3**
Other EU-25	Number of deals	0	0	0	0	0	**0**
	Deal volume (USD bn)	0	0	0	0	0	**0**
	Average deal volume (USD bn)	n/a	n/a	n/a	n/a	n/a	**n/a**
Norway	Number of deals	0	0	1	0	0	**1**
	Deal volume (USD bn)	0.0	0.0	0.5	0.0	0.0	**0.5**
	Average deal volume (USD bn)	n/a	n/a	0.5	n/a	n/a	**0.5**
Switzerland	Number of deals	16	0	0	2	16	**34**
	Deal volume (USD bn)	44.4	0	0.0	2.4	20.0	**66.9**
	Average deal volume (USD bn)	2.8	n/a	n/a	1.2	1.3	**2.0**
Total	Number of deals	**106**	**3**	**2**	**4**	**61**	**176**
	Deal volume (USD bn)	**174.1**	**2.0**	**4.4**	**3.8**	**69.0**	**253.3**
	Average deal volume (USD bn)	**1.6**	**0.7**	**2.2**	**1.0**	**1.1**	**1.4**

Source: Thomson Financial SDC platinum, Dealogic M&A database, press research

Figure 17: Regional focus of transactions

insurers with 34 transactions worth USD 66.9 bn, but only involved 4 times as target. The leading role of British insurers in European M&A is also reflected in the data sample of Cummins and Weiss (2004).

Figure 19 presents the relative transaction volumes compared to the market value of the acquirers at announcement. On average, transactions amounted to 10.8% of the acquirers' market capitalization. Large acquirers tend to focus on cross-border world deals, while small players mostly concentrate on national or cross-border EU deals. Only recently, between 1998 and 2005, large players were more involved in cross-border EU transactions than in cross-border world deals.

Acquirer country			Target country: EU-15 FR	BE	DE	DK	ES	FI	GB	IE	IT	LU	NL	SE	Tot.	EU-25 CZ	HU	PL	Tot.	Norway NO	Swiss CH	World AU	BM	BR	CA	CL	HK	IL	JP	LK	MX	SG	TW	US	Tot.	Overall Total
EU-15	FR	No.	4	3	1				3	1			2		14						1	1		1	1		1		1					4	9	24
		USD bn.	13.5	4.1	0.5				2.4	0.2			3.1		23.7						0.2	0.8		0.5	0.3		0.1		2.0					2.3	5.9	29.9
	AT	No.									1				1	1	1		2																	3
		USD bn.									0.1				0.1	0.1	1.7		1.8																	2.0
	BE	No.		2											2																					2
		USD bn.		1.1											1.1																					1.1
	DE	No.	1		5					1	3	1		1	12																			5	5	17
		USD bn.	5.2		5.8					0.4	1.3	0.1		0.1	12.9																			10.6	10.6	23.5
	DK	No.				3								1	4																			1	1	5
		USD bn.				0.5								0.5	1.1																			0.6	0.6	1.7
	ES	No.					1								1																					1
		USD bn.					0.3								0.3																					0.3
	FI	No.						2							2			1	1																	3
		USD bn.						0.4							0.4			0.2	0.2																	0.5
	GB	No.	2		1		1		24	1		1	1	1	32							1	1		2	1			1			1	1	9	17	49
		USD bn.	2.3		0.3		0.3		49.4	0.4		1.3	0.8	7.0	61.8							0.2	0.2		0.7	0.1			0.2			0.2	0.1	6.8	8.5	70.4
	IE	No.								1					1																					1
		USD bn.								2.7					2.7																					2.7
	IT	No.	3		2						15				20						1							1						1	2	23
		USD bn.	1.2		5.5						17.6				24.3						1.2							0.3						0.3	0.6	26.1
	NL	No.							1						1										3	1					2			5	11	12
		USD bn.							1.2						1.2										0.8	0.1					1.0			20.8	22.7	23.9
	SE	No.																		1																1
		USD bn.																		3.8																3.8
Total		No.	10	5	9	3	2	2	28	4	19	2	3	3	90	1	1	1	3	1	2	2	1	1	6	2	1	1	2		2	1	1	25	45	141
EU-15		USD bn.	22.3	5.2	12.0	0.5	0.6	0.4	53.0	3.7	19.0	1.4	3.9	7.6	129.7	0.1	1.7	0.2	2.0	3.8	1.4	1.0	0.2	0.5	1.7	0.2	0.1	0.3	2.2		1.0	0.2	0.1	41.4	49.0	185.9
Norway	NO	No.																		1																1
		USD bn.																		0.5																0.5
Swiss	CH	No.	3	2	1		2		6		1		1		16						2									1	1			14	16	34
		USD bn.	1.3	0.2	1.1		0.4		40.8		0.4		0.3		44.4						2.4									0.1	0.1			19.8	20.0	66.9
Overall		No.	13	7	10	3	4	2	34	4	20	2	4	3	106	1	1	1	3	2	4	2	1	1	6	2	1	1	2	1	3	1	1	39	61	176
Total		USD bn.	23.6	5.4	13.1	0.5	1.0	0.4	93.8	3.7	19.4	1.4	4.2	7.6	174.1	0.1	1.7	0.2	2.0	4.4	3.8	1.0	0.2	0.5	1.7	0.2	0.1	0.3	2.2	0.1	1.1	0.2	0.1	61.2	69.0	253.3

Country codes: FR - France, AT - Austria, BE - Belgium, DE - Germany, DK - Denmark, ES - Spain, FI - Finland, GB - Great Britain, IE - Ireland, IT - Italy, LU - Luxembourg, NL - Netherlands, SE - Sweden, CZ - Czech Republic, HU - Hungary, PL - Poland
NO - Norway, CH - Switzerland, AU - Australia, BM - Bermuda, BR - Brazil, CA - Canada, CL - Chile, HK - Hong Kong, IL - Israel, JP - Japan, LK - Sri Lanka, MX - Mexico, SG - Singapore, TW - Taiwan, US - United States of America

Sources: Thomson Financial SDC Platinum, Dealogic M&A database, press research

Figure 18: Number and volume of transactions by country

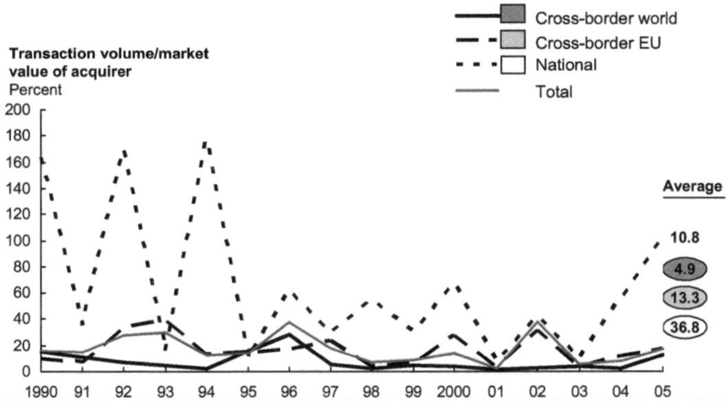

		1990	91	92	93	94	95	96	97	98	99	2000	01	02	03	04	05	
Average market value of acquirers* in USD bn	Cross-border world	8.8	n/a	1.9	2.0	4.7	4.3	7.6	18.5	20.8	39.3	32.1	37.2	n/a	20.5	10.9	20.8	23.3
	Cross-border EU*	2.4	3.2	1.2	3.4	5.6	n/a	4.9	17.2	27.7	17.6	13.0	18.9	2.4	8.3	6.0	21.3	12.3
	National	0.3	1.2	0.2	0.8	0.1	3.1	3.0	4.1	5.6	8.1	6.1	8.0	2.2	4.9	n/a	1.2	4.3
	Total	**5.3**	**2.2**	**1.1**	**2.4**	**4.8**	**3.8**	**4.4**	**11.5**	**18.7**	**22.5**	**19.2**	**29.9**	**2.3**	**8.7**	**7.3**	**13.6**	**13.4**

* Total market value of acquirers at announcement date in the respective year, divided by number of transactions in this year

Source: Thomson Financial SDC platinum, Dealogic M&A database, press research

Figure 19: Characteristics of acquirers and transactions

However, with respect to relative deal volume, national transactions were the largest: In few instances, the transaction volume even exceeded the acquirer's market capitalization. Further on, the relative deal volumes reveal a strong cyclicality: Years with high ratios are typically followed by a short period with lower size ratios, whereas changing acquirer size is not the major driver. A possible interpretation is that insurers tend to carry out deals in years where others do, and that they collectively require an integration period with lower activity afterwards.

This sample of transactions provides the basis for examining the question whether M&A in the European insurance industry creates value over a short-term horizon, discussed in section 4.3, and over a long-term horizon, discussed in section 4.4. These analyses shall not only provide insights into average value creation across all firms in the sample, but also identify explanations for variation of value creation between firms in the sample. Consequently, the following sub-section presents characteristics of several potential determinants of value creation derived from the deal sample.

4.2.3 Determinants of value creation

Cross-sectional analyses of value creation shall provide insights into determinants of short- and long-term value creation. Sections 4.3 and 4.4 examine the following determinants:

- Transaction strategy and properties: Geographical and industry focus (*STRATEGY*), timing of the transaction (*TIMING*).
- Acquirer properties: Region of origin (*ACQREGION*), industry (*ACQINDUSTRY*), natural logarithm of size[166] (*LNSIZE*), growth[167] (*GROWTH*), transaction experience[168] (*EXPERIENCE*).
- Target properties: Region of origin (*TARREGION*), industry (*TARINDUSTRY*), natural logarithm of relative transaction volume[169] (*LNRELVOLUME*), listing (*TARNOTLISTED*).

The categorical variable *STRATEGY* is introduced to test the hypothesis of relative importance of economies of scope or risk diversification through geographical or industry diversification, compared to economies of scale through industry focus or increase in market power through geographical focus.[170] If cross-border or cross-industry transactions generate more value than national or within-industry transactions, economies of scope or risk diversification are assumed to be larger than regional market power effects or scale economies.[171] *STRATEGY* is

166 Size is measured as market value at announcement date.

167 Growth is measured as relative change of market value over the estimation window. If market value data is not available at the beginning or the end of the estimation window, growth computed from available data is scaled to the length of the estimation window.

168 Number of transactions of the same acquirer in the long-term deal sample during the last 3 years. This measure thus restricts experience rightfully to targets within the insurance industry or asset management industry.

169 Transaction volume divided by acquirer size. Absolute transaction volume is not modeled because its logarithm is perfectly linear in the logarithms of transaction volume and acquirer size.

170 This is the most commonly analyzed cross-section in prior research. Cummins and Xie (2005) include geographical and industry focus in their multi- and univariate analyses, Floreani and Rigamonti (2001) examine the geographical dimension in their multi- and univariate analyses, and Cummins and Weiss (2004) analyze geographical univariate cross-sections. Boubakri et al. (2006) introduce two separate independent variables for geographical and industry focus in their multivariate analysis.

171 The current level of geographical or industry diversification is not controlled for, see Cummins and Xie (2005).

implemented as a polytomous dummy variable,[172] carrying the parameter values national/within-industry,[173] national/cross-industry, cross-border within EU[174]/ within-industry, cross-border within EU/cross-industry, cross-border world/within-industry, cross-border world/cross-industry. Fully focused transactions (national/within-industry) are chosen as the dummy reference so that superiority of diversification strategies can be tested against them.

The categorical variable *TIMING* controls for the timing of the transaction with regard to the phase in the M&A cycle.[175] If transactions in the peak phase of the M&A cycle generate less value than transactions in other phases, evidence for the "bandwagon effect" is provided. *TIMING* is operationalized by categorizing the announcement years into several phases. The typical 2-phase classification into positive growth and negative growth (e.g., Hamilton, 1989) is extended by further differentiating between peak and bottom phases due to superiority of the respective regression model.[176] The resulting classification is bottom (years 1990-1995, 2001-2005), upswing (1996), peak (1997-1999), and downturn (2000). The bottom phase is chosen as the dummy reference to test peak phase abnormal returns against it.

The categorical variables *ACQREGION*[177], *TARREGION*, *ACQINDUSTRY*[178], and *TARINDUSTRY*[179] control for differences in value creation across

---

172 E.g., Backhaus (2006, p. 8). A polytomous variable with m parameter values is implemented as m-1 dichotomous (indicator) variables.

173 The industry dimension is defined based on the industry classification as discussed in section 4.2.2.

174 EU is not further separated into EU-25, Switzerland and Norway in order to keep degrees of freedom small. The independent variables *ACQREGION* and *TARREGION* control for country-specific variations.

175 Cycle effects are not examined in prior research. However, Floreani and Rigamonti (2001) include the announcement year in their regression analysis and thus test for a linear trend in abnormal returns across time, but obtain insignificant results.

176 Alternative classification techniques (e.g., two or four phases, by quartiles or relative amount to peak) are evaluated based on the fit of the respective multivariate short-term and long-term models. The chosen classification technique, four phases relative to peak volume, results in regression models with superior average and ranked R-square, adjusted R-square and F-test significance across tested event windows and time horizons.

177 Floreani and Rigamonti (2001) analyze cross-sections of the acquirers' regions (U.S., Europe, Australia).

178 Akhigbe and Madura (2001) introduce an indicator variable to distinguish between life vs. non-life acquirers in their multivariate analysis.

regions and industries. The variable region of origin distinguishes between Western European countries (EU-15), Central and Eastern European countries (other EU-25), and Switzerland and Norway as the two European countries which are not member of the EU and thus operate in different jurisdictions. The industry variable differentiates life, P&C, reinsurance, agents/brokers, investment management and other industries, following the classification introduced in section 4.2.2.

The metric variable *LNSIZE* is introduced to test whether large institutions are better at identifying synergy potentials, negotiating the transaction, and realizing synergy potentials.[180] The hypothesis is supported if the estimated coefficient is significantly positive.[181] The metric variable *GROWTH* is used to examine whether fast growing acquirers are better or worse at generating value from M&A transactions than slowly growing acquirers. If transactions of fast growing acquirers generate less value than transactions of other acquirers, this indicates difficulties at integrating the target.[182]

The categorical variable *EXPERIENCE* is incorporated into the regression to test for an experience effect of acquirers in successfully choosing, negotiating and executing takeovers of insurers or investment managers. If transactions by more experienced acquirers yield higher abnormal returns, existence of a positive experience effect is supported. Due to its superior statistical properties[183] compared to other frequency or volume based measures,[184] *EXPERIENCE* is modeled as a polytomous variable with quartiles of transaction volume as parameter values.

179 Floreani and Rigamonti (2001) compare sub samples where acquirer and target are both a life insurer, both a reinsurer and other transactions. Boubakri et al. (2006) separate agencies/ brokers and other targets.

180 A test of the narrower hypothesis whether large acquirers are better at integrating targets, i.e. realizing synergy potential, would require controlling for synergy potential and transaction premium.

181 Size is logarithmized before introduction into the regression model, see e.g., Floreani and Rigamonti (2001) and Cummins and Xie (2005).

182 This test does not control for existing synergy potential and transaction premium.

183 This measure yields superior R-Square, adjusted R-Square and F-test significance across analyzed short- and long-term event windows.

184 Similarly, Cummins and Xie (2005) include bidder frequency as an indicator variable in their study. They distinguish between acquirers which buy more than once in a year and those that do not. Boubakri et al. (2006) include number of transactions of the acquirer in the same year as a metrical independent variable.

The metric variable *LNRELVOLUME* is introduced to examine whether institutions are better at handling transactions with relatively smaller targets.[185] A significantly positive regression coefficient would support this hypothesis.[186] The dichotomous variable *TARNOTLISTED* controls for differences between the short- and long-term data samples in the long-term analyses.[187] Descriptive statistics on the variables are presented as part of the multivariate analyses in sections 4.3.2.2 and 4.4.2.2.

The deal sample and these determinants of value creation are the basis for a profound analysis of value creation through M&A in the European insurance industry. The following chapter discusses in detail value creation across a short-term period before and after announcement of these transactions, whereas section 4.4 examines value creation through these transactions on a long-term horizon.

4.3 Analysis of short-term value creation

4.3.1 Methodology

4.3.1.1 Measurement of abnormal returns and benchmark construction

The short-term event study model follows the methodology devised by Dodd and Warner (1983), and Brown and Warner (1985), who compute cumulative abnormal returns (CARs) relative to a market benchmark model. A detailed specification of the approach is given in chapter 3.3.1.1 and chapter 3.3.1.2.

The abnormal return $AR_{i,t}$ of firm i at time t is measured as the difference between daily total returns to shareholder $R_{i,t}$ of firm *i* and the benchmark return $E(R_{i,t})$ for firm *i*

$$AR_{i,t} = R_{i,t} - E(R_{i,t}) \qquad (20)$$

185 Akhigbe and Madura (2001), and Floreani and Rigamonti (2001), and Cummins and Xie (2005) also control for relative transaction volume in their multivariate analyses.

186 The natural logarithm is applied to the relative transaction volume, see e.g., Floreani and Rigamonti (2001).

187 Akhigbe and Madura (2001) control for target listing in their multivariate analyses, too.

Abnormal returns of the acquirer $AR_{acquirer,t}$ and the target $AR_{target,t}$ are weighted with their market values MV_t to compute the combined entity return $AR_{transaction,t.}$

$$AR_{transaction,t} = \frac{AR_{acquirer,t} \cdot MV_{acquirer,t} + AR_{target,t} \cdot MV_{target,t}}{MV_{acquirer,t} + MV_{target,t}} \tag{21}$$

Benchmark returns are defined as the OLS-regression estimate of the standard market model on the estimation window at times t between [–270; –21] trading days before announcement, following Lorenz (2006)

$$R_{i,t} = \alpha_i + \beta_i \cdot R_{M,t} + \varepsilon_{i,t} \tag{22}$$

The market return $R_{M,t}$ is defined as the daily TRS of the Datastream European Insurance Index. The CARs are the equally-weighted average of the abnormal returns on a specified event period from times t_{e1} to t_{e2} between [–20; +20] trading days around announcement

$$CAR = \frac{1}{n} \sum_{i=1}^{n} \sum_{t=t_{e1}}^{t_{e2}} AR_{i,t} \tag{23}$$

Figure 20 illustrates the applied time periods for regression model estimation and measurement of value creation. The models are calibrated to the following data:

- Daily market values in EUR for acquirers and targets.
- Daily simple[188] TRS in local currency[189] for acquirers and targets.
- Daily simple TRS in EUR for market portfolio (Datastream European Insurance Index).

188 Total return to shareholders is computed as the simple return, i.e. index value at time t divided by index value one trading day earlier, not as the continuously compounded return, following the methodology applied in prior studies (e.g., Lorenz, 2006).

189 Return data is generated based on a local currency TRS index in order to eliminate overnight exchange rate effects from the analysis.

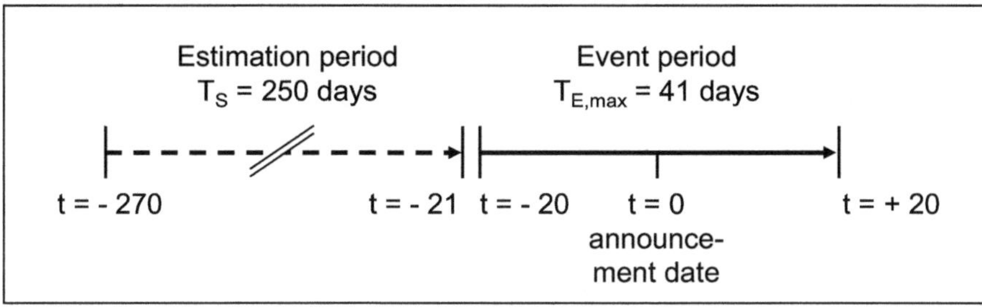

Figure 20: Estimation and event windows for short-term analyses

4.3.1.2 Tests for significance of abnormal returns

The significance of mean cumulative abnormal returns is tested with the parametric Dodd-Warner Z-statistic (Equation (21)), and the Boehmer test-statistic (Equation (22)).[190] All tests are briefly introduced here, and discussed in detail in section 3.3.1.3.

$$Z_{DW} = \frac{1}{\sqrt{n}} \cdot \sum_{i=1}^{n} \left(\frac{1}{\sqrt{t_{e2,i} - t_{e1,i}}} \cdot \sum_{t=t_{e1,i}}^{t_{e2,1}} \frac{AR_{i,t}}{\hat{\sigma}_{i,t}} \right) \qquad (24)$$

$$\text{With } \hat{\sigma}_{i,t} = \sqrt{\sigma^2_{S,i} \cdot \left(1 + \frac{1}{T_S} + \frac{(R_{M,t} - \overline{R}_M)^2}{\sum_{s=t_{S1}}^{t_{S2}} \left(R_{M,s} - \overline{R}_M \right)^2} \right)}$$

The null hypothesis that the observations have mean zero is rejected if $|Z_{DW}| > N(0{,}1;1 - \frac{\alpha}{2})$.

$$Z_B = \frac{1}{\sqrt{t_{e2,i} - t_{e1,i} + 1}} \sum_{t=t_{e1,i}}^{t_{e2,1}} Z_{B,t} \qquad (25)$$

190 Corrado's (1989) statistic is not implemented, see section 3.3.1.3.

$$\text{With } Z_{B,t} = \frac{\frac{1}{n_t}\sum_{i=1}^{n_t} SAR_{i,t}}{\sqrt{\frac{1}{n_t(n_t-1)}\sum_{i}^{n_t}\left(SAR_{i,t} - \sum_{i=1}^{n_t}\frac{SAR_{i,t}}{n_t}\right)^2}}$$

The null hypothesis that the observations have mean zero is rejected if $|Z_B| > N(0,1;1-\frac{\alpha}{2})$. Additionally, the significance of median abnormal returns and cumulative abnormal returns are tested with the nonparametric Wilcoxon signed rank test (Equation (23)), and the Generalized sign test (Equation (24))).

$$T^* = \frac{T^+ - \frac{1}{4}n\cdot(n+1)}{\sqrt{\frac{1}{24}n\cdot(n+1)(2n+1)}} \tag{26}$$

$$\text{With } T^+ = \sum_{1}^{n} c_i \cdot R_i$$

The null hypothesis that the observations are symmetrically distributed around zero is rejected if $|T^*| > N(0,1;1-\frac{\alpha}{2})$.

$$Z_{GST} = \frac{w - n\hat{p}}{\sqrt{n\hat{p}(1-\hat{p})}} \tag{27}$$

$$\text{With } \hat{p} = \frac{1}{n}\sum_{i=1}^{n}\frac{1}{T_S}\sum_{t=t_{s1}}^{t_{s2}} S_{i,t}$$

The null hypothesis that the observations are symmetrically distributed around zero is rejected if $|Z_{GST}| > N(0,1;1-\frac{\alpha}{2})$.

The significance of the difference between mean cumulative abnormal returns of two samples is tested with the parametric two-sample *t*-test (Equation (25)), and between median abnormal returns and cumulative abnormal returns with the Wilcoxon rank sum test (Equation (26)).

$$t = \frac{\frac{1}{n_1}CAR_1 - \frac{1}{n_2}CAR_2}{\sqrt{\frac{\left(n_1 \cdot \sigma_1^2 + n_2 \cdot \sigma_2^2\right)}{n_1 + n_2 - 2} \cdot \frac{n_1 + n_2}{n_1 \cdot n_2}}} \tag{28}$$

With $\sigma_i^2 = \frac{\sum_{j=1}^{n_j}\left(CAR_{ij} - \overline{CAR}_i\right)}{n_i - 1}$

The null hypothesis that $CAR_1 = CAR_2$ is rejected if $|t| > t\left(n_1 + n_2 - 2;1 - \frac{\alpha}{2}\right)$.

$$T^* = \frac{T_{n_1;n_2} - \frac{n_1(n_1 + n_2 + 1)}{2}}{\sqrt{\frac{n_1 n_2 (n_1 + n_2 + 1)}{12}}} \tag{29}$$

With $T_{n_1;n_2} = \sum_{i=1}^{n_{12}} r(x_{12,i})$

The null hypothesis that observations of two samples are identically distributed is rejected if $T^* < N(0,1;\frac{\alpha}{2})$ or $T^* > n_1(n_1 + n_2 + 1) - N(0,1;\frac{\alpha}{2})$.

4.3.2 Results

4.3.2.1 Results on entire data sample

Market model regression results

The market model is estimated on $N = 250$ observations for acquirers and targets. Missing acquirer data limits observations of the transactions between Old Mutual PLC and United Asset Management Corporation to $N = 225$. Missing target data limits observations of the transaction between Brit Insurance Holdings PLC and

Table 1: Market model regression statistics for acquirers

	Mean		Bottom 20		Top 20	
Observations	250		248		250	
Unknown variables	2		2		2	
Regression statistics	Statistic	p-value	Statistic	p-value	Statistic	p-value
R-Squared	0.2213	-	0.0213	-	0.5162	-
Adjusted R-Squared	0.2181	-	0.0174	-	0.5143	-
F-statistic	103.4423	4.2%	5.5016	20.8%	323.4438	0.0%
Coefficient estimates	Coefficient	Standard error	Coefficient	Standard error	Coefficient	Standard error
Constant	0.0005	0.0011	-	0.0016	-	0.0006
Beta(1)	0.7545	0.1022	-	0.1601	-	0.0570
Coefficient t-statistics	Statistic	p-value	Statistic	p-value	Statistic	p-value
Constant	0.4779	53.6%	-	87.9%	-	15.8%
Beta(1)	8.3094	4.2%	-	20.8%	-	0.0%

PRI Group PLC to N = 185. The OLS fitted market model explains the return variance well (average R-square of 0.22). Table 1 and Table 2 present averages as well as bottom and top 20% quantiles of further regression statistics. The high F-statistic and the low average p-values indicate significant estimates for the beta coefficient.

Table 2: Market model regression statistics for targets

	Mean		Bottom 20		Top 20	
Observations	249		244		250	
Unknown variables	2		2		2	
Regression statistics	Statistic	p-value	Statistic	p-value	Statistic	p-value
R-Squared	0.0858	-	0.0010	-	0.2501	-
Adjusted R-Squared	0.0821	-	-0.0031	-	0.2471	-
F-statistic	26.7589	17.1%	0.2488	67.6%	83.9687	0.0%
Coefficient estimates	Coefficient	Standard error	Coefficient	Standard error	Coefficient	Standard error
Constant	0.0005	0.0012	-	0.0020	-	0.0007
Beta(1)	0.4068	0.1234	-	0.2243	-	0.0583
Coefficient t-statistics	Statistic	p-value	Statistic	p-value	Statistic	p-value
Constant	0.5608	46.3%	-	90.0%	-	5.2%
Beta(1)	3.7633	17.1%	-	67.6%	-	0.0%

Normality property of abnormal returns

The hypothesis tests for abnormality of returns are based on the assumption, that the average abnormal returns on the estimation window are normally distributed. Table 3 shows that this assumption cannot be rejected: The Kolmogorov-Smirnov test yields high p-values.

Table 3: Distribution of abnormal returns

	Acquirer	Target	Combined Entity
Observations	250	250	250
Normal parameters	0	0	0
Mean	0.000002	0.000002	-0.000003
Sigma	0.002501	0.003139	0.002184
Most extreme differences	0.0000	0.0000	0.0000
Absolute	0.008747	0.010792	0.006221
Positive	0.008747	0.010792	0.006221
Negative	0.006092	0.010158	0.005981
Kolmogorov-Smirnov test	0	0	0
Statistic	0.0323	0.0442	0.0365
Asymptotic p-value	95.4%	70.3%	88.8%

Value generation and abnormal returns

The M&A transactions in the entire short-term deal sample generated a total net value of USD 1.8 bn (1.7%)[191] for investors. 26 deals generated value of USD 5.3 bn, whereas 28 deals destroyed value of USD 3.5 bn, see Figure 21. The overall positive net value is thus driven by higher average value generation for successful deals (USD 0.2 bn) than average value destruction by unsuccessful deals (USD 0.1 bn).

Although mean CERs are positive on all analyzed event windows, significant value creation is only observed shortly around the announcement date in the event windows [–5; 0] with 1.22%, [0; +10] with 1.45%, and [–10; +10] with 2.06% at the 10% level. Especially around announcement, the CERs are strongly right skewed.

The detailed results are documented in Table 4. In this table, "CER%" presents the mean and median CERs across firms. A higher mean than median indicates a right skewed distribution of firm CERs, i.e. there are few firms with high CERs. The further analyses focus on mean CERs as the predominant measure of prior academic work. "Sign of CERs" gives the number of observations in the

191 The computation of net value generated is based on the cumulative abnormal returns in [-20; +20] days around the announcement day and the market value of acquirers and targets at the end of the estimation period [-21].

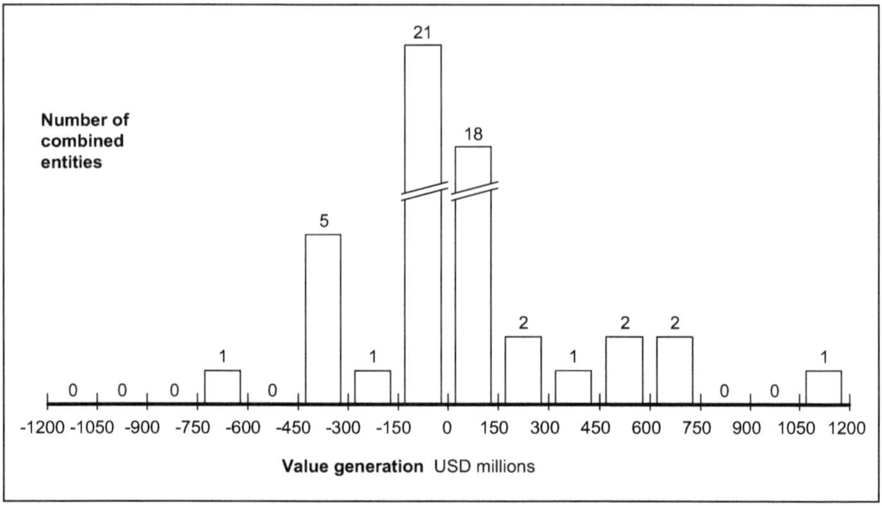

Figure 21: Distribution of value generation in short-term deal sample

sample with positive and negative CER. A large difference between both figures indicates qualitatively that the null hypothesis of zero CER could be rejected. The following columns display parametric and nonparametric tests of the null hypothesis that the mean and median CER are zero, respectively. If test statistics are high and *p*-values are low, the null hypotheses can be rejected.

In contrast, capital market reactions for targets were significantly positive at 1% level in all analyzed event windows except for the mean CAR in [0; +20] with a Boehmer p-value of 1.5%. The abnormal returns are strongest around the announcement date (maximum at mean CAR of 14.02% in [–20; +20] at 1% level), and lowest on the day of the announcement (mean CAR of 6.26% at 0.1% level). The distribution of the CARs is strongly right skewed. Table 5 presents the detailed results.

Acquirer CARs are mostly statistically insignificant; the only statistically significant result at 10% level or better occurs in [–2; +2] with CAR of –0.93% according to the Boehmer test. CARs in all other event windows are insignificant by any of the used test statistics. A detailed overview of the results is presented in Table 6.

Table 4: Significance of CERs on short-term deal sample ($N = 54$)

Event window	CER%		Sign of CERs		Dodd-Warner		Boehmer		Generalized Sign		Wilcoxon Signed Rank	
	mean	**median**	Pos	Neg	Statistic	p-value	Statistic	p-value	Statistic	p-value	Statistic	p-value
[-20; +0]	1.07%	1.65%	32	22	1.1334	25.7%	0.1800	85.7%	1.8648	6.2%	1.8038	7.1%
[-10; +0]	1.22%	1.52%	34	20	2.1307	3.3%	1.0103	31.2%	2.4104	1.6%	2.1482	3.2%
[-5; +0]	1.22%	0.93%	32	22	3.2340	0.1%	1.9176	5.5%	1.8648	6.2%	2.2688	2.3%
[-2; +0]	0.72%	0.12%	29	25	3.1363	0.2%	0.9998	31.7%	1.0464	29.5%	1.2356	21.7%
[-1; +0]	0.85%	0.12%	29	25	4.3292	0.0%	1.8380	6.6%	1.0464	29.5%	1.2614	20.7%
[+0; +0]	0.61%	0.11%	28	26	4.9773	0.0%	1.5035	13.3%	0.7737	43.9%	0.8912	37.3%
[+0; +1]	0.64%	0.06%	30	24	3.2442	0.1%	0.8690	38.5%	1.3192	18.7%	0.7792	43.6%
[+0; +2]	0.41%	-0.07%	26	28	2.0124	4.4%	0.1372	89.1%	0.2281	82.0%	0.3143	75.3%
[+0; +5]	0.46%	-0.25%	26	28	1.5153	13.0%	0.3569	72.1%	0.2281	82.0%	-0.0560	95.5%
[+0; +10]	1.45%	1.21%	32	22	2.5809	1.0%	2.0211	4.3%	1.8648	6.2%	1.8125	7.0%
[+0; +20]	1.23%	0.70%	29	25	1.9822	4.7%	1.5193	12.9%	1.0464	29.5%	1.1495	25.0%
[-1; +1]	0.87%	0.16%	28	26	3.3100	0.1%	1.3422	18.0%	0.7737	43.9%	0.8739	38.2%
[-2; +2]	0.52%	-0.10%	27	27	1.7622	7.8%	0.2083	83.5%	0.5009	61.6%	0.7276	46.7%
[-5; +5]	1.07%	0.51%	30	24	2.0068	4.5%	1.2265	22.0%	1.3192	18.7%	1.4680	14.2%
[-10; +10]	2.06%	1.97%	33	21	2.3238	2.0%	1.8659	6.2%	2.1376	3.3%	2.1999	2.8%
[-20; +20]	1.69%	-0.55%	26	28	1.4524	14.6%	0.9813	32.6%	0.2281	82.0%	1.4508	14.7%

Table 5: Significance of target CARs on short-term deal sample ($N = 54$)

Event window	CAR%		Sign of CARs		Dodd-Warner		Boehmer		Generalized Sign		Wilcoxon Signed Rank	
	mean	**median**	Pos	Neg	Statistic	p-value	Statistic	p-value	Statistic	p-value	Statistic	p-value
[-20; +0]	10.35%	4.21%	38	16	8.5521	0.0%	2.6618	0.8%	3.8747	0.0%	3.6034	0.0%
[-10; +0]	10.29%	3.35%	35	19	12.0088	0.0%	4.0508	0.0%	3.0526	0.2%	3.7411	0.0%
[-5; +0]	8.74%	3.22%	37	17	13.4138	0.0%	3.8459	0.0%	3.6007	0.0%	4.1286	0.0%
[-2; +0]	8.59%	2.91%	36	18	18.3239	0.0%	4.8792	0.0%	3.3267	0.1%	4.1975	0.0%
[-1; +0]	7.84%	1.42%	37	17	20.4023	0.0%	4.4267	0.0%	3.6007	0.0%	3.9306	0.0%
[+0; +0]	6.26%	0.93%	36	18	23.8375	0.0%	3.7540	0.0%	3.3267	0.1%	3.6464	0.0%
[+0; +1]	7.80%	1.57%	37	17	19.5007	0.0%	3.3242	0.1%	3.6007	0.0%	3.5431	0.0%
[+0; +2]	8.73%	1.75%	36	18	18.2539	0.0%	3.2170	0.1%	3.3267	0.1%	3.6636	0.0%
[+0; +5]	9.62%	3.57%	37	17	13.9934	0.0%	3.6629	0.0%	3.6007	0.0%	4.2147	0.0%
[+0; +10]	9.79%	3.81%	39	15	11.1013	0.0%	3.3023	0.1%	4.1487	0.0%	4.4127	0.0%
[+0; +20]	9.92%	6.05%	39	15	8.0143	0.0%	2.4230	1.5%	4.1487	0.0%	4.2147	0.0%
[-1; +1]	9.38%	2.45%	36	18	18.8181	0.0%	4.1612	0.0%	3.3267	0.1%	3.9392	0.0%
[-2; +2]	11.06%	4.41%	38	16	17.6726	0.0%	4.5924	0.0%	3.8747	0.0%	4.1458	0.0%
[-5; +5]	12.10%	6.14%	40	14	13.0543	0.0%	4.4138	0.0%	4.4228	0.0%	4.7055	0.0%
[-10; +10]	13.82%	7.87%	40	14	11.5241	0.0%	4.5026	0.0%	4.4228	0.0%	4.4558	0.0%
[-20; +20]	14.02%	10.03%	39	15	8.1334	0.0%	3.0528	0.2%	4.1487	0.0%	4.2491	0.0%

Table 6: Significance of acquirer CARs on short-term deal sample ($N = 54$)

Event window	CAR%		Sign of CARs		Dodd-Warner		Boehmer		Generalized Sign		Wilcoxon Signed Rank	
	mean	**median**	Pos	Neg	Statistic	p-value	Statistic	p-value	Statistic	p-value	Statistic	p-value
[-20; +0]	-0.09%	0.14%	28	26	0.0014	99.9%	-0.0776	93.8%	0.7100	47.8%	0.4865	62.7%
[-10; +0]	0.06%	0.37%	28	26	0.2836	77.7%	0.2775	78.1%	0.7100	47.8%	0.3057	76.0%
[-5; +0]	0.09%	-0.51%	24	30	0.6075	54.3%	0.6483	51.7%	-0.3806	70.3%	-0.2798	78.0%
[-2; +0]	-0.34%	-0.36%	22	32	-0.3712	71.0%	-0.7361	46.2%	-0.9259	35.4%	-1.0634	28.8%
[-1; +0]	-0.11%	-0.31%	20	34	0.2139	83.1%	0.0727	94.2%	-1.4712	14.1%	-0.9859	32.4%
[+0; +0]	-0.09%	-0.12%	25	29	0.4103	68.2%	0.2188	82.7%	-0.1080	91.4%	-0.4434	65.7%
[+0; +1]	-0.19%	-0.21%	24	30	-0.0207	98.4%	-0.0804	93.6%	-0.3806	70.3%	-0.7964	42.6%
[+0; +2]	-0.68%	-0.63%	21	33	-1.2921	19.6%	-1.3237	18.6%	-1.1986	23.1%	-1.4422	14.9%
[+0; +5]	-0.77%	-1.54%	20	34	-1.1497	25.0%	-1.0402	29.8%	-1.4712	14.1%	-1.5455	12.2%
[+0; +10]	0.32%	-0.04%	27	27	0.4138	67.9%	0.7505	45.3%	0.4373	66.2%	0.1162	90.7%
[+0; +20]	0.24%	-0.17%	27	27	0.3898	69.7%	0.5827	56.0%	0.4373	66.2%	0.2368	81.3%
[-1; +1]	-0.21%	-0.45%	23	31	-0.0791	93.7%	-0.1326	89.5%	-0.6533	51.4%	-0.7706	44.1%
[-2; +2]	-0.93%	-0.66%	21	33	-1.4719	14.1%	-1.6934	9.0%	-1.1986	23.1%	-1.3906	16.4%
[-5; +5]	-0.59%	-0.29%	24	30	-0.5241	60.0%	-0.3554	72.2%	-0.3806	70.3%	-0.6587	51.0%
[-10; +10]	0.47%	0.53%	28	26	0.4152	67.8%	0.6963	48.6%	0.7100	47.8%	0.4693	63.9%
[-20; +20]	0.25%	0.06%	27	27	0.2159	82.9%	0.3273	74.3%	0.4373	66.2%	0.3229	74.7%

Developing of CARs across the event window

At the announcement date, the target CAR jumps notably by 6.26%, probably due to high takeover premiums offered to target shareholders, see Figure 22. The fast reaction of targets' shareholders indicates efficiency of capital markets.

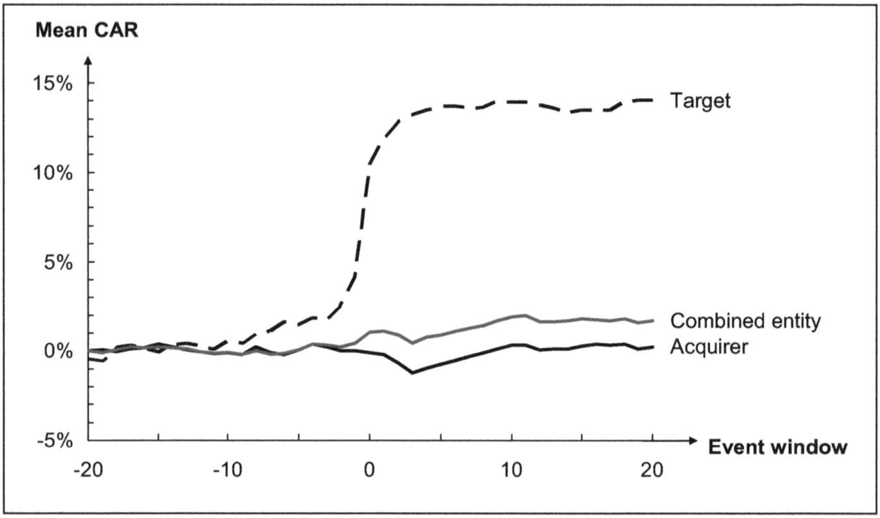

Figure 22: Developing of mean CAR on short-term deal sample

Comparison of results to prior research

This study finds that CERs are significantly positive on most analyzed event windows, reaching a maximum in [–10; +10] with 2.06% at the 10% level. Other studies on insurance M&A also find positive CERs, whereas those in the U.S. or global market are notably higher even in smaller event windows. Akhigbe and Madura (2001) observe positive significant CERs of 13.11% in [–1; 0] at 5% level for the U.S. market. Floreani and Rigamonti (2001) report a CER of 5.27% in the event window [–20; +2] on their sample comprising U.S., European, and Australian insurers. Cummins and Xie (2005) find significant positive CERs of 3.71% in [–1; +1] at 1% level for the U.S. market.[192]

192 Cummins and Weiss (2004) do not examine CERs on their Western European sample.

Further on, the analyses in this study show that target CARs are significantly positive in all analyzed event windows, with a maximum of 14.02% across the entire event period. This outcome is in line with prior research, but again abnormal returns in the U.S. and global markets are higher. Akhigbe and Madura (2001) and Cummins and Xie (2005) detect significantly positive abnormal returns for the U.S. market above 20%.[193] Floreani and Rigamonti's (2001) analyses on the U.S., European, and Australian market yield positive and mostly significant CARs with a maximum CAR of 18.80%. For Western Europe, Cummins and Weiss (2004) report consistently positive and significant CARs with a maximum 8.85%.

Acquirer CARs in this study are mostly statistically insignificant. The results of prior event studies are inhomogeneous in this respect. For the U.S. market, Akhigbe and Madura (2001) detect significantly positive and negative CARs depending on the event window, but Cummins and Xie (2005) obtain consistently positive, and partially significant CARs with a maximum of 1.19%. BarNiv and Hathorn (1997) observe mostly insignificantly positive CARs on their U.S. P&C sample. Floreani and Rigamonti (2001) find mostly positive CARs with a maximum of 3.65% for across U.S., European, and Australian transactions. Cummins and Weiss (2004) analyses yield mostly insignificantly negative CARs for the West European market.

4.3.2.2 Results of multivariate analysis

Determinants of value creation are identified based on a multivariate regression analysis of abnormal returns. The linear regression model is fitted following the ordinary least squares (OLS) approach. Three major assumptions of the OLS method are tested:

- The model specification is tested with Ramsey's (1969) Reset test. If introduction of squared and cubic predicted dependent variables as independent variables into the regression equation leads to a significant change in the

193 BarNiv (1997) find significantly positive CARs in [–250, +250] at 1% level for distressed targets, and insignificantly negative or positive CARs for financially sound targets for the U.S. P&C market. The height of the CARs for these sub samples depends on the chosen classification methodology.

F-statistic, the null hypothesis that the model is well specified can be rejected.

- The absence of or weak multicollinearity is assessed based on Variance Inflation Factors (VIF). Small VIFs indicate weak multicollinearity, whereas 5 or 10 are typically assumed as critical values.[194]

- The normal distribution of regression residuals is examined with the Kolmogorov-Smirnov (K-S) test. If the K-S test statistic is significant, the null hypothesis of normal distribution can be rejected.

The explanatory power of the model is evaluated based on unadjusted and adjusted R-squares. An F-test and t-tests are used to assess joint and individual significance of the coefficients of independent variables.

Equation (27) specifies the full regression model with CERs, acquirer CARs, and target CARs as dependent variables, and the determinants of value creation introduced in section 4.2.3 as independent variables.

$$\begin{aligned} CER / CAR = {} & constant + \beta_{STRATEGY} \cdot STRATEGY + \beta_{TIMING} \cdot TIMING + \\ & \beta_{ACQREGION} \cdot ACQREGION + \beta_{ACQINDUSTRY} \cdot ACQINDUSTRY + \\ & \beta_{LNSIZE} \cdot LNSIZE + \beta_{GROWTH} \cdot GROWTH + \beta_{EXPERIENCE} \cdot EXPERIENCE \\ & + \beta_{TARREGION} \cdot TARREGION + \beta_{TARINDUSTRY} \cdot TARINDUSTRY + \\ & \beta_{LNRELVOLUME} \cdot LNRELVOLUME \end{aligned} \quad (30)$$

The categorical independent variable *STRATEGY* is modeled as five dichotomous variables with reference "national/within-industry" to test diversification against focus, *TIMING* is modeled as three dichotomous variables with reference category "bottom phase" in order to test peak time against bottom time transactions, *ACQREGION* and *TARREGION* as four dichotomous variables with reference "EU-15", *ACQINDUSTRY* and *TARINDUSTRY* as four dichotomous variables with reference "P&C", and *EXPERIENCE* as three dichotomous variables with reference "no experience" to test transactions of experienced acquirers against those of inexperienced acquirers. Table 58 in the appendix shows the

194 E.g., Chatterjee and Price (1991).

detailed coding of the categorical variables and presents descriptive statistics for metric and categorical variables.

Table 7 presents the regression results of the full model on abnormal returns in the event window [–5; +5] days around announcement. The CER and acquirer CAR model are well specified according to the Ramsey Reset test. Only weak multicollinearity is present between independent variables: All VIFs are below the critical value of 10.[195] The hypothesis of normally distributed regression residuals cannot be rejected. In the chosen event window, CERs and CARs are well explained compared to prior research. The regression yields an R-square of 0.67 and an adjusted R-square of 0.43 on $N = 54$ observations,[196] which is high compared to prior research.[197] The independent variable coefficients are jointly significant for CERs and acquirer CARs at 1% and 10% level respectively according to the F-test.[198] Most indicators variables of *STRATEGY* and *TIMING* are significant for CERs, acquirer CARs and target CARs.

Before interpreting these results, two robustness tests shall be conducted. Firstly, a model with weaker multicollinearity is tested. The model is set up by omitting the independent variables *ACQREGION* and *STRATEGY*,[199] which yields a maximum VIF below 5. The adjusted R-square is reduced by .0115, but model and coefficient significance remains strong. Secondly, a reduced model[200]

---

195 The VIFs of *LNSIZE* and *EXPERIENCE3* are above 5. A linear OLS regression of all independent variables except for *LNSIZE* against the dependent variable *LNSIZE* reveals that multicollinearity is driven by *EXPERIENCE*, STRATEGY, and *ACQREGION* (R-square of 0.8444, adjusted R-square of 0.7339, and an F-test significance of 0.0%).

196 Explanation of other tested event windows for combined entity returns yield similar model fit and overall significance. The worst fit is achieved for CER [–1; +1] with an R-square of 56% and an adjusted R-square of 25%. Given the uncertain date of actual information leakage before announcement to certain market participants and time lagged reaction to information amongst market participants, the chosen 5-day event windows seems reasonable.

197 Akhigbe and Madura (2001) obtain an R-square of 0.05 ($N = 61$), Cummins and Xie (2005) report between 0.49 and 0.57 (N between 103 and 107), and Floreani and Rigamonti (2001) achieve between 0.27 and 0.30 ($N = 56$).

198 The indicator variable *TARREGION4* is omitted because its is perfectly linear in *STRATEGY4* and *STRATEGY5*.

199 Amongst the suspects *LNSIZE*, *EXPERIENCE*, *STRATEGY*, and *ACQREGION*, stepwise removal of *ACQREGION* and *STRATEGY* shows least significant reduction of F-statistic, and yields a model with all VIFs below 5.

200 Based on the full model, coefficients with change of F-statistic less significant than 10% are excluded stepwise. The following independent variables are excluded (in order): *LNRELVOLUME*, *ACQINDUSTRY* , *ACQREGION*, *EXPERIENCE*, *GROWTH*, *LNSIZE*, *STRATEGY*.

is examined. This model has higher explanatory power according to the adjusted *R*-square than the full model, but notably lower *R*-square. The independent variables are jointly significant, and individual significances for the remaining independent variables change only slightly.[201] In both models, coefficients change compared to the full model, but the order of coefficients remains constant amongst indicators for categorical independent variables. Thus, interpretation of results shall be generally based on the full model, taking into account additionally significant variables in the robustness test models. Table 59 in the appendix presents detailed regression results of both robustness tests.

The results of the full model show that capital markets appreciate diversifying transactions from a combined entity perspective. Relative to focused transactions, most value is created through cross-border transactions within the European Union and across industries (coefficient 0.0671, significant at 10% level), and cross-border world transactions within the acquirer's industry (coefficient 0.0646, significant at 5% level). The coefficient of an indicator variable is interpreted as additional (or fewer) abnormal return of the respective type of transaction relative to the reference type of transaction. The above reported coefficient of 0.0671 thus means that cross-border within EU/cross-industry transactions obtain 6.7% higher abnormal returns than fully focused transactions. Overall, investors thus believe that economies of scope or risk diversification[202] outweigh economies of scale or regional market power effects.

These results are consistent with Floreani and Rigamonti's (2001) observation that cross-border transactions within Europe have negative impact on the acquirers' CARs, whilst cross-border world deals by European acquirers positively affect their CARs. However, Cummins and Xie (2005) find on their P&C U.S. sample that any geographical or industry diversification is significantly worse than full geographical and industry focus with respect to CARs of acquirers.

Afterwards, independent variables more significant than 10% would be included stepwise. No variable fulfills this criterion.

201 In the model with weaker multicollinearity, *EXPERIENCE1* and *TARINDUSTRY1* are additionally significant. In the reduced model, *TARREGION4* and *TARINDUSTRY1* are additionally significant.

202 Results for acquirers and targets are not interpreted because only one *STRATEGY* indicator variable is significant.

Table 7: Results of short-term multivariate regression model (full model)

	CER		CAR Acquirer		CAR Target		VIF
Model specification	DF	sig DF	DF	sig DF	DF	sig DF	
Ramsey Reset	0.0279	97.3%	0.0702	93.2%	8.5751	0.1%	
Normality of residuals	Z	asy sig	Z	asy sig	Z	asy sig	
K-S	0.5882	88.0%	0.8644	44.4%	0.5206	94.9%	
Model fit	R-square	Adj. R-square	R-square	Adj. R-square	R-square	Adj. R-square	
R-square	0.6686	0.4145	0.5592	0.2213	0.4707	0.0650	
Model significance	Coeff.	F/t	Coeff.	F/t	Coeff.	F/t	
Entire model		2.6313 ***		1.6549 *		1.1601	
(Constant)	0.0610	0.7823	-0.0101	-0.1086	0.7179	1.8283 *	
STRATEGY1	-0.0144	-0.5953	-0.0166	-0.5725	0.0903	0.7429	2.2
STRATEGY2	0.0479	1.9539 *	0.0501	1.7043 *	0.1838	1.4891	3.1
STRATEGY3	0.0671	1.7142 *	0.0326	0.6947	0.2639	1.3385	3.6
STRATEGY4	0.0646	2.2481 **	0.0558	1.6200	0.3173	2.1928 **	4.2
STRATEGY5	0.0446	1.7624 *	0.0181	0.5958	0.1508	1.1818	3.8
TIMING1	0.1126	4.1876 ****	0.0616	1.9093 *	0.3455	2.5502 **	2.8
TIMING2	0.0526	2.6292 **	0.0571	2.3795 **	0.2480	2.4586 **	3.4
TIMING3	0.0605	2.4905 **	0.0407	1.3986	0.2053	1.6778	2.0
ACQREGION2	-0.0223	-1.0837	-0.0064	-0.2605	-0.0942	-0.9083	2.2
ACQINDUSTRY1	0.0128	0.6250	0.0071	0.2900	-0.1601	-1.5470	3.2
ACQINDUSTRY2	-0.0148	-0.5119	-0.0260	-0.7504	-0.3119	-2.1407 **	3.9
ACQINDUSTRY3	0.0233	0.4583	0.0318	0.5226	-0.1103	-0.4309	1.6
EXPERIENCE1	-0.0663	-1.4705	-0.1270	-2.3494 **	-0.1028	-0.4523	2.5
EXPERIENCE2	-0.0003	-0.0146	-0.0352	-1.4483	0.1105	1.0820	2.4
EXPERIENCE3	0.0335	1.1316	-0.0135	-0.3800	0.2136	1.4300	6.0
LNSIZE	-0.0150	-1.6740	-0.0046	-0.4299	-0.0492	-1.0907	6.4
GROWTH	-0.0250	-1.2676	-0.0217	-0.9195	-0.3476	-3.5044 ***	1.9
TARREGION2	0.0521	0.7705	0.0483	0.5960	0.1040	0.3054	2.8
TARREGION3	0.1382	2.5827 **	0.1185	1.8467 *	-0.2120	-0.7864	1.8
TARINDUSTRY1	0.0344	1.6601	0.0248	0.9958	0.0321	0.3076	3.6
TARINDUSTRY3	0.0059	0.1977	0.0351	0.9756	-0.1606	-1.0619	1.6
TARINDUSTRY4	0.0101	0.3913	0.0125	0.4016	-0.0840	-0.6433	3.9
LNRELVOLUME	0.0010	0.1824	-0.0004	-0.0643	-0.0245	-0.8476	3.2

DF: Change in F-statistic between initial and extended regression model according to Ramsey Reset test.
sig DF: Significance of change in F-statistic DF. Z: Kolmogorov-Smirnov Z-statistic.
asy sig: Asymptotic significance of Z-statistic Z. F/t: F-statistic for entire model, t-statistics for coefficients.
VIF: Variance Inflation Factors for coefficients.
STRATEGY indicates the geographical and industry focus of the transaction (national, cross-border EU, and cross-border world transactions, further separated into within- and cross-industry transactions; reference case is national within-industry), TIMING categorizes bottom (reference case), upswing, peak and downturn phases of the M&A market, ACQREGION and TARREGION distinguishes transactions into EU-15 (reference), Swiss and Norwegian acquirers and targets, ACQINDUSTRY and TARINDUSTRY separates transactions into P&C (reference), Life, Re, Agents/Brokers and other acquirer and target industries, EXPERIENCE indicates transaction experience of the acquirer (reference case no; then little, extensive, and most experience), LNSIZE and GROWTH the size and growth of the acquirer, and LNRELVOLUME the relative volume of the target compared to the acquirer. See section 4.2.3 for detailed descriptions of the explanatory variables.
*-**** Statistically significant at 10%, 5%, 1% or 0.1% level according to t-test.

Further on, capital markets valued transactions in the upswing, peak or downturn phase of the M&A cycle highest compared to the M&A market bottom. Highest abnormal returns are observed during the upswing (additional CER of 11.3%, significant at 1% level). These results imply that investors do not believe in the "bandwagon effect" or the overpayment hypothesis during market peaks, but rather highly appreciate transactions during these phases. These results are also valid for acquirer and target CARs. The latter experience a 34.6% higher CAR during market upswing than during the bottom phase of the cycle. Reviewed prior research in insurance M&A does not analyze this determinant.

In addition, the model with weaker multicollinearity indicates that transaction experience of the acquirers has a significant effect on CERs. Acquirers with little experience achieve an 8.6% lower CER, significant at 10% level, than acquirers without any transaction experience. Transactions by extensively or most experienced acquirers yield only insignificantly lower CERs than those of inexperienced acquirers. Seemingly, capital markets do not assume existence of an experience effect according to their short-term reactions.[203]

The two control variables *TARREGION* and *TARINDUSTRY* proved significant for CERs. Norwegian targets yield significantly higher CERs than transactions with targets within the EU-15 in the full model, and transactions with targets operating in the life insurance industry obtain significantly higher CERs compared to transactions with P&C targets in the reduced model. Prior research does not address these determinants.

Three further determinants proved insignificant in this study, but significant in previous research: Acquirer size (*LNSIZE*), acquirer industry (*ACQINDUSTRY*), and relative transaction volume (*LNRELVOLUME*). For the former determinant, this study finds that acquirer CARs and CERs insignificantly decrease with increasing market value of the acquirer. These results are consistent with prior research. Floreani and Rigamonti (2001) and Cummins and Xie (2005) find that acquirer CARs decrease with the size of the acquirer. With respect to acquirer industry, the results of this study show that transactions carried out by acquirers operating in life insurance create insignificantly more value in terms of

203 Similarly, Cummins and Xie (2005) observe that acquirers' abnormal returns are significantly lower (more than 1%, depending on the regression model), if they carry out more than one transaction within a year.

acquirer CARs and CERs than transactions by P&C insurers. Akhigbe and Madura (2001) observe the opposite. Acquirers' CARs in their analysis are higher for nonlife acquirers compared to life acquirers. For the relative transaction volume, the coefficient is only insignificantly different from zero. Cummins and Xie (2005) and Akhigbe and Madura (2001) obtain the same results. Only Floreani and Rigamonti (2001) find that CARs of acquirers increases significantly with the relative transaction volume.

The following section presents further descriptive analyses on the significant, hypotheses-related dimensions geographical and industry focus (*STRATEGY*), timing of the transaction (*TIMING*), and transaction experience (*EXPERIENCE*). *STRATEGY* is analyzed separately for geographical and industry focus of transactions in order to obtain sufficient observations in each sub sample for interpretation. The independent variable acquirer growth (*GROWTH*) is included due to its significance in the long-term analyses. The obtained results are only indicative with respect to the actual influence of these determinants on value creation; the final assessment on the importance of these determinants draws on the results of the multivariate analysis.

4.3.2.3 Results of descriptive analyses on major cross-sections

4.3.2.3.1 Geographical focus

Value generation in sub samples

Highest transaction volumes were recorded for national (USD 55.5 bn) and cross-border world (USD 54.8 bn) transactions, see Table 8, which were mostly driven by the number of deals. The average deal sizes for national and cross-border EU transactions reach about USD 3 bn, and the slightly lower average size in cross-border world transactions of USD 2.5 bn is compensated by higher number of transactions.

National and cross-border EU deals generated value (each USD 1.1 bn), and cross-border world deals destroyed value (USD -0.5 bn). The reasons for this difference in value creation are twofold: Firstly, successful cross-border world deals only generated little average value in comparison to national and cross-border

Table 8: Overview CARs depending on geographical focus of transactions

	National			**Cross-border EU**			**Cross-border world**		
Descriptive statistics									
Deal volume (USD bn)	55.5			42.0			54.8		
Number of deals	18			14			22		
Average deal volume (USD bn)	3.1			3.0			2.5		
Value generation (USD mn)	Value	Deals	V/D	Value	Deals	V/D	Value	Deals	V/D
Total value	1,127	18	63	1,134	14	81	-496	22	-23
Value generation	2,621	10	262	1,753	8	219	926	8	116
Value reduction	-1,493	8	-187	-619	6	-103	-1,422	14	-102
CAR analysis	Mean CAR%	Boehmer p-value		Mean CAR%	Boehmer p-value		Mean CAR%	Boehmer p-value	
Mean CER									
[-1; +1]	0.50%	77.0%		1.40%	21.0%		0.84%	24.6%	
[-2; +2]	-0.16%	70.9%		0.81%	74.3%		0.90%	27.1%	
[-5; +5]	-0.38%	92.7%		2.21%	45.9%		1.53%	7.1%	
[-10; +10]	1.32%	47.5%		4.42%	16.4%		1.16%	28.3%	
[-20; +20]	1.52%	96.4%		4.71%	25.2%		-0.10%	93.1%	
Mean CAR target									
[-1; +1]	5.27%	12.6%		8.33%	4.3%		13.40%	0.0%	
[-2; +2]	6.33%	6.9%		12.07%	1.9%		14.29%	0.0%	
[-5; +5]	7.08%	4.4%		13.95%	11.8%		15.03%	0.1%	
[-10; +10]	11.70%	0.0%		13.58%	17.3%		15.70%	2.3%	
[-20; +20]	9.78%	16.4%		11.79%	97.5%		18.90%	0.3%	
Mean CAR acquirer									
[-1; +1]	-1.19%	68.1%		1.17%	38.2%		-0.29%	45.8%	
[-2; +2]	-2.87%	3.4%		0.55%	69.7%		-0.28%	73.5%	
[-5; +5]	-3.16%	17.7%		1.92%	50.4%		-0.07%	86.0%	
[-10; +10]	-1.99%	46.5%		4.72%	6.3%		-0.23%	89.6%	
[-20; +20]	-0.56%	74.3%		4.66%	19.5%		-1.90%	49.4%	

EU deals. Secondly, almost twice as many deals destroyed value as generated value.

The combined entities in cross-border EU deals showed highest, yet insignificant mean CERs with 4.71% in [–20; +20] and 4.42% in [–10; +10]. The only significant mean CER is achieved by cross-border world transactions at 1.53% in [–5; +5] at 10% level.[204] Targets always showed positive and for most event windows even significant abnormal returns. Acquirer mean CARs in national and cross-border world transactions were always negative, in [–2; +2] even significantly negative for national transactions. In contrast, acquirers achieved a consis-

204 Analysis of Dodd Warner and nonparametric test statistics results in higher number of significant event windows, see further below.

tently positive abnormal return in cross-border EU transactions, in [–10; +10] even significant at 10% level.[205,206]

Developing of CERs across the event window

The CERs developed quite differently across the event window for the three sub samples, see Figure 23. Only cross-border EU transactions showed almost steadily increasing cumulative abnormal returns throughout the event window, reaching their maximum at day 15 after announcement with 5.70%. Seemingly, investors were informed early and had a positive view on the announced transactions. On the contrary, capital market reactions to cross-border world deals were negative shortly after announcement, indicating investors' disbelieve in anticipated synergies.

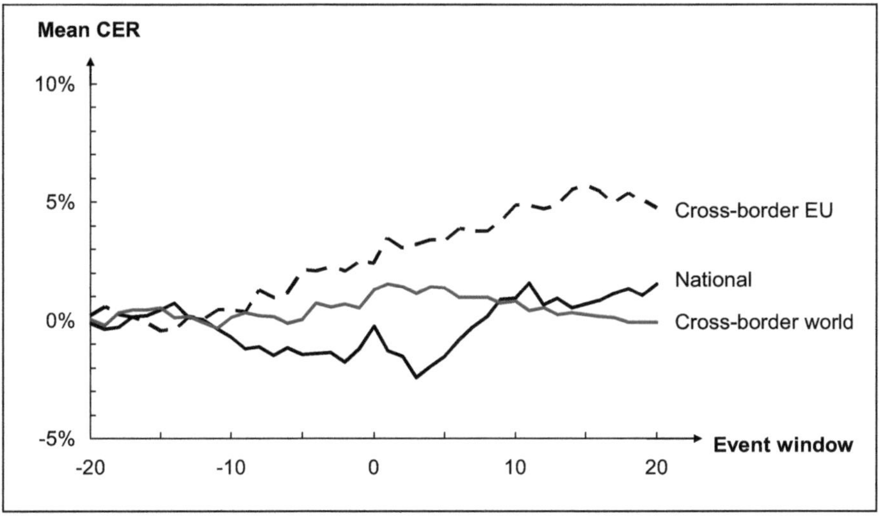

Figure 23: Developing of mean CER depending on geographical focus of transactions

205 Table 60 to 62 in the appendix present further test statistics.
206 In contrast, Beitel (2002, pp. 177) found significantly negative CARs for acquirers in the banking sector.

Comparison of CERs between sub samples

Cross-border EU transactions yield significantly higher mean abnormal returns than national transactions around the announcement date in [–1; +1] and [–5; +5] at 10% level, and also a significantly higher mean abnormal return than cross-border world transactions in [–20; +20] according to the t-statistic at 10% level. However, there is no significant order of value generation between national and cross-border world transactions. The latter generate significantly less value than national transactions in [0; +20], but partially more value than national transactions in [–5; +5]. Table 9 illustrates both findings.

Table 9: Significance of difference between CERs depending on geographical focus of transactions

		Cross-border EU				Cross-border world			
		dCER mean%	t-stat. p	dCER median%	Wilcox. p	dCER mean%	t-stat. p	dCER median%	Wilcox. p
National	[-20; +0]	2.65%	29.7%	1.41%	29.6%	1.57%	48.5%	-1.45%	96.7%
	[-10; +0]	1.82%	36.6%	1.15%	24.7%	1.54%	39.6%	2.03%	19.7%
	[-5; +0]	0.37%	82.6%	1.91%	23.1%	0.57%	68.1%	2.77%	8.4%
	[-2; +0]	-0.96%	58.5%	0.00%	98.5%	-0.34%	81.0%	0.99%	63.4%
	[-1; +0]	-1.21%	47.5%	-0.06%	92.4%	-0.90%	51.8%	0.01%	71.4%
	[+0; +0]	-1.08%	52.6%	-0.35%	83.4%	-0.13%	92.5%	-0.38%	79.6%
	[+0; +1]	1.02%	63.1%	0.83%	48.2%	1.10%	50.5%	0.96%	22.6%
	[+0; +2]	0.86%	68.9%	0.84%	53.1%	1.26%	44.2%	1.32%	28.3%
	[+0; +5]	1.14%	63.8%	4.41%	26.2%	1.21%	52.5%	3.43%	14.6%
	[+0; +10]	0.21%	92.9%	-0.30%	92.4%	-1.83%	31.6%	-1.25%	32.1%
	[+0; +20]	-0.54%	83.1%	-0.51%	69.0%	-3.33%	7.8%	-2.33%	17.8%
	[-1; +1]	0.89%	66.0%	3.09%	7.1%	0.34%	82.9%	3.30%	10.0%
	[-2; +2]	0.97%	65.7%	1.90%	37.2%	1.05%	51.8%	2.36%	24.8%
	[-5; +5]	2.59%	27.0%	3.84%	7.7%	1.91%	28.6%	2.21%	8.4%
	[-10; +10]	3.11%	26.7%	0.95%	26.2%	-0.16%	94.4%	0.09%	98.9%
	[-20; +20]	3.19%	38.4%	1.58%	35.2%	-1.63%	56.7%	-5.78%	57.7%
Cross-border	[-20; +0]	-	-	-	-	-1.07%	57.6%	-2.86%	22.4%
EU	[-10; +0]	-	-	-	-	-0.29%	85.1%	0.87%	93.5%
	[-5; +0]	-	-	-	-	0.19%	84.1%	0.86%	91.0%
	[-2; +0]	-	-	-	-	0.62%	40.6%	0.99%	37.2%
	[-1; +0]	-	-	-	-	0.31%	69.5%	0.07%	75.8%
	[+0; +0]	-	-	-	-	0.94%	23.2%	-0.03%	54.8%
	[+0; +1]	-	-	-	-	0.08%	94.4%	0.13%	70.9%
	[+0; +2]	-	-	-	-	0.40%	73.1%	0.48%	30.7%
	[+0; +5]	-	-	-	-	0.08%	95.9%	-0.98%	88.4%
	[+0; +10]	-	-	-	-	-2.03%	21.8%	-0.96%	33.8%
	[+0; +20]	-	-	-	-	-2.80%	15.2%	-1.82%	32.2%
	[-1; +1]	-	-	-	-	-0.55%	61.8%	0.21%	100.0%
	[-2; +2]	-	-	-	-	0.08%	94.1%	0.47%	35.5%
	[-5; +5]	-	-	-	-	-0.68%	61.1%	-1.63%	70.9%
	[-10; +10]	-	-	-	-	-3.26%	12.7%	-0.86%	21.2%
	[-20; +20]	-	-	-	-	-4.81%	9.3%	-7.36%	11.6%

Comparison of results to prior research

The results indicate that capital markets believed in value creation by cross-border transactions within Europe, since these created most value per deal and achieved significantly higher abnormal returns than national transactions. However, capital markets did not support further geographical diversification through worldwide transactions. Investors seem to value increasing market power higher than economies of scope or risk diversification. Prior research obtains similar results. Floreani and Rigamonti (2001) show that within country transactions have in average higher CERs than cross border transactions. For acquirer CARs, there is no clear difference between the sub samples. Cummins and Weiss (2004) identify that within country transactions perform slightly worse than cross border transactions. The former yield partially significant negative acquirer CARs around the announcement date (e.g., –0.63% in [0; +2] at 0.1%) , whereas the latter transactions only realize insignificant positive and negative CARs. However, their analysis of target CARs draws a different picture. Within country transactions have higher CARs than cross border transactions on 15 out of 16 analyzed event windows. Cummins and Xie's (2005) analyses show that geographically focused transactions have high CERs, e.g., insignificant 4.08% in [–1; +1], whereas geographically diversified transactions have somewhat smaller, but still positive CERs, e.g., insignificant 3.64% in [–1; +1].

4.3.2.3.2 Industry focus

Value generation in sub samples

Transactions were highly focused on within-industry deals with a total deal volume of USD 129.5 bn compared to USD 22.8 bn for cross-industry deals, see Table 10. Major driver for the difference is the significantly larger deal volume of within-industry transactions (USD 4.2 bn vs. USD 1.0 bn). Within-industry transactions created value (USD 3.6 bn) while cross-industry transactions destroyed value (USD –1.8 bn). Two factors drive this outcome: Firstly, the success ratio of within-industry deals is higher (60% vs. 35%). Secondly, successful within-industry transactions created almost 3 times the value destroyed by un-

Table 10: Overview CARs depending on industry focus of transaction

	Within-industry			Cross-industry		
Descriptive statistics						
Deal volume (USD bn)	129.5			22.8		
Number of deals	31			23		
Average deal volume (USD bn)	4.2			1.0		
Value generation (USD mn)	Value	Deals	V/D	Value	Deals	V/D
Total value	3,592	31	116	-1,827	23	-79
Value generation	4,936	18	274	364	8	46
Value reduction	-1,344	13	-103	-2,191	15	-146
CAR analysis	Mean CAR%	Boehmer p-value		Mean CAR%	Boehmer p-value	
Mean CER						
[-1; +1]	1.44%	10.0%		0.10%	75.5%	
[-2; +2]	1.48%	21.2%		-0.76%	6.2%	
[-5; +5]	1.90%	12.5%		-0.05%	57.2%	
[-10; +10]	3.39%	1.5%		0.26%	73.3%	
[-20; +20]	3.74%	5.4%		-1.07%	23.1%	
Mean CAR target						
[-1; +1]	7.72%	0.2%		11.61%	1.5%	
[-2; +2]	10.72%	0.0%		11.51%	18.2%	
[-5; +5]	12.27%	0.0%		11.87%	28.4%	
[-10; +10]	14.09%	0.0%		13.45%	12.0%	
[-20; +20]	14.06%	1.2%		13.97%	32.4%	
Mean CAR acquirer						
[-1; +1]	0.79%	31.0%		-1.56%	9.2%	
[-2; +2]	0.23%	85.1%		-2.50%	0.5%	
[-5; +5]	0.48%	76.7%		-2.02%	16.0%	
[-10; +10]	2.10%	9.2%		-1.74%	28.2%	
[-20; +20]	2.38%	19.7%		-2.62%	23.8%	

successful transactions, whilst successful cross-industry transaction only created a third of the value destroyed by unsuccessful transactions. Mean CERs in within-industry transactions are significantly positive in [–10; +10] with 3.39% at 5% level and in [–20; +20] with 3.74% at 10% level. On the contrary, cross-industry transactions mostly showed negative CERs, in [–2; +2] even significantly negative with –0.76% at 10% level. The positive combined entity results of within-industry transactions are driven by positive CARs of targets and acquirers.[207]

207 Table 63 and Table 64 in the appendix present further test statistics.

Developing of CERs across the event window

The consistently positive development of mean cumulative abnormal returns indicate a positive view of investors on within-industry transactions, see Figure 24. In contrast, cross-industry yielded negative and decreasing mean CERs almost across the entire event window.

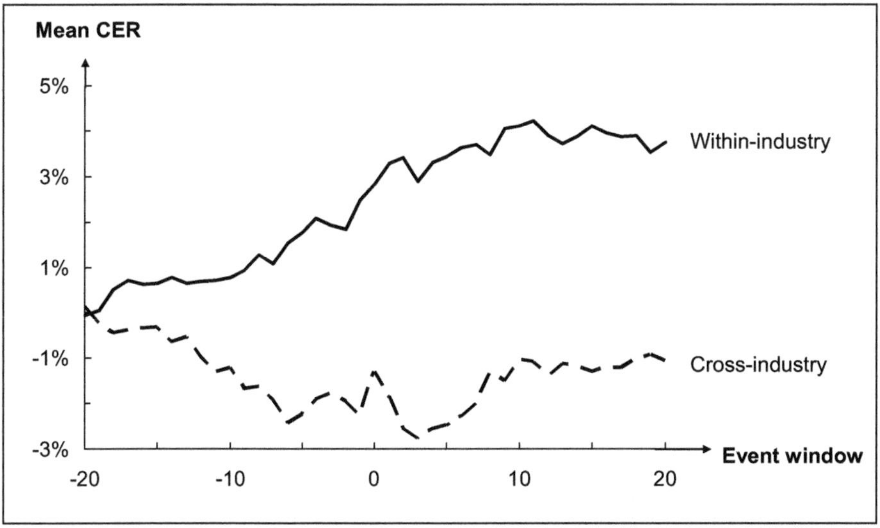

Figure 24: Developing of mean CER depending on industry focus of transactions

Comparison of CERs between sub samples

Table 11 provides evidence that within-industry transactions generate significant more value than cross-industry transactions in [–20; +20] at 5% level, and for [–10; +10] and [–2; +2] at 10% level.

Table 11: Significance of difference between CERs depending on industry focus of transaction

		Cross-industry			
		dCER mean%	t-stat. p	dCER median%	Wilcox. p
Within-	[-20; +0]	-4.13%	1.9%	-3.04%	0.7%
industry	[-10; +0]	-2.12%	13.6%	-3.71%	7.3%
	[-5; +0]	-0.16%	88.4%	-1.00%	86.8%
	[-2; +0]	-0.43%	69.4%	-1.10%	43.6%
	[-1; +0]	-0.34%	75.3%	-0.28%	58.2%
	[+0; +0]	0.61%	57.5%	0.24%	44.7%
	[+0; +1]	-0.40%	76.6%	-0.03%	69.4%
	[+0; +2]	-1.21%	36.3%	-0.57%	19.2%
	[+0; +5]	-1.18%	44.6%	-1.29%	37.7%
	[+0; +10]	-0.40%	79.5%	0.33%	80.0%
	[+0; +20]	-0.07%	96.6%	-1.22%	69.4%
	[-1; +1]	-1.34%	28.6%	-1.59%	15.4%
	[-2; +2]	-2.24%	8.7%	-2.63%	3.7%
	[-5; +5]	-1.95%	18.6%	-1.01%	12.2%
	[-10; +10]	-3.13%	9.8%	-3.09%	3.8%
	[-20; +20]	-4.81%	5.0%	-6.39%	4.5%

Comparison of results to prior research

Investors seem to value economies of scale through industry focus higher than potential synergies from economies of scope or risk diversification through industry diversification. Within-industry transactions achieved significantly positive CERs, cross-industry deals partly significantly negative CERs, and the difference between both is significant on part of the analyzed event windows. Again, these results are comparable to the outcome of prior research. Floreani and Rigamonti (2001) show that CERs and acquirer CARs of Reinsurance companies are positive and higher than those of life and other insurance players. Cummins and Xie (2005) find positive CERs for within-industry transactions (e.g., insignificant 5.01% in [–1; +1]), and small, mostly negative CERs for cross-industry transactions (e.g., –0.20% in [–1; +1]).

4.3.2.3.3 Timing of the transaction

Value generation in sub samples

Acquirers were most active in the peak and bottom phase of the M&A market (56% and 20% of deals, respectively), see Table 12. The sub samples of transactions during the upswing and downturn shall not be interpreted because less than 10 transactions were carried out during these two phases. During the peak phase, the largest transactions were announced with an average deal size of USD 2.6 bn. Only these transactions generated value, driven by higher value creation of successful deals (USD 146 mn) than value destruction of unsuccessful deals (USD –81 mn) compared to the bottom of the M&A cycle (USD 27 mn and USD –141 mn, respectively). Consistent with these results, CERs in the peak phase are (insignificantly) positive, while CERs in the bottom are partly significantly negative. In the event window [–5; +5], the abnormal return of the combined entity is –3.1%, significant at 5% level. Again, target CARs are positive across all event

Table 12: Overview CARs depending on timing of the transaction

	Bottom			Upswing			Peak			Downturn		
Descriptive statistics												
Deal volume (USD bn)	15.9			19.8			77.3			39.2		
Number of deals	11			7			30			6		
Average deal volume (USD bn)	1.4			2.8			2.6			6.5		
Value generation (USD mn)	Value	Deals	V/D	Value	Deals	V/D	Value	Deals	V/D	Value	No. deals	V/D
Total value	-878	11	-80	-571	7	-82	521	30	17	2,693	6	449
Value generation	107	4	27	536	4	134	1,901	13	146	2,756	5	551
Value reduction	-984	7	-141	-1,107	3	-369	-1,380	17	-81	-63	1	-63
CAR analysis	Mean CAR%	Boehmer p-value		Mean CAR%	Boehmer p-value		Mean CAR%	Boehmer p-value		Mean CAR%	Boehmer p-value	
Mean CER												
[-1; +1]	-1.33%	17.8%		5.40%	9.5%		0.83%	40.4%		-0.14%	96.6%	
[-2; +2]	-2.25%	8.9%		5.26%	24.5%		0.31%	58.3%		1.16%	36.8%	
[-5; +5]	-3.10%	1.8%		5.99%	57.0%		0.97%	39.1%		3.47%	0.8%	
[-10; +10]	-3.26%	14.5%		6.33%	35.1%		1.98%	36.4%		7.23%	1.2%	
[-20; +20]	-3.80%	32.3%		2.94%	36.3%		1.81%	64.1%		9.68%	5.3%	
Mean CAR target												
[-1; +1]	5.18%	4.0%		8.86%	4.1%		10.76%	0.1%		10.76%	52.1%	
[-2; +2]	4.83%	22.8%		11.05%	4.9%		13.02%	0.0%		12.68%	15.1%	
[-5; +5]	5.54%	31.6%		11.65%	19.9%		13.89%	0.1%		15.69%	8.7%	
[-10; +10]	4.49%	87.7%		15.59%	0.3%		16.01%	1.3%		17.91%	5.0%	
[-20; +20]	3.83%	69.5%		14.44%	33.2%		16.89%	15.3%		17.83%	13.3%	
Mean CAR acquirer												
[-1; +1]	-2.19%	2.5%		1.64%	72.4%		0.22%	71.6%		-0.91%	75.9%	
[-2; +2]	-3.06%	5.5%		-0.15%	32.4%		-0.49%	20.5%		-0.15%	87.8%	
[-5; +5]	-3.33%	4.5%		-0.56%	19.6%		0.08%	85.6%		1.08%	9.6%	
[-10; +10]	-2.13%	49.0%		-1.66%	24.9%		0.89%	78.7%		5.57%	1.2%	
[-20; +20]	-1.17%	97.6%		-4.67%	3.5%		0.61%	86.8%		6.77%	1.6%	

windows, and significantly positive up to 10 days around announcement for transactions during the peak of the M&A cycle. Even acquirer CARs are (insignificantly) positive in this phase.[208]

Developing of CERs across the event window

CERs of transactions during the bottom and the peak phase develop quite differently. The former show increasingly negative CERs almost persistently throughout the event window, while the latter increasingly generate value. Figure 25 presents the evidence.

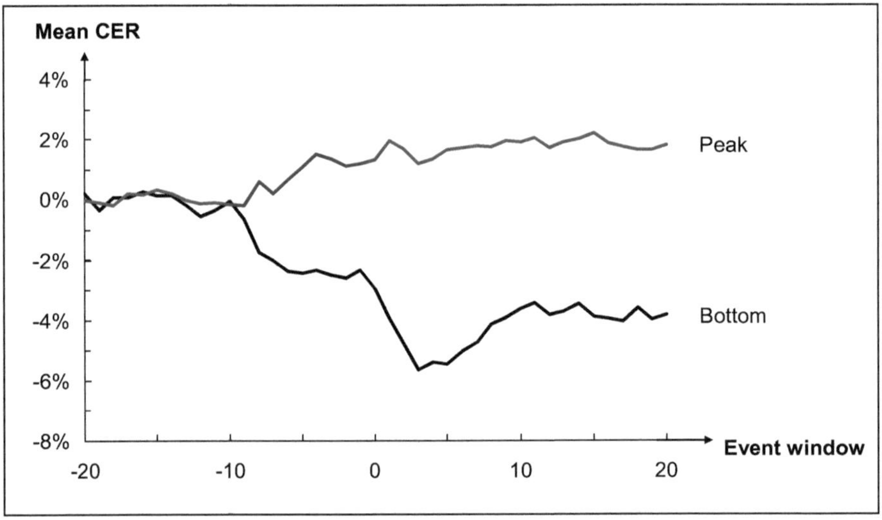

Figure 25: Developing of mean CER depending on timing of the transaction

Comparison of CERs between sub samples

The superior abnormal performance of combined entities for peak-phase acquisitions compared to acquisitions during the bottom is significant in many of the tested event windows, and for mean and median CERs, see Table 13.

208 Table 65 and Table 66 in the appendix present further test statistics on bottom and peak phase transactions.

Table 13: Significance of difference between CERs depending on phase of M&A cycle

		Peak			
		dCER mean%	t-stat. p	dCER median%	Wilcox. p
Bottom	[-20; +0]	4.28%	3.2%	1.66%	16.2%
	[-10; +0]	4.01%	1.3%	2.70%	6.2%
	[-5; +0]	1.26%	22.3%	1.65%	17.1%
	[-2; +0]	0.42%	66.3%	0.12%	60.7%
	[-1; +0]	0.55%	56.4%	-0.20%	94.1%
	[+0; +0]	0.76%	44.0%	0.51%	27.0%
	[+0; +1]	2.36%	9.2%	1.82%	2.4%
	[+0; +2]	2.91%	4.6%	1.17%	9.6%
	[+0; +5]	3.57%	3.0%	3.27%	1.3%
	[+0; +10]	1.99%	21.3%	-0.23%	35.4%
	[+0; +20]	2.10%	24.2%	-1.39%	33.9%
	[-1; +1]	2.15%	11.0%	0.84%	8.5%
	[-2; +2]	2.56%	9.8%	0.55%	35.4%
	[-5; +5]	4.07%	0.8%	2.67%	0.6%
	[-10; +10]	5.23%	1.6%	3.49%	2.4%
	[-20; +20]	5.62%	5.7%	1.86%	12.2%

Comparison of results to prior research

The results show that capital markets valued transactions during the peak phase higher than those during the bottom: The former generated positive CERs, the latter significantly lower and negative CERs. Prior research does not study his cross-section.

4.3.2.3.4 Growth of acquirer

Value generation in sub samples

The fastest growing acquirers achieved an average growth[209] of 74.9%, medium growing insurers of 19.8% and slowest growing acquirers shrank by 8.1%. The

209 Growth is measured as relative change of market value over the estimation window. If market value data is not available at the beginning or the end of the estimation window, growth computed from available data is scaled to the length of the estimation window.

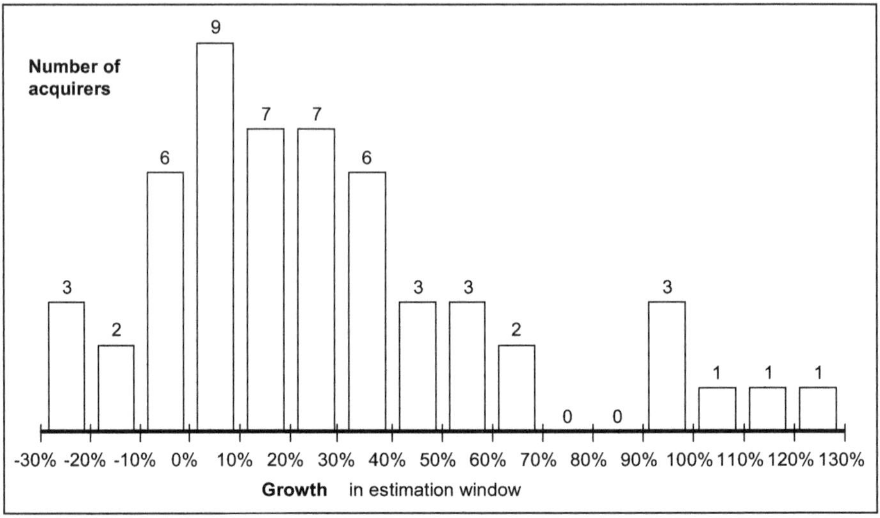

Figure 26: Distribution of acquirer growth

histogram in Figure 26 documents the growth distribution for all acquirers. Medium growing acquirers carried out the largest deals with an average deal volume of USD 3.5 bn compared to USD 2.0 bn for fastest growing companies and USD 2.4 for insurers with slowest growth, see Table 14.

Slowest growing acquirers created more than double the value compared to medium growing insurers (USD 2.5 bn vs. USD 1.2 bn), and top growth companies even destroyed USD –1.9 bn of value. This result is largely driven by the fact that almost all deals carried out by fast growing companies turned out to be unsuccessful, whereas slowest growing acquirers achieved a 70% success ratio. They also generated the highest value on a per deal basis (USD 179 mn). Mean CERs confirm these results. Slowest growing acquirers achieve a significantly positive mean CER of 3.75% in [–20; +20] at 5% level, whereas fastest growing companies show a significantly negative mean CER of –3.28% in the same event window at 5% level. This outcome is explained by several factors. Firstly, targets of slowest growing acquirers accomplish significant positive CARs on all analyzed event windows around the announcement day of above 17% at 1% level. Se-

Table 14: Overview CARs depending on growth of acquirer

	14 fastest growing acquirers			**26 medium growing acquirers**			**14 slowest growing acquirers**		
Descriptive statistics									
Deal volume (USD bn)	27.7			90.3			34.2		
Number of deals	14			26			14		
Average deal volume (USD bn)	2.0			3.5			2.4		
Average performance	174.9%			119.8%			91.9%		
Value generation (USD mn)	Value	Deals	V/D	Value	Deals	V/D	Value	Deals	V/D
Total value	-1,945	14	-139	1,199	26	46	2,511	14	179
Value generation	48	2	24	2,587	14	185	2,665	10	267
Value reduction	-1,994	12	-166	-1,388	12	-116	-154	4	-38
CAR analysis	Mean CAR%	Boehmer p-value		Mean CAR%	Boehmer p-value		Mean CAR%	Boehmer p-value	
Mean CER									
[-1; +1]	1.50%	81.9%		1.47%	10.1%		-0.86%	61.2%	
[-2; +2]	0.41%	9.2%		1.29%	37.4%		-0.78%	92.7%	
[-5; +5]	1.35%	59.3%		1.72%	46.8%		-0.42%	42.5%	
[-10; +10]	0.31%	31.4%		3.23%	4.9%		1.62%	14.4%	
[-20; +20]	-3.28%	1.2%		3.26%	23.7%		3.75%	3.1%	
Mean CAR target									
[-1; +1]	6.03%	2.9%		7.05%	1.9%		17.05%	0.9%	
[-2; +2]	5.43%	55.8%		9.72%	0.4%		19.17%	0.2%	
[-5; +5]	7.10%	5.7%		10.30%	2.5%		20.45%	0.2%	
[-10; +10]	8.32%	12.6%		12.38%	0.5%		22.00%	1.0%	
[-20; +20]	5.11%	49.8%		12.49%	8.7%		25.75%	0.4%	
Mean CAR acquirer									
[-1; +1]	-0.41%	35.3%		0.85%	29.5%		-1.98%	11.1%	
[-2; +2]	-1.57%	0.9%		0.13%	83.8%		-2.27%	19.3%	
[-5; +5]	-1.33%	8.8%		0.90%	80.4%		-2.60%	48.9%	
[-10; +10]	-2.55%	8.3%		2.48%	14.1%		-0.26%	74.8%	
[-20; +20]	-6.11%	0.4%		3.14%	21.7%		1.22%	25.2%	

condly, acquirer abnormal returns on the entire event window are significantly negative with –6.11% mean CAR in [–20; +20] at 1% level.[210]

Developing of CERs across the event window

Further investigation of the development of mean CERs across time gives an explanation of these results. Capital market reactions to deals of fastest growing acquirers were strongly negative already around 10 days before announcement, and not compensated afterwards. However, slowest and medium growing acquirers almost steadily increased mean CERs across the event window, see Figure 27.

210 Table 67 to 69 in the appendix present further test statistics. The results are comparable.

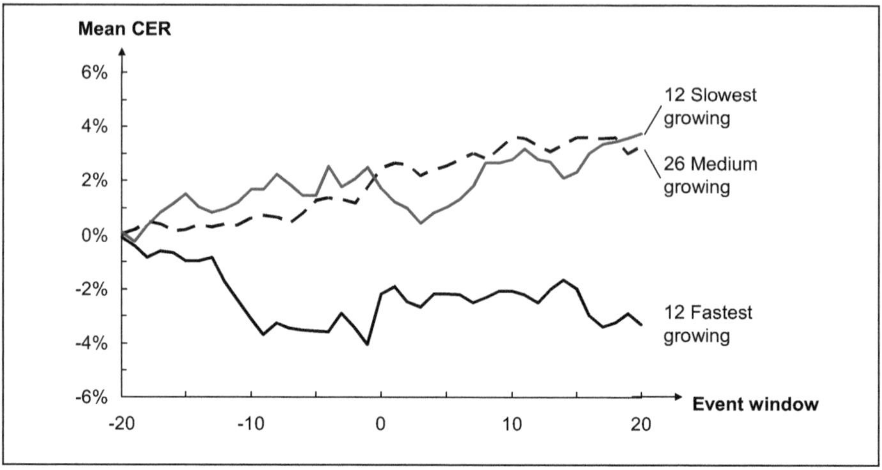

Figure 27: Developing of mean CER depending on growth of acquirers

Comparison of CERs between sub samples

Consequently, both slowest and medium growing acquirers achieve significant excess CERs above fastest growing insurers only in the event intervals [–20; 0] and [–20; +20] at 5% level. Shortly after and shortly around the announcement day, fastest growing companies even generate higher value than other sub samples, see Table 15.

Comparison of results to prior research

The results give no clear indication whether or not fast growth leads to difficulties in integrating the target. Prior research does not study this cross-section.

4.3.2.3.5 Transaction experience

Value generation in sub samples

Inexperienced acquirers carried out most transactions in terms of number of deals, whilst transactions of most experienced acquirers were the largest in average (USD 4.4 bn). The sub sample of acquirers with little experience is disregarded due to its sample size below 10 observations. More experienced acquir-

Table 15: Significance of difference between CERs depending on growth of acquirer

		26 medium growing acquirers				14 slowest growing acquirers			
		dCER mean%	t-stat. p	dCER median%	Wilcox. p	dCER mean%	t-stat. p	dCER median%	Wilcox. p
14 fastest growing acquirers	[-20; +0]	4.60%	5.0%	5.06%	1.1%	3.89%	3.3%	5.02%	3.3%
	[-10; +0]	1.88%	33.1%	3.02%	17.8%	0.32%	81.5%	1.61%	80.0%
	[-5; +0]	0.28%	84.7%	-0.83%	83.2%	-1.10%	37.2%	-0.02%	42.1%
	[-2; +0]	0.43%	76.5%	0.78%	66.0%	-0.79%	56.4%	1.00%	98.2%
	[-1; +0]	0.01%	99.2%	0.24%	72.3%	-1.62%	20.7%	0.12%	47.6%
	[+0; +0]	-1.20%	39.2%	-0.20%	47.0%	-2.63%	5.3%	-0.25%	24.1%
	[+0; +1]	-1.25%	45.4%	-0.35%	23.9%	-3.37%	4.4%	-0.20%	26.0%
	[+0; +2]	-0.75%	66.4%	-0.28%	72.3%	-3.04%	5.7%	-0.50%	16.1%
	[+0; +5]	-1.10%	58.9%	-0.92%	60.0%	-3.31%	11.7%	-1.58%	17.5%
	[+0; +10]	-0.16%	94.1%	0.14%	96.6%	-1.64%	40.1%	-0.67%	80.0%
	[+0; +20]	0.74%	74.8%	2.06%	47.0%	0.52%	83.0%	3.46%	28.0%
	[-1; +1]	-0.03%	98.3%	0.85%	87.6%	-2.36%	10.1%	0.17%	26.0%
	[-2; +2]	0.88%	62.1%	2.17%	31.4%	-1.19%	41.1%	0.81%	83.6%
	[-5; +5]	0.37%	85.0%	1.44%	70.2%	-1.78%	34.6%	-0.14%	53.5%
	[-10; +10]	2.92%	25.5%	2.86%	16.0%	1.31%	50.5%	2.39%	19.0%
	[-20; +20]	6.54%	4.2%	8.43%	2.1%	7.03%	1.2%	9.70%	0.6%
26 medium growing acquirers	[-20; +0]	-	-	-	-	-0.72%	75.0%	-0.04%	68.1%
	[-10; +0]	-	-	-	-	-1.56%	40.2%	-1.41%	21.7%
	[-5; +0]	-	-	-	-	-1.37%	31.6%	0.81%	66.0%
	[-2; +0]	-	-	-	-	-1.22%	35.5%	0.22%	72.3%
	[-1; +0]	-	-	-	-	-1.64%	19.9%	-0.12%	56.1%
	[+0; +0]	-	-	-	-	-1.43%	26.4%	-0.06%	54.2%
	[+0; +1]	-	-	-	-	-2.12%	19.3%	0.15%	78.8%
	[+0; +2]	-	-	-	-	-2.29%	15.6%	-0.22%	26.3%
	[+0; +5]	-	-	-	-	-2.20%	20.6%	-0.66%	43.5%
	[+0; +10]	-	-	-	-	-1.48%	41.1%	-0.81%	70.2%
	[+0; +20]	-	-	-	-	-0.22%	90.6%	1.41%	62.0%
	[-1; +1]	-	-	-	-	-2.33%	13.2%	-0.68%	26.3%
	[-2; +2]	-	-	-	-	-2.07%	20.9%	-1.36%	13.7%
	[-5; +5]	-	-	-	-	-2.15%	22.0%	-1.59%	19.7%
	[-10; +10]	-	-	-	-	-1.61%	50.5%	-0.46%	43.5%
	[-20; +20]	-	-	-	-	0.49%	87.1%	1.27%	94.3%

ers generated USD 1.1 bn value through their M&A transactions, driven by higher value creation of successful deals compared to value destruction of unsuccessful deals. This imparity even offset the low success ratio of merely 30% of most experience acquirers. Inexperience acquirers destroyed value, driven by large average value destruction of unsuccessful deals. Combined entity returns and target CARs are positive, whereas extensively experienced acquirers achieved highest CERs, with a maximum of 4.0% in [–10; +10], significant at 10% level, but targets of most experienced acquirers obtained highest CARs above 17% and significant at 5% level in event windows shortly around

Table 16: Overview CARs depending on transaction experience of acquirers

	No experience			Little experience			Extensive experience			Most experience		
Descriptive statistics												
Deal volume (USD bn)	44.5			7.4			34.0			66.3		
Number of deals	25			2			12			15		
Average deal volume (USD bn)	1.8			3.7			2.8			4.4		
Value generation (USD mn)	Value	Deals	V/D	Value	Deals	V/D	Value	Deals	V/D	Value	No. deals	V/D
Total value	-1,069	25	-43	581	2	290	1,153	0	12	1,100	15	73
Value generation	1,142	12	95	581	2	290	1,639	7	234	1,938	5	388
Value reduction	-2,211	13	-170	0	0	n/a	-486	5	-97	-839	10	-84
CAR analysis	Mean CAR%	Boehmer p-value		Mean CAR%	Boehmer p-value		Mean CAR%	Boehmer p-value		Mean CAR%	Boehmer p-value	
Mean CER												
[-1; +1]	1.60%	11.3%		-4.05%	27.2%		0.33%	86.5%		0.75%	49.2%	
[-2; +2]	0.72%	69.5%		-5.10%	21.1%		1.00%	34.6%		0.57%	76.0%	
[-5; +5]	1.44%	62.3%		-6.08%	10.9%		1.18%	53.0%		1.32%	32.4%	
[-10; +10]	1.35%	64.1%		3.12%	0.0%		3.95%	5.0%		1.59%	45.2%	
[-20; +20]	1.28%	89.0%		9.70%	0.1%		2.80%	65.6%		0.41%	88.6%	
Mean CAR target												
[-1; +1]	5.80%	3.1%		1.32%	82.0%		8.17%	7.3%		17.37%	2.0%	
[-2; +2]	5.39%	34.1%		1.75%	88.0%		15.54%	0.8%		18.17%	3.5%	
[-5; +5]	6.42%	12.2%		3.59%	34.3%		16.42%	8.1%		19.24%	3.3%	
[-10; +10]	8.34%	4.1%		9.12%	2.2%		18.72%	8.9%		19.65%	10.6%	
[-20; +20]	9.50%	12.1%		11.98%	0.0%		16.77%	87.7%		19.62%	41.2%	
Mean CAR acquirer												
[-1; +1]	0.38%	64.7%		-5.91%	28.7%		-0.34%	72.3%		-0.33%	54.8%	
[-2; +2]	-0.59%	29.7%		-7.38%	18.5%		-1.06%	26.0%		-0.54%	47.8%	
[-5; +5]	0.09%	95.4%		-9.89%	3.4%		-1.17%	32.8%		0.00%	98.6%	
[-10; +10]	0.21%	86.6%		-0.92%	0.0%		1.52%	62.0%		0.22%	82.6%	
[-20; +20]	0.55%	75.1%		6.76%	0.2%		0.57%	76.5%		-1.39%	55.6%	

announcement. Abnormal returns for acquirers are insignificantly different from zero, independent of their transaction experience.[211] Table 16 presents an overview of the results.

211 Table 70 to 72 in the appendix present further test statistics. The results are comparable.

Developing CERs across the event window

Abnormal returns of combined entities develop similarly across the event window independent of their transaction experience, see Figure 28.

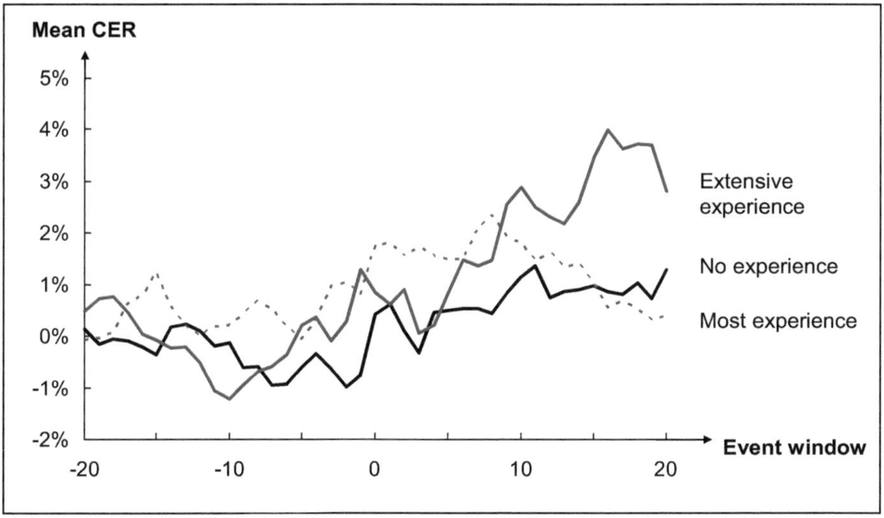

Figure 28: Developing of mean CER depending on transaction experience of acquirers

Significance of sub sample CERs

Acquirers without transaction experience achieve positive mean CERs in all analyzed event windows, but negative median CERs shortly after announcement and on the entire event window [–20; +20]. Thus, a left skew is present in the distribution of CERs. The parametric and the generalized sign test agree that CERs in [–1; +0] are significantly positive at 10% level or better, see Table 70. Extensively experienced acquirers destroy value shortly after announcement in the average, but mostly generate value in all other analyzed event windows. All tests agree that the CER of 1.3% in [–10; +10] is significant at 10% level or better, see Table 71. For most experienced acquirers, significantly positive CERs are observed shortly around and particularly before the announcement date, depending on the applied test statistic. The results are presented in Table 72.

Table 17: Significance of differences between CERs depending on transaction experience of acquirer

		Extensive experience				Most experience			
		dCER mean%	t-stat. p	dCER median%	Wilcox. p	dCER mean%	t-stat. p	dCER median%	Wilcox. p
No experience	[-20; +0]	0.42%	87.1%	1.63%	63.8%	1.35%	55.7%	1.42%	75.9%
	[-10; +0]	1.29%	53.4%	1.90%	40.8%	0.96%	61.2%	1.43%	50.3%
	[-5; +0]	-0.15%	92.3%	0.37%	75.8%	0.24%	85.7%	1.53%	26.4%
	[-2; +0]	-0.11%	94.2%	0.54%	54.8%	-0.25%	85.7%	0.45%	50.3%
	[-1; +0]	-0.84%	58.6%	-0.43%	59.2%	-0.67%	62.7%	-0.28%	95.5%
	[+0; +0]	-1.62%	29.2%	-0.26%	46.5%	-0.20%	87.6%	0.21%	41.8%
	[+0; +1]	-2.04%	28.7%	-0.33%	59.2%	-0.38%	81.0%	0.23%	41.8%
	[+0; +2]	-1.23%	52.8%	0.17%	100.0%	-0.10%	95.1%	0.36%	59.6%
	[+0; +5]	-1.73%	42.3%	1.19%	91.0%	-0.57%	77.6%	0.36%	71.6%
	[+0; +10]	-0.31%	88.9%	-0.18%	83.3%	-0.92%	65.2%	-0.96%	73.7%
	[+0; +20]	-0.51%	83.2%	0.37%	83.3%	-2.42%	28.3%	-1.34%	45.1%
	[-1; +1]	-1.27%	48.9%	-0.86%	85.8%	-0.84%	60.4%	0.84%	65.5%
	[-2; +2]	0.28%	88.4%	1.27%	54.8%	-0.15%	93.4%	-0.30%	75.9%
	[-5; +5]	-0.26%	90.3%	0.17%	91.0%	-0.12%	95.1%	0.02%	82.3%
	[-10; +10]	2.60%	34.6%	3.24%	14.9%	0.24%	92.2%	-1.14%	75.9%
	[-20; +20]	1.53%	65.9%	6.35%	46.5%	-0.86%	78.2%	0.14%	93.3%
Extensive experience	[-20; +0]	-	-	-	-	0.93%	63.4%	-0.21%	94.2%
	[-10; +0]	-	-	-	-	-0.33%	82.1%	-0.47%	67.8%
	[-5; +0]	-	-	-	-	0.39%	74.6%	1.15%	71.4%
	[-2; +0]	-	-	-	-	-0.13%	88.1%	-0.10%	100.0%
	[-1; +0]	-	-	-	-	0.17%	85.4%	0.15%	54.2%
	[+0; +0]	-	-	-	-	1.41%	21.5%	0.47%	15.0%
	[+0; +1]	-	-	-	-	1.67%	26.3%	0.56%	15.0%
	[+0; +2]	-	-	-	-	1.12%	44.4%	0.18%	54.2%
	[+0; +5]	-	-	-	-	1.16%	47.6%	-0.83%	94.2%
	[+0; +10]	-	-	-	-	-0.61%	69.0%	-0.78%	51.0%
	[+0; +20]	-	-	-	-	-1.91%	28.9%	-1.71%	29.4%
	[-1; +1]	-	-	-	-	0.42%	70.0%	1.70%	44.9%
	[-2; +2]	-	-	-	-	-0.42%	70.4%	-1.57%	75.1%
	[-5; +5]	-	-	-	-	0.14%	91.9%	-0.15%	98.1%
	[-10; +10]	-	-	-	-	-2.36%	24.0%	-4.38%	23.2%
	[-20; +20]	-	-	-	-	-2.39%	42.4%	-6.21%	34.1%

Comparison of CERs between sub samples

The differences in cumulative abnormal performance of combined entities depending on the transaction experience of acquirers are not significant, see Table 17.

Comparison of results to prior research

The results indicate that capital markets do not significantly value transaction experience in the short-term. Prior research does not study this cross-section.

4.4 Analysis of medium- and long-term value creation

4.4.1 Methodology

4.4.1.1 Event time approach with control firm benchmark

4.4.1.1.1 Measurement of abnormal returns and benchmark construction

The basic methodology of analyzing long-term value creation according to control firm buy-and-hold abnormal returns is presented in section 3.3.2.1. This section discusses the specific application the methodology in the context of this study. Buy-and-hold abnormal returns $BAHR_i$ for individual acquirers are computed from monthly firm TRS $R_{i,t}$ and benchmark TRS $E(R_{i,t})$ based on the model

$$BAHR_i = \prod_{t=1}^{t_{e2}} \left(1 + R_{i,t}\right) - \prod_{t=1}^{t_{e2}} \left(1 + E(R_{i,t})\right) \tag{31}$$

The benchmark TRS $E(R_{i,t})$ is defined as the control firm TRS. Control firms are selected annually from the historical constituents of the Datastream European Insurance Index[212] (DEII) based on firm size,[213] and book-to-market ratio[214]

- For each acquirer and each period in the event window, a short list of DEII constituents with firm size between 70% and 130% of the acquirer[215] is created.[216]

212 According to Datastream, the exact historical composition of the DEII cannot be traced back. However, it can be assumed that the current constituents, including currently zero-weighted firms, were included into the index at the point in time when market data became available in Datastream.

213 Firm size is defined as market value of common equity at 30.6. in year t for the period 1.7·*t* – 30.6·*t* + 1.

214 Book-to-market ratio for the period 1.7·*t* – 30.6·*t*+1 is defined as book value of common equity end of year *t* – 1, divided by market value of common equity at 31.12. of year t-1.

215 If there is no benchmark firm in the original size range, lower and upper bound of the size range are extended by 10 percentage points until a benchmark firm can be identified.

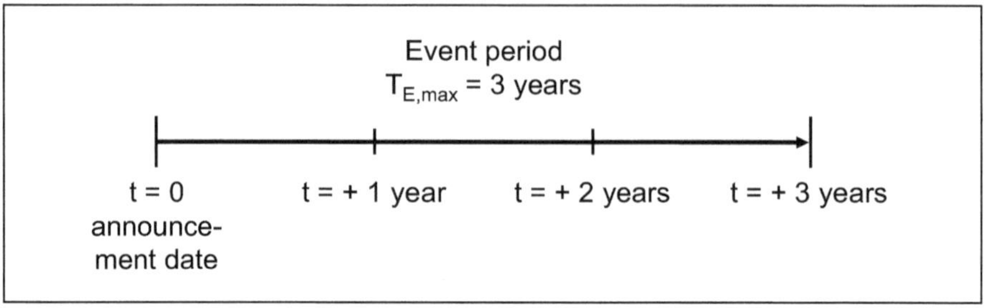

Figure 29: Event window for long-term BAHR analyses

- For each acquirer and each period in the event window, a single control firm from this short list based on the lowest difference in book-to-market ratio between the firms contained in the short list and the acquirer is selected.

Value generation is studied in the event window for times *t* between [0; +1 years], [0; +2 years], and [0; +3 years] after the announcement date, see Figure 29. Following the approach of Mußhoff (2007), deals from the long-term data sample are only included in the analyses, if capital market data is available until 3 years after announcement.[217] Thus, 18 transactions are excluded from the event time analysis, reducing the sample size from 176 to 158 firms. The model is calibrated to monthly simple TRS in local currency for acquirers, and monthly simple TRS in local currency for control firms.

4.4.1.1.2 Tests for significance of abnormal returns

The utilized tests follow the methodology presented in section 3.3.2.1.3. The significance of BAHRs is tested with the two-sided *t*-statistic (Equation (29)), and the skewness-adjusted two-sided *t*-statistic (Equation (30)).

$$t_{conv} = \sqrt{n} \cdot \frac{\overline{BAHR}}{\sigma(BAHR)} \qquad (32)$$

216 Acquirers which are also represented in the DEII are removed from the list of constituents before selecting a control firm.

217 All transactions announced at or after 1.7.2003 are excluded from the analyses. The date is chosen consistently with the validity period of control firms.

The null hypothesis that the observations have mean zero is rejected if $\left|t_{conv}\right| > t\left(n-1;1-\frac{\alpha}{2}\right)$.

$$t_{sa} = \sqrt{n} \cdot \left(\frac{t_{conv}}{\sqrt{n}} + \frac{\hat{\gamma} \cdot t_{conv}^2}{3n} + \frac{\hat{\gamma}}{6n} \right) \tag{33}$$

With $\hat{\gamma}$ the estimated coefficient of skewness

The null hypothesis that the observations have mean zero is rejected if $\left|t_{sa}\right| > t\left(n-1;1-\frac{\alpha}{2}\right)$.

Further on, a bootstrapped version of the skewness-adjusted two-sided *t*-statistic is implemented, following the procedure devised by Lyon et al. (1999). From the original sample, draw 1,000 bootstrapped resamples with size $n_b = n/4$ and recompute t_{sa}^b in each of these resamples. Compute lower critical value x_l^* and the upper critical value x_u^* as the lower and upper $\alpha/2$ quantile of the distribution of t_{sa}^b, where α is the level of significance. The null hypothesis is rejected if either $t_{sa} < x_l^*$ or $t_{sa} > x_u^*$. In order to test for significance of difference between mean abnormal returns of two samples, the parametric two-sample t-test, see section 3.3.2.1.3, is applied.

4.4.1.2 Calendar time approach based on Fama-French-Three-Factor model

4.4.1.2.1 Measurement of abnormal returns and benchmark construction

Analyses of long-term value creation in this study shall draw both on the BAHR and the calendar time approach, since a clear recommendation for application of either one cannot be given based on their fundamental statistical properties.[218] The examination of overall value creation on the entire sample assigns equal relevance to the result of either approach in the final assessment of value creation. However, the analysis of determinants of value creation shall attach greater

218 See section 3.3.2 for a detailed discussion.

importance to the results of the BAHR approach, since the CTAR approach does not allow for a multivariate analysis of several influencing factors.

The calendar time methodology follows the Fama-French-Three-Factor model approach presented in section 3.3.2.2. Total returns of acquirers show abnormal performance, if the regression of the market portfolio excess return $R_{m,t} - R_{f,t}$, the return differential between small stocks and big stocks SMB_t, and the return differential between high and low book-to-market stocks HML_t against the calendar time portfolio excess return $R_{p,t} - R_{f,t}$ yields an intercept which is significantly different from zero

$$R_{p,t} - R_{f,t} = \alpha + \beta \cdot \left(R_{m,t} - R_{f,t}\right) + s \cdot SMB_t + h \cdot HML_t + \varepsilon_t \tag{34}$$

The calendar time portfolios for the 3-year event period study are constructed from the long-term deal sample, and contain all acquirers which announced a transaction in the calendar month or in any of the 35 months prior to announcement, see Figure 30. The following data is used to calibrate the model:

- Monthly simple TRS in local currency for acquirers.
- Market values in USD of acquirers.
- Monthly simple TRS in EUR of market portfolio, small stocks, big stocks, high book-to-market stocks, and low book-to-market stocks.
- Average 3-month FIBOR in percent to represent the risk-free rate.[219]

The SMB and HML returns are computed following the approach described by Fama and French (1993). The market portfolio is defined as the constituents of the Datastream European Insurance Index (DEII). The procedure for each calendar month can be summarized as follows:

219 Event studies use different approximations to specify the risk-free rate, typically 3-month Treasury bills. Since Treasury bills are issued on an European level, and the EURIBOR does not cover the entire calendar time period, this study utilizes the FIBOR as the predecessor of the EURIBOR.

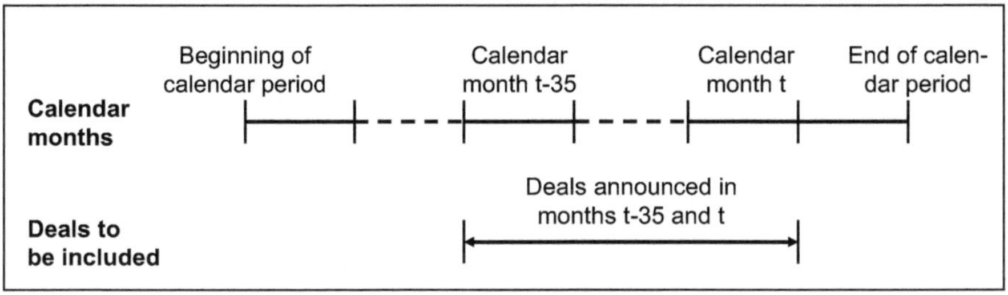

Figure 30: Calendar time and calendar time portfolio specification

- The DEII constituents are partitioned into small stocks and big stocks at the size median.
- The DEII constituents are partitioned into stocks with low, medium, and high book-to-market ratio at the 30% and 70% quantile of the book-to-market distribution.
- The value-weighted returns for the six intersecting portfolios are computed.
- The equally-weighted average returns on the small stock, big stock, high book-to-market ratio, and low book-to-market ratio portfolios are computed.
- SMB is calculated as the difference between the average small stock and big stock portfolio returns.
- HML is calculated as the difference between the average high book-to-market ratio and low book-to-market ratio portfolio returns.

Following the approach of Mußhoff (2007), the regression models are calibrated to CTA portfolio returns between 1.12.1992 and 31.12.2005 only, since 3-years of transaction history is required to form complete CTA portfolios. Thus, the eleven transactions between 1.1.1990 and 30.11.1992 are excluded from the analyses.

4.4.1.2.2 Tests for significance of abnormal returns

The applied test statistics follow the methodology laid out in section 3.3.2.2.2. The regression model intercept is tested for significant difference from zero with the two-sided t-statistic

$$t_0 = \frac{b_0}{s \cdot \sqrt{c_{00}}} \tag{35}$$

based on the regression intercept b_0, the estimated variance s, and c_{00} the (1,1)-element of the inverse squared design matrix $C = (X^T X)^{-1}$. The null hypothesis that the intercept is zero is rejected if $|t_0| > t\left(n - p - 1; 1 - \frac{\alpha}{2}\right)$. In order to test for equality of intercepts of two multiple regressions, an indicator variable model[220] is utilized

$$y = \alpha_1 + \beta_1 \cdot x + \alpha_2 \cdot z + \beta_2 \cdot x \times z + \varepsilon \tag{36}$$

where z is the indicator variable (0 for the first sub sample, 1 for the second sub sample). The intercepts are significantly different, if the null hypothesis $\alpha_2 = 0$ can be rejected according to the standard t-statistic.

4.4.2 Results in event time

4.4.2.1 Results on entire data sample

Value generation and abnormal returns

The transactions in the long-term BAHR sample generated a total net value of USD 20.6 bn[221] for the investors, equivalent to USD 130 mn per deal. 49% of the deals were conducted successfully, creating a value of USD 350.9 bn over a 3-year horizon. Thus, the overall positive effect is mostly driven by a slightly higher average value generation of successful deals (USD 4.6 bn) compared to un-

220 Larsen (2006), pp. 6.

221 The computation of the net value generated is based on the buy-and-hold abnormal return over 3 years, and the market value of the acquirer one day before the announcement day.

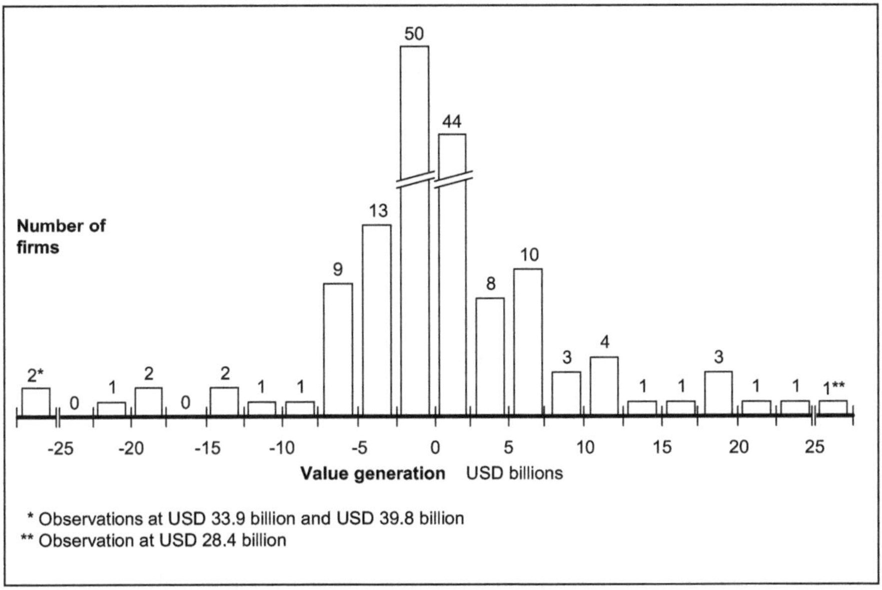

Figure 31: Distribution of value generation in long-term BAHR deal sample

successful deals (USD –4.1 bn). Figure 31 presents the distribution of the value generated.

Although total value generated is positive, observed BAHRs are negative on all analyzed event windows, and even significantly negative one year (–4.73%) and two years (–9.98%) after announcement at 10% level, see Table 18. BAHRs and value generation differ due to equal-weighting of BAHRs across acquirers as opposed to value-weighting of abnormal performance when analyzing value generation. Thus, larger acquirers are able to extract more value from transactions than small acquirers. Only Boubakri et al. (2006) analyze value creation of insurance transactions on the long-term horizon, however restricted to U.S. P&C acquirers. In contrast to the results of this study, they find a strongly positive market-return adjusted BAHR of 57.3% on a 3-year horizon based on 177 observations.

Compared to short-term CARs, long-term abnormal returns are more likely to result from an overlay of several effects, especially multiple M&A activity of

Table 18: Significance of BAHRs on long-term BAHR deal sample

		Sign of BAHR		conventional t		skewness adj. t		bootstrap s.a. t
Event window	BAHR%	Pos	Neg	Statistic	p-value	Statistic	p-value	p-value
[0; +1y]	-4.73%	73	85	-1.6956	9.2%	-1.6943	9.2%	41.6%
[0; +2y]	-9.98%	75	83	-2.0692	4.0%	-2.0478	4.2%	44.4%
[0; +3y]	-6.57%	78	80	-1.0924	27.6%	-1.0898	27.7%	62.6%

acquirers in the event window. In order to separate multi-bidder effects, Antoniou and Zhao (2006) filter their deal sample for single-bidders and clusters of multiple-bidders. The long-term BAHR data sample contains 72 deals from single-bidders, and 86 deals from multiple-bidders, whereas most multiple-bidders carried out two deals over a 3-year horizon. The difference between BAHRs of the entire sample, the multiple-bidder and the single-bidder sub sample are statistically insignificant.[222]

4.4.2.2 Results of multivariate analysis

A multivariate analysis is conducted to examine the cause-effect relationship between transaction strategy and properties, properties of the acquirer and the target, and buy-and-hold abnormal returns. The model is estimated and tested based on the statistics laid out in the multivariate short-term analysis in section 4.3.2.2. Equation (37) specifies the full regression model, with BAHRs as dependent variables, and the determinants of value creation introduced in section 4.2.3 as independent variables.

$$\begin{aligned}
&BAHR = constant + \beta_{STRATEGY} \cdot STRATEGY + \beta_{TIMING} \cdot TIMING + \\
&\beta_{ACQREGION} \cdot ACQREGION + \beta_{ACQINDUSTRY} \cdot ACQINDUSTRY + \\
&\beta_{LNSIZE} \cdot LNSIZE + \beta_{GROWTH} \cdot GROWTH + \beta_{EXPERIENCE} \cdot EXPERIENCE \\
&+ \beta_{TARREGION} \cdot TARREGION + \beta_{TARINDUSTRY} \cdot TARINDUSTRY + \\
&\beta_{LNRELVOLUME} \cdot LNRELVOLUME + \beta_{TARNOTLISTED} \cdot TARNOTLISTED
\end{aligned} \quad (37)$$

The categorical independent variable *STRATEGY* is modeled as five dichotomous variables with reference "national/within-industry" to test diversification against focus, *TIMING* is modeled as three dichotomous variables with reference

222 *p*-values above 70% on the three year horizon.

category "bottom phase" in order to test peak time against bottom time transactions, *ACQREGION* and *TARREGION* as four dichotomous variables with reference "EU-15", *ACQINDUSTRY* and *TARINDUSTRY* as four dichotomous variables with reference "P&C", and *EXPERIENCE* as three dichotomous variables with reference "no experience" to test transactions of experienced acquirers against those of inexperienced acquirers. Table 73 in the appendix shows the detailed coding of the categorical variables and presents descriptive statistics for metric and categorical variables. Additionally, the dichotomous variable *TARNOTLISTED* is included to distinguish between listed (N = 51, *TARNOTLISTED* = 0) and non-listed targets (N = 107, *TARNOTLISTED* = 1), i.e. to control for differences between the short- and long-term deal sample.

Table 19 presents the regression results of the full model and the reduced model[223] on 3-year BAHRs.[224] Both models are well specified according to the Ramsey Reset test. The independent variables are only weakly multicollinear. The hypothesis of normally distributed regression residuals cannot be rejected.

Both models explain BAHRs well, but slightly worse than prior research.[225] All independent variables are jointly significant above 5% level. However, the only individually significant independent variables are acquirer growth, target industry, and transaction experience. The reduced model additionally indicates significance of the transaction strategy and the regression constant.[226]

With respect to the transaction strategy, acquirers pursuing a full diversification strategy (*STRATEGY5*) are rewarded according to the reduced model. They achieve a 38.3% higher BAHR, significant at 10% level, compared to insurers conducting a full focus transaction. However, insurers which executed a cross-border EU/within-industry transaction (*STRATEGY2*) destroyed significant

---

223 Based on the full model, coefficients with change of F-statistic less significant than 10% are excluded stepwise. The following independent variables are excluded (in order): *LNRELVOLUME*, *ACQINDUSTRY* , *ACQREGION*, *EXPERIENCE*, *GROWTH*, *LNSIZE*, *STRATEGY*. Afterwards, independent variables more significant than 10% would be included stepwise. No variable fulfills this criterion.

224 2-year BAHRs are similarly well explained. However, the regression on 1-year BAHRs yields an R-square of only 18%.

225 Boubakri et al. (2006) obtain an R-square between 0.30 and 0.51 (N between 152 and 177).

226 These results are mostly consistent with regressions on 1-year and 2-year BAHRs. The former additionally obtains significant target region of origin, the latter phase of the M&A cycle.

Table 19: Results of multivariate regression analyses

	BAHR			**BAHR** (Reduced)		
Model specification	DF	sig DF		DF	sig DF	
Ramsey Reset	0.0028	99.7%		0.0317	96.9%	
Normality of residuals	Z	asy sig		Z	asy sig	
K-S	0.8467	47.0%		0.8781	42.4%	
Model fit	R-square	Adj. R-square		R-square	Adj. R-square	
R-square	0.2645	0.1125		0.2486	0.1626	
Model significance	Coeff.	F/t	VIF	Coeff.	F/t	VIF
Entire model		1.7405 **			2.8902 ****	
(Constant)	-0.9090	-1.4860		-0.8520	-2.8610 ***	
STRATEGY1	0.1820	0.7170	1.88	0.1510	0.6410	1.72
STRATEGY2	-0.3190	-1.5580	1.82	-0.3390	-1.8130 *	1.61
STRATEGY3	-0.1030	-0.3800	2.25	-0.1020	-0.4290	1.83
STRATEGY4	-0.1150	-0.4990	2.04	-0.1250	-0.5980	1.80
STRATEGY5	0.3880	1.5280	2.94	0.3830	1.6710 *	2.55
TIMING1	-0.2160	-0.9100	1.49			
TIMING2	-0.1060	-0.6220	2.08			
TIMING3	-0.0330	-0.1400	1.38			
ACQREGION2	-0.0830	-0.4560	1.54			
ACQINDUSTRY1	0.2810	1.2150	3.01	0.1930	0.9300	2.59
ACQINDUSTRY2	-0.0880	-0.3090	3.21	-0.2380	-0.9850	2.47
ACQINDUSTRY3	0.8980	1.1160	1.18	0.8650	1.1250	1.14
EXPERIENCE1	-0.5740	-1.5800	1.26	-0.6460	-1.9410 *	1.12
EXPERIENCE2	-0.3160	-1.8660 *	1.45	-0.3260	-2.0880 **	1.30
EXPERIENCE3	-0.0280	-0.1230	3.04	-0.0900	-0.5560	1.65
LNSIZE	0.0190	0.2590	3.83			
GROWTH	0.3830	2.5140 **	1.51	0.3700	2.9190 ***	1.11
TARREGION1	0.3940	0.6680	1.26			
TARREGION2	-0.1960	-0.4760	1.21			
TARREGION3	-0.2430	-0.4430	1.09			
TARINDUSTRY1	0.4640	2.3870 **	2.69	0.5040	2.7860 ***	2.46
TARINDUSTRY3	-0.1840	-0.6050	1.45	-0.1710	-0.5940	1.37
TARINDUSTRY4	0.2320	1.0650	2.06	0.2690	1.3660	1.79
LNRELVOLUME	0.0430	0.7220	2.99			
TARNOTLISTED	-0.0340	-0.2210	1.48			

DF: Change in F-statistic between initial and extended regression model according to Ramsey Reset test.
sig DF: Significance of change in F-statistic DF. Z: Kolmogorov-Smirnov Z-statistic.
asy sig: Asymptotic significance of Z-statistic Z. F/t: F-statistic for entire model, t-statistics for coefficients.
VIF: Variance Inflation Factors for coefficients.
STRATEGY indicates the geographical and industry focus of the transaction (national, cross-border EU, and cross-border world transactions, further separated into within- and cross-industry transactions; reference case is national within-industry), TIMING categorizes bottom (reference case), upswing, peak and downturn phases of the M&A market, ACQREGION and TARREGION distinguishes transactions into EU-15 (reference), EU-25, Swiss and Norwegian acquirers and targets, ACQINDUSTRY and TARINDUSTRY separates transactions into P&C (reference), Life, Re, Agents/Brokers and other acquirer and target industries, EXPERIENCE indicates transaction experience of the acquirer (reference case no; then little, extensive, and most experience), LNSIZE and GROWTH the size and growth of the acquirer, and LNRELVOLUME the relative volume of the target compared to the acquirer, TARNOTLISTED for listing of the target. See section 4.2.3 for detailed descriptions of the explanatory variables.
*-**** Statistically significant at 10%, 5%, 1% or 0.1% level according to t-test.

value (coefficient of –0.3390, significant at 10% level) compared to players with a full focus strategy. These results support the hypothesis that economies of scope or risk diversification outweigh economies of scale or benefits from increased regional market power. These results are contrary to findings of Boubakri et al. (2006), who observe significantly lower BAHRs for cross-border transactions on their U.S. P&C-focused sample.[227]

Further on, strongly growing acquirers generate significantly more value than weakly growing or shrinking acquirers. The additional BAHR over acquirers with zero growth is between 37.0% and 38.3%, significant above 5% level. The presumption that acquirers looking back on a history of fast growth are worse at integrating targets can thus be rejected. The reviewed prior research does not analyze this determinant.

For transaction experience, both the full and reduced model indicate that acquirers with little transaction experience generate significantly less value than insurers without transaction experience: Acquirers with only little experience destroy value of 64.6% (significant at 10% level) in the reduced model compared to insurers without a transaction history. However, most experienced acquirers generate similar value compared to inexperienced acquirers.[228] Thus, successful acquirers may be separated into two classes: Insurers with a focus on organic growth, and insurers with a strong tendency to inorganic growth. Insurers only carrying out few transactions may suffer from difficulties to choose or integrate the target. The findings of Boubakri et al. (2006) are directionally consistent: They report that BAHRs increase significantly with the number of transactions by the acquirer in the same year.[229]

Finally, acquisitions of life insurers are significantly more successful than P&C acquisitions. The additional BAHRs in both regression models are above 46% and significant at 5% level or better. The reviewed prior research does not analyze this determinant.

The following section presents further descriptive analyses on the significant, hypotheses-related dimensions geographical and industry focus (*STRAT-*

227 The estimated coefficients depend considerably on the applied regression model.

228 The null hypothesis that *EXPERIENCE3* is zero cannot be rejected.

229 All regression models yield results of above 4% increase of BAHR per additional acquirer transaction in the same year.

EGY), acquirer growth (*GROWTH*), and transaction experience (*EXPERIENCE*). The dimension announcement year (*TIMING*) is included due to its significance in the short-term analyses. The obtained results are only indicative with respect to the actual influence of these determinants on value creation; the final assessment on the importance of these determinants draws on the results of the multivariate analysis.

4.4.2.3 Results of descriptive analyses on major cross-sections

4.4.2.3.1 Geographical and industry focus

Value generation and abnormal returns in sub samples

National within-industry transactions dominated European insurance M&A (22% of deals, 34% of total deal volume). Only these fully focused and cross-border world deals created value, whereas the latter proved to be most successful with an average value creation between USD 1.4 bn and USD 1.6 bn per deal. However, only fully diversifying transactions achieved a significantly positive BAHR (14.0% over a 3-year horizon, significant at 10% level). Fully focused transactions also showed positive, yet insignificant BAHRs over 3-years.

Table 20: Overview BAHRs depending on geographical and industry focus of transaction (1/2)

	National Within-industry			**National Cross-industry**			**Cross-border EU Within-industry**		
Descriptive statistics									
Deal volume (USD bn)	77.4			12.2			50.3		
Number of deals	36			18			29		
Average deal volume (USD bn)	2.2			0.7			1.7		
Value generation (USD bn)	Value	Deals	V/D	Value	Deals	V/D	Value	Deals	V/D
Total value	13.8	36	0.4	-18.2	18	-1.0	-58.0	29	-2.0
Value generation	36.7	22	1.7	6.1	6	1.0	46	8	5.7
Value reduction	-22.9	14	-1.6	-24.3	12	-2.0	-103.7	21	-4.9
BAHR analysis	BAHR%	skew. adj. p	(boot-str.)	BAHR%	skew. adj. p	(boot-str.)	BAHR%	skew. adj. p	(boot-str.)
[0; +1y]	-4.51%	51.4%	72.4%	-2.02%	82.3%	92.6%	-2.93%	74.0%	97.4%
[0; +2y]	-10.99%	32.4%	56.4%	-24.82%	12.2%	32.6%	-10.84%	21.9%	56.8%
[0; +3y]	9.40%	55.5%	85.8%	-12.96%	64.6%	64.6%	-26.18%	0.6%	0.6%

Table 21: Overview BAHRs depending on geographical and industry focus of transaction (2/2)

	Cross-border EU Cross-industry			Cross-border World Within-industry			Cross-border World Cross-industry		
Descriptive statistics									
Deal volume (USD bn)	29.8			37.5			21.6		
Number of deals	19			25			31		
Average deal volume (USD bn)	1.6			1.5			0.7		
Value generation (USD bn)	Value	Deals	V/D	Value	Deals	V/D	Value	Deals	V/D
Total value	-0.2	19	0.0	40	25.0	1.6	44	31.0	1.4
Value generation	32.2	9	3.6	132	14.0	9.4	99	18.0	5.5
Value reduction	-32.3	10	-3.2	-92	11.0	-8.4	-55	13.0	-4.2
BAHR analysis	BAHR%	skew. adj. p	(boot-str.)	BAHR%	skew. adj. p	(boot-str.)	BAHR%	skew. adj. p	(boot-str.)
[0; +1y]	-16.37%	6.0%	23.6%	1.12%	79.8%	88.8%	-5.84%	18.4%	43.2%
[0; +2y]	-37.95%	0.4%	17.2%	2.86%	79.6%	81.4%	7.38%	27.4%	57.0%
[0; +3y]	-29.51%	5.7%	17.8%	-10.26%	53.8%	90.4%	13.98%	8.5%	48.0%

Acquirers with cross-border EU transactions within their own industry destroyed most value (USD 2.0 bn per deal), driven by a low success ratio of merely 28%. Their abnormal return of -26% is significant to 1% level. Industry-diversifying cross-border EU transactions show an even worse significant BAHR. The results are presented in Table 20 and Table 21.

Developing of BAHRs across the event window

While the overperformance of full focus or full diversification strategies begins to materialize two years after announcement, capital markets penalize acquirers for European industry-diversifying strategies already one year after announcement. The evidence is presented in Figure 32.

Comparison of BAHRs between sub samples

The overperformance of national within-industry transactions over cross-border EU within-industry transactions is significant at 10% level over a 3-year horizon. Fully diversifying transactions are significantly superior to cross-border EU transactions. Table 22 and Table 23 present the evidence.

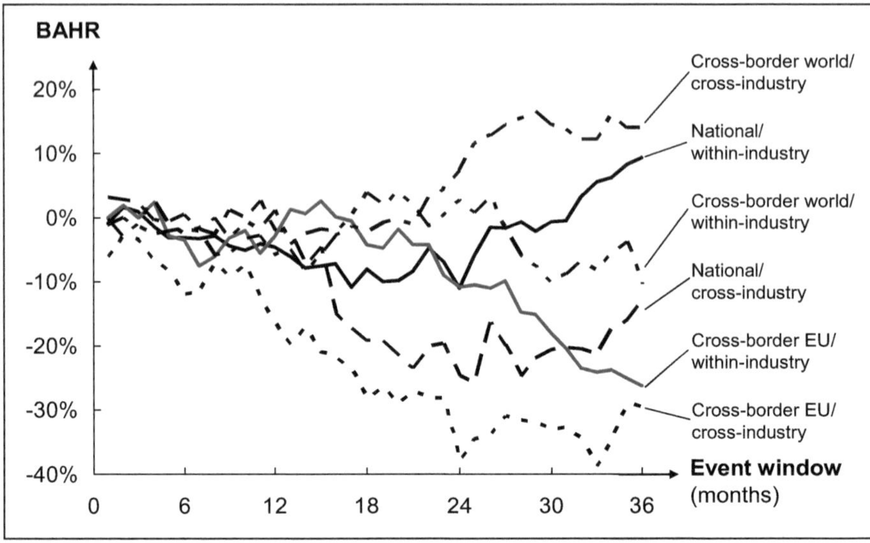

Figure 32: Developing of BAHR depending on geographical and industry focus of transaction

Table 22: Significance of difference between BAHRs depending on geographical and industry focus of transactions (1/2)

		National Cross-industry		**Cross-border EU Within-industry**		**Cross-border EU Cross-industry**	
		dBAHR%	t-statistic p	dBAHR%	t-statistic p	dBAHR%	t-statistic p
National Within-industry	[0; +1y]	2.48%	82.9%	1.58%	87.9%	-11.87%	32.4%
	[0; +2y]	-13.84%	49.9%	0.15%	99.2%	-26.97%	15.2%
	[0; +3y]	-22.35%	42.1%	-35.57%	6.8%	-38.91%	11.6%
National Cross-industry	[0; +1y]	-	-	-0.90%	94.0%	-14.35%	28.7%
	[0; +2y]	-	-	13.98%	43.5%	-13.13%	54.8%
	[0; +3y]	-	-	-13.22%	57.0%	-16.56%	58.0%
Cross-border EU Within-industry	[0; +1y]	-	-	-	-	-13.45%	29.0%
	[0; +2y]	-	-	-	-	-27.11%	8.6%
	[0; +3y]	-	-	-	-	-3.34%	85.9%

Table 23: Significance of difference between BAHRs depending on geographical and industry focus of transactions (2/2)

		Cross-border World Within-industry		Cross-border World Cross-industry	
		dBAHR%	t-statistic p	dBAHR%	t-statistic p
National Within-industry	[0; +1y]	5.63%	53.4%	-1.33%	87.7%
	[0; +2y]	13.85%	46.0%	18.36%	19.6%
	[0; +3y]	-19.66%	39.0%	4.58%	80.3%
National Cross-industry	[0; +1y]	3.14%	72.5%	-3.82%	67.3%
	[0; +2y]	27.69%	23.5%	32.20%	5.2%
	[0; +3y]	2.70%	92.4%	26.93%	22.4%
Cross-border EU Within-industry	[0; +1y]	4.05%	66.4%	-2.91%	74.6%
	[0; +2y]	13.70%	42.3%	18.22%	11.7%
	[0; +3y]	15.92%	39.7%	40.15%	0.4%
Cross-border EU Cross-industry	[0; +1y]	17.49%	8.9%	10.53%	29.1%
	[0; +2y]	40.81%	5.6%	45.33%	0.2%
	[0; +3y]	19.25%	42.6%	43.49%	1.6%
Cross-border World Within-industry	[0; +1y]	-	-	-6.96%	29.1%
	[0; +2y]	-	-	4.51%	77.4%
	[0; +3y]	-	-	24.24%	17.4%

Comparison of results to prior research

These results support the hypotheses of economies of scope or risk diversification, since acquirers pursuing a full diversification strategy generate most value. Nevertheless, fully focusing acquirers prove similarly successful, suggesting that economies of scale or market power effects may offset scope or diversification benefits.In contrast, Boubakri et al. (2006) find that focused transactions are superior to diversifying transactions in separate analyses on the geographical and industry dimension. National transactions generate a BAHR of 63.1%, which is significantly higher at 5% level than the BAHR of 28.5% of international transactions. Acquirers involved in within-industry transactions achieve a BAHR of 76.3%, compared to 37.1% for those carrying out cross-industry transactions, while the difference is significant at the 5% level.

4.4.2.3.2 Timing of the transaction

Value generation and abnormal returns in sub samples

Most transactions were carried out in the peak and bottom phase of the M&A market (69 and 58 deals, respectively). The highest total deal volume was achieved in the peak phase (USD 123 bn), but largest transactions took place during the downturn (USD 2.8 bn). Transactions in the latter phase created most value per deal (USD 3.8 bn), driven by a high success ratio of almost 70% and the fact that successful deals created more than double the value unsuccessful deals destroyed. The only significant abnormal returns are observed for transactions during M&A market upswing with BAHR of –15% over the one year horizon, and in the peak phase with BAHR of –13% over the two year horizon. The results are presented in Table 24.

Developing of BAHRs across the event window

BAHRs of acquirers which carried out a transaction in the upswing phase of the M&A cycle develop notably worse than BAHRs of other acquirers. They experience negative abnormal returns almost consistently across the entire 3-year time horizon, as illustrated in Figure 33.

Comparison of BAHRs between sub samples

The underperformance of acquirers in the upswing phase is significant at 10% level relative to acquirers that announced a transaction during the bottom phase, see Table 25.

Comparison of results to prior research

In summary, the "bandwagon effect" or the overpayment hypothesis are weakly supported by these results. Acquirers carrying out transactions in the upswing or peak phase destroy value but generate only insignificantly negative BAHRs. However, their BAHRs are significantly lower than those of acquirers which announced deals during the bottom of the M&A cycle. Prior research does not analyze this determinant.

Table 24: Overview BAHRs depending on timing of the transaction

	Bottom			Upswing			Peak			Downturn		
Descriptive statistics												
Deal volume (USD bn)	37.6			26.7			123.2			41.6		
Number of deals	58			16			69			15		
Average deal volume (USD bn)	0.6			1.7			1.8			2.8		
Value generation (USD bn)	Value	Deals	V/D	Value	Deals	V/D	Value	Deals	V/D	Value	Deals	V/D
Total value	51.2	58	0.9	-17.8	16	-1.1	-69.6	69	-1.0	56.8	15	3.8
Value generation	122.9	27	4.6	29.3	6	4.9	129.4	33	3.9	69.3	11	6.3
Value reduction	-71.7	31	-2.3	-47.0	10	-4.7	-199.0	36	-5.5	-12.5	4	-3.1
BAHR analysis	BAHR%	skew.adj. p-value		BAHR%	skew.adj. p-value		BAHR%	skew.adj. p-value		BAHR%	skew.adj. p-value	
[0; +1y]	-1.67%	59.8%	80.6%	-15.34%	9.7%	9.7%	-4.61%	36.9%	36.9%	-5.82%	51.7%	51.7%
[0; +2y]	-1.28%	83.7%	96.6%	-34.11%	33.9%	33.9%	-13.45%	3.3%	3.3%	-1.96%	86.0%	89.6%
[0; +3y]	-8.23%	44.2%	70.0%	-23.47%	42.9%	42.9%	-4.03%	63.7%	63.7%	6.23%	46.1%	46.1%

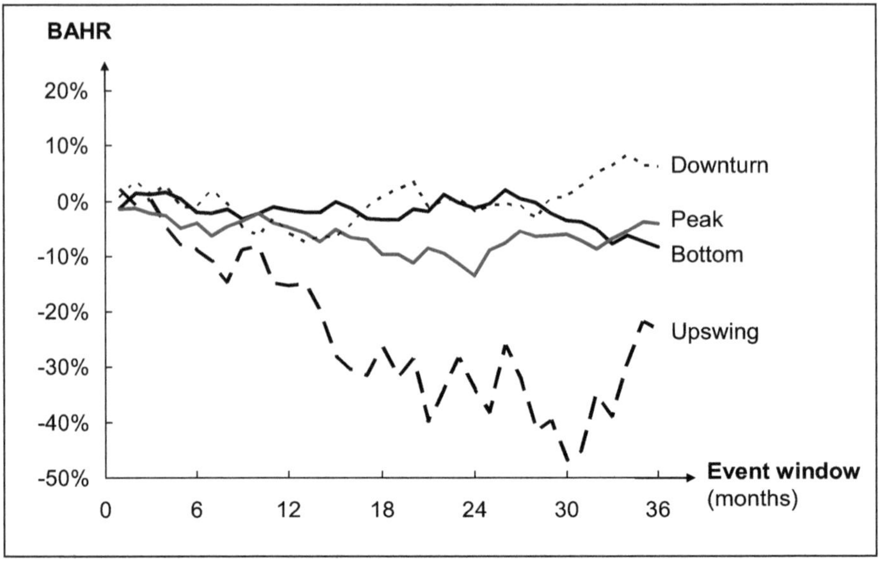

Figure 33: Developing of BAHR depending on timing of the transaction

Table 25: Significance of difference between BAHRs depending on timing of the transaction

		Upswing		Peak		Downturn	
		dBAHR%	t-statistic p	dBAHR%	t-statistic p	dBAHR%	t-statistic p
Bottom	[0; +1y]	-13.67%	9.3%	-2.94%	64.0%	-4.16%	61.0%
	[0; +2y]	-32.83%	9.6%	-12.16%	19.7%	-0.68%	96.0%
	[0; +3y]	-15.24%	55.6%	4.20%	75.4%	14.46%	51.4%
Upswing	[0; +1y]	-	-	10.73%	34.9%	9.52%	48.6%
	[0; +2y]	-	-	20.66%	30.2%	32.15%	33.0%
	[0; +3y]	-	-	19.44%	37.0%	29.71%	33.9%
Peak	[0; +1y]	-	-	-	-	-1.21%	91.7%
	[0; +2y]	-	-	-	-	11.48%	45.8%
	[0; +3y]	-	-	-	-	10.26%	56.3%

4.4.2.3.3 Growth of acquirer

Value generation and abnormal returns in sub samples

The 40 fastest growing acquirers[230] achieved to increase their market value by 91.5% across the estimation window, the 78 medium growing insurers realized a growth of 22.1%, and the 40 slowest growing companies shrank by 22.5%. The histogram in Figure 34 presents the distribution of growth.

The medium growing insurers carried out the largest deals in average (USD 1.8 bn), closely followed by the fastest growing companies (USD 1.6 bn), see Table 26. Only medium growing acquirers achieved to generate value (USD

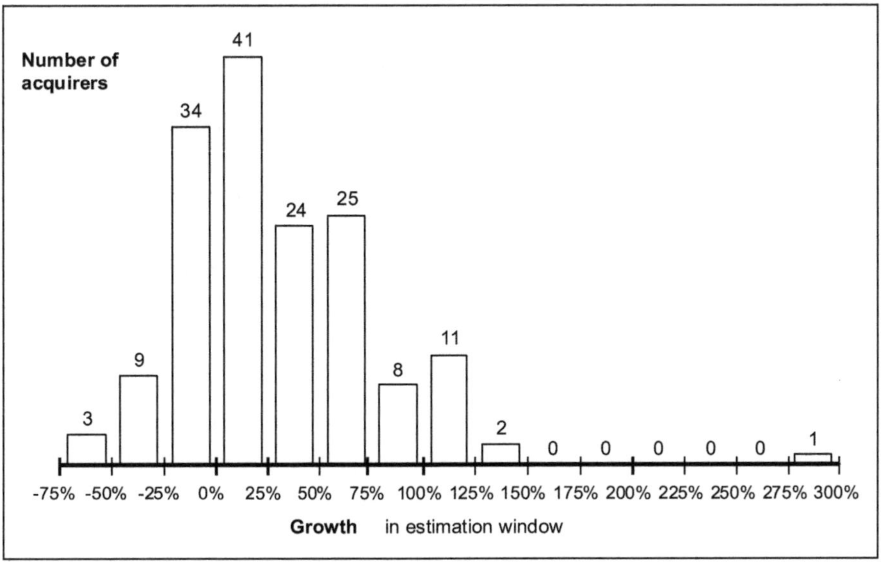

Figure 34: Distribution of acquirer growth

230 Growth is measured as relative change of market value over the short-term analysis estimation window. If market value data is not available at the beginning or the end of the estimation window, growth estimated from available data is scaled to the length of the estimation window. The acquirers are classified according to their quantile in the distribution of growth in the data sample. Those acquirers with a growth rate in the upper quartile are labelled "fastest growing acquirers", and those ones with a growth rate in the lower quartile "slowest growing acquirers". All other acquirers are allocated to the class of "medium growing acquirers".

Table 26: Overview BAHRs depending on growth of acquirer

	40 Fastest growing acquirers			78 Medium growing acquirers			40 Slowest growing acquirers		
Descriptive statistics									
Deal volume (USD bn)	62.5			136.8			29.7		
Number of deals	40			78			40		
Average deal volume (USD bn)	1.6			1.8			0.7		
Average performance	191.5%			122.1%			77.5%		
Value generation (USD bn)	Value	Deals	V/D	Value	Deals	V/D	Value	Deals	V/D
Total value	-33.0	40	-0.8	108.1	78	1.4	-54.4	40	-1.4
Value generation	76.6	19	4.0	240.7	45	5.3	33.6	13	2.6
Value reduction	-109.6	21	-5.2	-132.6	33	-4.0	-88.0	27	-3.3
BAHR analysis	BAHR%	skew. adj. p	(boot-str.)	BAHR%	skew. adj. p	(boot-str.)	BAHR%	skew. adj. p	(boot-str.)
[0; +1y]	-1.77%	76.7%	88.4%	-5.17%	19.2%	71.0%	-6.84%	20.7%	48.6%
[0; +2y]	-3.03%	70.1%	90.0%	-11.06%	14.9%	71.2%	-14.83%	13.7%	51.4%
[0; +3y]	13.75%	13.5%	47.4%	-9.17%	25.8%	61.4%	-21.81%	12.2%	45.8%

108.1 bn), driven by both a high success ratio of 58% and higher value creation per deal of successful deals than of unsuccessful deals. Slowest growing acquirers destroyed most value on a per deal basis (USD –1.4 bn). However, BAHRs for medium growing and for slowest growing acquirers are continuously negative. Only top growth companies achieved a positive BAHR on the 3-year horizon, although all BAHRs are insignificant. Again, the discrepancy to the examined value generation is rooted in the equal-weighting of the BAHRs.

Developing of BAHRs across the event window

Capital markets reacted negatively to the announcement of transactions for all acquirers. Only top performing acquirers again gained confidence of the investors in the 2nd year after the announcement, and created value thereafter. Figure 35 illustrates this development.

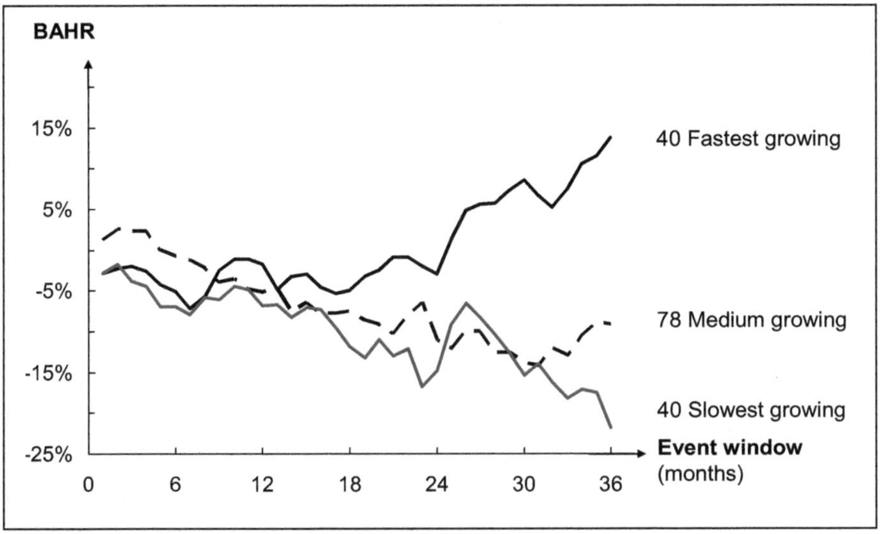

Figure 35: Developing of BAHR depending on growth of acquirer

Comparison of BAHRs between sub samples

On the 3-year horizon, the over-performance of top performers compared to bottom performers is significant at the 5% level, see Table 27. These results counter the hypothesis that fast growing insurers face difficulties at integrating takeover targets. The 40 fastest growing acquirers are the only ones to achieve

Table 27: Significance of difference of BAHRs depending on growth of acquirer

		78 Medium growing acquirers		40 Slowest growing acquirers	
		dBAHR%	t-statistic p	dBAHR%	t-statistic p
40 Fastest growing acquirers	[0; +1y]	-3.40%	62.4%	-5.07%	54.9%
	[0; +2y]	-8.03%	49.0%	-11.80%	37.2%
	[0; +3y]	-22.93%	10.4%	-35.56%	4.2%
78 Medium growing acquirers	[0; +1y]	-	-	-1.67%	80.2%
	[0; +2y]	-	-	-3.77%	76.6%
	[0; +3y]	-	-	-12.63%	40.8%

positive BAHRs 3 years after announcement, which are significantly higher than abnormal returns generated by the 40 slowest growing acquirers.

Comparison of results to prior research

These results counter the hypothesis that fast growing insurers face difficulties at integrating take over targets. Prior research does not analyze this determinant.

4.4.2.3.4 Transaction experience

Value generation and abnormal returns in sub samples

Most transactions are carried out by acquirers without M&A experience (46% of deals). The sub sample of acquirers with little experience contains only five transactions and shall thus not be further interpreted. Acquirers with most experience carried out the largest deals (USD 2.1 bn per deal). They also created most value per deal (USD 2.3 bn), driven by a higher value creation of successful deals compared to value destruction of unsuccessful deals. Together with inexperienced acquirers they are the only ones to achieve positive, but insignificant BAHRs 3 years after announcement. Only the underperformance of acquirers with extensive experience is significant over a 2-year horizon (BAHR –23.5% at 5% level). Table 28 presents the evidence.

Developing of BAHRs across the event window

While BAHRs of acquirers without and with most experience develop similar over time, acquirers with extensive transaction experience consistently destroy value over almost the entire 3-year time horizon, see Figure 36.

Comparison of BAHRs between sub samples

The abnormal performance of acquirers with extensive experience is significantly worse than BAHRs of most experienced acquirers already 2 years after announcement, see Table 29. These results imply that possibly existing positive experience effects are at least partly offset by other factors not controlled for in the univariate analysis.

Table 28: Overview BAHRs depending on transaction experience of acquirer

	No experience			Little experience			Extensive experience			Most experience		
Descriptive statistics												
Deal volume (USD bn)	63.6			11.7			56.9			90.2		
Number of deals	67			5			33			42		
Average deal volume (USD bn)	0.9			2.3			1.7			2.1		
Value generation (USD bn)	Value	Deals	V/D	Value	Deals	V/D	Value	Deals	V/D	Value	Deals	V/D
Total value	-36.5	67	-0.5	-8.9	5	-1.8	-22.9	33	-0.7	96.3	42	2.3
Value generation	81.3	36	2.3	2.4	1	2.4	35.9	13	2.8	229.8	23	10.0
Value reduction	-117.8	31	-3.8	-11.3	4	-2.8	-58.8	20	-2.9	-133.5	19	-7.0
BAHR analysis	BAHR%	skew. adj. p	(boot-str.)	BAHR%	skew. adj. p	(boot-str.)	BAHR%	skew. adj. p	(boot-str.)	BAHR%	skew. adj. p	(boot-str.)
[0; +1y]	-2.07%	68.0%	87.6%	-18.18%	0.3%	-*	-9.17%	15.5%	62.0%	-4.97%	22.7%	49.0%
[0; +2y]	-3.18%	73.6%	86.4%	-61.39%	14.5%	-*	-23.50%	1.1%	15.6%	-4.49%	38.2%	68.6%
[0; +3y]	2.78%	80.7%	87.6%	-61.71%	16.2%	-*	-26.84%	12.8%	82.6%	3.49%	45.6%	69.8%

* Insufficient observations for bootstrapping.

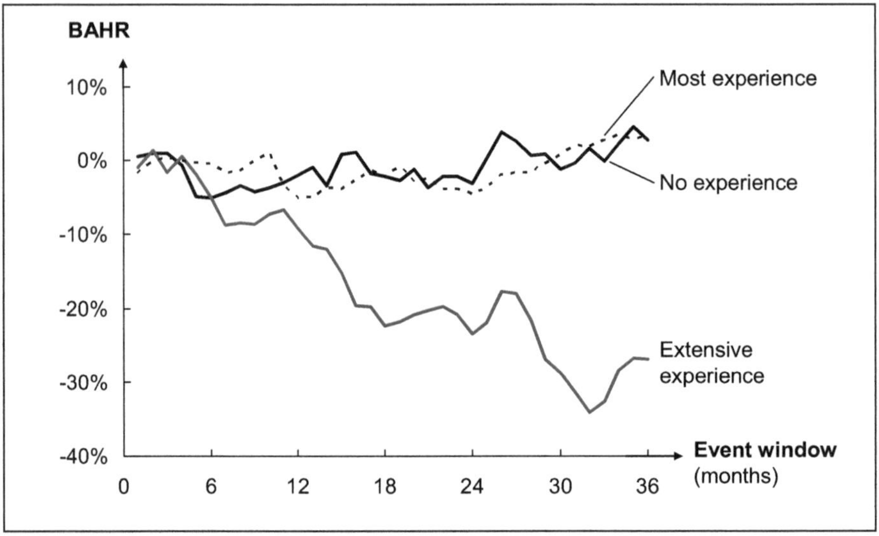

Figure 36: Developing of BAHR depending on transaction experience of acquirer

Table 29: Significance of difference between BAHRs depending on transaction experience of acquirer

		Extensive experience		**Most experience**	
		dBAHR%	t-statistic p	dBAHR%	t-statistic p
No experience	[0; +1y]	-7.10%	39.5%	-2.90%	68.7%
	[0; +2y]	-20.32%	17.3%	-1.31%	91.5%
	[0; +3y]	-29.62%	12.6%	0.71%	96.1%
Extensive experience	[0; +1y]	-	-	4.20%	59.3%
	[0; +2y]	-	-	19.01%	9.0%
	[0; +3y]	-	-	30.33%	4.0%

4.4.3 *Results in calendar time*

4.4.3.1 Results on entire data sample

In the previous subsection, long-term value creation is assessed following the BAHR methodology. In order to round off the perspective on long-term value creation, this section presents the results of the calendar time analyses. The final assessment of overall value creation on the entire sample assigns equal relevance to the result of the BAHR analysis in the previous section and the CTAR approach in this section. However, the analysis of determinants of value creation shall attach greater importance to the results of the BAHR approach, since the CTAR approach does not allow for a multivariate analysis of several influencing factors.

Market model regression results

The market model for the entire sample is estimated on $N = 157$ observations.[231] A low standard error of regression, and high (adjusted) R-square show, that the Fama-French-Three-Factor model explains the excess returns of the CTA portfolio well, see Table 30. Additionally, the low p-values of the F-test and the t-tests indicate mostly significant estimates for the intercept and the beta coefficients.

Table 30: Fama-French-Three-Factor model regression results on entire sample

	Entire sample (equally-weighted)		**Entire sample** (value-weighted)	
Regression model	Statistic	p-value	Statistic	p-value
R-Squared	0.8168		0.8484	
Adjusted R-Squared	0.8132		0.8454	
F-statistic	227.3503	0.0%	285.3611	0.0%
Coefficients	Coeff.	p-value	Coeff.	p-value
Intercept	-0.0037	15.9%	-0.0039	14.4%
Index excess return	0.7884	0.0%	0.8144	0.0%
SBM return	-0.1600	2.1%	-0.3366	0.0%
HML return	0.1424	1.4%	0.0290	62.3%

231 In the CTA analysis, observations are the number of calendar months included in the regression model.

Table 31: Normality tests of residuals of Fama-French-Three-Factor model

	Entire sample (equally-weighted)	Entire sample (value-weighted)
Observations	157	157
Normal parameters		
Mean	0.0000	0.0000
Sigma	0.0272	0.0281
Most extreme differences		
Absolute	0.0884	0.0850
Positive	0.0884	0.0669
Negative	0.0766	0.0850
Kolmogorov-Smirnov test		
Statistic	0.0369	0.0319
Asymptotic p-value	98.1%	99.7%

Normality property of regression residuals

The hypothesis tests for abnormality of returns are based on the assumption, that regression residuals are normally distributed. Table 31 shows that this assumption cannot be rejected according to the Kolmogorov-Smirnov test.

Abnormal returns

Table 32 presents the findings on the entire sample and the sub samples according to the bidding frequency of acquirers. The entire sample shows insignificant negative CTARs of about –0.4% per month, i.e. the excess return on the calendar time portfolio is insignificantly lower than the return on a combination of the market, SMB and HML portfolios. These results are comparable to the findings in event time, which yield an insignificantly negative BAHR of –6.57% on a 3-year horizon.[232] Following the discussion for the analysis in event time, overlay effects of multiple-bidding is examined. The performance differential between the entire sample, multiple-bidders and single-bidders is again not significant.[233]

232 BAHRs on 1- and 2-year horizons (–4.73%, and –9.98%, respectively) are significantly negative according to the conventional and skewness-adjusted *t*-statistic, but not according to the bootstrapped version of the latter.

233 p-values above 55% for equally- and value-weighted CTARs.

Table 32: Significance of CTARs on long-term CTA sample

Descriptive statistics		
Deal volume (USD bn)	253.3	
Number of deals	176	
Average deal volume (USD bn)	1.4	
CTA analysis	Intercept	p-value
Equally-weighted	-0.37%	15.9%
Value-weighted	-0.39%	14.4%

4.4.3.2 Results of descriptive analyses on major cross-sections

Geographical and industry focus

National within-industry transactions dominated European insurance M&A between 1990 and 2005, both in terms of number and volume of deals. The analyses yield significant CTARs only for fully diversified transactions. Theses deals achieve a negative abnormal performance of –0.67% per month in the average, significant at 5% level, which is significantly lower than the insignificant positive abnormal performance of cross-border world within-industry transactions. Table 33 to Table 36 present the respective evidence. These results indicate, contrary to the analyses in event time, that potential benefits from economies of scope or risk diversification do not outweigh scale economies or benefits from increase in market power: Fully diversifying acquirers perform worse than acquirers pursuing other strategies, while the comparative underperformance is partly even significant.

The outcome of the calendar time analysis is contrary to the results of the event time analysis in section 4.4.2.3.1. There, fully diversifying transaction yield a significantly positive 3-year BAHR of 13.98%, whereas cross-border world within-industry transactions achieve a negative (yet insignificant) 3-year BAHRs of –10.26%. The deviations may occur due to differences in the under-

Table 33: Overview CTARs depending on geographical and industry focus of transaction (1/2)

	National Within-industry		**National Cross-industry**		**Cross-border EU Within-industry**	
Descriptive statistics						
Deal volume (USD bn)	81.8		12.6		58.9	
Number of deals	40		20		32	
Average deal volume (USD bn)	2.0		0.6		1.8	
CTA analysis	Intercept	p-value	Intercept	p-value	Intercept	p-value
Equally-weighted	-0.56%	25.0%	-0.41%	40.9%	-0.11%	76.2%
Value-weighted	-0.76%	12.6%	-0.22%	65.6%	-0.56%	17.6%

Table 34: Overview CTARs depending on geographical and industry focus of transaction (2/2)

	Cross-border EU Cross-industry		**Cross-border World Within-industry**		**Cross-border World Cross-industry**	
Descriptive statistics						
Deal volume (USD bn)	31.0		39.6		29.4	
Number of deals	23		29		32	
Average deal volume (USD bn)	1.3		1.4		0.9	
CTA analysis	Intercept	p-value	Intercept	p-value	Intercept	p-value
Equally-weighted	-0.23%	59.5%	0.18%	63.5%	-0.67%	4.9%
Value-weighted	0.04%	92.9%	0.24%	54.6%	-0.53%	13.0%

lying transaction sample,[234] or different statistical properties of both approaches.[235] However, as argued in the introduction of this chapter, this univariate cross-sectional analysis delivers only indicative, descriptive results. Final conclusions with respect to the influence of individual determinants, such as geographical and industry focus, on value creation can only be drawn on the results of multivariate regression analyses. Only these multivariate studies allow for accurately separating the simultaneous influence of several determinants. The respective results are discussed in section 4.4.2.2.

234 For the long-term analysis according to the BAHR approach, the last 18 transactions need to be dropped (see section 4.4.2.1), whereas for the CTAR analyses, the first 11 transactions need to be disregarded (see section 4.4.3.1).

235 See section 3.4 for a detailed discussion.

Table 35: Significance of difference between CTARs depending on geographical and industry focus of transaction (1/2)

		National Cross-industry		Cross-border EU Within-industry		Cross-border EU Cross-industry	
		dIntercept%	t-stat. p	dIntercept%	t-stat. p	dIntercept%	t-stat. p
National Within-industry	Eq.weight.	0.15%	82.6%	0.45%	45.9%	0.32%	62.1%
	Val.weight.	0.54%	43.8%	0.20%	75.6%	0.79%	22.2%
National Cross-industry	Eq.weight.	-	-	0.30%	62.7%	0.17%	79.4%
	Val.weight.	-	-	-0.34%	59.5%	0.26%	69.3%
Cross-border EU Within-industry	Eq.weight.	-	-	-	-	-0.12%	82.7%
	Val.weight.	-	-	-	-	0.60%	31.1%

Table 36: Significance of difference between CTARs depending on geographical and industry focus of transaction (2/2)

		Cross-border World Within-industry		Cross-border World Cross-industry	
		dIntercept%	t-stat. p	dIntercept%	t-stat. p
National Within-industry	Eq.weight.	0.74%	23.5%	-0.11%	85.5%
	Val.weight.	1.00%	12.0%	0.23%	70.3%
National Cross-industry	Eq.weight.	0.59%	35.0%	-0.26%	66.4%
	Val.weight.	0.46%	47.1%	-0.31%	60.6%
Cross-border EU Within-industry	Eq.weight.	0.29%	58.1%	-0.56%	26.1%
	Val.weight.	0.80%	16.5%	0.03%	95.5%
Cross-border EU Cross-industry	Eq.weight.	0.41%	47.7%	-0.43%	43.2%
	Val.weight.	0.21%	72.3%	-0.57%	29.8%
Cross-border World Within-industry	Eq.weight.	-	-	-0.85%	9.3%
	Val.weight.	-	-	-0.77%	14.6%

Timing of the transaction

Acquirers achieve the highest positive, yet insignificant CTARs in the upswing and peak phase of the M&A cycle. Nevertheless, the former perform significantly better than acquirers, which carry out a transaction during the bottom of the M&A market. Table 37 and Table 38 present the respective evidence. These results counter the "bandwagon effect" and the overpayment hypothesis. Acquirers carrying out transactions during the upswing or peak phase of the M&A cycle show the best performance, even compared to acquirers that announce deals during the bottom.

Table 37: Significance of CTARs depending on timing of the transaction

	Trough		**Upswing**		**Peak**		**Downturn**	
Descriptive statistics								
Deal volume (USD bn)	61.9		26.7		123.2		41.6	
Number of deals	76		16		69		15	
Average deal volume (USD bn)	0.8		1.7		1.8		2.8	
CTA analysis	Intercept	p-value	Intercept	p-value	Intercept	p-value	Intercept	p-value
Equally-weighted	-0.26%	45.8%	0.26%	67.6%	0.56%	48.8%	-0.88%	13.2%
Value-weighted	-0.30%	40.1%	1.03%	13.2%	0.52%	52.4%	-0.52%	41.6%

Table 38: Significance of difference between CTARs depending on phase in M&A cycle

		Upswing		Peak		Downturn	
		dIntercept%	t-stat. p	dIntercept%	t-stat. p	dIntercept%	t-stat. p
Trough	Eq.weight.	0.51%	45.2%	0.81%	28.0%	-0.63%	38.6%
	Val.weight.	1.33%	6.3%	0.82%	28.7%	-0.22%	76.4%
Upswing	Eq.weight.	-	-	0.30%	78.3%	-1.14%	18.3%
	Val.weight.	-	-	-0.51%	65.2%	-1.55%	10.1%
Peak	Eq.weight.	-	-	-	-	-1.44%	21.5%
	Val.weight.	-	-	-	-	-1.04%	38.3%

Again, the event time analyses yield contrary results: The only significant BAHRs are obtained for transactions during the upswing (BAHR of –15.34% on a 1-year horizon) and the peak phase (BAHR of –13.45% on a 2-year horizon). As argued in section 4.4.3.2.1, deviations between these indicative univariate results may occur due to differences in the underlying transaction sample or different statistical properties of both approaches, but final conclusions with respect to the influence of determinants of success on value creation may only be drawn from multivariate analyses presented in section 4.4.2.2.

Growth of acquirer

The results presented in Table 39 suggest, that the faster an acquirer grew before a transaction, the less abnormal return it generates thereafter, while the difference is not significant.[236] However, from a value-weighted perspective, the 44 slowest growing acquirers[237] performed worst with a significant negative CTAR of –0.90% at 5% level. The difference to their equally-weighted CTAR indicates that especially large and slowly growing or shrinking acquirers destroyed most value compared to fastest, medium or other slowly growing acquirers.

236 See Table 40.

237 The number of acquirers in each of the categories fastests, medium and slowest growing acquirers deviate from bin sizes in the respective event time analysis in section 4.4.2.3.3, because the number of transactions in the underlying data samples differ. The event time analyses excludes the 18 transactions announced after 1.7.2003 (see section 4.4.1.1.1), whereas the calendar time analyses excludes the 11 transactions before 30.11.1992 (see section 4.4.1.2.1).

Table 39: Overview CTARs depending on growth of acquirer

	44 Fastest growing acquirers		**88 Medium growing acquirers**		**44 Slowest growing acquirers**	
Descriptive statistics						
Deal volume (USD bn)	63.8		158.9		30.6	
Number of deals	44		88		44	
Average deal volume (USD bn)	1.4		1.8		0.7	
Average growth	188.0%		119.9%		77.6%	
CTA analysis	Intercept	p-value	Intercept	p-value	Intercept	p-value
Equally-weighted	-0.71%	10.2%	-0.48%	15.1%	-0.47%	32.5%
Value-weighted	-0.67%	15.2%	-0.38%	24.5%	-0.90%	5.0%

Table 40: Significance of difference between CTARs depending on growth of acquirer

		88 Medium growing acquirers		**44 Slowest growing acquirers**	
		dIntercept%	t-stat. p	dIntercept%	t-stat. p
44 Fastest growing acquirers	Eq.weight.	0.22%	67.9%	0.24%	70.8%
	Val.weight.	0.29%	60.3%	-0.23%	72.3%
88 Medium growing acquirers	Eq.weight.	-	-	0.02%	97.9%
	Val.weight.	-	-	-0.52%	34.7%

The results are ambivalent with respect to the hypothesis that fast growing acquirers face difficulties at integrating takeover targets. On the one hand, slowest growing acquirers show worse abnormal performance than fastest growing acquirers, but the difference is insignificant. On the other hand, medium growing acquirers destroy less value than fastest growing acquirers, but again the difference is not significant. The corresponding event time analyses only yields insignificant results.

Transaction experience

The abnormal performance of inexperienced acquirers is significantly negative, while large acquirers even perform worse: The value-weighted CTAR of –0.68% per month is significant at 5% level. However, the CTARs of inexperienced acquirers are not significantly lower than the abnormal performance of acquirers

Table 41: Overview CTARs depending on transaction experience of acquirers

	No experience		Little experience		Extensive experience		Most experience	
Descriptive statistics								
Deal volume (USD bn)	77.0		11.7		67.8		90.2	
Number of deals	77		5		41		42	
Average deal volume (USD bn)	1.0		2.3		1.7		2.1	
CTA analysis	Intercept	p-value	Intercept	p-value	Intercept	p-value	Intercept	p-value
Equally-weighted	-0.51%	9.8%	-0.63%	37.6%	-0.24%	57.4%	-0.28%	54.6%
Value-weighted	-0.68%	4.9%	-0.73%	36.5%	-0.50%	19.4%	-0.27%	57.0%

with more experience. The results weakly support the hypothesis that positive transaction experience effects exist, and that these effects may even offset other negative effects of frequent transactions: Most experienced acquirers achieve higher abnormal returns than other acquirers, but the difference is insignificant. Table 41 and Table 42 present the results of the respective analyses.

In contrast, the event time analyses yield significantly negative BAHRs for acquirers with little experience (BAHR of –18.18% over a 1-year horizon), and those with extensive experience (BAHR of –23.50% over a 2-year horizon). As argued in section 4.4.3.2.1, deviations may occur due to differences in the underlying transaction sample or different statistical properties of both approaches.

Table 42: Significance of difference between CTARs depending on transaction experience of acquirers

		Little experience		Extensive experience		Most experience	
		dIntercept%	t-stat. p	dIntercept%	t-stat. p	dIntercept%	t-stat. p
No experience	Eq.weight.	-0.12%	85.9%	0.28%	59.7%	0.23%	68.2%
	Val.weight.	-0.04%	95.3%	0.19%	71.5%	0.42%	47.3%
Little experience	Eq.weight.	-	-	0.39%	61.4%	0.35%	67.9%
	Val.weight.	-	-	0.23%	76.7%	0.46%	60.0%
Extensive experience	Eq.weight.	-	-	-	-	-0.05%	93.9%
	Val.weight.	-	-	-	-	0.23%	70.4%

4.5 Summary

4.5.1 Results of short-term analysis in the context of recent academic work

4.5.1.1 Results on entire data sample

The completed transactions generated a total net value of USD 1.8 bn equivalent to USD 32.7 mn per deal for investors. This study finds that CERs are significant and positive on most analyzed event windows, with a maximum CER of 2.06% in [–10; +10], significant at the 10% level. These results are generally consistent with prior research:

- Akhigbe and Madura (2001) observe positive significant CERs of 13.11% in [–1; 0] at 5% level, and insignificant positive abnormal returns in the event windows [–11; –2] and [+1; +10] for the U.S. market.
- Only Floreani and Rigamonti (2001) report significantly positive abnormal returns in all studied event windows at 5% significance level except on the announcement day, with highest CER of 5.27% in the event window [–20; +2]. They analyze the U.S., European, and Australian market.
- Cummins and Weiss' (2004) study on the Western European market does not include analysis of the combined entity. They document small positive returns around the announcement date for acquirers, and strong positive returns (CAR above 20%, at 0.1% level of significance) around announcement for acquirers, so that CERs are likely to be significantly positive for these event windows, too.
- Cummins and Xie (2005) find significant positive CERs of 3.71% in [–1; +1] at 1% level for the U.S. market.

Further on, the analyses in this study show that target CARs are significant and positive in all analyzed event windows. This outcome again is typical for prior research:

- The analyses of BarNiv and Hathorn (1997) on the U.S. P&C market result in significantly positive CARs in [–250, +250] at 1% level for distressed targets, and insignificantly negative or positive CARs for financially sound targets.[238]

- Akhigbe and Madura (2001) compute significantly positive abnormal returns, with a maximum at 20.78% in [–1; 0] at 1% level.
- Floreani and Rigamonti's (2001) analyses yield positive and mostly significant CARs, with a maximum CAR of 18.80% in the event window [–40; +40], significant at 1% level.
- Cummins and Weiss (2004) also report consistently positive and significant CARs in all analyzed event windows between [–15; +15], with a maximum 8.85% in [–15; +15] at 1% level.
- Cummins and Xie (2005) also find significantly positive CARs in all event windows between [–15; +15], mostly significant at better than 0.1% level. The highest abnormal return is achieved in the event window [–15; +15] with 24.98%.

However, acquirer CARs in this study are mostly statistically insignificant. The results of prior event studies are inhomogeneous in this respect:

- BarNiv and Hathorn (1997) observe negative abnormal returns only for one classification of distressed acquirers, with an outlier-driven CAR of –138.63% at 10% level. CARs for either financially sound or differently classified distressed acquirers are insignificantly positive.
- Akhigbe and Madura (2001) report small negative returns (–0.28% in [–11; –2] at 10% level, and insignificant –0.23% in [+1; +10]), and significant positive abnormal returns (2.21% in [–1; +0] at 1% level).
- Floreani and Rigamonti (2001) discover positive CARs for all analyzed event windows between [–40; +40]. The only exception is found in [+3; +40] with an insignificantly negative CAR of –0.76%. The largest positive CAR is recorded between [–20; +2] with 3.65%, significant at 1% level.

238 The height of the CARs for these sub samples depends on the chosen classification methodology.

Author	Industry focus	Geography focus	Time frame	Event study results: Method	CERs	Target AR	Acquirer AR
This study	• Acquirer is insurance, target is insurance or asset manager	• Acquirer in EU-25, Switzerland or Norway	1990 - 2005	• CAR, CER, BAHR, CTA	• Always positive, significant in some event windows	• Positive significant in all analyzed event windows	• Small positive and negative, significant negative only in one event window
BarNiv and Hathorn, 1997	• P&C insurance	• US	1985 - 1992	• CAR	• -	• Significant positive CARs for distressed tar-gets, small posi-tive or negative for financially sound targets	• Small positive or significant negative CARs for distressed acquirers, small positive for financially sound acquirers
Akhigbe and Madu-ra, 2001	• Acquirer and target is insurance	• US	1985 - 1995	• CAR, CAR regres-sion models, CER	• Always positive, significant in some event windows	• Always positive and mostly significant	• Positive significant in some event windows
Floreani and Rigamonti, 2001	• Insurance	• US, Europe, and Australia	1996 - 2000	• CAR, CER, BAHR	• Positive significant in all event windows	• Always positive and mostly significant	• Always positive with one exception, mostly significant
Cummins and Weiss, 2004	• Acquirer or target is insurance company	• Western EU	1990 - 2002	• CAR	• -	• Positive significant in all analyzed event windows	• Mostly small, but insignificantly negative
Cummins and Xie, 2005	• Acquirer or target is P&C insurance company	• US	1997 - 2003	• CAR, CER	• Positive significant in shortly around announcment date	• Positive significant in all studied event windows	• Always positive, partially significant in some event windows

Source: Own research

Figure 37: Qualitative comparison of results of this event study with prior event studies on entire data sample

- Cummins and Weiss (2004) analyses yield mostly small, but insignificantly negative CARs (lower than –0.5%) with the exception of 0.02% CAR in [–1; 0].

- Cummins and Xie (2005) obtain consistently positive CARs with a maximum of 1.19%. However, only abnormal returns in the event windows [0; +1], [–1; +1] and [–5; +5] are statistically significant at 1% or 5% level.

Figure 37 summarizes these findings for the entire data sample.

4.5.1.2 Results of multivariate analysis

Three hypothesis-related determinants have significant influence on the combined entity performance: Geographical and industry focus of the transaction (*STRATEGY*), timing of the transaction (*TIMING*), and transaction experience of the acquirer (*EXPERIENCE*):

- *Geographical and industry focus (STRATEGY):* With respect to the first determinant, this study finds that acquirer CARs and CERs in geographical or industry diversifying transactions are significantly higher than acquirer CARs and CERs in fully focused transactions. Capital markets thus believe that economies of scope or risk diversification outweigh economies of scale and regional market power effects. These results are consistent with Floreani and Rigamonti's (2001) observation that cross-border transactions within Europe have negative impact on the acquirers' CARs, whilst cross-border world deals by European acquirers positively affect their CARs. However, Cummins and Xie (2005) find on their P&C U.S. sample that any geographical or industry diversification is significantly worse than full geographical and industry focus with respect to CARs of acquirers.

- *Timing of the transaction (TIMING):* This study find that transactions during upswing, peak or downturn phase generate significantly higher abnormal returns for acquirers and combined entities. The results imply that investors do not believe in a "bandwagon effect" or the overpayment hypothesis in hot markets, but rather appreciate transactions during these phases in the M&A cycle. The reviewed prior research does not analyze this factor.

- *Transaction experience (EXPERIENCE):* In addition, a reduced regression model indicates that transaction experience of the acquirers has a significant effect on CERs: Acquirers with little experience achieve significantly smaller CERs than acquirers without any transaction experience. The hypothesis of a positive experience effect is thus not supported. Prior research does not address this determinant.

Two control variables are significant for explanation of CERs:

- *Target region of origin (TARREGION):* Norwegian targets yield significantly higher CERs than transactions with targets within the EU-15. Prior research does not address this variable.
- *Target industry (TARINDUSTRY):* Transactions with targets operating in the life insurance industry obtain significantly higher CERs compared to transactions with P&C targets in the reduced models. Prior research does not address this variable.

Three further determinants proved insignificant in this study, but significant in previous research: Acquirer size (*LNSIZE*), acquirer industry (*ACQINDUSTRY*), and relative transaction volume (*LNRELVOLUME*). The results compare as follows:

- *Acquirer size (LNSIZE):* With respect to the acquirer size, this study finds that acquirer CARs and CERs insignificantly decrease with increasing market value of the acquirer. These results are consistent with prior research. Floreani and Rigamonti (2001) and Cummins and Xie (2005) find that acquirer CARs decrease with the size of the acquirer.[239]
- *Acquirer industry (ACQINDUSTRY):* The results of this study show that transactions carried out by acquirers operating in life insurance create insignificantly more value in terms of acquirer CARs and CERs than transactions by P&C insurers. Akhigbe and Madura (2001) observe the opposite. Acquirers' CARs in their analysis are higher for nonlife acquirers compared to life acquirers.

239 The effect in Cummins and Xie's (2005) analysis is significant.

- *Relative transaction volume (LNRELVOLUME):* This study observes that the effect of the relative transaction volume is only insignificantly different from zero. Floreani and Rigamonti (2001) find that CARs of acquirers increases significantly with the relative transaction volume.

4.5.1.3 Results of descriptive analyses on major cross-sections

Four significant, hypotheses-related dimensions are examined further in univariate descriptive analyses: Geographical and industry focus (*STRATEGY*), timing of the transaction (*TIMING*), and transaction experience of the acquirer (*EXPERIENCE*). *STRATEGY* is analyzed separately for geographical and industry focus of transactions in order to obtain sufficient observations in each sub sample for interpretation. The independent variable acquirer growth (*GROWTH*) is included due to its significance in the long-term analyses.

- *Geographical focus of transaction:* Only national and cross-border EU deals generated value (each USD 1.1 bn). Cross-border EU deals generated the highest value on a per deal basis (USD 81 mn). Cross-border EU deals yielded highest, but insignificant mean CERs above 4%. However, these CERs are significantly higher than the CERs of national and cross-border world transactions. Seemingly, investors were informed early and had a positive view on cross-border EU deals. These results are comparable to prior research. Floreani and Rigamonti (2001) show that within country transactions have in average higher CERs than cross border transactions. For acquirer CARs, there is no clear difference between the sub samples. Cummins and Weiss (2004) identify that within country transactions perform slightly worse than cross border transactions. The former yield partially significant negative acquirer CARs around the announcement date (e.g., –0.63% in [0; +2] at 0.1%) , whereas the latter transactions only realize insignificant positive and negative CARs. However, their analysis of target CARs draws a different picture. Within country transactions have higher CARs than cross border transactions on 15 out of 16 analyzed event windows. Cummins and Xie's (2005) analyses show that geographically focused transactions have high CERs, e.g., insignificant 4.08% in [–1; +1], whereas geographically diversified transactions have somewhat smaller, but still positive CERs, e.g., insignificant 3.64% in [–1; +1].

- *Industry focus of transaction:* Within-industry transactions created tremendous value (USD 3.6 bn), whereas cross-industry transactions destroyed value (USD –1.8 bn). CERs in within-industry transactions are consistently, and partially significantly, positive; even acquirer mean CARs are partially significantly positive. Cross-industry transactions mostly showed partially significant negative mean CERs. The over-performance of within-industry transactions is partially significant. Investors seem to value economies of scale from industry focus higher than economies of scope from industry diversification. Again, these results are comparable to the outcome of prior research. Floreani and Rigamonti (2001) show that CERs and acquirer CARs of reinsurance companies are positive and higher than those of life and other insurance players. Cummins and Xie (2005) find positive CERs for within-industry transactions (e.g., insignificant 5.01% in [–1; +1]), and small, mostly negative CERs for cross-industry transactions (e.g., –0.20% in [–1; +1]).

- *Timing of the transaction (TIMING):* Transactions in the trough of the M&A cycle destroyed value, while those in peak of the cycle generated value (USD –0.9 bn vs. USD 0.5 bn). Consistent with these results, CERs in the trough were significantly negative shortly around announcement (e.g., –3.5% in [–5; +5]), and insignificantly positive during the peak phase. The performance differential between both phases is significant. Thus, investors did not believe in the existence of a "bandwagon effect" or the overpayment hypothesis during M&A market highs.

- *Growth of acquirer (GROWTH):* Slowest growing acquirers generated more than double the value compared to medium performers (USD 2.5 bn vs. USD 1.2 bn), and fastest growing insurers even destroyed USD –1.9 bn of value. The former also generated the highest value on a per deal basis (USD 179 mn), and achieved a significantly positive mean CER of 3.75% across the event window, whereas the latter showed a significantly negative CER of –3.28%. The negative overall CER of fastest growing acquirers is caused by strongly negative CERs between 20 days before announcement and 11 days before the announcement which are not compensated for thereafter. However, even reduction of the event window to [–10; +20] does only mitigate, but not neutralize the value destruction of their transactions.

- *Transaction experience (EXPERIENCE):* Inexperienced acquirers destroyed value of USD –1.1 bn, while extensively and most experienced acquirers generated value of USD 1.1 bn. The latter also generated most value on a per deal basis (USD 73 mn). However, only extensively experienced acquirers achieved a significant CER of 4.0% at 5% level in [–10; +10][240]. The difference of abnormal returns between sub samples are not significant. Thus, capital markets do not value transaction experience in the short-term.

4.5.2 Results of medium- and long-term analysis in the context of recent academic work

4.5.2.1 Results on entire data sample

Overall, the analyzed transactions created a total net value of USD 20.6 bn, or USD 130 mn per deal. This study finds that acquirers achieved an insignificant and negative BAHR of –6.6% on a 3-year horizon. CTARs are insignificant and negative at about –0.40% per month. Only Boubakri et al. (2006) analyze value creation of insurance transactions on the long-term horizon, however restricted to U.S. P&C acquirers. In contrast to the results of this study, they find a strongly positive market-return adjusted BAHR of 57.3% on a 3-year horizon based on 177 observations.

4.5.2.2 Results of multivariate analysis

Three hypothesis-related determinants show significant influence on the buy-and-hold abnormal returns of acquirers: Geographical and industry focus of the transaction (*STRATEGY*), acquirer growth (*GROWTH*), and transaction experience of the acquirer (*EXPERIENCE*). The results are:

240 Sub sample of acquirers with little experience excluded from analysis due to small sample size ($N = 2$).

- *Geographical and industry focus (STRATEGY):* This study finds that acquirers pursuing a full diversification strategy create significantly more value than fully focusing acquirers. Further on, acquirers executing a cross-border EU transaction within their industry destroyed significant value compared to fully focusing acquirers. Thus, economies of scope or risk diversification outweigh economies of scale or benefits from increased regional market power. These results are contrary to findings of Boubakri et al. (2006), who observe significantly lower BAHRs for cross-border transactions on their U.S. P&C-focused sample.
- *Acquirer growth (GROWTH):* Acquirers with a history of strong growth achieve significantly higher BAHRs than weaker growing acquirers. The hypotheses that strongly growing acquires may face difficulties integrating targets can thus be rejected. The reviewed prior research does not analyze this determinant.
- *Transaction experience (EXPERIENCE):* Acquirers with little experience generate significantly less value than acquirers without transaction experience. Acquirers with most experience create similar value compared to these inexperienced acquirers. Thus, there may be two distinct classes of insurers: Those focused on organic growth and those "in the M&A game". The findings of Boubakri et al. (2006) are directionally consistent: They report that BAHRs increase significantly with the number of transactions by the acquirer in the same year.

The control variable target industry also proved significant in the multivariate model. Acquisitions of life insurers were significantly more successful than acquisitions of P&C insurers.

4.5.2.3 Results of descriptive analyses on major cross-sections

Three significant, hypotheses-related dimensions are examined further in univariate descriptive analyses: Geographical and industry focus (*STRATEGY*), acquirer growth (*GROWTH*), and transaction experience (*EXPERIENCE*). The independent variable announcement year (*TIMING*) is included due to its significance in the short-term analyses.

- *Geographical and industry focus of transactions (STRATEGY):* Value was only created by national within-industry transactions (USD 13.8 bn), and cross-border world deals (USD 40 bn within-industry, and USD 44 bn cross-industry). The latter transactions created the highest value per deal (USD 1.6 bn, and USD 1.4 bn, respectively), and yield significantly better BAHRs than cross-border European transactions, which suffer from BAHRs below –26%, significant at 10% level or better. These results suggest that economies of scope or risk diversification may or may not outweigh economies of scale and regional market power benefits in the long run. It seems to be more important for insurers to pursue an "all-or-nothing" strategy of either full or no diversification. However, the calendar time analyses yield different results.[241] Only fully diversified transactions achieve significant CTARs, but they are significantly negative with –0.67% abnormal return per month at 5% level. These results indicate that potential benefits from economies of scope or risk diversification do not outweigh scale economies or benefits from increase in market power. Both results are contrary to the findings of Boubakri et al. (2006), who report superiority of focused transactions in separate analyses on the geographical and industry dimension. National transactions generate a BAHR of 63.1%, which is significantly higher at 5% level than the BAHR of 28.5% of international transactions. Acquirers involved in within-industry transactions achieve a BAHR of 76.3%, compared to 37.1% for those carrying out cross-industry transactions, while the difference is significant at the 5% level.

- *Timing of the transaction (TIMING):* Transactions in the downturn and bottom phase of the M&A cycle were the only ones to generate value (USD 56.8 bn, and USD 51.2 bn, respectively), whereas the former achieved largest value creation per deal (USD 3.8 bn). The only significant BAHRs are observed during the market upswing (–15.3% after one year), and peak (–13.5% after two years), whereas the former is significantly worse than one and two year BAHRs in the bottom phase. These results weakly support

241 The deviations may occur due to differences in the underlying transaction sample or different statistical properties of both approaches. A final assessment of the influence of geographical and industry focus of the transactions shall be based on findings of the multivariate analysis in the previous section.

existence of "bandwagon effect" or overpayment during hot market phases. Again, the calendar time analysis yields different results. Acquirers only achieve positive (yet insignificant) CTARs in the upswing phase (value-weighted 1.03% per month), and the peak phase (value-weighted 0.52% per month) of the M&A cycle, whereas the former are significantly higher than CTARs of transactions in the bottom phase of the market (value-weighted CTAR of -030% per month).[242] These results counter the "bandwagon effect" and the overpayment hypothesis. Prior research does not analyze this determinant.

- *Growth of acquirer (GROWTH):* Only medium growing acquirers created value (USD 108.1 bn equivalent to USD 1.4 bn per deal). However, fastest growing acquirers were the only acquirers to achieve positive BAHRs. On 3-year horizon, their BAHR is significantly higher than the BAHR of slowest growing acquirers. The only significant abnormal returns are achieved by slowest growing acquirers with a value-weighted CTAR of –0.90%, significant at 5% level. Both results counter the hypothesis that fast growing insurers face difficulties at integrating takeover targets. Results from the calendar time analysis are similar. Prior research does not analyze this determinant.

- *Transaction experience (EXPERIENCE):* Most experienced acquirers are the only ones to create value through their M&A transactions (USD 96.3 bn, equivalent to USD 2.3 bn per deal). However, the only significant BAHRs are achieved by extensively experienced acquirers, with –23.5% significant at 5% level two years after announcement. The superior performance of most experienced acquirers compared to extensively experienced acquirers is significant at 10% level or better after two and three years. These results suggest that other factors than experience effects may ultimately determine value creation of transactions. In contrast, the calendar time analysis supports the hypothesis that experience increases value extraction from M&A,

242 The deviations may occur due to differences in the underlying transaction sample or different statistical properties of both approaches. A final assessment of the influence of geographical and industry focus of the transactions shall be based on findings of the multivariate analysis in the previous section.

since the only significant results are obtained for inexperienced acquirers with a value-weighted CTAR of –0.68%, significant at 5% level.[243] Prior research does not analyze this determinant.

4.5.3 Comparison of short- and long-term results

4.5.3.1 Industry perspective

Previous event study results in this study indicate that the influence of determinants of value creation may depend on the time horizon of the analysis. This section examines which factors historically lead to value creation according in the short run, and how these factors compare to those driving value creation in the long run. The results may support management in choosing the appropriate strategy depending on their time horizon or in communicating strategies more effectively to investors. The analysis draws on three regression models.

- A CER model as presented in section 4.3.2.2.[244]
- An analogous regression model on acquirer CARs, but with the deal sample extended to all deals, which are included in the long-term BAHR analysis. Additionally, the target listing (*TARNOTLISTED*) is introduced in order to control for difference between the short- and long-term deal sample.
- A BAHR regression model as presented in section 4.4.2.2.

The regression results are presented in Table 43. All three models are well specified according to the Ramsey Reset test. The hypotheses that the regression residuals are normally distributed cannot be rejected. The models show good explanatory power for the variance of the dependent variables with an *R*-square of 0.66 for the CER model and *R*-squares above 0.22 for the CAR and the BAHR

---

243 However, the difference of CTARs to more experienced acquirers is not significant. The deviations may occur due to differences in the underlying transaction sample or different statistical properties of both approaches. A final assessment of the influence of geographical and industry focus of the transactions shall be based on findings of the multivariate analysis in the previous section.

244 Three transactions which are not part of the long-term deal sample for BAHR analysis are excluded from the short-term deal sample.

Table 43: Results of multivariate regression models on industry perspective

	CER[a]			CAR Acquirer[b]			BAHR[c]		
Model specification	DF	sig DF		DF	sig DF		DF	sig DF	
Ramsey Reset	0.0158	98.4%		0.9204	40.1%		0.0028	99.7%	
Normality of residuals	Z	asy sig		Z	asy sig		Z	asy sig	
K-S	0.6593	77.8%		0.6463	79.8%		0.8467	47.0%	
Model fit	R-square	Adj. R-square		R-square	Adj. R-square		R-square	Adj. R-square	
R-square	0.6625	0.3749		0.2228	0.0622		0.2645	0.1125	
Model significance	Coeff.	F/t	VIF	Coeff.	F/t	VIF	Coeff.	F/t	VIF
Entire model		2.3040 **			1.3872			1.7405 **	
(Constant)	0.0486	0.5596		-0.0127	-0.2497		-0.9090	-1.4860	
STRATEGY1	-0.0124	-0.4862	2.3	0.0132	0.6261	1.9	0.1820	0.7170	1.9
STRATEGY2	0.0505	1.8717 *	3.1	0.0222	1.3075	1.8	-0.3190	-1.5580	1.8
STRATEGY3	0.0597	1.3527	3.1	0.0107	0.4755	2.2	-0.1030	-0.3800	2.2
STRATEGY4	0.0659	2.1351 **	4.0	0.0224	1.1759	2.0	-0.1150	-0.4990	2.0
STRATEGY5	0.0448	1.6711	3.8	0.0033	0.1575	2.9	0.3880	1.5280	2.9
TIMING1	0.1103	3.3579 ***	3.7	0.0437	2.2134 **	1.5	-0.2160	-0.9100	1.5
TIMING2	0.0512	1.8913 *	5.2	0.0475	3.3404 ***	2.1	-0.1060	-0.6220	2.1
TIMING3	0.0564	1.7859 *	3.0	0.0429	2.1976 **	1.4	-0.0330	-0.1400	1.4
ACQREGION2	-0.0216	-0.9743	2.2	-0.0075	-0.4992	1.5	-0.0830	-0.4560	1.5
ACQINDUSTRY1	0.0133	0.5345	4.1	0.0156	0.8152	3.0	0.2810	1.2150	3.0
ACQINDUSTRY2	-0.0144	-0.4231	4.9	-0.0110	-0.4654	3.2	-0.0880	-0.3090	3.2
ACQINDUSTRY3	0.0222	0.4134	1.6	0.0462	0.6913	1.2	0.8980	1.1160	1.2
EXPERIENCE1	-0.0705	-1.4649	2.5	-0.0595	-1.9691 *	1.3	-0.5740	-1.5800	1.3
EXPERIENCE2	-0.0069	-0.2747	3.1	-0.0274	-1.9463 *	1.4	-0.3160	-1.8660 *	1.4
EXPERIENCE3	0.0264	0.7599	7.3	-0.0027	-0.1423	3.0	-0.0280	-0.1230	3.0
LNSIZE	-0.0132	-1.2910	7.4	-0.0030	-0.5129	3.8	0.0190	0.2590	3.8
GROWTH	-0.0245	-1.1670	1.9	-0.0102	-0.8044	1.5	0.3830	2.5140 **	1.5
TARREGION1				-0.0237	-0.4828	1.3	0.3940	0.6680	1.3
TARREGION2	0.0514	0.7242	2.8	-0.0421	-1.2343	1.2	-0.1960	-0.4760	1.2
TARREGION3	0.1332	2.2576 **	1.9	0.0550	1.2100	1.1	-0.2430	-0.4430	1.1
TARINDUSTRY1	0.0361	1.6232	3.6	0.0019	0.1160	2.7	0.4640	2.3870 **	2.7
TARINDUSTRY3	0.0079	0.2496	1.6	-0.0138	-0.5465	1.4	-0.1840	-0.6050	1.4
TARINDUSTRY4	0.0102	0.3691	3.8	-0.0062	-0.3403	2.1	0.2320	1.0650	2.1
LNRELVOLUME	0.0015	0.2368	3.1	-0.0002	-0.0478	3.0	0.0430	0.7220	3.0
TARNOTLISTED				0.0083	0.6565	1.5	-0.0340	-0.2210	1.5

DF: Change in F-statistic between initial and extended regression model according to Ramsey Reset test.
sig DF: Significance of change in F-statistic DF. Z: Kolmogorov-Smirnov Z-statistic.
asy sig: Asymptotic significance of Z-statistic Z. F/t: F-statistic for entire model, t-statistics for coefficients.
VIF: Variance Inflation Factors for coefficients.

STRATEGY indicates the geographical and industry focus of the transaction (national, cross-border EU, and cross-border world transactions, further separated into within- and cross-industry transactions; reference case is national within-industry), TIMING categorizes bottom (reference case), upswing, peak and downturn phases of the M&A market, ACQREGION and TARREGION distinguishes transactions into EU-15 (reference), EU-25, Swiss and Norwegian acquirers and targets, ACQINDUSTRY and TARINDUSTRY separates transactions into P&C (reference), Life, Re, Agents/Brokers and other acquirer and target industries, EXPERIENCE indicates transaction experience of the acquirer (reference case no; then little, extensive, and most experience), LNSIZE and GROWTH the size and growth of the acquirer, and LNRELVOLUME the relative volume of the target compared to the acquirer, TARNOTLISTED for listing of the target. See section 4.2.3 for detailed descriptions of the explanatory variables.

*-**** Statistically significant at 10%, 5%, 1% or 0.1% level according to t-test.

[a] CERs in event window [-5; +5]. Data sample: Transactions of short-term deal sample included in BAHR analysis.

[b] Acquirer CARs in event window [-5; +5]. Data sample: Transactions which are included in BAHR analysis.

[c] BAHRs across 3-year time horizon.

model. The coefficients in the CER and the BAHR model are jointly significant according to the F-test. However, none of the independent variables is significant in all three models. For this reason, interpretation of coefficients shall rely on both significant and insignificant variables, keeping in mind that coefficients of insignificant variables may not necessarily be different from zero or might even carry different signs on a data sample with more observations.[245]

For hypothesis-related independent variables with significant coefficient estimates, the regression results imply:

- *Geographical and industry focus (STRATEGY):* In the short-term, any diversification strategy created value compared to full focus strategies, but in the long-term, only full focus or full diversification strategies created value.
- *Timing of the transaction (TIMING):* In the short-term, transactions in the peak phase of the M&A market were rewarded by investors compared to transactions during the bottom, but in the long-term, transactions in the bottom phase proved superior.
- *Acquirer growth (GROWTH):* In the short-term, value creation decreased with speed of acquirer growth, but in the long-term, faster growing acquirers generated more value than slower growing acquirers.
- *Transaction experience (EXPERIENCE):* In the short-term and the long-term, medium experienced acquirers destroyed value compared to inexperienced and most experienced acquirers.

These findings are summarized in Figure 38.

---

245 Reduced models are not tested for two reasons. Firstly, stepwise reduction of independent variables would result in different remaining variables in the three models. Secondly, the applied regression models prove robust with respect to included variables as tested in section 4.3.2.2 and 4.4.2.2.

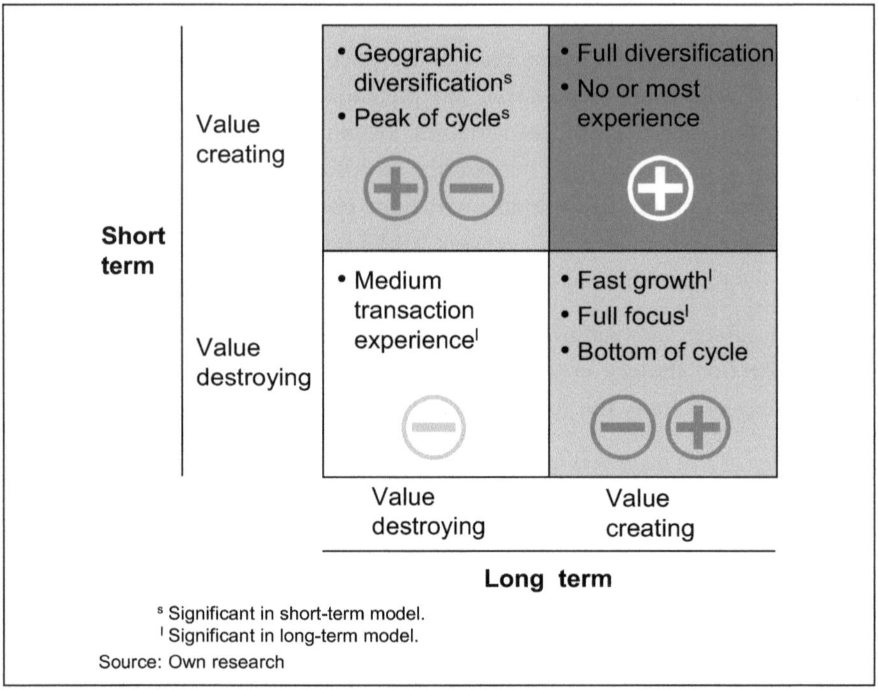

Figure 38: Comparison of influence of determinants on value creation depending on time horizon of the analysis

4.5.3.2 Investor perspective

Long-term value creation may be related to investors' initial assessment of announced M&A transactions. If this is the case, one could argue that the initial assessment of the capital market is adequate with respect to value creation potential and its realization. However, one could also argue that the initial assessment is "sticky" and actual potential and its realization only have minor influence on capital markets assessment in the long run.[246] Still, important recommendations for investors' mid-term investment strategy can be derived.

In order to test the relationship between short- and long-term value creation, the BAHR regression model as presented in section 4.4.2.2 is extended by short-

246 In other words, the direction of the cause-and-effect relationship is unclear.

term value creation as another independent variable. Application of this regression model to CERs, restricted to those transactions in the short-term deal sample which are also included in the BAHR analysis, does not yield significant estimates for the CER variable for any long-term horizon against any short-term event window. This also applies to regressions with acquirer and target CAR as dependent variable. However, application of the BAHR regression model to acquirers CARs on the long-term BAHR sample does yield significant coefficient estimates against the event window [–20; +20] days.[247] The regression results of the full model excluding acquirer CARs (the "base model"), the full model and the reduced model[248] including acquirer CARs (the "extended models") are presented in Table 44.

All three models are well specified according to the Ramsey Reset test. The hypotheses that the regression residuals are normally distributed cannot be rejected. The extended models show even better explanatory power than the base model according to unadjusted and adjusted R-squares. The coefficients in all models are jointly significant according to the F-test. Significance of independent variables (other than acquirer CAR) in the extended models changes only slightly compared the base model: The reduced extended model also indicates significance of a *STRATEGY* indicator variable, and a *TARINDUSTRY* indicator variable. However, directions of coefficients are comparable in all models.

The extended models show that the acquirer CAR is a strong indicator for long-term value creation. With each percentage point increase of short-term acquirer CARs, the BAHRs after three years increase two to four percentage points, depending on the regression model. The relation between both variables is significant at 1% level.

In summary, shareholders may appreciate that European insurance M&A created value in the average on a short-term horizon, and that the expected next

247 This event window is chosen as independent variable since its introduction into the regression model most significantly changes the F-statistic. It is not necessary to include further short-term CARs in other event windows, because the respective change in F-statistic is worse than 10% in all cases.

248 Based on the full model, coefficients with change of F-statistic less significant than 10% are excluded stepwise. The following independent variables are excluded (in order): *TARNOTLISTED*, *TARREGION*, *LNSIZE*, *ACQREGION*, *LNRELVOLUME*, *TIMING*, and *ACQINDUSTRY*. Afterwards, independent variables more significant than 10% would be included stepwise. No variable fulfills this criterion.

Table 44: Results of multivariate regression models on capital market perspective

	BAHR (base model)		**BAHR incl. CAR Acquirer** (full model)		**BAHR incl. CAR Acquirer** (reduced model)		
Model specification	DF	sig DF	DF	sig DF	DF	sig DF	
Ramsey Reset	0.0028	99.7%	0.1139	89.2%	0.9368	39.5%	
Normality of residuals	Z	asy sig	Z	asy sig	Z	asy sig	
K-S	0.8467	47.0%	0.7427	64.0%	0.7586	61.3%	
Model fit	R-square	Adj. R-square	R-square	Adj. R-square	R-square	Adj. R-square	
R-square	0.2645	0.1125	0.3353	0.1913	0.2770	0.2063	
Model significance	Coeff.	F/t	Coeff.	F/t	Coeff.	F/t	VIF
Entire model		1.7405 **		2.3283 ***		3.9189 ****	
(Constant)	-0.9090	-1.4860	-0.8857	-1.5161	-0.7874	-3.0877 ***	
STRATEGY1	0.1820	0.7170	0.0820	0.3362	0.0605	0.2644	1.7
STRATEGY2	-0.3190	-1.5580	-0.3235	-1.6568	-0.3454	-1.8980 *	1.6
STRATEGY3	-0.1030	-0.3800	-0.0953	-0.3687	-0.1283	-0.5609	1.8
STRATEGY4	-0.1150	-0.4990	-0.1173	-0.5351	-0.1371	-0.6757	1.8
STRATEGY5	0.3880	1.5280	0.3379	1.3933	0.3225	1.4839	2.4
TIMING1	-0.2160	-0.9100	-0.2884	-1.2671			
TIMING2	-0.1060	-0.6220	-0.2305	-1.3814			
TIMING3	-0.0330	-0.1400	-0.1998	-0.8718			
ACQREGION2	-0.0830	-0.4560	-0.1144	-0.6597			
ACQINDUSTRY1	0.2810	1.2150	0.1419	0.6342			
ACQINDUSTRY2	-0.0880	-0.3090	-0.0955	-0.3522			
ACQINDUSTRY3	0.8980	1.1160	0.6701	0.8690			
LNSIZE	0.0190	0.2590	0.0237	0.3479			
GROWTH	0.3830	2.5140 **	0.4764	3.2267 ***	0.3829	3.1127 ***	1.1
EXPERIENCE1	-0.5740	-1.5800	-0.7314	-2.0904 **	-0.7856	-2.4232 **	1.1
EXPERIENCE2	-0.3160	-1.8660 *	-0.2259	-1.3817	-0.2232	-1.4782	1.3
EXPERIENCE3	-0.0280	-0.1230	0.0381	0.1755	-0.0799	-0.5130	1.6
TARREGION1	0.3940	0.6680	0.4023	0.7147			
TARREGION2	-0.1960	-0.4760	0.1315	0.3266			
TARREGION3	-0.2430	-0.4430	-0.5515	-1.0413			
TARINDUSTRY1	0.4640	2.3870 **	0.4421	2.3796 **	0.5369	3.1006 ***	2.4
TARINDUSTRY3	-0.1840	-0.6050	-0.1781	-0.6126	-0.0576	-0.2116	1.3
TARINDUSTRY4	0.2320	1.0650	0.2620	1.2596	0.3206	1.7165 *	1.7
LNRELVOLUME	0.0430	0.7220	0.0439	0.7654			
TARNOTLISTED	-0.0340	-0.2210	-0.0443	-0.3038			
CAR Acquirer [-20; +20]			2.2723	3.5756 ****	2.1135	3.7095 ****	1.1

DF: Change in F-statistic between initial and extended regression model according to Ramsey Reset test.
sig DF: Significance of change in F-statistic DF. Z: Kolmogorov-Smirnov Z-statistic.
asy sig: Asymptotic significance of Z-statistic Z. F/t: F-statistic for entire model, t-statistics for coefficients.
VIF: Variance Inflation Factors for coefficients.
STRATEGY indicates the geographical and industry focus of the transaction (national, cross-border EU, and cross-border world transactions, further separated into within- and cross-industry transactions; reference case is national within-industry), TIMING categorizes bottom (reference case), upswing, peak and downturn phases of the M&A market, ACQREGION and TARREGION distinguishes transactions into EU-15 (reference), EU-25, Swiss and Norwegian acquirers and targets, ACQINDUSTRY and TARINDUSTRY separates transactions into P&C (reference), Life, Re, Agents/Brokers and other acquirer and target industries, EXPERIENCE indicates transaction experience of the acquirer (reference case no; then little, extensive, and most experience), LNSIZE and GROWTH the size and growth of the acquirer, and LNRELVOLUME the relative volume of the target compared to the acquirer, TARNOTLISTED for listing of the target. See section 4.2.3 for detailed descriptions of the explanatory variables.
*-**** Statistically significant at 10%, 5%, 1% or 0.1% level according to t-test.

wave of transactions may again create value due to similarity of its transaction motives with those of the previous wave. However, insurers need to carefully decide on their M&A strategy, since past transactions did not create value in the average on a long-term horizon. Nevertheless, some insurers achieved to create tremendous value through their transactions, and the above analyses identified industry and geographical focus, timing of the transaction and acquirer growth prior to the transaction as significant determinants of success. Still, further research on drivers of value creation, especially on a longer term horizon, is crucial as previous research often obtains contradictory results for those determinants included in several studies.[249] Therefore, recent academic work on value creation in M&A turned to additionally analyzing individual cases in order to examine the influence of process-related determinants of success. The following chapter shall thus enrich the empirical findings by examining two major transactions, Munich Re's acquisition of American Re (1996), and CGU's merger with Norwich Union to form Aviva (2000).

249 For example, Floreani and Rigamonti (2001) find on their U.S.-dominated sample that in the short-term, fully diversifying transaction strategies pay off for investors in the combined entity, but Cummins and Xie (2005) find on their U.S. sample that any geographical or industry diversification is significantly worse than full geographical and industry focus.

5 Case Studies on Value Creation by M&A in the European Insurance Industry

5.1 Objectives

Empirical studies on insurance M&A conclude that completed transactions created value over a short- and long-term horizon. The empirical analyses in this study find that European transactions between 1990 and 2005 created an average value of USD 30 mn per deal in the short-term,[250] and USD 130 mn per deal in the long-term.[251] Prior research, mostly focused on the U.S. P&C insurance industry and short-term effects around announcement of transactions, found even stronger value creation.[252]

However, the question of determinants of success has not yet been answered satisfactory. Prior research analyzes mostly different sets of determinants, and obtains contradictory results for those determinants included in several studies. For example, this study and Floreani and Rigamonti (2001) observe that in the short-term, fully diversifying transaction strategies pay off for investors in the combined entity, but Cummins and Xie (2005) obtain the result that any geographical or industry diversification is significantly worse than full geographical and industry focus.[253]

Consequently, recent research on value creation in M&A in general turned from examining large samples of transactions to analyzing individual cases, in order to better account for specifics of transactions.[254] This study shall thus

250 Event window [–20; +20] days around announcement, see section 4.3.2.1.

251 3-year time horizon, see section 4.4.2.1.

252 For a detailed overview and comparison to findings of this study, see section 4.5.1 and 4.5.2.

253 See section 4.5.1.2.

254 E.g., Calomiris and Karceski (1998), Pilloff and Santomero (1998), Calomiris (1999) employ-case study techniques to analyze efficiency gains of and value creation from bank mergers.

broaden the perspective of prior research on value creation in insurance M&A[255] by employing case study techniques to individual transactions by European insurers. Specifically, two cases shall be analyzed on the level of the transactions partners. The objectives for these case studies are twofold: Firstly, occurrence of drivers and hurdles for M&A[256] shall be tested. Secondly, the influence of the transaction conduct ("process perspective") on value extraction shall be further investigated.

Section 5.2 develops an analysis approach that supports both objectives based on quantitative[257] and qualitative evidence[258] along motives, conduct and outcome of the transactions. Hypotheses of sources of value creation are tested by identifying M&A motives, linking these motives to concrete performance measures where possible, and comparing pre- and post-transaction performance to the market median. Theory on the influence of the transaction conduct on value creation is elaborated and extended by identifying root causes for (under-)-achievement of planned M&A benefits in the pre- and post-acquisition process. Jemison and Sitkin (1986) introduced this "process perspective" to the field of M&A success studies in the mid-1980s, and Pablo et al. (1996) argue that "although better outcomes [of transactions] are associated with choosing a better target, negotiating a better financial deal, or expertly identifying and successfully sharing key strategic complementarities, the degree to which these events are likely to occur depends upon characteristics of the process used to make and implement acquisition decisions".

Section 5.3 selects cases following a theoretical sampling approach.[259] The cases shall include extreme transaction types such as "long-term value creating" vs. "long-term value destroying", and replicate insurance industry specifics through focusing on long-tailed businesses reinsurance and life insurance (as opposed to P&C insurance). Further on, a short overview of the selected cases is provided. Section 5.4 and section 5.5 present evidence on the two transactions,

255 Prior case study research in the financial institution industry focuses on bank mergers.
256 See chapter 2.3.
257 E.g., capital market reactions, market share, financial performance.
258 E.g., management reports, comments of financial analysts, statements of rating agencies.
259 Eisenhardt (1989) argues that for theory-building case study research, statistical sampling is not preferable. In fact, theoretical sampling allows to "fill theoretical categories and provide examples of polar types".

and analyze case data along the approach laid out in section 5.2. The findings are reviewed in the context of prior research. Section 5.6 summarizes determinants of value creation identified in the case studies, and discusses these in the context of the event study results.

5.2 Analysis approach

5.2.1 General approach

The transactions shall be discussed following the four-step approach illustrated in Figure 39. Firstly, motives for the transactions are derived from an analysis of the general market environment and the specific position and development of the transaction partners. The general market environment is captured through examination of the market concentration, the momentum in the M&A market, and fundamental drivers for M&A. After a short review of the history and organization of the transaction partners, their business model and financial performance[260] is discussed in detail. The utilized financial performance measures are developed in section 5.2.2. From these descriptive analyses, drivers and hurdles of the transaction are derived along the framework presented in chapter 2.3.2. The potential M&A benefits are linked to concrete performance levers which they seek to address.

Secondly, the conduct of the transaction is described in three sections. The first section portrays the transaction process along the framework developed in chapter 2.2.3, compares it with the evolution of market rumors, and draws inference on the pursued transaction strategy. The second section discusses core elements of the deal structure. The third section presents core aspects of the post-merger integration process.

Thirdly, value creation by the transaction is examined. This step begins with an analysis of short- and long-term capital market reactions to the announcement

260 The analysis includes the stand-alone performance of the transaction partners, as well as their performance compared to their industry peers ("market-adjusted performance").

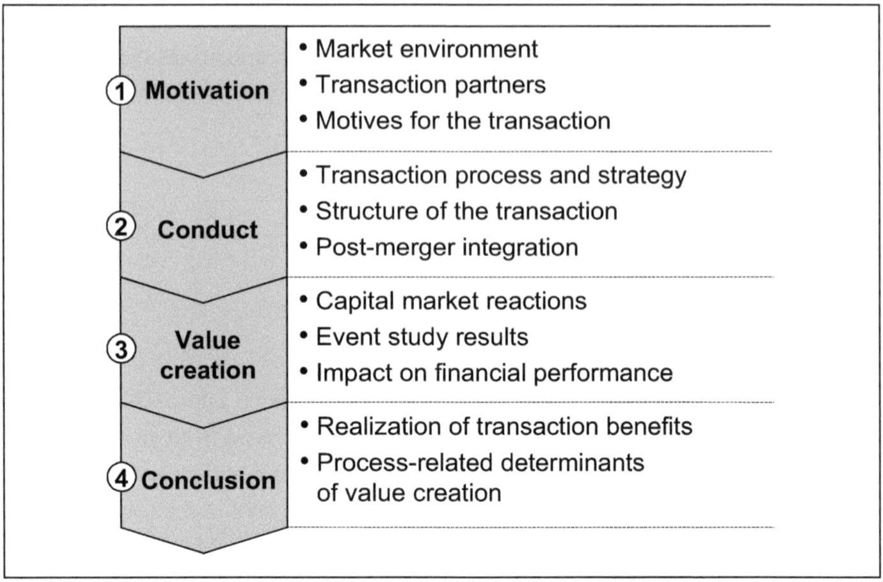

Figure 39: Case study analysis approach

and execution of the transaction. These reactions are discussed in light of major events during the conduct of the transaction. Afterwards, the event study results of chapter 4 for the particular transactions are examined to gain insights into abnormal returns and value creation. Finally, the development of the acquirers' and targets' financial performance is studied.

As the fourth and last step, the core findings of each previous step are reviewed. Hypotheses on M&A benefits (derived in step 1) are tested through comparing linked pre- and post transaction financial performance (presented in step 3). Process-related determinants of value creation are identified in the light of the conduct of the transaction ("process perspective", illustrated in step 2).

5.2.2 Measurement of financial performance

The analysis of the transaction partners' financial performance is a central element of the case studies. Planned M&A benefits are linked to drivers of financial performance where possible. Thus, comparison of pre- and post-merger performance drivers allows to objectively assess the transaction success.

The measurement of financial performance shall be derived from a capital market perspective. According to McKinsey & Company (2005, p. 55), company value can generally be decomposed into the drivers cash flows to shareholders, expected growth of these cash flows, and cost of capital reflecting the riskiness of a business. For insurance companies, the common valuation basis are earnings minus excess capital accumulated in the respective period of time (not cash flows).[261] Due to limited data availability, this study shall analyze several profitability measures derived directly from earnings as reported.[262] Further on, riskiness is assessed based on several insurance specific measures. Discussion of these solvency measures is additionally important since they also capture capital strength from a company perspective (going concern) or a narrower[263] policyholder perspective (ability to meet obligations) according to Pentikäinen (1967). The following subsections review and select measures of solvency, profitability, and growth for assessment of the financial performance of the transaction partners.

Solvency

O'Neil (1984) defines solvency as a state of an insurance company where the surplus[264] satisfies a certain condition, e.g., being larger than a certain level of minimum required surplus or larger than zero.[265] Concrete definitions of solvency differ by stakeholders such as supervisors and rating agencies, by jurisdic-

261 The Actuarial Standards Board (1991, p. 7) requires to use earnings, not cash flows, for actuarial appraisal. Toole and Herget (2005, p. 112) base their appraisal methodology on after-tax earnings minus increase in required capital. Tremblay (2006, p. 5) reviews a methodology to compute embedded value and employs an analogous approach.

262 Accumulation and decumulation of (excess) capital is also visible in the solvency analyses, see further below.

263 The policyholder perspective is narrower since it allows for liquidation of the company.

264 Surplus is the statutory term for the difference of the long-term value of assets and liabilities. Accounting term would be capital.

265 Other terms typically used in the context of capitalization of insurance companies are solidity and solvency margin. O'Neil (1984) defines the former as a state where the insurer additionally has long-term capacity to pay claims, expenses, sufficient dividends, retain earnings for growth and continue its operations. Pentikäinen (1967) uses the latter term interchangeably with surplus. However, nowadays solvency margin is typically understood as the ratio between current surplus (available capital) and minimum required surplus (required capital).

tion, and by time period. For example, current European regulatory requirements ("Solvency I") are merely a function of premiums, claims, reserves, sum at risk and capital. Investment risk is not accounted for explicitly.[266] However, the current U.S. American regulation with respect to capitalization, Risk Based Capital, includes three types of investment risks.[267] The European Solvency II measure, with expected implementation date between 2009 and 2012,[268] offers an even more sophisticated factor-based model, linked to company specific risk exposure and diversification.[269] The current rating model of Standard & Poor's already includes detailed breakdown to risk drivers, both on the investment and insurance side. However, even simple solvency measures such as Solvency I are neither published nor computable from public account data.[270] Thus, alternative, simpler measures need to be selected.

For P&C insurance, Settnik (2006, pp. 279) proposes to use equity plus equalization reserves divided by gross premiums earned. McKinsey & Company (2006a) additionally increases equity by unrealized investment gains, and uses the sum of a factor-based estimate for insurance, investment and general risk as the denominator. Standard & Poor's (1996, p. 23) defines the reciprocal value (net premiums earned divided by shareholders' equity) as "operating leverage". In addition, they report reserves leverage (technical reserves divided by pre-tax net income), and reserves ratio (technical reserves divided by net premiums earned). For life insurance, Settnik (2006, pp. 279) use equity divided by gross technical reserves ("equity reserves ratio"). McKinsey & Company (2006b) additionally increases equity by unrealized investment gains, unallocated provisions for premium refunds and terminal surplus shares. The sum of the estimated investment, mortality and general business risk is the denominator.

This study reports all of the above mentioned ratios and additionally includes the equity ratio (shareholders' equity divided by total assets) as the standard measure of capitalization of financial institutions for the sake of complete-

266 See European Council (1973, 1979, 2002a, 2002b).
267 See Zeppetella (2002).
268 E.g., ING (2006) assumes 2012, Towers Perrins Tillinghast (2006) assumes at the beginning of 2010, and CEA (2007) assumes during 2009.
269 European Commission (2002a, 2002b).
270 Sum at risk and other significant input factors are not publicly reported.

ness. The granularity of each measure is limited due to unavailability of detailed industry peer data. Figure 40 presents the detailed definitions.

Profitability

This study utilizes relative profitability measures as opposed to absolute profitability measures in order to ensure comparability between the acquirer, the target, and their industry peers. The following discussion of applicable measures is focused on accounting measures, since value based measures (e.g., present value of profits divided by present value of future premiums) are not publicly reported. Major relative, accounting based measures comprise return on equity and return on premiums.

- *Return on equity:* Amel et al. (2003) use return on equity to measure performance for insurance companies.[271] The Geneva Association (2004) finds that large European insurance groups typically use return on equity to measure profitability, whereas definition of equity ranges from risk adjusted capital, IFRS equity, economic capital to embedded value.[272] Standard & Poor's (2007a, 2007b) uses return on equity besides return on assets and return on revenues, but with less emphasis due to its dependency on the capital structure of the company.[273] McKinsey & Company (2006a, 2006b) uses after tax return on equity[274] for P&C and life.
- *Return on premiums:* Settnik (2006, p. 289) measures profitability as return on revenue, which relates profit[275] to gross earned premiums. Standard & Poor's (2006) uses return on revenue defined as pretax operating income divided by the sum of net premiums earned, net investment income, and other income. McKinsey & Company (2006a, 2006b) uses return on gross earned premiums for P&C[276] and life.[277] Standard & Poor's (2007a, 2007b)

271 Detailed specification of the used return and equity measures is not given.
272 The return measure is not specified further.
273 Neither the return nor the equity measure is specified further.
274 Return including change of equalization reserves (P&C only). Uncalled capital is subtracted from equity.
275 Settnik (2006, p. 289) uses unadjusted profits after tax for life and health insurance, and profits after tax for P&C. Unadjusted profits equal profits plus cost of premium refund.
276 Return is before change of equalization reserves and before tax. Earned premiums are adjusted for change of premium refund provisions.

argue that return on revenues best measures operating profit because it is independent of leverage and includes underwriting and investments results as sources of value.

- *Other measures:* Standard & Poor's (2007a, 2007b) additionally draws on return on assets.[278] They note that return on assets is their principal measure for life insurance companies, because many life insurance segments (except for risk lines such as term life or annuities) are asset accumulation business. Another popular profitability measure for life insurance companies is return on reserves. Technical reserves are regulated and thus not as prone to management decisions as equity or earned premiums. Further on, technical reserves are less sensitive to the life insurance business mix between single and recurring premium contracts than return on premiums.[279]

This study shall analyze profitability based on all of these measures except for return on assets since profitability of the investment management function is captured separately, see further below. The granularity of return, equity and premium definitions is limited due to unavailability of detailed industry peer data. Figure 40 presents the chosen profitability measures and their detailed definitions.

Profitability shall be further decomposed into its drivers to capture effectiveness and efficiency of the insurance company. Major drivers of the common nominator return are premiums, losses and loss adjustment expenses (LAE), operating expenses, and net investment result.[280]

For P&C insurers and reinsurers, underwriting effectiveness is measured as losses and LAE relative to premiums, and typically referred to as "claims ratio" or "loss ratio". Underwriting efficiency is measured as operating expenses[281] re-

277 Return is unadjusted profit plus cost of premium refund plus direct refund. Settnik (2006, p. 289) uses a similar definition.

278 Return is after tax and after policyholder dividends.

279 Increased sensitivity to business mix traditional vs. unit-linked contracts of this measure is not an issue, because the latter contracts are of minor importance for transaction partners in the life study at the relevant point in time.

280 See Rockel et al. (2005), pp. 220.

281 Operating expenses exclude investment expenses and thus only relate to underwriting business, see Rockel et al. (2005), pp. 221.

	Indicator	Nominator	Denominator
Size	Earnings	Net income after taxes and minorities	
	Premiums	Net premiums earned	
	Reserves	Net insurance provisions	
	Shareholders' Equity	Shareholders' equity including minorities	
	Assets	Total assets	
Solvency	Equity ratio	Shareholders' equity including minorities	Total assets
	Equity reserves ratio	Shareholders' equity including minorities	Net insurance provisions
	Operating leverage	Net premiums earned	Shareholders' equity including minorities
	Reserves leverage	Net insurance provisions	Net income before taxes and minorities
	Reserves ratio	Net insurance provisions	Net premiums earned
Profitability	Return on reserves	Net income before taxes and minorities	Net insurance provisions
	Return on equity	Net income before taxes and minorities	Shareholders' equity including minorities
	Return on premiums	Net income before taxes and minorities	Net premiums earned
	Combined ratio	Loss ratio + expense ratio	-
	Loss ratio	Net losses and loss adjustment expenses	Net premiums earned
	Expense ratio	Net commissions and admin. expenses	Net premiums earned
	Net investment result ratio	Net investment income	Net premiums earned
	Net investment yield	Net investment income	Total assets
Growth	Earnings	Change of net income after taxes and minorities	
	Premiums	Change of net premiums earned	
	Reserves	Change of net insurance provisions	
	Shareholders' Equity	Change of shareholders' equity incl. minorities	
	Assets	Change of total assets	

Source: Own research

Figure 40: Definitions of financial performance measures

lative to premiums, and typically referred to as "expense ratio". The sum of both ratios is known as "combined ratio". Calandro and Lane (2002) and Swiss Re (2006) define the relevant premium basis for the claims ratio as earned premiums, and for the expense ratio as written premiums. McKinsey & Company (2006a) consistently uses earned premiums for both ratios,[282] but introduces further adjustments.[283] Swiss Re (2006) further on suggests to use an economic combined ratio based on net present values of claims, expenses, and policyholder dividends. Klumpes (2006) summarizes further, more granular efficiency measures for utilization in data envelopment analyses.

For life insurers, McKinsey & Company (2006a) uses an analogous definition for claims and expense ratios. Correctly, they do not explicitly compute the combined ratio as a result since measures should be interpreted with care (if at all) for life insurers. Major pitfall of the claims ratio as a measure of underwriting effectiveness in life insurance is that incurred losses relate to contracts originated many years ago, but premiums mostly relate to new business.[284] Most important shortcomings of the expense ratio are that acquisition costs are mostly driven by sum of premiums as the major component of the provisioning model, and administration costs are mostly driven by number of contracts in the in-force book.

This study utilizes combined ratio, claims ratio, and expense ratio as indicators for underwriting effectiveness and efficiency. Due to unavailability of detailed industry peer data, earned premiums are chosen as the reference basis for these ratios. In addition, net investment result divided by total assets is reported ("net investment yield")[285] to capture effectiveness and efficiency of the investment management. For consistency with assessment of the underwriting func-

282 The rationale is to use earned instead of written premiums in jurisdictions where acquisition costs are deferred.

283 The "extended combined ratio" for P&C insurers is defined as claims ratio plus expense ratio plus other expenses/revenues ratio. Claims are defined as claims payments plus change of reserves minus direct credit, divided by earned premiums.

284 Earned premiums include annual premium payments of in-force recurring premium contracts.

285 Total assets include non-operative investments such as strategic participations and receivables. Due to unavailability of detailed industry peer data, the indicator cannot be adjusted for these non-operative investments. Further on, "fair" assessment of investment management performance may consider restrictions imposed by underwriting or ALM, and riskiness of the asset allocation. Required data for respective adjustment is not publicly reported.

tion, net investment result divided by earned premiums is also shown ("net investment result ratio"). Figure 40 presents the chosen profitability measures and their detailed definitions.

Growth

In McKinsey & Company's (2005, p. 55) discussions, growth as a driver for company value refers to annual percentage change of cash flow. Since insurance appraisal is based on earnings, not cash flows, this study reports percentage change of earnings. Further on, growth of premiums is additionally included as a flow measure, and growth of total assets, technical reserves, and shareholders' equity as stock measures. Growth of premiums is included because it is the basis for market share comparisons. Growth of total assets is reported to account for the importance of investment management especially for life insurers, but also for reinsurers.[286] Technical reserves are reported because they indicate the size of the in-force business. Shareholders' equity complements the balance sheet. Additionally, the respective bases to measure growth are reported in a separate category "size" for the sake of completeness. Figure 40 presents the detailed definitions.

5.3 Overview of selected cases

5.3.1 Selection of case studies

The case studies are selected from the long-term data sample[287] along the five criteria acquirer and target industry, value creation, announcement date, transaction volume, and acquirer and target country.[288] They should fulfill the following characteristics:

---

286 The mere underwriting function of reinsurers is often unprofitable: Market average combined ratios between 1989 and 1996 are well above 100%, see Figure 46.

287 See section 4.2.

288 These are all data sample filter criteria (complemented by value creation), which allow observations with multiple parameter values to remain in the deal sample. E.g., acquirer country includes all European countries, Switzerland and Norway.

- *Acquirer and target industry:* The case studies should include a reinsurer and a life insurer transaction due to their long-tailed business.[289]
- *Value creation:* The case studies should include a long-term value creating, and a long-term value destroying deal.
- *Announcement date:* The two case studies should capture different phases of the M&A cycle. The empirical analyses in section 4.2.3 defined the bottom phase to range from 1990 to 1995 and from 2001 to 2005, the upswing phase as the year 1996, the peak phase from 1997 to 1999, and the downturn phase as the year 2000.
- *Transaction volume:* The transaction volume should be sufficiently large compared to the acquirer size in order to ensure visibility of M&A effects in capital market reactions and financial performance measures.
- *Acquirer and target country:* The case studies should include a cross-border transaction.

Figure 41 presents a short list of transactions that satisfy the criterion "acquirer and target industry is reinsurance". Munich Re's acquisition of American Re is selected as the first case study, since it presents the largest transaction ever in this industry for European acquirers between 1990 and 2005. Further on, it marks the starting point for European involvement in the transatlantic reinsurance consolidation wave beginning in 1995. Finally, it fulfills the "transaction volume" criterion with a relative transaction volume of almost 30%.

Figure 42 presents a short list of transactions, which satisfy the criterion "acquirer and target industry is life insurance". Further on, "announcement date" is restricted to transactions in the peak of the M&A market in the life insurance industry (1999) and the year of the downturn (2000), since the first case study examines a transaction in the upswing, and five years of operative performance data should be available after the transaction given the long-term nature of the life insurance business. The merger between CGU and Norwich Union is selec-

289 The characteristics of these business lines are highly specific for insurance companies, and may be only partially captured even through long-term even study analyses.

Acquirer/ Target		Munich Re buys American Re (Selected)	Swiss Re buys Mercantile and General Re	Swiss Re buys SAFR	Swiss Re buys Life Re	Tryg-Baltica buys Danbyg	Swiss Re buys Underwriters Re	SCOR buys PartnerRe Life	Swiss Re buys Lincoln Re	Hannover Re buys HDI Re (Ireland)
Announcement date		1996	1996	1997	1998	1999	1999	2000	2001	2003
Transaction volume	Absolute (USD bn)	3.3	0.5	1.8	0.1	2.7	0.3	0.7	2.0	0.4
	Relative (Percent of MV acquirer)	29	29	5	6	26	2	8	5	18
Country		DE - US	CH - GB	CH - FR	CH - US	DK - DK	CH - US	FR - US	CH - US	DE - IE
Industry		Re - Re	Re - Re	Re - Re	Re - Re	Re - Re	Re - Re	Re - Re	Re - Re	Re - Re
Long-term value creation	BAHR (Percent)	-179.6	-138.5	-26.8	0.3	-141.2	14.3	-62.6	12.5	-66.4
	Value (USD bn)	-20.8	-12.5	-3.0	0.1	-1.7	4.2	-1.1	4.9	-1.3
Short-term value creation	CER (Percent)	6.4	-	3.8	-6.9	-	-	-3.1	-	-
	Value (USD mn)	76.6	-	21.5	-79.3	-	-	-62.9	-	-

Selected

Source: Long-term deal sample

Figure 41: Short list of possible transactions for reinsurance case study

Acquirer/ Target		AXA Colonia buys Albingia	Generali buys INA	CGU buys Norwich Union (Selected)	ERGO buys Bayerische Vita
Announcement date		1999	1999	2000	2000
Transaction volume	Absolute (USD bn)	1.0	10.2	11.9	0.6
	Relative (Percent of MV acquirer)	44	34	71	5
Country		DE - DE	IT - IT	GB - GB	DE - IT
Industry		Life - Life	Life - Life	Life - Life	Life - Life
Long-term value creation	BAHR (Percent)	3.2	21.1	25.1	18.5
	Value (USD bn)	0.1	6.6	4.2	2.0
Short-term value creation	CER (Percent)	-3.5	-4.8	5.6	19.3
	Value (USD mn)	-12.0	-392.4	697.8	147.9

Figure 42: Short list of possible transactions for life insurance case study

ted for the second case study, since the relative transaction volume is the highest amongst the presented transactions. Further on, this transaction built the nucleus for the highly successful UK life insurer Aviva.

5.3.2 Overview of case studies

The first case study examines Munich Re's acquisition of American Re, announced on 14 August 1996.[290] In that year, M&A momentum was picking up,

290 The first case study focuses its analyses on the two transaction partners Munich Re and American Re. Two other bidders were shortly involved, but their identity remained undisclosed.

possibly due to stagnating premium growth in the reinsurance market and strong margin pressure from underwriting and fixed income markets. Munich Re ("Münchener Rückversicherungsgesellschaft A.G.") is a public company established in 1880, and by the time of the acquisition the world's largest reinsurance provider by premiums. Although it had begun international expansion in 1886, its business was still strongly dependent on the European traditional reinsurance market. In the late 1990s, Munich Re came under pressure: Capital markets expressed high growth expectations in its valuation, but Munich Re's market share was declining for several consecutive years. American Re ("American Re-Insurance Company") was a private equity owned company established in 1917. It embarked on international expansion only in the 1970s, but remained focused on the North American traditional but also nontraditional reinsurance market. In 1996, American Re was the 11th largest reinsurer in the world and 3rd largest reinsurer in the U.S.[291]

On 14 August 1996, Munich Re announced to acquire American Re for USD 3.3 bn cash-only at 11% premium to previous day's closing. Munich Re negotiated the acquisition in a short controlled auction process, and reached agreement with American Re's Board of Directors and its controlling shareholder, KKR, for the equity acquisition through a reverse triangular merger. The post-acquisition integration can be separated into three phases: Integration of staff, integration and streamlining of the organization, followed by restructuring of the U.S. business. The latter became necessary after reserve issues of the U.S. liability business, partly written after the acquisition between 1997 and mid-2002, required total reserve strengthenings of USD 5.4 bn (equivalent to 2.6 percentage points of Munich Re's loss ratio). Capital markets lost faith in Munich Re's growth story, and Munich Re's market valuation spiraled downwards. Consistently, the event study finds CER of 6.4% in the event window [–20; +20] days around announcement, but a BAHR of –179.6% over three years. However, the post-transaction financial performance of Munich Re does not entirely support this reaction: Profitability improved slightly compared to the market me-

291 Whether or not there would have been strategic alternatives for Munich Re to grow inorganically besides American Re is difficult to assess from today's perspective. Given the dependence on Europe, international diversification was probably an adequate decision. In the U.S. market, American Re was the only reinsurer left for acquisition, see arguments above.

dian, premium growth picked up significantly, however solvency and credit ratings worsened notably.

The second case study examines CGU's merger with Norwich Union (NU) in the year 2000, which built the nucleus for the successful life insurer Aviva. The M&A cycle in the European insurance industry entered a downturn phase after having reached its peak in 1999. CGU was a public company, resulting from the mergers of Commercial Union, Hand-in-hand, and General Accident, and by the time of the merger Britains second largest life insurer and third largest non-life insurer, with a focus on the UK and European life insurance markets and a non-life orientation beyond Europe. NU converted from a mutual society to a public company in 1997, and was focused on the UK life market.

On 21 February 2000, CGU and NU announced that the Boards of both companies have agreed on a nil-premium all-shares merger on 18 February 2000 after week long negotiations. Post-merger integration began immediately afterwards, whereas three work streams can be distinguished: Retention and integration of staff, realignment of lines of businesses and distribution, and integration of operations. The integration process was reported as completed at the end of 2001. After a short share price drop of both transaction partners, capital markets reacted positively to the merger. The event study finds a CER of 5.6% in the event window [–20; +20] days around announcement, and a BAHR of 25.1% over three years. Indeed, the transaction partners realized economies of scale, although less so than planned, to improve their overall profitability and gained market share in the UK and European life markets. Figure 43 presents an overview of both case studies.

Phase		Case study A: Munich Re acquires American Re (1996)	Case study B: CGU merges with Norwich Union (2000)
1 Motivation	Market environment	M&A momentum, premium volume and profitability under pressure	M&A momentum, growth and profitability under pressure
	Transaction partners	MR public company with European traditional focus, AR PE-owned company with U.S. focus and nontraditional expertise	CGU public company with European focus, NU public company with UK life focus
	Motives for transaction	Increase growth, improve underwriting effectiveness	Become life insurer, and grow in this segment; avoid hostile takeover
2 Conduct	Transaction process and strategy	Four-week controlled auction	Week-long private negotiations
	Structure of transaction	All-cash acquisition of equity through reverse triangular merger; internal financing	Nil-premium all-share merger
	Post-merger integration	Three step integration (staff, organization, and business restructuring)	Three step integration (staff, business portfolio, operations)
3 Value creation	Capital market reaction	Downward spiral starting Nov 2001	Positive development
	Event study results	CER 6.4%, but BAHR -179.6%	CER 5.6%, BAHR 25.1%
	Impact on financial performance	Premium growth, but only marginal improvement of profitability	Life market share up, profitability slightly improved

Source: Own research

Figure 43: Overview of case studies

5.4 Case study A: Munich Re acquires American Re (1996)

5.4.1 Motivation for the transaction

5.4.1.1 Market environment

The acquisition of American Re by Munich Re marked the starting point for the consolidation of the global[292] reinsurance market. The 5-firm concentration ratios[293] between 1994 and 1998 were still rather low compared to the European primary non-life insurance market (average of 52% across European countries), and the European primary life insurance market (average of 62% European countries),[294] see Figure 44. However, market concentration rose notably in 1999: The 5-firm concentration ratio increased by 8 percentage points from 52% to 60%. The consolidation process was driven by largest insurers, as the 10-firm and especially 15-firm concentration ratios only increased marginally in these years.

M&A was a major driver for the observed reinsurance market concentration: The transaction data sample presented in Figure 45 shows an increasing M&A market momentum beginning in 1996 for the European reinsurance industry,[295] despite contradictory expectations for the global market.[296] Societe Commerciale de Reassurance was the first European reinsurer in the 1990s to pursue an M&A strategy by announcing the acquisition of The Allstate Life Insurance CO, a U.S.-based life primary insurer, on 23 July 1996 for USD 0.5 bn. Munich Re followed on 14 August 1996 by announcing its acquisition of American Re

---

292 The geographical scope of the reinsurance market is global: Swiss Re (1998) and Cummins and Weiss (2000) analyze consolidation of reinsurance providers on a global basis.

293 This section discusses market concentration following the methodology applied in section 2.3.1. The concentration of the global reinsurance market is measured by concentration ratios, defined as "the percentages of total industry output [...] which a given number of large firms account for", see OECD (1993). The total industry output is defined as net reinsurance premiums written, as provided by Standard & Poor's (1995-1999).

294 Section 2.3.1 provides detailed information on the status of consolidation of the respective markets.

295 Analysis based on long-term deal sample, see section 4.2.

296 Standard & Poor's (1997, p. 33) expects pace of consolidation to slow down compared to 1996.

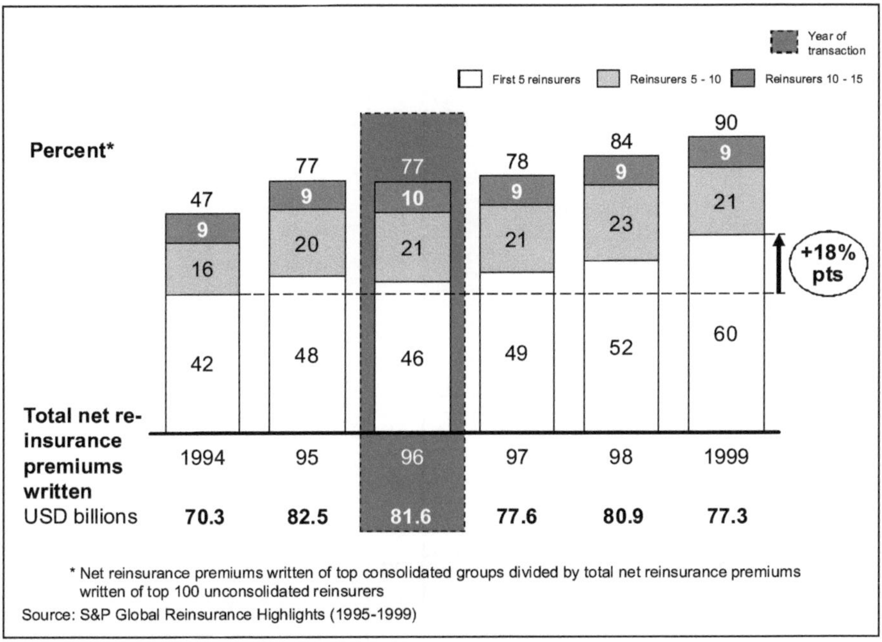

Figure 44: Development of global reinsurance market concentration

for USD 3.3 bn, the largest reinsurance-focused transaction recorded between 1990 and 2005 in Europe. Consolidation beyond Europe already began two years earlier when General Re, the third largest[297] U.S. based reinsurer, and Employers Re, the largest U.S. based reinsurer, announced to acquire Cologne Re and Frankona Re in June 1994 and March 1995, respectively.

The increase in momentum of the global reinsurance M&A market was driven by fundamental changes in underwriting markets.[298] Firstly, reinsurers' profitability was under pressure. Although their underwriting performance im-

297 Based on net written premiums 1994 according to Standard & Poor's (1995) list of world's 20 largest consolidated reinsurance groups.

298 By the time of the transaction, capital markets partially reflected these changes. In 1993, re-insurance carriers achieved a 22 percentage points higher TRS than the S&P 500 Composite index (10 percentage points higher TRS than the MSCI world index), but in 1995 a 10 percent-age points lower TRS (8 percentage points higher TRS).

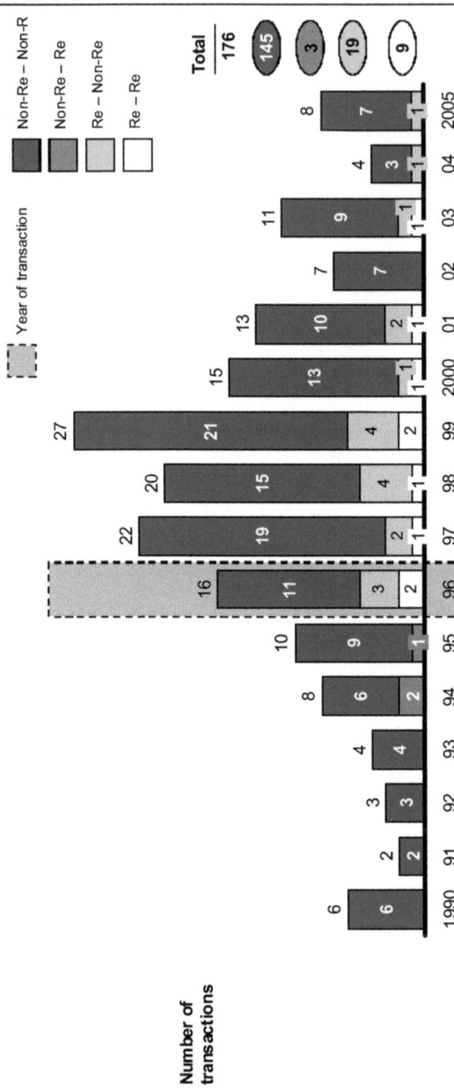

		1990	91	92	93	94	95	96	97	98	99	2000	01	02	03	04	2005	Total
Transaction volume USD billions	Non-Re – Non-Re	5.0	0.6	0.9	2.9	3.3	4.8	19.5	44.8	23.1	48.6	41.2	6.4	6.2	4.9	1.7	11.5	225.6
	Non-Re – Re	0.0	0.0	0.0	0.0	1.6	0.5	0.0	0.0	0.0	0.0	0.0	0.0	0.0	0.0	0.0	0.0	2.1
	Re – Non-Re	0.0	0.0	0.0	0.0	0.0	0.0	1.2	0.4	1.0	1.9	0.2	0.5	0.0	0.1	0.6	7.8	13.7
	Re – Re	0.0	0.0	0.0	0.0	0.0	0.0	6.0	0.5	1.8	1.0	0.1	2.0	0.0	0.4	0.0	0.0	11.8
	Total	**5.0**	**0.6**	**0.9**	**2.9**	**4.9**	**5.3**	**26.7**	**45.7**	**25.9**	**51.6**	**41.6**	**9.0**	**6.2**	**5.4**	**2.3**	**19.3**	**253.3**
Average transaction volume USD billions	Non-Re – Non-Re	0.8	0.3	0.3	0.7	0.6	0.5	1.8	2.4	1.5	2.3	3.2	0.6	0.9	0.5	0.6	1.6	1.6
	Non-Re – Re	n/a	n/a	n/a	n/a	0.8	0.5	n/a	n/a	n/a	n/a	n/a	n/a	n/a	n/a	n/a	n/a	0.7
	Re – Non-Re	n/a	n/a	n/a	n/a	n/a	n/a	0.4	0.2	0.3	0.5	0.2	0.3	n/a	0.1	0.6	7.8	1.3
	Re – Re	n/a	n/a	n/a	n/a	n/a	n/a	3.0	0.5	1.8	0.5	0.1	2.0	n/a	0.4	n/a	n/a	1.3
	Total	**0.8**	**0.3**	**0.3**	**0.7**	**0.6**	**0.5**	**1.7**	**2.1**	**1.3**	**1.9**	**2.8**	**0.7**	**0.9**	**0.5**	**0.6**	**2.4**	**1.4**

* Based on long-term data sample of event study in this thesis.

Source: Thomson Financial SDC platinum, Dealogic M&A database, press research

Figure 45: Development of M&A transactions* between 1990 and 2005

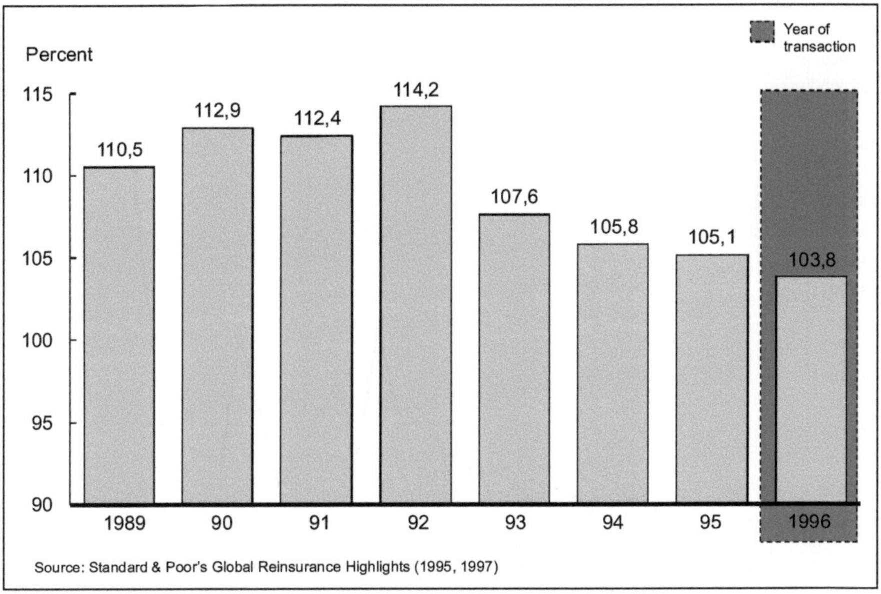

Figure 46: Development of global combined ratios (percent)

proved notably since 1992, see Figure 46, particularly traditional reinsurers were urged to strictly control combined ratios for three reasons:

- Bermudan reinsurers achieved significantly better underwriting performance. For 1994, Standard & Poor's (1996, p. 22) reported a combined ratio of only 69.2% (5-year weighted average of 83.7%), compared to combined ratios of 106.0% (110.2%) in Germany, and 106.0% (108.0%) in the United States. As a result, the pressure on renewal pricing increased in an already softening market: U.S. and European players needed to lower rates to be able to avoid losing volume to Bermudan reinsurers.

- Renewal rates decreased since the reinsurance market entered the soft phase of the underwriting cycle.[299] While a hard market prevailed between 1986

299 Rubin (2000) defines underwriting cycle (also known as price cycle) as the "tendency of property and liability insurance premiums, insurers' profits, and availability of coverage to rise

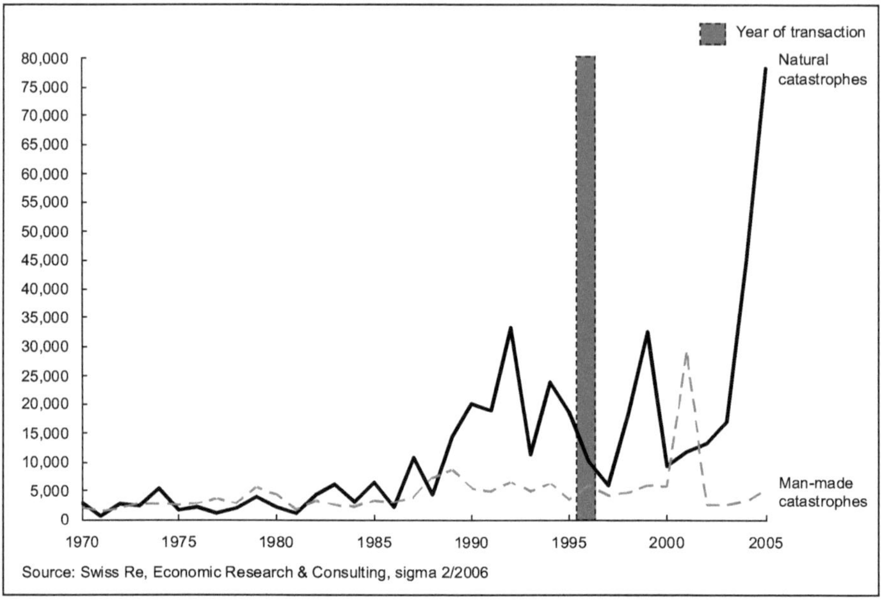

Figure 47: Development of insured losses (USD mn, 2005 prices)

and 1993,[300] anew falling prices in 1995/1996 renewals confirmed softening of the reinsurance cycle,[301] especially for the U.S. and European property market, and the South American catastrophe market. Standard & Poor's (1996, p. 15 and 25) additionally predicts increasing international competition in motor insurance[302] and large commercial risks,[303] leading to higher pressure on reinsurance pricing.

- Insured catastrophe losses increased strongly after 1988 (see Figure 47), adding to uncertainty but possibly also necessity to re-estimate expected

and fall with some regularity over time." The market phase of high premiums, high profits, and lower coverage are called "hard market", the opposite situation "soft market", see e.g., Leng and Meier (2002).

300 See World Insurance Report (16 June 1995).

301 See Reactions (26 February 1996).

302 Direct (phone) sales became increasingly popular in the primary insurance market. Direct physical presence in the target market was not required, thus increasing international competition.

303 German "Konsortialkommissionen" for evaluating large commercial risks were abolished, thus increasing openness of the market to international players.

losses as more data becomes available.[304] Besides increasing catastrophe losses, Standard & Poor's (1996, p. 10) expects further reserve strengthening for environment and asbestos liability for primary insurers, with significant spill over to reinsurance carriers.

At the same time, especially American reinsurers may not have been able to compensate rising loss ratios through an increase in investment performance: They were invested by two thirds in fixed income instruments, and only by one fifth in shares[305] in an environment of sharply declining interest rates[306] but favorably equity markets, see Figure 48 and Figure 49. The situation is less severe

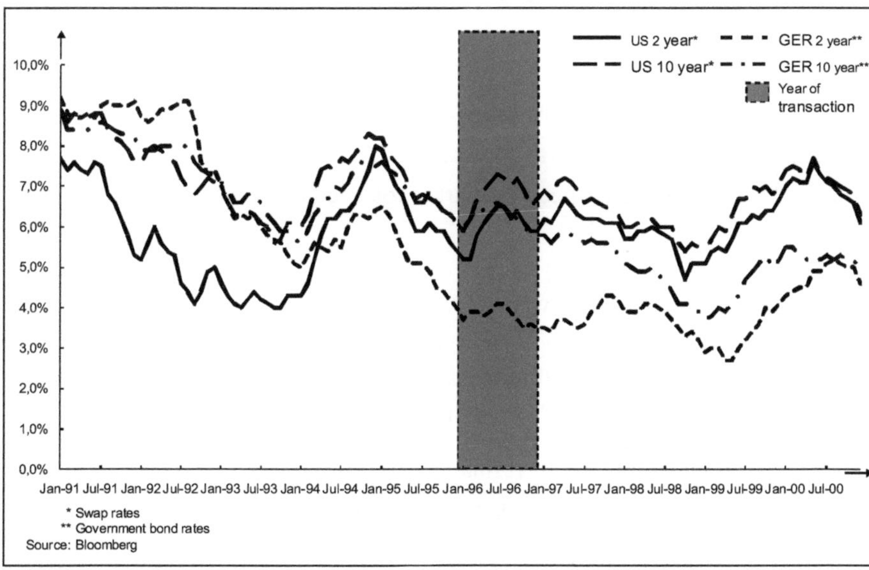

Figure 48: Development of U.S. and German fixed income rates

304 Reinsurers acknowledged this fact by signing a co-operation pact to help arrest global warming after voicing concerns over worsening trend in storm damage and global warming leading to increased volatility of weather conditions on inter-governmental climate summit in Berlin/Germany (Reactions, 16 January 1996).

305 Standard &Poor's (1996, p. 23).

306 In times of falling interest rates, the asset-short duration mismatch leads to faster increase of liability value than increase of fixed income instrument value.

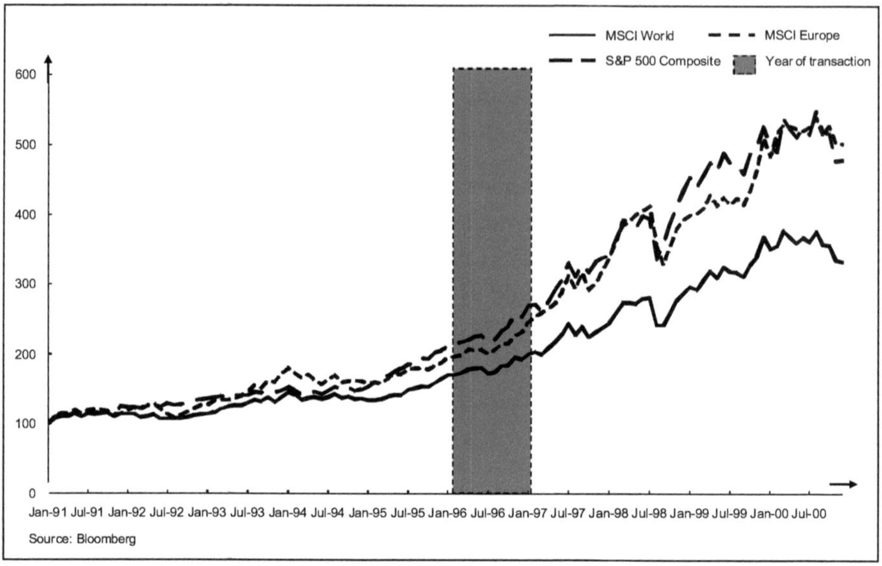

Figure 49: Development of equity market total return to shareholders (indexed, 31.1.1991 = 100)

for German reinsurers, which were invested only by one fourth in fixed income instruments but by almost 50% in equity.

Secondly, premium growth rates were declining since 1986, see Figure 50. Nevertheless, Standard & Poor's predicted growth from three sources in 1996:

- Nontraditional reinsurance ("financial reinsurance") was to become more popular, and reinsurers would see themselves more and more as "providers of capital" instead of providers of reinsurance.[307]
- Increasing volume and complexity of primary life insurance markets would lead to an increase in demand for experienced reinsurers.[308]
- Primary insurance cover picked up in Southeast Asian and Latin American, thus increasing total reinsurance demand in these markets.[309]

307 Standard & Poor's (1996, p. 8).
308 Standard & Poor's (1996, p. 17).
309 Standard & Poor's (1996, p. 8).

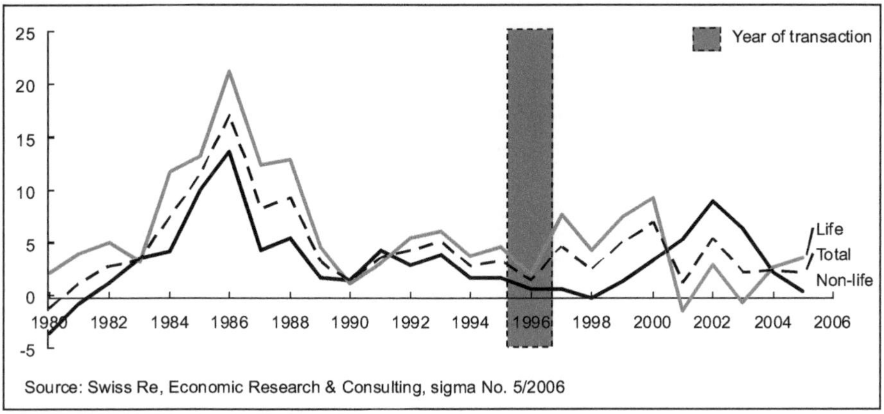

Figure 50: Development of real reinsurance premium growth rates (percent)

Thirdly, solvency margins were likely to deteriorate. Available capital of reinsurers could decline as profits were under pressure, but also because reinsurers may have been forced to increase dividend payout ratios: Standard & Poor's (1996, p. 15) argue that increasing investor sophistication and international transparency would increase pressure on dividending, and lead to declining capital adequacy ratios and decreasing run-off profits. Secondly, the cost of equity increased with rising risk free rates, see Figure 48. The two following sections illustrate that these market conditions generally applied to Munich Re, and discuss the specific situation of Munich Re leading to its bid for American Re.

5.4.1.2 The transaction partners: Munich Re

Munich Re was established in 1880 by Carl Thieme, who was then employee of Cologne Re, the worldwide first reinsurance company, founded 34 years earlier. Already 6 years after its foundation, Munich Re opened offices across Europe, and went to the stock market only 8 years later. In 1899, it opened an office in the United States, and further expanded its international activities even throughout difficult times of the first and second world war. In 1955, Munich Re opened a P&C reinsurance subsidiary in New York, closely followed by a life subsidiary in Atlanta in 1959. Although growth in North and Latin America strengthened afterwards, management was not yet satisfied and consequently decided in 1996

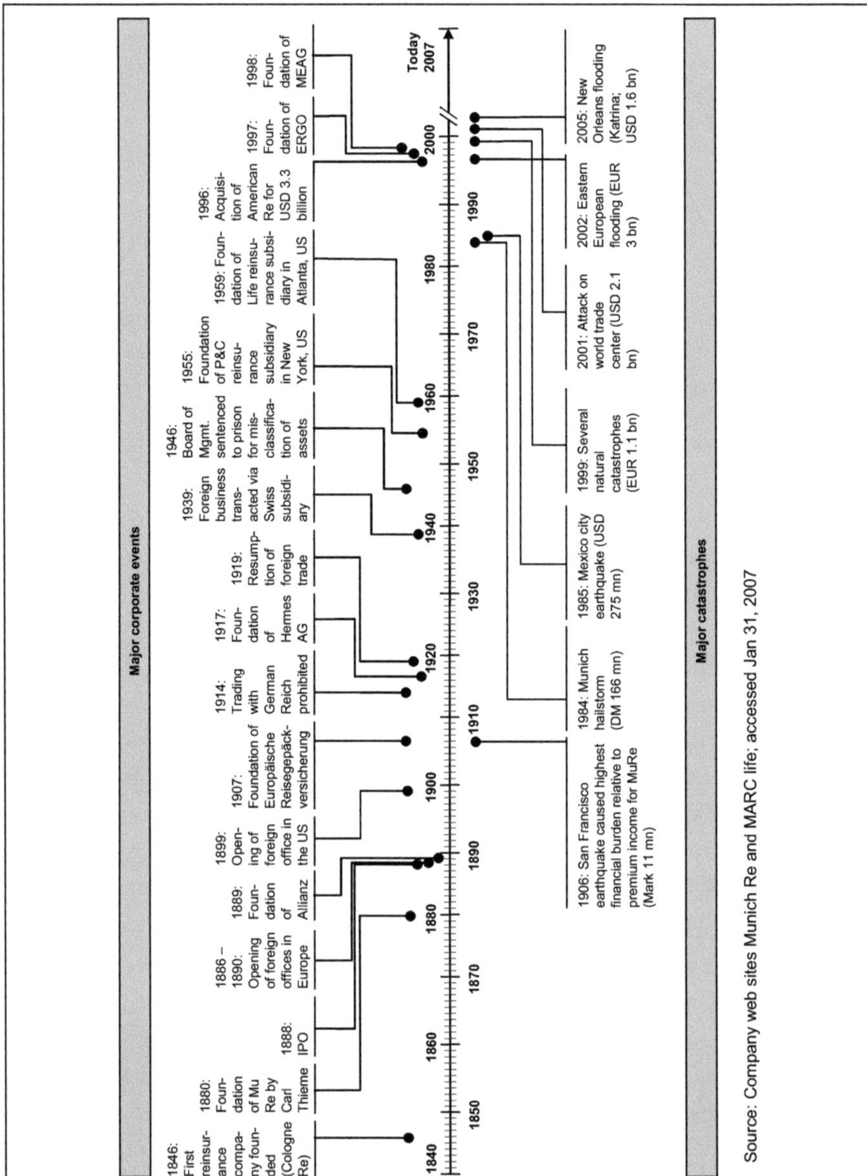

Source: Company web sites Munich Re and MARC life; accessed Jan 31, 2007

Figure 51: History of Munich Re

to pursue the landmark acquisition of American for USD 3.3 bn. Figure 51 presents the history in further detail.

Munich Re is a publicly listed German company ("Aktiengesellschaft"). Five block holders held 60% of its paid-in capital of DM 813 mn (USD 535 mn) as of 30 June 1996.[310] The remaining 40% of share holdings were free float. The consolidated Munich Re Group embraces the Munich Reinsurance Company, which is writer of the largest part of the reinsurance business, and 13 major[311] reinsurance and primary insurance subsidiaries, see Figure 52. With a global market share of 14% of total net written premiums in 1995, Munich Re was the largest reinsurance group worldwide,[312] but strongly dependent on the European market as 69% of its gross premium income was written in this region. The business lines aviation, motor and life dominated Munich Re's portfolio, each accounting for about 20% of total gross premium income.

Despite its leading position in the global reinsurance market and strong capital market performance, Munich Re came under pressure in the mid 1990s. After outperforming its industry peers[313] in 1993 and 1994 on the capital market,[314] Munich Re suffered from a TRS of -17% compared to a TRS of the reinsurance market of 5% in 1995. Three fundamental factors drove the devaluation of Munich Re. Firstly, investors expected high growth from Munich Re: 82% of its market valuation was driven by earnings growth expectations[315] at the beginning of 1996. However, Munich Re lost 1.9 percentage points market share between 1994 and 1996 (down from 15.2%) in a global reinsurance market that grew by 7.7% CAGR in the same period of time.[316] Further on, the valuation

310 Allianz held 25%, Bayerische Vereinsbank, Deutsche Bank, and Dresdner Bank each held 10%, and Commercial Union Assurance Company held 5%.

311 Subsidiaries of Munich Re with consolidated equity above DM 100 mn in 1995.

312 Standard & Poor's (1996) list of world's 20 largest consolidated reinsurance groups.

313 Market median computed based on account data of 42 major worldwide reinsurance providers, as reported by Research Insight/GV.

314 In 1993 and 1994, Munich Re achieved a TRS of 13% and 46% compared to a TRS of -7% and 32% of its industry peers.

315 Computed as 1 minus (3-year average of after tax earnings / (cost of equity x market value)). Cost of equity calculated with 5% risk premium, risk free rate as average of 10 year U.S. government bond rate and 10 year German Sovereign rate, and beta based on 3-year covariance with MSCI world index.

316 Based on total net written premiums as reported by Standard & Poor's (1995-1997).

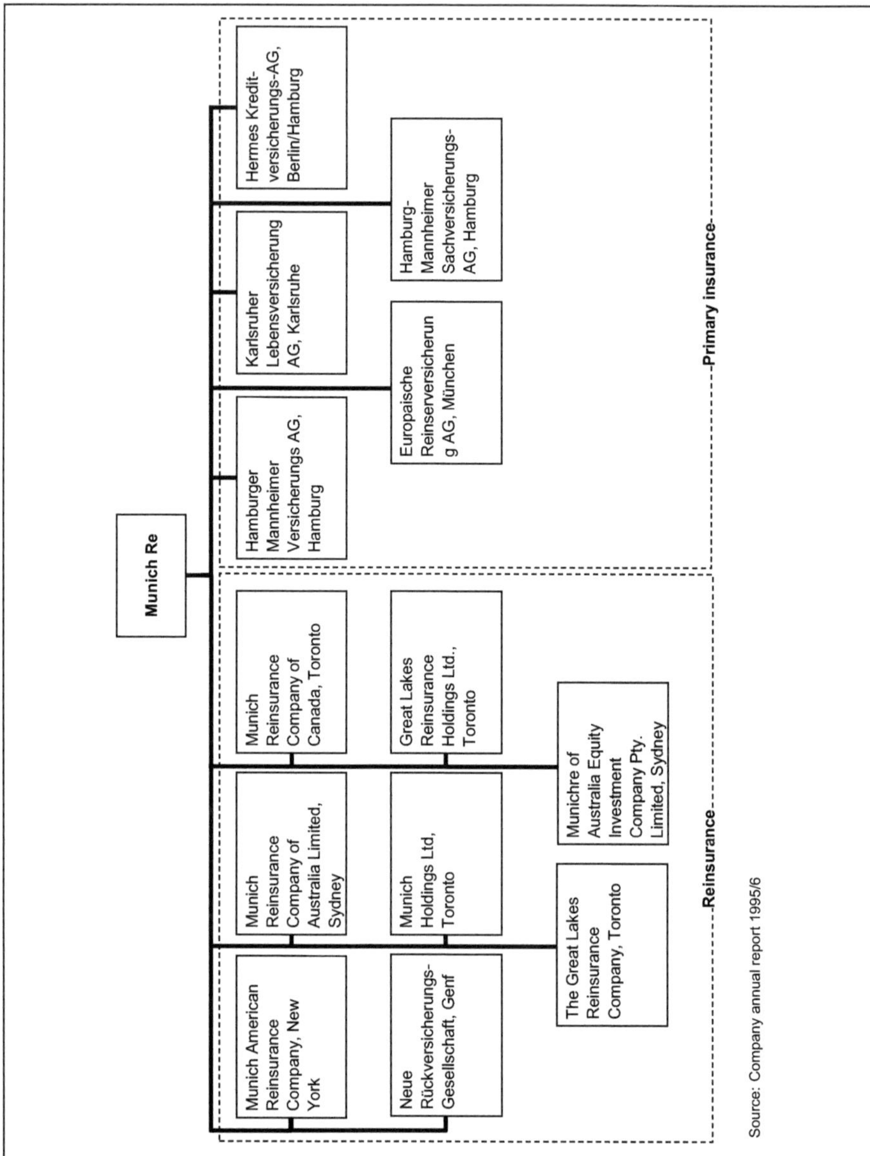

Figure 52: Subsidiaries of Munich Re with consolidated equity over DM 100 mn

Table 45: Financial performance of Munich Re (1991–1995)

MUNICH RE	Unit	1991	1992	1993	1994	1995
Size						
Earnings	USD mn	103.9	104.6	110.3	177.5	346.7
Premiums	USD bn	8.9	13.7	14.4	16.7	18.2
Reserves	USD bn	23.0	52.8	54.5	64.6	75.0
Assets	USD bn	27.6	60.7	62.8	75.7	88.2
Shareholders' Equity	USD bn	1.8	2.2	2.5	2.9	3.7
Solvency						
Equity ratio	%	6.7%	3.7%	3.9%	3.8%	4.2%
Equity reserves ratio	%	8.0%	4.2%	4.5%	4.4%	5.0%
Operating leverage	times x	4.9	6.1	5.8	5.8	4.9
Reserves leverage	times x	96.6	151.3	142.6	138.0	95.0
Reserves ratio	times x	2.6	3.8	3.8	3.9	4.1
Profitability						
Return on reserves	bp	103.6	66.1	70.1	72.4	105.2
Return on equity	%	13.0%	15.6%	15.5%	16.3%	21.1%
Return on premiums	%	2.7%	2.5%	2.7%	2.8%	4.3%
Combined ratio	%	118.7%	128.1%	123.8%	119.8%	116.9%
Loss ratio	%	86.6%	99.5%	96.2%	93.1%	91.3%
Expense ratio	%	32.1%	28.6%	27.6%	26.7%	25.6%
Net investment result ratio	%	20.3%	27.8%	25.0%	24.2%	30.2%
Net investment yield	%	6.6%	6.3%	5.7%	5.3%	6.3%
Growth						
Growth of earnings	%	73.4%	0.6%	5.4%	61.0%	95.3%
Growth of premiums	%	7.8%	53.9%	4.8%	15.9%	9.6%
Growth of reserves	%	7.9%	129.3%	3.2%	18.7%	16.0%
Growth of assets	%	7.0%	120.3%	3.5%	20.5%	16.5%
Growth of equity	%	5.1%	21.9%	9.8%	16.6%	30.5%

implied growth rate[317] of 8.6% ranged well above the long-term market average premium growth of 5.4%.[318] Munich Re's ability to increase its earnings, premiums and assets by more than 30% CAGR between 1991 and 1995, see Table 45, could not countervail its long-term negative revenue outlook. Secondly, Munich Re only achieved by 1995 to return to its profitability levels of 1991 as measured

317 Computed as (combined market value x cost of equity – combined earnings) / (combined market value + combined earnings).

318 Average between 1980 and 1995 based on Swiss Re (2006).

Table 46: Market adjusted financial performance of Munich Re (1991–1995)

MUNICH RE (market adj.)	**Unit**	**1991**	**1992**	**1993**	**1994**	**1995**
Size						
Earnings	x times market	1.2	1.7	1.9	2.7	6.3
Premiums	x times market	3.5	6.6	5.0	5.5	6.3
Reserves	x times market	3.8	6.8	6.2	6.3	9.8
Assets	x times market	3.2	5.8	5.1	5.9	9.6
Shareholders' Equity	x times market	1.8	1.9	1.8	2.0	4.4
Solvency						
Equity ratio	Δ%pts to market	-2.7%	-5.9%	-6.2%	-6.5%	-6.3%
Equity reserves ratio	Δ%pts to market	-3.5%	-6.6%	-7.5%	-7.7%	-8.0%
Operating leverage	Δtimes x to marke	2.0	3.9	3.4	3.6	2.6
Reserves leverage	Δtimes x to marke	32.1	70.3	71.5	75.3	45.2
Reserves ratio	Δtimes x to marke	-0.3	0.4	0.6	0.7	1.2
Profitability						
Return on reserves	Δbp to market	-50.7	-57.1	-67.7	-86.9	-85.2
Return on equity	Δ%pts to market	-1.1%	4.5%	2.5%	2.8%	5.9%
Return on premiums	Δ%pts to market	-1.7%	-1.7%	-1.7%	-2.1%	-1.8%
Combined ratio	Δ%pts to market	13.0%	27.5%	28.8%	30.5%	25.4%
Loss ratio	Δ%pts to market	8.3%	25.5%	26.2%	27.0%	22.2%
Expense ratio	Δ%pts to market	4.7%	2.0%	2.6%	3.6%	3.2%
Net investment result ratio	Δ%pts to market	-1.2%	2.6%	0.0%	1.4%	8.7%
Net investment yield	Δ%pts to market	-0.1%	0.5%	-0.6%	-0.3%	0.2%
Growth						
Growth of earnings	Δ%pts to market	n/a*	30.9%	9.7%	50.5%	111.4%
Growth of premiums	Δ%pts to market	106.8%	48.9%	-30.3%	8.7%	6.7%
Growth of reserves	Δ%pts to market	3.0%	106.7%	-16.2%	11.4%	12.4%
Growth of assets	Δ%pts to market	2.5%	98.6%	-15.1%	12.4%	16.6%
Growth of equity	Δ%pts to market	n/a*	9.9%	-5.5%	9.1%	71.1%

* Market figures not available for 1990.

by return on reserves, while its industry peers continuously improved their performance in this period of time. The profitability gap widened from –51 bp return on reserve in 1991 to –85 bp in 1995, see Table 46. In the same period of time, Munich Re's already below market underwriting effectiveness worsened to a loss ratio 22 percentage points above the market median, which it could only partly compensate by reducing expenses and increasing the investment yield.[319] Thirdly, Munich Re's capitalization weakened. Its equity ratio declined by 2.5

319 Munich Re only improved return on equity compared to the market. However, this effect was driven by the eroding capital base, see further below.

percentage points to 6.3% percentage points below the market median, while its leverage increased compared to the market median by all measures.

In summary, the mid 1990s brought dramatic change to Munich Re, as it stepped from comfortably holding the position of the global market leader to being under strong pressure to grow profitably. Munich Re's management considered M&A as a prompt solution, and did this probably rightfully so. Firstly, organic growth may realize too late compared to M&A-driven growth of Munich Re's competitors, or it may come at high cost as the market power of its competitors increases with accelerating consolidation of the global reinsurance market. Secondly, coming from a history of purely organic growth, Munich Re may have hoped for enthusiastic reactions of investors, since the decision to pursue M&A emphasized their eagerness to change pace and to secure its position as the world market leader.

5.4.1.3 The transaction partners: American Re

American Re was founded in 1917. Besides two national acquisitions in 1950 and 1963, American Re remained a rather quiet player until the 1970s, when it eventually began international expansion. In 1979, the acquisition of American Re by Aetna Life and Casualty Insurance Company for USD 340 mn heralded a time of frequent ownership changes. On 30 September 1992, the private equity firm Kohlberg Kravis Roberts (KKR) invested USD 1.43 bn in American Re. The newly created holding company American Re Corporation was owned by 91% by KKR and American Re senior management, with 9% remaining in hands of Aetna. Only four months later, on 29 January 1993, KKR successfully placed 24% of American Re Corporation on the capital market. KKR remained controlling shareholder with roughly owning 70% of share holdings. After further international expansion especially into the eastern hemisphere, already three years later in August 1996, KKR sold American Re to Munich Re for USD 3.3 bn. Figure 53 presents the detailed timeline.

Before its acquisition by Munich Re, American Re was publicly listed with KKR as a dominant shareholder controlling 64% of the paid-in capital of USD 711 mn (31 December 1995). Further 20% were in private hands, and 16%

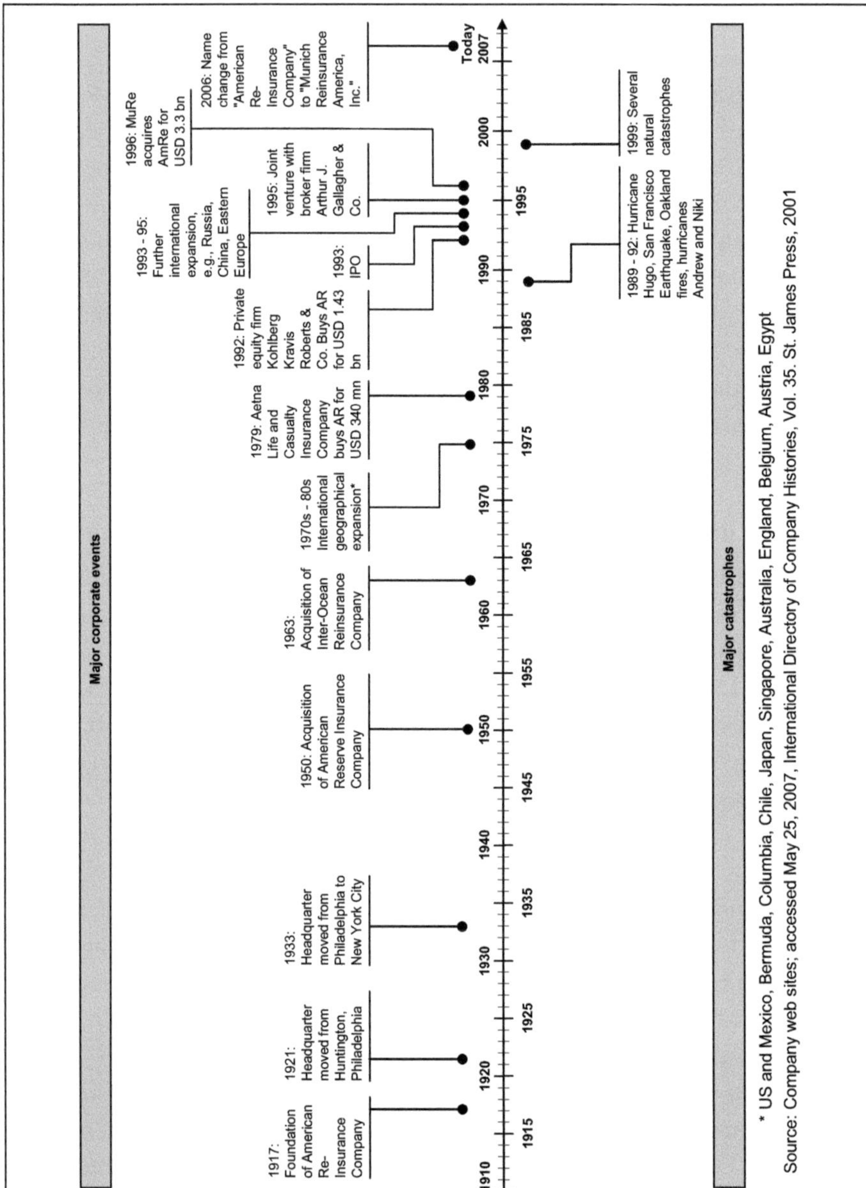

Figure 53: History of American Re

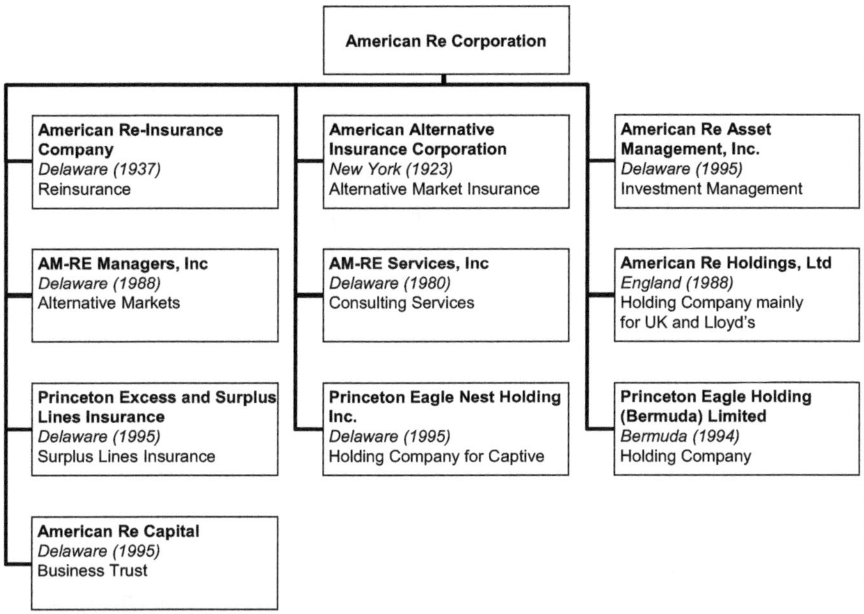

Source: Company annual report 1995

Figure 54: Direct subsidiaries of American Re in 1995

dominated by institutional investors. American Re held 10 subsidiaries, thereof two foreign subsidiaries incorporated in Bermuda and the UK, see Figure 54.

With a global market share of 2% of total net written premiums, American Re was the 11th largest player in the global reinsurance market, and the third largest reinsurance carrier in the U.S. in 1995.[320] Its portfolio was dominated by liability lines and workers' compensation, which contributed a third and a fourth to the total net written premiums in 1995, respectively. American Re wrote 82% of its business in North America, and was acknowledged as an experienced underwriter of nontraditional reinsurance,[321] a product market gaining importance according to Standard & Poor's (1996). Figure 55 and Figure 56 illustrate the

320 Standard & Poor's (1996) survey on world's 20 largest consolidated reinsurance groups.
321 Munich Re (14 August 1996).

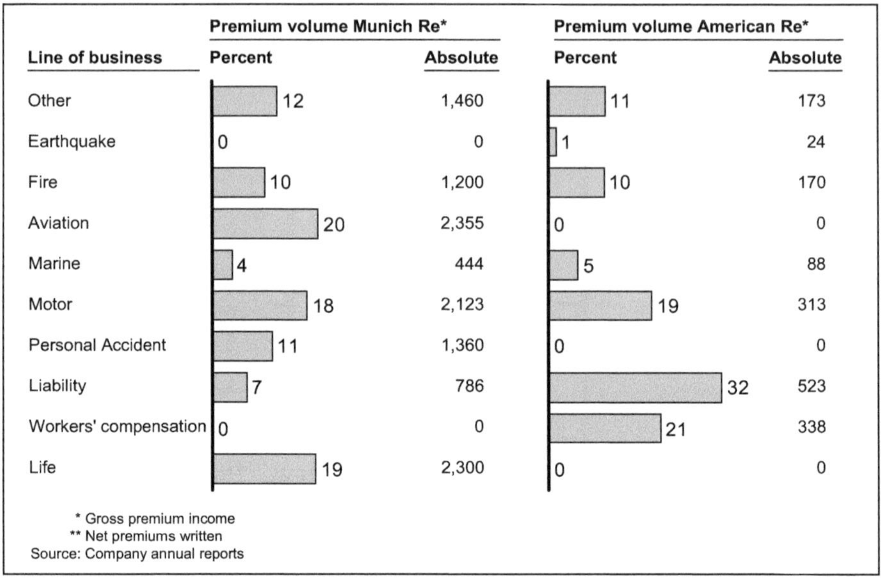

Figure 55: Complementarity of Munich Re and American Re business mix by lines of business (USD mn, 1995)

complementarity of American Re's and Munich Re's business mix, promising product and especially geographical diversification benefits from a combination of the portfolios by reducing the strong dependency of both reinsurers on their home markets.

Superficially, American Re's operations looked healthy by its fundamental account data. It grew in line with the global reinsurance market by slightly extending its market share from 2.2% in 1994 to 2.3% in 1996.[322] Further on, in the five years prior to the transaction, American Re outgrew the market median by increasing its premiums by 13% CAGR, growing its asset base by 20% CAGR, and increasing its reserves by 29% CAGR, see Table 47.[323] However, American Re bought growth through relaxation of its underwriting discipline. Between

322 Standard & Poor's (1996) survey on world's 20 largest consolidated reinsurance groups.

323 Only shareholder equity shrank by 3% CAGR due to an increase in gearing after refinancing by KKR in 1992.

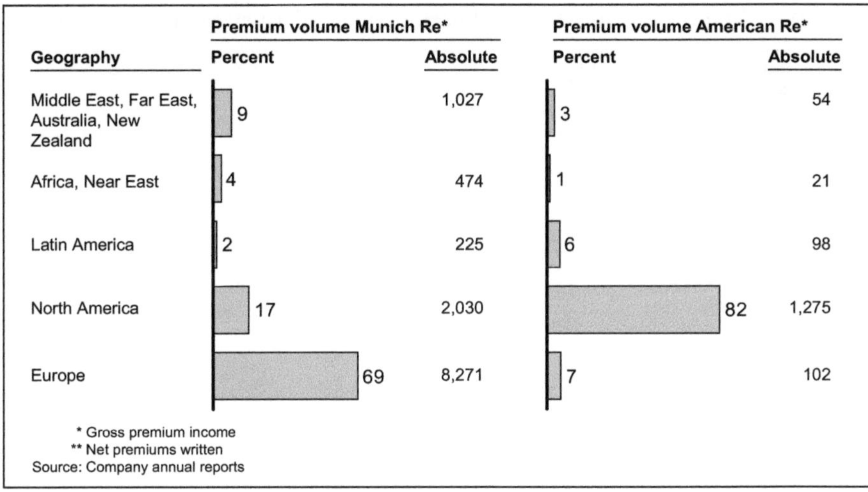

Figure 56: Complementarity of Munich Re and American Re business mix by geography (USD mn, 1995)

Table 47: Financial performance of American Re (1991–1995)

AMERICAN RE	Unit	1991	1992	1993	1994	1995
Size						
Earnings	USD mn	158.1	94.8	98.4	97.5	-87.6
Premiums	USD bn	0.9	1.0	1.2	1.5	1.5
Reserves	USD bn	2.1	4.1	4.3	4.7	5.6
Assets	USD bn	3.8	5.5	5.4	6.7	7.8
Shareholders' Equity	USD bn	1.0	0.4	0.8	0.8	0.8
Solvency						
Equity ratio	%	25.3%	7.0%	14.7%	11.8%	10.8%
Equity reserves ratio	%	46.8%	9.5%	18.4%	16.8%	15.0%
Operating leverage	times x	1.0	2.5	1.6	1.9	1.8
Reserves leverage	times x	10.2	34.5	30.0	39.0	-35.4
Reserves ratio	times x	2.2	4.2	3.5	3.2	3.7
Profitability						
Return on reserves	bp	983.0	289.8	333.2	256.6	-282.4
Return on equity	%	21.0%	30.7%	18.1%	15.3%	-18.8%
Return on premiums	%	21.8%	12.3%	11.5%	8.3%	-10.4%
Combined ratio	%	100.4%	103.3%	96.0%	99.2%	117.1%
Loss ratio	%	72.9%	69.9%	63.8%	69.2%	87.5%
Expense ratio	%	27.5%	33.4%	32.3%	30.1%	29.6%
Net investment result ratio	%	23.7%	17.1%	15.1%	15.2%	16.2%
Net investment yield	%	5.8%	3.0%	3.5%	3.3%	3.2%
Growth						
Growth of earnings	%	4.5%	-40.1%	3.8%	-0.9%	-189.8%
Growth of premiums	%	11.8%	3.6%	29.7%	16.9%	4.8%
Growth of reserves	%	-1.0%	98.0%	5.8%	8.8%	20.1%
Growth of assets	%	1.8%	44.3%	-1.2%	22.9%	17.0%
Growth of equity	%	10.0%	-60.0%	106.4%	-1.0%	7.3%

Table 48: Market adjusted financial performance of American Re (1991–1995)

AMERICAN RE (market adj.)	**Unit**	**1991**	**1992**	**1993**	**1994**	**1995**
Size						
Earnings	x times market	1.8	1.5	1.7	1.5	-1.6
Premiums	x times market	0.4	0.5	0.4	0.5	0.5
Reserves	x times market	0.3	0.5	0.5	0.5	0.7
Assets	x times market	0.4	0.5	0.4	0.5	0.9
Shareholders' Equity	x times market	0.9	0.3	0.6	0.5	1.0
Solvency						
Equity ratio	Δ%pts to market	15.9%	-2.5%	4.5%	1.6%	0.3%
Equity reserves ratio	Δ%pts to market	35.3%	-1.4%	6.4%	4.6%	2.0%
Operating leverage	Δtimes x to mark	-1.9	0.3	-0.9	-0.4	-0.5
Reserves leverage	Δtimes x to mark	-54.3	-46.5	-41.1	-23.8	-85.2
Reserves ratio	Δtimes x to mark	-0.7	0.8	0.3	0.1	0.8
Profitability						
Return on reserves	Δbp to market	828.8	166.6	195.4	97.2	-472.8
Return on equity	Δ%pts to market	6.9%	19.6%	5.0%	1.8%	-34.1%
Return on premiums	Δ%pts to market	17.4%	8.0%	7.1%	3.3%	-16.6%
Combined ratio	Δ%pts to market	-5.3%	2.7%	1.1%	9.9%	25.6%
Loss ratio	Δ%pts to market	-5.4%	-4.1%	-6.2%	3.0%	18.5%
Expense ratio	Δ%pts to market	0.2%	6.8%	7.3%	6.9%	7.2%
Net investment result ratio	Δ%pts to market	2.3%	-8.1%	-9.9%	-7.6%	-5.4%
Net investment yield	Δ%pts to market	-0.8%	-2.7%	-2.8%	-2.3%	-2.9%
Growth						
Growth of earnings	Δ%pts to market	n/a*	-9.8%	8.1%	-11.4%	-173.8%
Growth of premiums	Δ%pts to market	110.8%	-1.4%	-5.4%	9.8%	1.9%
Growth of reserves	Δ%pts to market	-6.0%	75.4%	-13.6%	1.6%	16.5%
Growth of assets	Δ%pts to market	-2.6%	22.6%	-19.8%	14.7%	17.1%
Growth of equity	Δ%pts to market	n/a*	-72.0%	91.1%	-8.5%	48.0%

* Market figures not available for 1990.

1991 and 1994, it was more profitable than the market median in terms of return on reserves, return on equity and return on premiums, but the profitability gap between American Re and the market median narrowed ever more, Table 48. Although American Re was strongly exposed to rather long tailed lines of business such as liability and workers compensation, its loss ratio rose above market median level already in 1994. At the same time, relative expenses increased and investments only yielded weak returns. Accordingly, American Re's solvency compared to the market median declined strongly.

Thus, warning signs with respect to the sustainability of American Re's results and risk comprised in the portfolio were clearly observable, emphasized by Standard & Poor's (1996, p. 10) statement that they expect further reserve strengthening for environment and asbestos liability for primary insurers, with significant spill over to reinsurance carriers. Its growth combined with worsening relative loss ratios indicated a top-line focus of top management already three years after American Re's acquisition by KKR.

5.4.1.4 Benefits of the transaction

In the mid 1990s, Munich Re came under pressure to grow significantly faster and profitably. In these years, market growth was expected to mainly come from traditional reinsurance in Latin America and South-East Asia, and non-traditional reinsurance in global markets.[324] Munich Re believed to achieve geographical expansion in traditional product lines organically, because it was experienced in the business, or may not have found reasonable, "right-sized" takeover targets in these geographies. However, the profitable but heavily expertise-based business of nontraditional reinsurance was more difficult to develop for Munich Re based on internal resources and capabilities. Following this argumentation, the acquisition of an experienced U.S. carrier was a rationale step.[325] However, Munich Re reached out to the U.S. market rather late, because the largest U.S. reinsurer Employers Re and second largest U.S. reinsurer General Re acquired Frankona Re and Cologne Re two years earlier, and thus became too large to be taken over by Munich Re. Further on, smaller U.S. reinsurers suffered from low ratings, publicly known portfolio issues (environmental and asbestos exposure), or insignificant size (below USD 1 bn premium volume), leaving American Re as the only rational takeover candidate.

Munich Re stated as main motives for the acquisition of American Re the above average growth, sustainable high profitability, closeness to customers, highly specialized expertise in the areas of financial reinsurance and alternative markets, and managements' reputation for its extraordinary professionalism.[326] As the discussion in section 5.4.1.3 show, the first to reasons may be doubted as American Re grew at the expense of lowering its underwriting discipline. Munich Re did not attach concrete financial targets to the acquisition, but expected

324 Standard & Poor's (1996, p. 8).

325 U.S. and Bermudan carriers dominated the market of nontraditional reinsurance, but Bermudan carriers were considered intransparent.

326 Munich Re (14 August 1996).

	Market environment	Specifics of transaction partners	Merger benefits and obstacles
Motives that create value	• M&A market for reinsurers in upswing (especially U.S.)		• Value creation by – Avoiding transaction in M&A peak – Acquiring before market is cleared
• **Profitability**	• Profitability in reinsurance market under pressure*	• MR underwriting less effective than AR underwriting	• Economies of scope (skill transfer primarily for underwriting effectiveness)
• **Growth**	• Growth of reinsurance market declining	• MR's valuation strongly based on growth • MR's market share declining, AR's market share constant	• Further organic growth through – Market power increase** – Revenue economies of scale due to "Flight to Quality" – Economies of scope (skill transfer nontraditional reinsurance)
• **Solvency**	• Solvency margins deteriorating	• MR capitalized worse than market, AR better • MR is European player, AR has North American focus	• Strengthening of capitalization • Risk reduction through – Global and product diversification – Less proportional business
Other motives	• Acquisition of German reinsurers by U.S. reinsurers		• Empire building

* Softening cycle, increasing natural catastrophes, rising interest rates

** U.S. traditional and European non-traditional markets

Source: Own research

Figure 57: Merger benefits and obstacles

that 1997 earnings would be hurt, synergies would be visible in 1998 results,[327] and future earnings per share would be positively affected.[328] In the following, Munich Re's motives are discussed in the context of drivers and hurdles for M&A as identified in section 2.3.2.[329]

Value creating motives. The empirical analysis on value creation by M&A in section 4.4.2.2 indicates that in the long-term, transactions in the peak phase create less value than transactions in the through phase.[330] Since the reinsurance M&A market was just picking up but has not yet reached its peak, Munich Re may have chosen the transaction timing well. Whether or not the acquisition generated value is examined based on its CARs and BAHRs.

Profitability. The acquisition of American Re promised Munich Re to realize *economies of scope* from skill transfer in traditional reinsurance. Through the transaction it would obtain access to the underwriting skills of American Re: Munich Re's underwriting effectiveness as measured by the loss ratio was 21 percentage points lower in the average between 1991 and 1995.[331] On the other hand, Munich Re may hope to increase American Re's underwriting efficiency and net investment yield up to its own level. Due to the nature of these economies of scope it is imperative for Munich Re during the integration process to retain senior management of American Re, as they carry underwriting expertise and own the client contact, and to ensure rapid capability transfer to its own underwriters, e.g., by rotating staff or building integrated underwriting centers. The realization of these economies of scope shall be tested through examining pre- and post-transaction claims ratios, expense ratios and investment yield indicators compared to the market. If claims ratios fall relative to the market but Munich Re's premium market share remains constant or increases, underwriting skills of

327 Dow Jones International News (4 September 1996), Reuters News (4 September 1996).

328 Munich Re (14 August 1996).

329 The analysis of motives is focused on Munich Re's perspective The clear benefit for American Re's controlling shareholder is the sevenfold increase in value of its stakes over merely 4 years together with the all-cash compensation proposed by Munich Re.

330 However, relevant coefficient estimate s in regression model are not significant.

331 However, although American Re's historically achieved a loss ratio 5 percentage points better than the market median, the gap between American Re and the market was narrowing for consecutive 5 years and in 1995, American Re's loss ratio even exceeded the market median by 18.5 percentage points.

Munich Re are advancing. If expense ratios decrease relative to the market, underwriting efficiency of Munich is improving. If net investment yields pick up without increasing investment risk compared to the market,[332] Munich Re's underwriting efficiency and effectiveness is developing positively.

Growth. The acquisition of American Re may lead the combined entity back on the path of growth for three reasons. Firstly, Munich Re strengthens its *market power* in the U.S., where it sees strong growth opportunities,[333] as the acquisition of American Re drives up their combined market share to 15.6%. Secondly, Munich Re may realize *revenue economies of scale*. As a consequence of Hurricane Andrew in 1992, a "flight to quality" emerged in the global reinsurance market,[334] describing the effect that buyers of reinsurance contracts are attracted by well capitalized reinsurers with large balance sheets especially in times of higher losses.[335] Both market power effects and revenue economies of scale would be indicated by an increase in Munich Re's premium market share after the acquisition, if profitability remains at the same level compared to the market median or even improves.

Thirdly, Munich Re may realize *economies of scope* from skill transfer in nontraditional reinsurance. Standard & Poor's (1995, p. 24) say that competition is increasing from nontraditional reinsurance sources such as capital market hedging instruments (cat ILS) and cat-triggered surplus notes (cat bonds), where investment banks enter the field as natural competitors. Additionally, new entrants especially from the U.S. and Bermuda, offer to unbundle risk (i.e. tailoring coverage to the specific risk) and thus increase competition.[336] American Re's underwriters distinguished themselves through closeness to clients due to their direct sales approach and highly specialized know how in the profitable areas of

332 If investment risk for Munich Re and the market would be available, combined risk-return measures (e.g., Sharpe ratio) were preferable. However, investment risk is neither available for Munich Re nor its industry peers.

333 Munich Re (14 August 1996).

334 E.g., European Commisson (2007b, p. 78) and Standard & Poor's (1997, p. 10).

335 Standard & Poor's (1995, p. 24) argues that reinsurers with larger capital bases outperformed their smaller competitors and are better able to meet the challenges presented by natural catastrophes and competitive forces.

336 Standard & Poor's (1996, p.8).

financial reinsurance and alternative markets.[337] Munich Re may hope to further expand American Re's acknowledged skills to bundle both players' competitive power against new entrants in the U.S. market, and transfer American Re's skills to the still less sophisticated European market and beyond. Again, it is crucial for Munich Re to retain senior management and facilitate early skill exchange to foster realization of these economies of scope. An increase of Munich Re's premium market share in nontraditional markets after the acquisition at constant or improving underwriting effectiveness would indicate successful exploitation of these economies of scope. This hypothesis cannot be tested, since a premium split into traditional and nontraditional reinsurance is neither available for Munich Re nor the market.

Solvency. The prevalent market environment exerted pressure on earnings and thus capitalization of reinsurance providers. Munich Re may be especially affected due to its already weak capitalization compared to its competitors, so that a combination with the historically strongly capitalized American Re seems advantageous. This *strengthening of the available capital base* is assessed by comparing those solvency measures, which include shareholders' equity in their definition,[338] against the market. Further on, an acquisition of American Re may lead to a reduction of required capital, or *risk reduction*, due to the especially geographically, but also product-wise complementary business mix of Munich Re and American Re. In addition, combination of the business may lower the ratio of proportional business in Munich Re's portfolio, thus immunizing Munich Re to some extent against primary insurance price cycles. The effect of risk reduction cannot be tracked based on available financial performance measures, since required risk computations (e.g., based on internal models) are unavailable.

Other (non-value generating) motives. After the acquisition of Frankona Re and Cologne Re by world number two and three reinsurers Employers Re and General Re in 1995, Munich Re may now be urged to secure its position in the market, relating to the motive of *empire building*.

337 Munich Re (14 August 1996).

338 I.e., equity ratio, equity reserves ratio, and operating leverage.

In summary, numerous motives and potential benefits – value generating and non-value generating – can be identified for Munich Re's acquisition of American Re. However, realization of hypothesized acquisition benefits put forward several requirements towards the transaction process and the post-acquisition integration process. Firstly, Munich Re needed to pick up warning signals with respect to American Re's current underwriting issues, and consequently seek to gain further transparency on American Re's in-force book of business, especially in risky liability lines, and to initiate an independent actuarial appraisal of these lines during due diligence. Secondly, Munich Re was required to ensure transparency on and control of underwriting of new business in these lines, although it is significantly less familiar with the type of product and geographical specifics of the North American market. Thirdly, key success factor for integration is the retention of senior management and rapid facilitation of skill transfer in order to realize economies of scope. An analysis of the conduct of the transaction reveals that these three important points were not achieved.

5.4.2 Conduct of the transaction

5.4.2.1 Transaction process and strategy

Munich Re acquired American Re in a four-week controlled auction. Figure 58 summarizes the major steps of the transaction along the process framework laid out in chapter 2.2.3.[339] After rumors that Munich Re and less so American Re may be interested in acquiring National Re on 1 July 1996,[340] the CEO of one of American Re's principal U.S. based competitors (Company 1) opened the first round bid by contacting the Chairman of the Board of American Re to explore the possibility of a strategic combination. American Re decided to get in the lead. In the middle of July, American Re's financial advisor, Goldman Sachs & Co., contacted five possible buyers, including Munich Re and Company 1. American Re entered into confidentiality agreements with Munich Re, Company

339 Most of the information is drawn from the Schedule 14A Statement (23 October 1996), unless other sources are stated explicitly.

340 Dow Jones International News (1 July 1996).

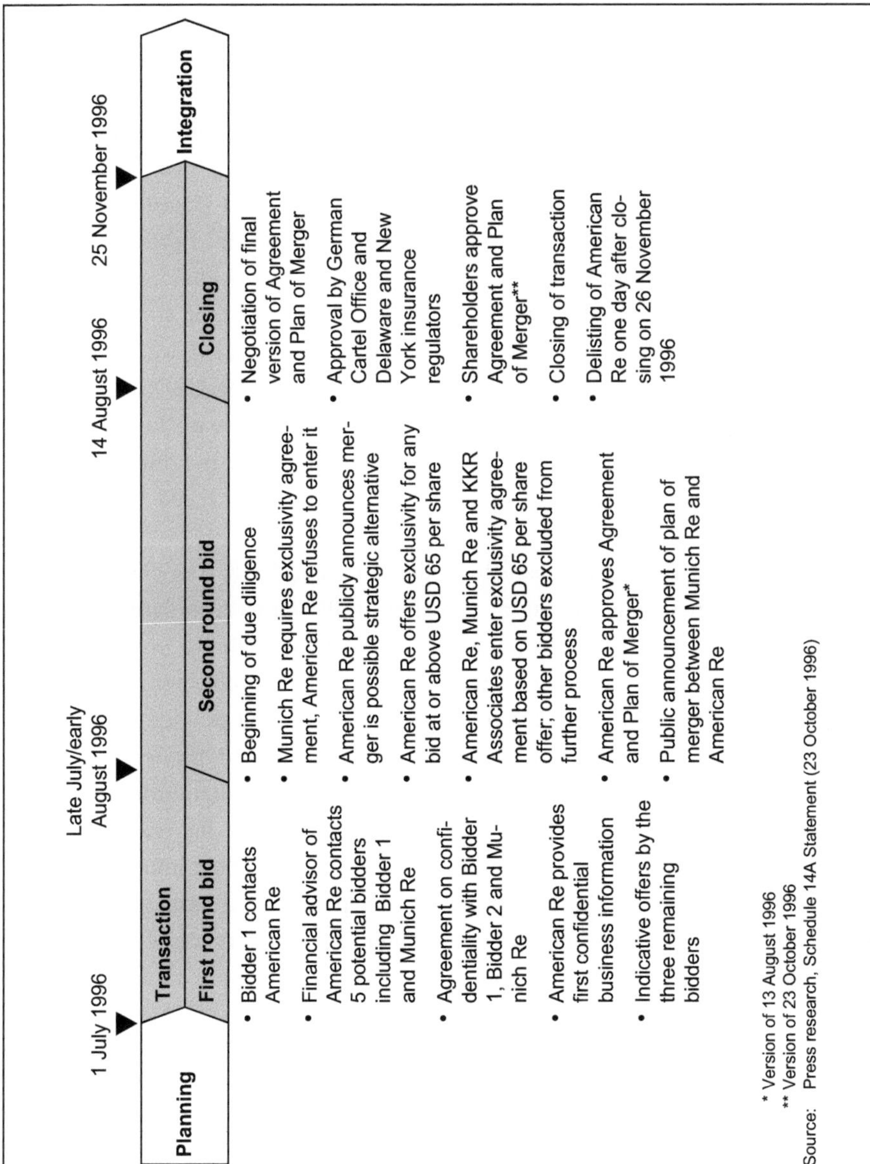

Figure 58: Transaction process of Munich Re's acquisition of American Re

1 and an unnamed Company 2. All three potential buyers were granted access to certain confidential business information such as premiums by division, projected results and pro forma expense analyses.

During late July and early August, the second round bidding was initiated. Munich Re required an exclusivity agreement to complete its due diligence review and negotiate the transaction, but on 5 August 1996, the Board of Directors of American Re countered by making the auction public. In a press release, it stated that is in the best interests of the company and its stockholders to explore strategic alternatives, including the possible merger or sale of the company.[341] At the same time, it notified the three prospective bidders that it would consider entering into exclusivity agreements with any bidder offering USD 65 per share or higher subject to confirmatory due diligence and acceptable exclusivity conditions.[342] Company 1 and 2 indicated interest in due diligence but did not commit to a price, and their prospective indicative offers did not exceed USD 65 per share.

On 7 August 1996, American Re, Munich Re and KKR Associates reached an exclusivity agreement, aiming at agreeing on the terms of a definite merger agreement by 15 August 1996 pursuant to which Munich Re would acquire American Re at a price of USD 65 per share in cash and other terms. In accordance with the exclusivity agreement, American Re did not provide further confidential information to other potential bidders and terminated discussions. On 13 August 1996, the Board of Directors of American Re Corporation unanimously approved the merger. Amongst other reasons for its decision, the Board said that it appreciated Munich Re's indication to be willing to enter into the merger agreement immediately. At that time, an independent actuarial appraisal of American Re's reserves had not yet been conducted, nor were terms of the transaction linked to the outcome of such a reserve review in the near future.[343]

341 Business Wire (5 August 1996).

342 Munich Re's indicative offer at that time was USD 60 per share. American Re, whose common shares were valued at USD 57.25 per share at that time, declined.

343 According to Select Federal Filings Newswires (24 October 1996), Goldman Sachs reviewed loss and loss adjustment reserves, but no independent actuarial appraisal was made.

On 14 August 1996, the transaction was announced, but still subject to approval by shareholders of American Re, German[344] and U.S. cartel officials, the Department of Insurance of the State of New York, and the Insurance Department of the State of Delaware, and certain other customary conditions and approvals.[345] The controlling shareholder KKR had already agreed to vote in favor of the transaction[346], and common stockholders of American Re voted to approve and to adopt the amended[347] Agreement and Plan of Merger on 21 November 1996. In the meanwhile, the approval of the Delaware and the New York insurance departments were obtained,[348] as well as the approval of the German Cartel Office. As expected by Munich Re,[349] the transaction was closed on 25 November 1996. One day later outstanding shares of American Re were unlisted.

Munich Re entered the auction with the strategy to achieve exclusivity early through a high non-binding offer compared to other bidders.[350] Its reason to seek a fast closing probably was it's angst of losing the last attractive opportunity to tap new sources for growth through M&A, or its fear of being forced into a possibly expensive bidding contest. American Re interpreted Munich Re's situation properly and responded smartly. Firstly, it increased pressure on Munich Re by publicly announcing its interest in a merger or sale of the company.[351] Secondly, at the same time, American Re offered Munich Re immediate exclusivity at a higher price than its original non-binding offer. Not only did Munich Re accept

344 The German Federal Cartel office said it was informed in advance and will probably handle the transaction, not the European Union cartel officials (Reuters News, 14 August 1996b).

345 Dow Jones News Service (14 August 1996a).

346 Busines Wire (14 August 1996).

347 On 23 October 1996, the Board of Directors of American Re approved an amended version of the merger agreement, and recommended shareholders to vote for approval and adoption. Major amendments included introduction of the walkaway date 28 February 1997, i.e. termination of the merger if it is not completed by this date, and a reduction of the termination fee from USD 32.5 mn to USD 26.0 mn, which American Re was to pay if it accepts a third party offer commenced after 13 August 1996 and either company fails to obtain shareholder approval (Select Federal Filings Newswires, 24 October 1996).

348 Business Wire (21 November 1996).

349 On 11 November 1996, Munich Re said that it expected the merger to be completed by the end of November, but American Re will not be consolidated into the Group until its 1997/1998 business year (Reuters News, 11 November 1996).

350 Generally, the price for American Re was considered hefty, see discussions in section 5.4.2.2.

351 On the one hand this move signals to existing bidders that none of the non-binding offers is considered adequate, but on the other hand it would also attract additional bidders to contact American Re.

American Re's offer prior to carrying out a thorough independent actuarial appraisal especially of the risky liability lines, but it also abandoned any linkage of results of such an actuarial appraisal in the near future to the terms of the transaction. It is American Re's in-force business in these liability lines which will cause major value and performance issues for Munich Re between 2001 and 2005, see section 5.4.2.3.

5.4.2.2 Structure of the transaction

Munich Re acquired American Re through an equity deal: All assets vested into the merged entity, and all liabilities were to be assumed by the merged entity.[352] The merger itself was structured as a reverse subsidiary merger: Puma Acquisition Corporation, a wholly owned subsidiary of Munich Re, is merged with and into the American Re Corporation on the effective date. Puma Acquisition Corporation's separate corporate existence ceased after the merger.[353] American Re-Insurance Company was maintained as separate legal entity and continued operations from its headquarters in Princeton, New Jersey.[354]

On 23 August 1996, Munich Re acquired an option on 63.9% of common shares of American Re Corporation, i.e. KKR's stake of 30,236,000 shares. The option was structured to terminate if the merger was not approved by American Re's shareholders, if American Re's board withdrew or modified its recommendation of the merger, or American Re breached its representations and warranties under the agreement.[355] Munich Re paid all-cash, thus immediately cutting strings to KKR without affecting its own shareholder structure. All shares issued and outstanding prior to the effective date were cancelled and converted into the right to receive USD 65 in cash per share.[356] Munich Re said that financing of the cash consideration would largely come from internal sources.[357] However, about 2 years later on 31 August 1998, Munich Re announced plans to raise USD

352 Schedule 14A Statement (23 October 1996).
353 Schedule 14A Statement (23 October 1996).
354 Bloomberg Business News (15 August 1996).
355 Select Federal Filings Newswires (23 August 1996).
356 Schedule 14A Statement (23 October 1996).
357 Reuters News (14 August 1996a) quoted a company spokesman on the announcement day that "the financing will be primarily bottom liquid assets. There is a possibility of a small element of external financing".

1.74 bn in capital in order to increase underwriting capacity, and to come in advance of stricter Solvency requirements.[358] Analysts however suppose that the capital increase may have been linked to insufficient free cash flow for full internal deal financing.[359]

Although KKR and the likewise participating senior management of American Re were not to receive a package premium,[360] it certainly was a good deal for them.[361] In September 1992, they invested USD 302 mn in cash, and were to receive back USD 2.1 bn for their remaining 64% stake in the year of the transaction, a sevenfold increase of the initial investment equivalent to an annual return of 63%. Consequently, both groups of shareholders expressed their appreciation of the deal. KKR general partner Saul Fox considered the merger to be "right move at the right time" for both companies, allowing American Re to continue as an industry leader.[362] Paul H. Inderbitzin, then Chairman, President and CEO of American Re commented that he is "delighted to have American Re become part of the Munich Re organization".[363]

But markets considered the price to be hefty for Munich Re,[364] which paid 4.3 times book value of American Re's equity,[365] thus valuing American Re much higher than other targets in the same phase of the M&A market cycle: Employers Re paid only 2.7 times book value for its acquisition of Frankona Re in 1995, and Swiss Re even acquired Société Anonyme Francaise de Reassurances for only 1.6 times its book value in 1997.[366] Stockholders of American Re earned an immediate 11.3% premium over 13 August 1996 closing share price of USD 58.375. The actual premium for Munich Re however is notably larger, as illustrated in Figure 59. Compared to the share price of USD 46.13 on 1 July 1996,

358 Equity stakes in other insurance companies cannot be counted towards solvency available capital anymore (effective 1999).
359 Reactions (31 August 1998).
360 Reuters (14 August 1996).
361 Bloomberg Business News (15 August 1996).
362 Business Wire (14 August 1996).
363 Business Wire (14 August 1996).
364 Dow Jones News Service (14 August 1996a).
365 Based on pre-transaction market-to-book ratios as reported by Thompson Financial Datastream and takeover premiums.
366 However, Swiss Re's paid 4.2 times book value for its acquisition of U.S.-based Life Re in 1998.

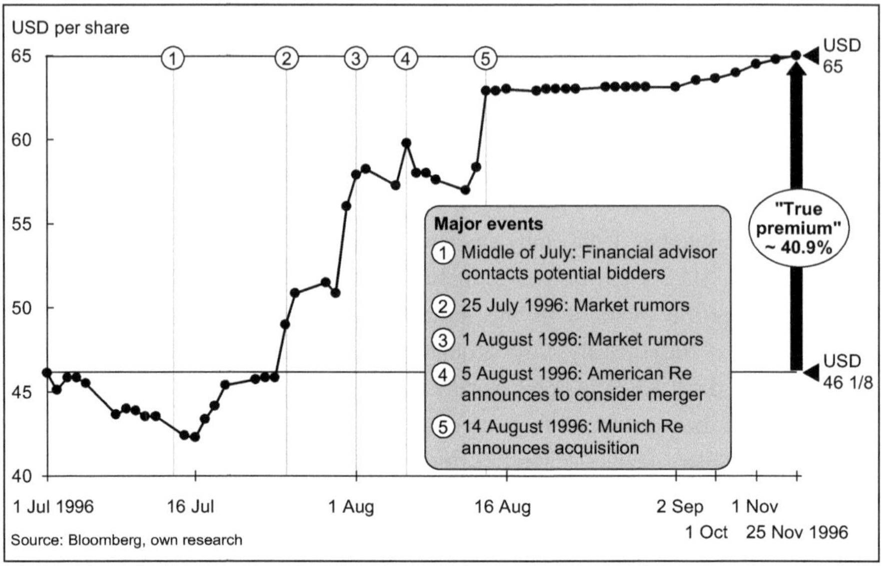

Figure 59: Development of American Re share price (USD)

when first rumors on American Re's involvement in M&A activity started, the "true premium" is 40.9% or USD 892 mn.[367]

5.4.2.3 Post-acquisition integration

The post-merger integration activities can be separated into three phases: Integration of staff, integration and streamlining of the organization, and restructuring of the U.S. business, see Figure 60.

Munich Re initiated integration of staff not until half a year after the announcement of the transaction, although being a major prerequisite for realizing economies of scope: On 5 February 1997, 23 executives, partly from Munich

367 However, since Munich Re's valuation is strongly based on earnings growth, it can easily create the market value equivalent for the "true premium" by slightly increasing its earnings base or growth. At current implied growth rate, Munich Re needs to its increase earnings base, e.g. through synergies, by only USD 16 mn. Alternatively, it could increase growth by 0.1 percentage points, leaving its earnings base unchanged.

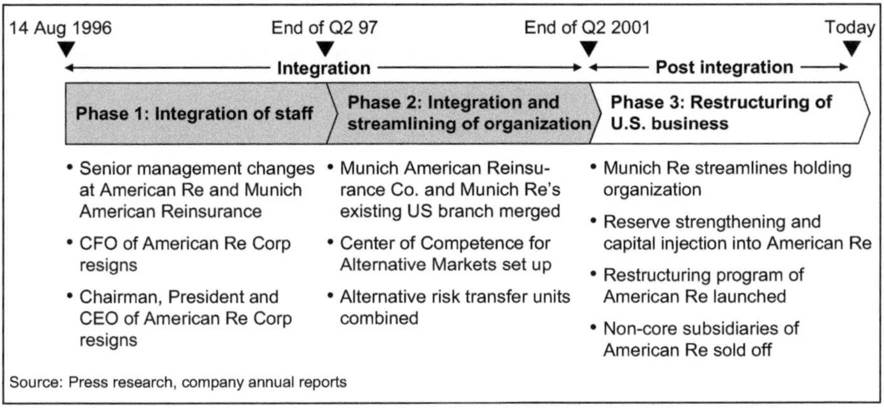

Figure 60: Post-acquisition integration process

American Reinsurance Company, were appointed Senior Vice Presidents of American Re-Insurance Company.[368] However, Munich Re was not able to retain top management of American Re, possibly impairing transaction prospects due to the loss of underwriting capabilities and threat of losing major client accounts: On 28 February 1997, James R. Fisher, CFO of American Re and president of American Re Financial Products, resigned,[369] and Paul H. Inderbitzin, Chairman, President and CEO of American Re Corporation followed his foothold, and resigns to pursue personal business interests on 15 March 1997.[370]

Organizational measures were launched even later, further putting realization of targeted economies of scope through skill transfer at risk. It was not until 7 July 1997 that Munich Re consolidated its U.S. businesses by merging Munich American Reinsurance Co. (MARC) and Munich Re's existing U.S. branch into American Re,[371,372] and that it set up a Center of Competence at American Re to

368 Business Wire (5 February 1997).

369 However, he would remain as a consultant to American Re until January 1999 (Review, 28 February 1997).

370 Edward J. Noonan, President of American Re-Insurance Company's Domestic Insurance Company Operations, succeeds as President, CEO, and Director of the Company. Dr. Hans-Jürgen Schinzler, then CEO of Munich Re, assumes the position of the Chairman (Business Wire, 15 March 1997).

371 Bestwire (7 July 1997).

provide know how for the entire Munich Re Group on alternative markets for risks of large industrial and service companies. More than two years after announcement of the transaction, on 2 November 1998, Munich Re and American Re combined their alternative risk transfer units: Am-Re Managers and some members of Munich Re's Oil and Gas unit were merged to form Munich American RiskPartners with headquarters in Princeton.[373] On 1 July 2001, Munich Re announced to restructure its governance from the top by replacing the historically grown matrix organization with 15 organizational units responsible for lines and products, and 15 organizational units responsible for markets and clients with a simpler organizational structure of seven operative divisions (4 regional, among those North America, and 3 supraregional, among those Special and Financial Risks).[374] On the one hand, this fundamental reorganization may be seen as the final step of the post-merger integration, but on the other hand, it could indicate that serious issues in the U.S. business had already come to Munich Re top managements' attention.

In late 2001, Munich Re's painful spiral of reserve strengthenings for its U.S. liability business initiated the restructuring phase of the post-merger integration process. In less than four years, Munich Re was required to strengthen reserves four times, mainly for its U.S. business.[375] On 15 November 2001, Munich Re spent USD 1.1 bn to strengthen capital base of American Re.[376] On 10 July 2002, Munich Re again boosted American Re reserves by USD 2 bn after reviewing especially liability and workers' compensation lines, and additionally strengthened reserves by USD 495 mn for potential losses from 11 September 2001.[377] On 6 August 2004, Munich Re reported to further push American Re reserves by USD 100 mn in the first half of 2004, and another USD 80 mn in the

372 Through this transaction, Allianz became minority shareholder of American Re when its stockholdings in MARC were converted into stockholdings of American Re after their merger (Bestwire, 7 July 1997). Only on 18 December 1998, Munich Re became full owner of American Re again after an equity stake swap with Allianz (Reuters News, 18 December 1998).

373 Business Wire (2 November 1998).

374 Munich Re (2000, p. 72).

375 National Post (11 July 2002a). Standard & Poor's (2005, p. 10) reported that reserve additions by Munich Re's American Re and Employers Re alone amounted to more than $5 billion in 2002, but that these companies were not the only ones affected.

376 Bestwire (15 November 2001).

377 Munich Re announced a capital increase by USD 1.4 bn subject to regulatory approval whereas financing would come from own resources, see Munich Re (30 September 2002).

second half of 2004.[378] On 19 July 2005, Munich Re announced a so far final reserve strengthening of USD 1.6 bn particularly for liability, workers' compensation, asbestos and environmental claims. Quite surprisingly, this most recent addition to reserves addressed liability and workers' compensation business written after American Re's acquisition between 1997 and mid-2002.[379] Thus, not only did Munich Re pay heavily for its failure to conduct a thorough review of reserves for in-force business written prior to the transaction, but also it did not achieve to gain transparency and to exert control on the underwriting of risky liability lines in the four years thereafter.

Munich Re tried to break the spiral of reserve strengthenings by exchanging management and deepening its ties with American Re. On 10 January 2002, John P. Phelan, then President and Director of Munich Reinsurance Company of Canada, succeeded Ed Noonan as President and CEO of American Re Corporation.[380] Three months later, Mr. Phelan was additionally appointed to the Board of Management of Munich Re.[381] On 27 May 2002, Mr. Schinzler said that American Re had been successful in "doing all [it] can to write reinsurance business at significantly improved prices and conditions." Subsequently, American Re was to focus on profitable business in the U.S. market,[382] leading to several sell offs of non-core and non-U.S. subsidiaries, and stricter underwriting.[383]

Although Munich Re took these corrective organizational measures relatively promptly, its communication to investors was not convincing. Until mid 2005,

378 This estimate proved too conservative: Eventually, American Re's reserves were increased by USD 195.4 mn in 2004 (Dow Jones International News, 6 August 2004; Munich Re, 8 November 2004).

379 Additionally, Munich Re planned to inject capital of USD 1.1 bn from existing resources, and to convert USD 1.6 bn of existing internal group financing into equity (Munich Re, 19 July 2005a).

380 Munich Re (10 January 2002).

381 Munich Re (10 July 2002).

382 Munich Re (27 May 2002).

383 On 20 October 2003, American Re announced the sale of Becher + Carlson Risk Management, a retail broker, risk management consultant and captive manager for large organizations and groups (Business Wire, 20 October 2003). The transaction closed on 17 November 2003 (Business Wire, 17 November 2003). On 3 November 2003, American Re reported to sell ARB International Ltd, its Lloyd's brokering house with headquarters in London. On 26 February 2004, American Re divested its 50% stake in its UK-based joint venture Risk Management Partners Ltd., which offered innovative insurance and risk management products to public companies in the UK (PR Newswire, 26 February 2004).

top management of American Re or Munich Re confirmed the healthy constitution of American Re's book of business and successful implementation of appropriate counter measures after each single strengthening of reserves.[384] Consequently, after the second such incidence, rating agencies doubted Munich Re's announcements in this respect. Standard & Poor's considered to lower Munich Re's AAA rating, reflecting "heightened concerns about American Re's earnings and capital adequacy".[385] Also A.M. Best anticipated further issues, reviewed Munich Re's rating, and posted a negative outlook without ruling out a downgrade.[386] Munich Re assumed a more concise communication only in 2005. On 15 February 2005, a Munich Re spokesman did not rule out the necessity to further strengthen reserves of American Re particularly due to asbestos claims,[387] and on 9 May 2005, Jörg Schneider, member of the Munich Re Board of Management, says that uncertainties regarding risks involved in calculating reserves for prior-year losses, particularly in the area of liability business, remain.[388] Further on, Munich Re failed to communicate the negligibility of reserve strengthenings compared to its total premium volume: The invested USD 5.4 bn between 2001 and 2005 increased the loss ratio by merely 2.6 percentage points in the average per anno. Given the doubtful communication and explicit concerns expressed by rating agencies, capital markets reacted with a strong devaluation of Munich Re, as discussed in the next section.

---

384 E.g., in July 2002, Mr. Phelan, CEO of American Re at that time, confirmed that realignment of American Re with respect to senior management, organization, cost reduction and target markets was then concluded. Munich Re's CEO, Mr. Schinzler, expected that American Re produced profits immediately. Mr. Schneider, another member of Munich Re's Board of Management, said he expected no extra capital injections into the ailing U.S. business in the foreseeable future (Reuters News, 10 July 2002; Munich Re, 10 July 2002; National Post, 11 July 2002a). Further on, in April 2003, Munich Re said that regular reserve reviews confirmed adequacy of reserves, e.g. for asbestos and environmental lines (Munich Re, April 2003).

385 National Post (11 July 2002b).

386 Süddeutsche Zeitung (14 July 2005).

387 Dow Jones-VWD Unternehmen Deutschland (15 February 2005).

388 Munich Re (9 May 2005).

5.4.3 Value creation by the transaction

5.4.3.1 Capital market reactions

Initial analyst reactions to the acquisition announcement were only partially positive. One analyst said that Munich Re needed American Re due to their underwriting expertise, as European contracts will become more similar to American contracts.[389] Another analyst acknowledged that "The purchase has filled one large hole in Munich Re's worldwide network."[390] A third analyst asked rhetorically: "Does this mean the "M" factor will now be replaced with the "S" factor?",[391] where "M" refers to Swiss Re's aggressive Chairman Mr. Mühlemann, and "S" to the Munich Re's less dominant Chairman Mr. Schinzler. However, most analysts were rather critical. The Economist (17 August 1996) comments that "Global reinsurance takes capital and expertise to where it is most needed. And it is clearly not needed in the United States". Another analysts is quoted saying that "The two companies have a difference of mind-set and culture and write very dissimilar books of business. [..] It won't be easy to merge that overnight."[392] Some other analysts downgrade Munich Re shares to "sell" due to fear that deal may be financed through rights issue, diluting the value of Munich Re shares.[393]

Capital markets reacted quite positively shortly before the acquisition announcement, but in accordance with analysts' comments rather cautiously shortly after the announcement, as depicted in Figure 61. After market rumors that American Re may be interested in acquiring National Re on 1 July 1996,[394] American Re's share price declined by 8% until 16 July 1996.[395] From this date onwards, coinciding with American Re's financial advisors beginning to solicit potential bidders, American Re's share price and share price volatility almost

389 Dow Jones News Service (14 August 1996a).
390 Dow Jones News Service (14 August 1996a).
391 Reactions (31 October 1996).
392 National Underwriter Property & Casualty-Risk & Benefits Management Edition (19 August 1996).
393 Dow Jones News Service (14 August 1996b).
394 Dow Jones International News (1 July 1996).
395 Negative (abnormal) short-term returns are typical for acquirers, see section 4.3.2 and 4.5.1.

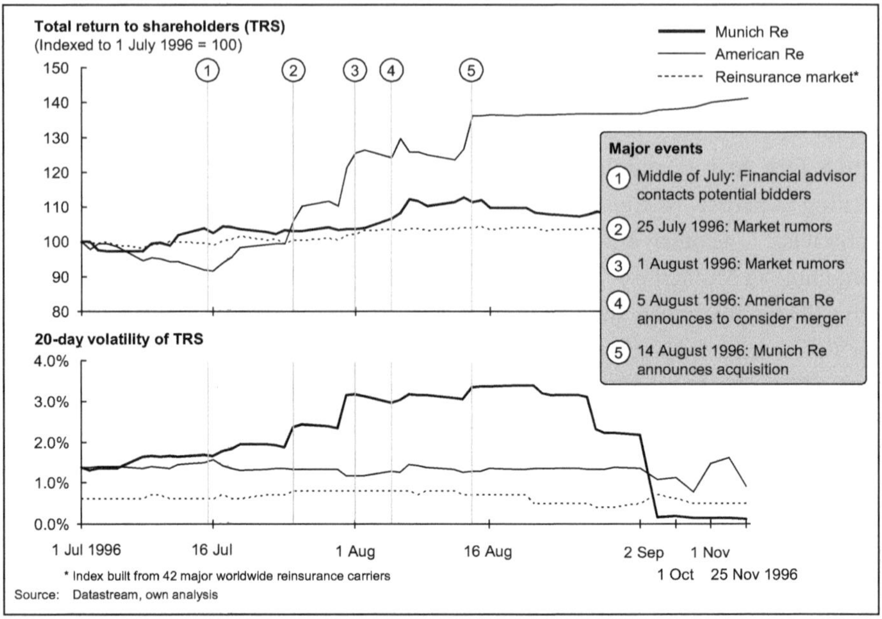

Figure 61: Short-term capital market reactions to events in transaction process

steadily increased. Munich Re's share price rose as well, although the company came into play as potential bidder for National Re on 1 July 1996 and American Re on 25 July 1996. After the announcement of the acquisition on 14 August 1996, the share price of American Re increased slowly from USD 63.88 to the takeover price of USD 65.00 at closing on 25 November 1996, indicating that investors did not expect termination of the acquisition. Munich Re's share price firstly declined from USD 84.99 to USD 79.74 after announcement, but started to pick up on 3 September, and again after a short setback on 22 September 1996 (two days before the Board of Directors of American Re approved the amendment to the merger agreement) to finally reach USD 88.54 on at closing. In the long run, Munich Re's TRS continued to develop positively compared to the reinsurance market, until the spiral of reserve strengthenings started in November 2001: Whilst the reinsurance market recovered after bearish times between 2001 and 2003, Munich Re's TRS stagnated, see Figure 62. Investors punished

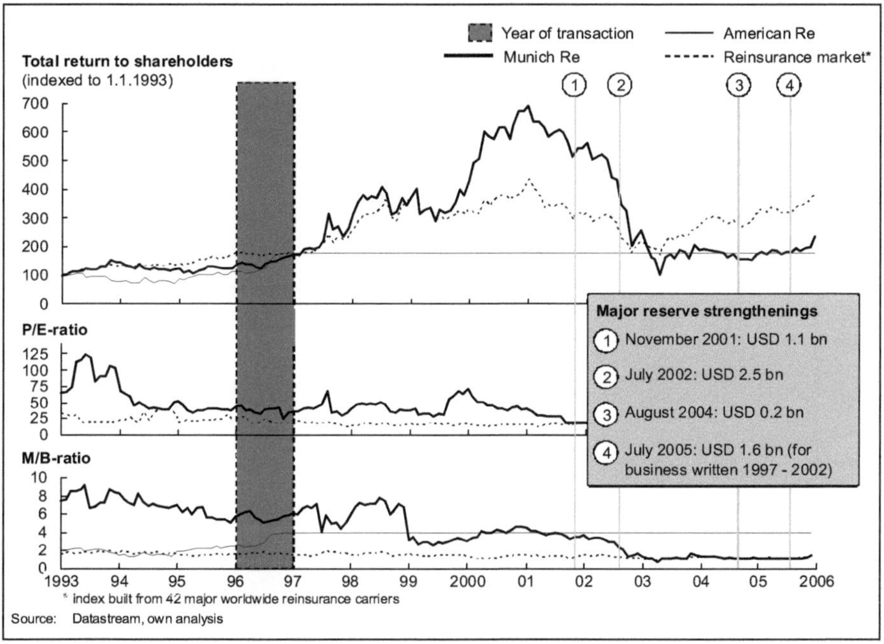

Figure 62: Long-term capital market reaction to acquisition announcement

Munich Re strongly for its reserving issues. In the time period between announcement of the first and so far last boosting of reserves, Munich Re market capitalization shrank by USD 43.8 bn, while total reserve strengthenings amounted only to USD 5.4 bn. Clearly, investors lost confidence in Munich Re's growth prospects, as implied by the steadily declining P/E ratio after 2000, dropping below market average in September 2002 and remaining there since then.

5.4.3.2 Event study results

In chapter 4, short- and long-term value creation is analyzed for European Insurance M&A transactions between 1990 and 2005. Figure 63 presents the results for Munich Re's acquisition of American Re. Investors' appreciated the announced transaction in the short-term: The combined entity achieved an abnormal return of 6.4% in the event window [–20; +20] days around announcement

Short-term*		Long-term	
Value generation	USD 77 mn	Value generation	USD -20.8 bn
CER	6.4%	BAHR 1 year	-153.8%
CAR acquirer	2.1%	BAHR 2 years	23.3%
CAR target	38.9%	BAHR 3 years	-179.6%

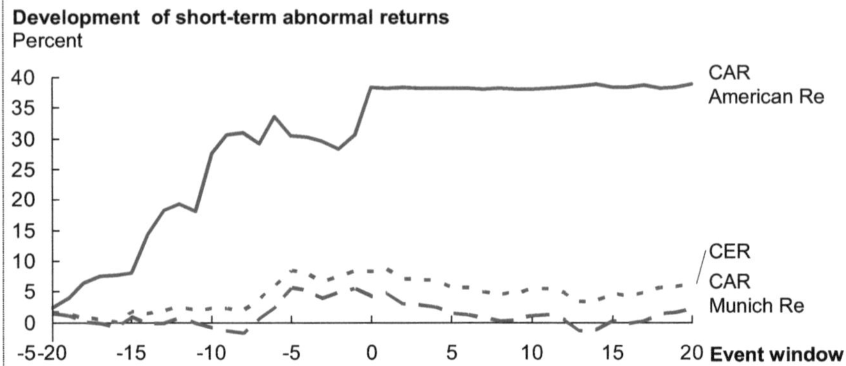

* Event window [-20; +20] trading days

Source: Own research

Figure 63: Event study results for Munich Re's acquisition of American Re

(corresponding to the 68% quantile of CERs of all transactions), and even Munich Re's CAR turned out positive. The development of short-term abnormal returns support the hypothesis of early information leakage to the market. Medium-term abnormal returns show that investors were uncertain about the value added by the transaction as the BAHR was strongly negative with –153.8% one year after announcement, but turned positive in the course of the following year. However, long-term abnormal returns turned out disastrous. The acquisition destroyed value of USD –20.8 bn, with a 3-year BAHR of –179.6%.[396] Thus, Munich Re did not achieve the overarching objective to generate value from the transaction as measured by BAHRs.

396 This is the 3rd worst BAHR of all transactions examined in the long-term event study in chapter 4.4.

5.4.3.3 Impact on financial performance

In the 10 years after the transaction, Munich Re roughly doubled its size in terms of premiums, reserves and assets, and even increased its earnings nine fold. In this respect, the prognosis of Mr. Schinzler, Chairman of Munich Re at the time of the transaction, that "the transaction is also expected to have a positive effect on the Munich Re's future earnings per share"[397] came true. Overall, Munich Re improved its comparative profitability but remained below market level. The average return on reserve differential went down from –70 bp (1991-1995) to –77 bp (2002-2006), but improved adjusted for the troubled U.S. portfolio to about 32 bp (2002-2006). The average return on premium differential increased from –1.8 percentage points to –0.7 percentage points, and even +1.3 percentage points adjusted for U.S. reserve strengthenings in the respective time periods. However, Mr. Schinzler's expectation that synergies would be visible in 1998 group profits, did not materialize: The average loss ratio differential to the market median increased from 21.8% (1991-1996) to 24.8% (1996-2001). Only thereafter, it improved to 16.1% (2002-2006), still remaining notably above the market median.[398] At the same time, Munich Re extended its market share in the U.S. and globally, see Figure 64. Thus, e*conomies of scope* through underwriting skill transfer in traditional reinsurance cannot be rejected, but the effect became visibly only late after the transaction.

However, Munich Re and American Re lost underwriting efficiency compared to the market: Munich Re's expense ratio differential went up from 3.2% in (1991-1995) to 8.0% in (2002-2006). American Re's expense ratio differential increased from 5.7% (1991-1995) to 12.2% in (1997-2000[399]). Nevertheless, both companies gained investment efficiency and effectiveness. Munich Re's investment yield differential went up from –0.1% (1991-1995) to 0.5% (2002-

397 Munich Re (14 August 1996).

398 The effect of American Re's troubled liability business on Munich Re's performance is negligible. American Re's loss ratio worsened by more than 10 percentage points compared to the market median between 1999 and 2000 (see Table 75 in the appendix), but successive reserve strengthenings by Munich Re hit the groups' loss ratio "only" by 2.6 percentage points in the average per anno (USD 5.4 bn against aggregated group premiums of USD 206.1 bn between 2001 to 2005).

399 More recent data for American Re not available.

Table 49: Financial performance of Munich Re before and after acquisition of American Re

MUNICH RE	Unit	1991	1992	1993	1994	1995	1996	1997	1998	1999	2000	2001	2002	2003	2004	2005	2006
Size																	
Earnings	USD mn	103.9	104.6	110.3	177.5	346.7	386.2	506.8	523.0	1,135.7	1,643.1	222.6	302.2	-547.4	2,491.5	3,150.6	4,536.2
Premiums	USD bn	8.9	13.7	14.4	16.7	18.2	18.8	22.5	27.4	25.0	26.4	28.2	38.1	47.4	49.7	42.7	47.1
Reserves	USD bn	23.0	52.8	54.5	64.6	75.0	88.0	105.6	116.3	132.8	132.5	133.5	160.0	194.9	217.4	189.4	208.9
Assets	USD bn	27.6	60.7	62.8	75.7	88.2	105.5	126.4	140.6	180.3	181.7	179.9	206.1	264.1	292.0	257.9	284.7
Shareholders' Equity	USD bn	1.8	2.2	2.5	2.9	3.7	4.3	5.5	7.3	20.6	24.4	18.1	15.2	24.4	28.2	29.1	34.9
Solvency																	
Equity ratio	%	6.7%	3.7%	3.9%	3.8%	4.2%	4.1%	4.4%	5.2%	11.4%	13.4%	10.1%	7.4%	9.3%	9.7%	11.3%	12.2%
Equity reserves ratio	%	8.0%	4.2%	4.5%	4.4%	5.0%	4.9%	5.2%	6.3%	15.5%	18.4%	13.6%	9.5%	12.5%	13.0%	15.4%	16.7%
Operating leverage	times x	4.9	6.1	5.8	5.8	4.9	4.4	4.1	3.8	1.2	1.1	1.6	2.5	1.9	1.8	1.5	1.4
Reserves leverage	times x	96.6	151.3	142.6	138.0	95.0	111.7	86.2	73.6	77.9	57.1	-232.5	348.2	116.6	61.4	42.8	30.6
Reserves ratio	times x	2.6	3.8	3.8	3.9	4.1	4.7	4.7	4.2	5.3	5.0	4.7	4.2	4.1	4.4	4.4	4.4
Profitability																	
Return on reserves	bp	103.6	66.1	70.1	72.4	105.2	89.5	116.0	136.0	128.4	175.0	-43.0	28.7	85.7	162.8	233.7	327.2
Return on equity	%	13.0%	15.6%	15.5%	16.3%	21.1%	18.4%	22.1%	21.6%	8.3%	9.5%	-3.2%	3.0%	6.8%	12.6%	15.2%	19.6%
Return on premiums	%	2.7%	2.5%	2.7%	2.8%	4.3%	4.2%	5.4%	5.8%	6.8%	8.8%	-2.0%	1.2%	3.5%	7.1%	10.4%	14.5%
Combined ratio	%	118.7%	128.1%	123.8%	119.8%	116.9%	115.7%	116.9%	116.7%	127.2%	131.9%	132.3%	110.3%	110.3%	110.8%	117.3%	107.8%
Loss ratio	%	86.6%	99.5%	96.2%	93.1%	91.3%	89.9%	90.4%	91.0%	101.2%	105.8%	107.8%	85.7%	86.4%	86.6%	92.1%	83.1%
Expense ratio	%	32.1%	28.6%	27.6%	26.7%	25.6%	25.8%	26.5%	25.7%	26.1%	26.1%	24.5%	24.6%	23.9%	24.2%	25.2%	24.7%
Net investment result ratio	%	20.3%	27.8%	25.0%	24.2%	30.2%	32.4%	32.7%	32.9%	38.2%	43.3%	32.9%	15.4%	19.0%	22.0%	29.9%	24.9%
Net investment yield	%	6.6%	6.3%	5.7%	5.3%	6.3%	5.8%	5.8%	6.4%	5.3%	6.3%	5.2%	2.9%	3.4%	3.7%	4.9%	4.1%
Growth																	
Growth of earnings	%	73.4%	0.6%	5.4%	61.0%	95.3%	11.4%	31.2%	3.2%	117.2%	44.7%	-86.5%	35.8%	-281.1%	-555.1%	26.5%	44.0%
Growth of premiums	%	7.8%	53.9%	4.8%	15.9%	9.6%	3.1%	19.7%	21.9%	-8.9%	5.6%	6.8%	35.1%	24.5%	4.7%	-14.0%	10.3%
Growth of reserves	%	7.9%	129.3%	3.2%	18.7%	16.0%	17.4%	20.0%	10.1%	14.2%	-0.2%	0.8%	19.8%	21.8%	11.5%	-12.9%	10.3%
Growth of assets	%	7.0%	120.3%	3.5%	20.5%	16.5%	19.6%	19.8%	11.3%	28.2%	0.8%	-1.0%	14.6%	28.1%	10.5%	-11.7%	10.4%
Growth of equity	%	5.1%	21.9%	9.8%	16.6%	30.5%	14.8%	29.1%	32.0%	182.1%	18.1%	-25.7%	-16.1%	60.9%	15.3%	3.2%	19.8%

Table 50: Market adjusted financial performance of Munich Re before and after acquisition of American Re

MUNICH RE (market adj.)	Unit	1991	1992	1993	1994	1995	1996	1997	1998	1999	2000	2001	2002	2003	2004	2005	2006
Size																	
Earnings	x times market	1.2	1.7	1.9	2.7	6.3	7.0	9.2	14.0	26.4	28.3	-9.0	26.4	-6.2	23.5	56.9	11.0
Premiums	x times market	3.5	6.6	5.0	5.5	6.3	10.2	20.4	27.2	15.8	12.5	10.8	12.8	16.2	18.0	16.1	11.8
Reserves	x times market	3.8	6.8	6.2	6.3	9.8	21.3	31.6	32.9	25.0	20.7	16.0	20.1	26.4	30.8	20.6	16.2
Assets	x times market	3.2	5.8	5.1	5.9	9.6	18.1	25.5	28.2	25.3	19.2	16.5	19.4	26.0	26.5	19.7	20.5
Shareholders' Equity	x times market	1.8	1.9	1.8	2.0	4.4	5.0	8.7	12.1	25.1	20.5	13.7	14.2	23.1	22.3	18.6	9.1
Solvency																	
Equity ratio	Δ%pts to market	-2.7%	-5.9%	-6.2%	-6.5%	-6.3%	-8.6%	-13.4%	-11.3%	-3.2%	-3.8%	-3.5%	-7.1%	-7.5%	-7.6%	-6.1%	-5.8%
Equity reserves ratio	Δ%pts to market	-3.5%	-6.6%	-7.5%	-7.7%	-8.0%	-11.0%	-22.5%	-18.7%	-5.3%	-8.5%	-4.0%	-10.0%	-11.9%	-11.9%	-11.3%	-8.3%
Operating leverage	Δtimes x to mark	2.0	3.9	3.4	3.6	2.6	2.2	2.5	2.2	-0.4	-0.1	0.1	0.5	0.4	0.0	0.1	0.3
Reserves leverage	Δtimes x to mark	32.1	70.3	71.5	75.3	45.2	59.3	58.7	31.3	31.9	0.0	-221.6	315.7	94.0	39.8	6.6	10.2
Reserves ratio	Δtimes x to mark	-0.3	0.4	0.6	0.7	1.2	1.9	2.1	1.2	1.8	2.0	1.3	1.3	1.3	1.6	1.2	0.4
Profitability																	
Return on reserves	Δbp to market	-50.7	-57.1	-67.7	-86.9	-85.2	-101.6	-168.8	-71.1	-67.7	2.6	12.7	-76.6	-214.0	-108.1	65.8	-50.2
Return on equity	Δ%pts to market	-1.1%	4.5%	2.5%	2.8%	5.9%	4.9%	6.4%	9.8%	-0.7%	0.1%	0.0%	-2.7%	-5.2%	0.0%	6.8%	0.0%
Return on premiums	Δ%pts to market	-1.7%	-1.7%	-1.7%	-2.1%	-1.8%	-2.0%	-4.8%	-0.8%	1.7%	3.6%	0.2%	-1.5%	-3.8%	0.0%	5.0%	-3.1%
Combined ratio	Δ%pts to market	13.0%	27.5%	28.8%	30.5%	25.4%	19.5%	27.6%	27.1%	35.4%	39.6%	29.0%	20.0%	24.0%	23.2%	27.2%	28.6%
Loss ratio	Δ%pts to market	8.3%	25.5%	26.2%	27.0%	22.2%	17.4%	22.8%	21.0%	27.9%	32.7%	19.3%	12.0%	18.1%	16.2%	17.6%	16.6%
Expense ratio	Δ%pts to market	4.7%	2.0%	2.6%	3.6%	3.2%	2.1%	4.8%	6.1%	7.5%	6.9%	9.6%	8.0%	5.9%	7.0%	9.6%	12.0%
Net investment result ratio	Δ%pts to market	-1.2%	2.6%	0.0%	1.4%	8.7%	9.0%	11.2%	12.3%	23.0%	22.3%	19.6%	-4.6%	-3.3%	0.5%	18.6%	12.4%
Net investment yield	Δ%pts to market	-0.1%	0.5%	-0.6%	-0.3%	0.2%	-0.4%	0.5%	2.0%	3.2%	3.9%	3.0%	-0.8%	-0.3%	-0.9%	2.6%	1.8%
Growth																	
Growth of earnings	Δ%pts to market	n/a*	30.9%	9.7%	50.5%	111.4%	10.8%	32.2%	35.0%	102.1%	9.6%	56.4%	181.8%	-950.2%	-575.7%	74.3%	-601.2%
Growth of premiums	Δ%pts to market	106.8%	48.9%	-30.3%	8.7%	6.7%	-1.4%	9.6%	18.6%	-29.9%	-8.9%	-11.0%	26.2%	27.5%	4.3%	-14.2%	9.3%
Growth of reserves	Δ%pts to market	3.0%	106.7%	-16.2%	11.4%	12.4%	11.9%	4.1%	0.6%	-16.4%	-7.5%	-17.3%	18.1%	21.1%	6.9%	-31.0%	9.6%
Growth of assets	Δ%pts to market	2.5%	98.6%	-15.1%	12.4%	16.6%	10.2%	0.2%	0.7%	-1.6%	-7.1%	-23.9%	15.5%	24.5%	3.3%	-29.5%	9.5%
Growth of equity	Δ%pts to market	n/a*	9.9%	-5.5%	9.1%	71.1%	15.2%	54.5%	37.3%	146.0%	-26.5%	-36.5%	2.7%	61.8%	-4.2%	-20.1%	-124.7%

* Market figures not available for 1990.

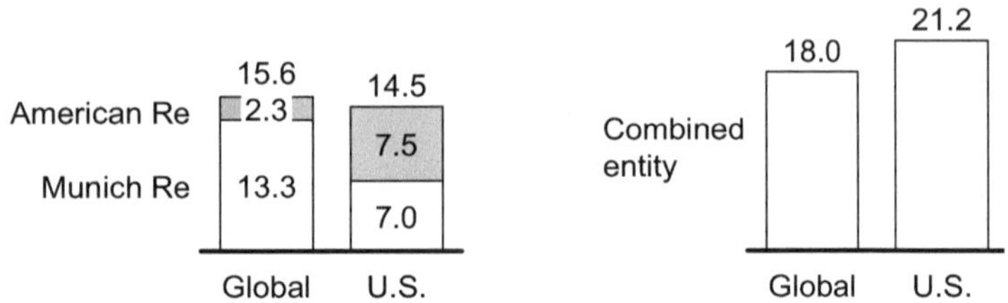

	1996 Global	1996 U.S.		2004 Global	2004 U.S.
Total net written premiums USD billion	**81.6**	**21.6**		**166.9**	**30.1**
• American Re	1.9	1.5		n/a	n/a
• Munich Re	10.9	1.4		n/a	n/a
• **Total**	**12.8**	**2.8**		**30.0**	**6.4**

4 major global competitors			
• Swiss Re	10.0 (12.3%)	• Swiss Re	25.8 (15.5%)
• General Re	6.7 (8.2%)	• Berkshire Hathaway	6.7 (4.0%)
• Employers Re	5.9 (7.2%)	• Hannover Re	5.9 (3.5%)
• Lloyd's	4.1 (5.0%)	• GE Insurance Solutions	4.1 (2.5%)

Source: S&P Global Reinsurance Highlights (1996), Reinsurance Association of America's "Reinsurance Underwriting Review: 2004 Industry Results, company annual reports

Figure 64: Development of market share (percent of total net reinsurance premiums written)

2006), while American Re's differential improved from –6.0% (1991-1995) to –3.8% (1997-2000).[400]

With respect to *growth*, Munich Re achieved its major objective to extend its market share in the U.S., but also globally. Figure 64 illustrates, that the combined U.S. market share of Munich Re and American Re increased from 14.5% to 21.2% between 1996 and 2004 due to an annual premium growth rate of 4.2%.[401] In the same time period, their global market share increased by 2.4 percentage points. In addition, Munich Re may have achieved to increase its *market power* and realize *revenue economies of scale*, since its loss ratio differential

400 Not adjusted for possible change of riskiness of asset allocation.

401 Estimates based on Reinsurance Association of America (2004), Munich Re (1996/97, 2004), and Standard & Poor's (1996, 1997).

improved marginally by 1.2 percentage points in the same time period. The realization of economies of scope from transfer of American Re's expertise in financial reinsurance and alternative market to the European market cannot be assessed since a split of results into both types of reinsurance contracts is not publicly reported.

Munich Re has not strengthened its *available capital base* compared to the market. Although its average equity reserves ratio increased from 12% (1991-1995) to 24% (2002-2006), lack of profitability lead to a decrease of the market differential from –7% to –11%.[402] Only in terms of operating leverage, Munich Re achieved to improve compared to the market, from average differential 3.1 down to 0.3.[403] Rating agencies assessment of Munich Re's solvency confirm these results. After initially careful, but positive reactions to the acquisition of American Re,[404] all rating agencies lowered Munich Re's and American Re's ratings shortly after the second round of reserve strengthenings became public mid of 2002, see Figure 65.[405]

402 It should be noted, that these measures are not risk adjusted, i.e. Munich Re might have carried less risk than the market median even before the acquisition of American Re, and may further reduce riskiness through geographical or product diversification, thus requiring less capital.

403 The finding does not change when estimating the effect of U.S. reserve strengthenings.

404 A.M. Best said it views the acquisition as a long-term positive business development for both organizations because it combines a leading U.S. market direct reinsurer with a global reinsurer. Still, it puts the rating of both companies and affected subsidiaries under review (Bestwire, 14 August 1996). Standard & Poor's argues that American Re would benefit via balance sheet strengthening because it carries less debt, and extends to global market with non-life facultative, finite risk, and alternative risk reinsurance. (Lloyd's List International, 17 August 1996), nonetheless it puts Munich Re on credit watch due to the "significant price, expected high level of goodwill and uncertainty regarding the complete financing arrangements of the transaction, and how it will affect the Munich Re balance sheet" (Post Magazine, 22 August 1996).

405 A.M. Best, Moody's and Fitch rating classes are mapped to Standard & Poor's rating classes in order to make them comparable, see mapping Table 76 in the appendix.

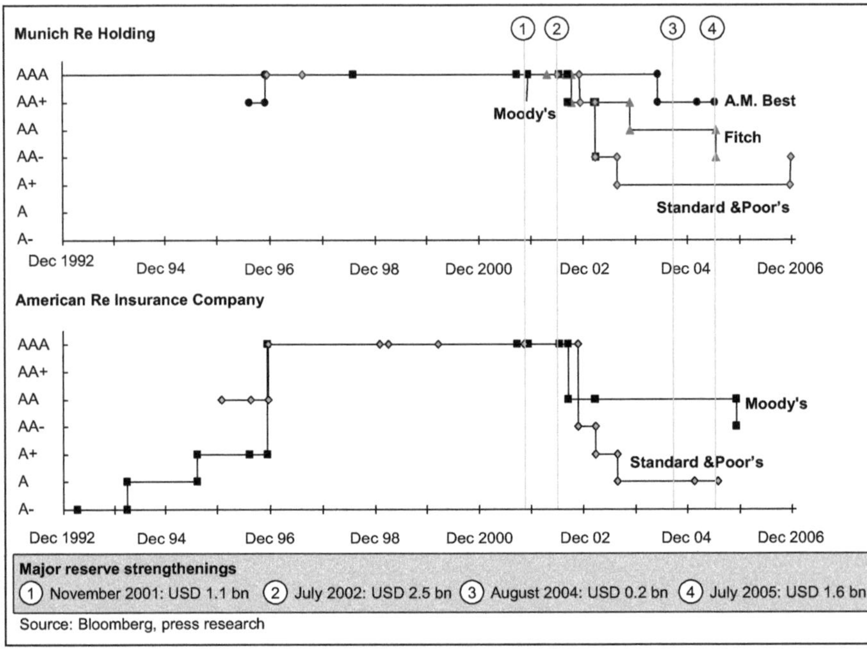

Figure 65: Development of Munich Re and American Re ratings

5.4.4 Conclusion

This section examines the case of Munich Re's acquisition of American Re in August 1996. This particular transaction is chosen for three reasons. It represented the largest reinsurance transaction of a European acquirer between 1990 and 2005, it marked the starting point for European involvement in the transatlantic reinsurance consolidation wave beginning in 1995, and it badly disappointed investors' initially high expectations with respect to value creation.

Motivation, conduct and value creation

In 1996, M&A momentum was picking up in a stagnating and less profitable global reinsurance market. Munich Re, a public company with a long-standing history and a focus on European traditional reinsurance contracts, was at that time still the world's largest reinsurance provider by premiums. Munich Re faced a severe issue: Although its valuation was strongly based on earnings growth expectations, its market share was declining for several consecutive years. Munich Re came to the conclusion that reviving growth and profitability must build on inorganic growth given the increasing market consolidation and resulting competition. American Re, a private equity firm-owned company with focus on the North American market and strong footprint in nontraditional reinsurance, was the 11th largest reinsurer in the world and 3rd largest in the U.S. market. On 14 August 1996, Munich Re announced to acquire American Re for USD 3.3 bn at 11% premium to previous day's closing. Munich Re hoped to create value primarily by fostering growth particularly in the U.S. traditional and European nontraditional reinsurance markets, by improving especially its underwriting profitability, through skill transfer and strengthening of its solvency position.

Munich Re negotiated the acquisition in a four-week controlled auction process, but obtained exclusivity already after two weeks for agreeing to pay USD 65 per share. However, it failed to carry out an actuarial appraisal especially of risky liability lines or to link the outcome of such an actuarial appraisal to the terms of the transaction. Further on, the price was considered hefty by markets, as it valued American Re at 4.3 times its book value and thus notably higher than transactions in the same phase of the M&A market cycle (between 1.6 and 2.7 times book value of the target). The all-cash equity acquisition was structured as a reverse triangular merger, thus maintaining the separate existence of American Re Corporation as a subsidiary of Munich Re.

The post-acquisition process can be separated into three phases. Integration of staff was initiated not until half a year after announcement of the transaction, and Munich Re failed to retain part of American Re's top management. Integration of the organizations (e.g., merging U.S. branches, setting up underwriting competence centers) was only implemented one year after announcement. Restructuring of the U.S. business became necessary after reserve issues of U.S. liability business, partly written after the acquisition between 1997 and mid-2002, required total reserve strengthenings of USD 5.4 bn (equivalent to 2.6 percentage points of loss ratio). Although Munich Re implemented organizational counter measures quickly, it failed to gain transparency and control on these business lines and did not communicate the extent and impact of the reserving issues concisely to investors. Capital markets reacted swiftly, leading to a downward spiral for Munich Re's market valuation. The event study results confirm: The transaction yielded a CER of 6.4% in the event window [–20; +20] days around announcement, but a BAHR of –179.6% over three years.

Realization of merger benefits

Value: Munich Re's market value developed worse than the reinsurance market beginning with the reserve strengthenings in late 2001. The event study results indicate that value was even destroyed over a 3-year horizon after announcement (BAHR of –179.6% over 3-year horizon, equivalent to USD –21 bn); only short-term results are positive (CER of 6.4% in [–20; +20], equivalent to USD 77 mn). Considering that the acquisition took place during the peak of the reinsurance M&A cycle, in particular with respect to the U.S. market, existence of a "bandwagon effect" cannot be rejected.

Profitability: The improvement in underwriting effectiveness from loss ratio of 21.8 percentage points (1991-1996) to 16.1 percentage points (2002-2006) above market while extending its market share may not be attributable to economies of scope through underwriting skill transfer from American Re to Munich Re due to its time-lagged occurrence after the acquisition. Economies of scope through skill transfer from Munich Re to American Re did not realize with respect to underwriting efficiency (expense ratio increased from 3.2% (1991-1995) to 8.0% (2002-2006) above market), but may have realized[406] with respect to investment efficiency and effectiveness (investment yield went up from –0.1% (1991-1995) to 0.5% (2002-2006) above market).

Growth: Munich Re achieved to revive organic growth by extending its U.S. market share from 14.5% to 21.2%, and its global market share from 15.6% to 18.0% of net written premiums between 1996 and 2004. However, it is difficult to assess whether Munich Re actually increased its market power and realized revenue economies of scale, since its loss ratio differential improved only marginally by 1.2 percentage points in the same time period. The realization of

406 Investment yield measures not adjusted for riskiness of asset allocation.

economies of scope from transfer of American Re's expertise in financial reinsurance and alternative market to the European market cannot be assessed based on public information.

Solvency: Munich Re did not improve its capitalization: Its equity reserves ratio increased from –7% (1991-1995) to –11% (2002-2006) below market, and rating agencies lowered ratings after the second round of reserve strengthenings. The potential benefit of risk reduction cannot be assessed based on public information.

Identification of process-related determinants of value creation

In the pre-acquisition process, Munich Re acted hasty. Although being relatively inexperienced in reinsuring asbestos and environmental risks, and despite widespread awareness of reserve issues in these lines in the U.S. market, Munich Re pushed for exclusivity early in the transaction process, and before actuarial appraisal of American Re's book.

This phenomenon of increasing desire to rapidly complete (or terminate) a transaction is known as *escalating momentum*[407]. Pablo et al. (1996) argue that once the acquirer chose the desired target (objective is to "avoid risk"), it thereafter focuses merely on achieving the best possible outcome (objective is to "manage risk").[408] In this case, Munich Re locked into its target early after being contacted by the financial advisors, and afterwards focused on reducing the risk of entering a bidding contest or entirely losing the target. Closely related is the notion of *ambiguous expectations* of acquirer management with respect to the outcome of a transaction, resulting in deferral of difficult issues to the post-acquisition phase.[409] In this case, proper appraisal of American Re's long-tailed businesses certainly would have imposed process and content issues.

Both drivers for fast closing are rather typical for risk-seeking decision makers, in that they perceive risk as opportunity,[410] whereas Munich Re top

407 See e.g., Jemison and Sitkin (1986).
408 Pablo et al. (1996) acknowledge supporting and contradicting empirical evidence for this hypothesis.
409 See e.g., Jemison and Sitkin (1986).
410 March and Shapira (1987).

management was considered rather conservative by the time of the transaction.[411] Even given Munich Re's priority of quick agreement, it could have either carried out a focused actuarial appraisal of the most risky (and publicly discussed) business lines, or it may have incorporated the right of termination into the merger agreement, in case issues significantly affecting American Re's valuation emerge. In harsh contrast, it seems that Munich Re not even sought transparency on American Re's book of business until 2003, since doubtful underwriting practices continued until mid-2002.

During the post-acquisition process, Munich Re failed to better control underwriting of risky liability lines between 1997 and mid-2002, and to properly communicate negligibility of related issues to external stakeholders.[412] Five reasons may explain the first shortcoming. Firstly, *different management styles* may result in M&A outcome to fall short of expectations.[413] This effect may occur in this case, given the conservative history of Munich Re and the more risk-affine, private equity-dominated governance of American Re. Secondly, Munich Re may not have carried out the postponed actuarial appraisal even after signing of the merger agreement or closing of the deal. Thirdly, *differences of reward schemes* may make M&A less successful, especially if they differ in terms of leverage and bonus.[414] Munich Re may have just not aligned American Re's incentive scheme with targeted acquisition benefits. Fourthly, *ineffective imposition of reward schemes* on the target may impair M&A performance.[415] Even if Munich Re aligned American Re's incentive scheme, management may still not have acted accordingly. Finally, Munich Re may have exercised too little control on American Re's operations.[416]

---

411 Reactions (31 October 1996).

412 It is not questioned whether or not Munich Re should have warned investors at all. Firstly, avoiding a timely publication would cast future doubt on Munich Re's credibility, negatively impacting its valuation, see further below. Secondly, Tucker (2007) finds that openness of firms with respect to warning on earnings shortfalls is not penalized by investors.

413 Buono and Bowditch (1985).

414 See Diven (1984) and Hayes (1979). However, Datta (1991) did not find respective empirical evidence based on 173 transactions in the U.S. manufacturing industry.

415 Jemison and Sitkin (1986).

416 The fact that American Re is notably smaller than Munich Re in terms of premiums (9% of group net premiums written in 1995; liability lines contribution merely 3% to group net premiums written) may have deceived from the inherent risks.

The second shortcoming of *low disclosure quality* can be attributed to two drivers. Firstly, Munich Re failed to adequately position the negligibility of its reserve strengthenings, which impaired its loss ratio by only 2.3 percentage points. The fundamental improvement of Munich Re's profitability compared to the market (although at the expense of growth in 2001 and 2002, see Table 50) remained unaffected. Secondly, several times it had to contradict its previous statements, that anew reserve strengthenings would be the ultimate ones. Although value relevancy of corporate disclosure quality is controversially discussed in prior research,[417] Gelb and Zarowin (2002) find that better disclosure as measured by AIMR-FAF annual corporate disclosure ratings is associated with greater share price informativeness.

Summary

Despite the flawed pre- and post-acquisition process, Munich Re achieved some of its targeted acquisition benefits, indicating that it reached a good level of integration,[418] see Figure 66. One may even argue that pressure from shortfalls during the acquisition process, culminating in a spiral of reserve strengthenings, eventually served as a catalyst for fundamental transformation of Munich Re's operations, which it may not have achieved otherwise. Still, earlier realization of acquisition benefits would have allowed Munich Re to participate more actively in the strong reinsurance and reinsurance M&A market until 1999 and after 2003. The loss of its position as the world's largest reinsurer to Swiss Re after acquisition of GE Insurance Solutions in 2006, which constitutes Munich Re's failure to achieve its possible motive of empire building, could potentially have been avoided. Ultimately, Munich Re might have been even better off entering the U.S. M&A market at least one year earlier, when acquisition options were broader and takeover premiums may have been lower.

---

417 Core (2001) reviews literature on disclosure quality and its effect on cost of capital, but emphasizes measurement problems and problems of joint hypotheses tests linking disclosure quality, information asymmetry and cost of capital.

418 Zollo and Singh (2004) argue that previous research found that a high level of integration may increase or decrease value extracted from M&A, but find a significant positive relation between integration and acquisition performance on their U.S. banking sample ($N = 228$).

	Planned merger benefits	Achieved results	Root causes for underachievement
Motives that create value	• Value creation by – Avoiding transaction in M&A peak – Acquiring before market is cleared	• Significant value destroyed	• (see below)
• **Profitability**	• Economies of scope (skill transfer primarily for underwriting effectiveness)	• Profitability improved only marginally, and underwriting effectiveness only 6-7 years after the merger	• Hastyness in pre-acquisition process (no actuarial appraisal of AR portfolio) • Failure to stop underwriting of risky liability business
• **Growth**	• Further organic growth through – Market power increase* – Revenue economies of scale due to "Flight to Quality" – Economies of scope (skill transfer nontraditional reinsurance)	• U.S. and global market share increased • Market power, revenues economies of scale, and economies of scope difficult to assess	• (achieved)
• **Solvency**	• Strengthening of capitalization • Risk reduction through – Global and product diversification – Less proportional business	• Leverage ratios reduced, but equity ratios still below market • Rating suffered from U.S. reserve strengthening	• Failure to communicate neglibility of U.S. reserve strengthenigs and contradiction of previous statements
Other motives	• Empire building	• Position as largest reinsurer maintained until 2006, afterwards lost to Swiss Re/GE Insurance Solutions	• Insufficient funds for inorganic growth (lack of profitability, high takeover premium)

* U.S. traditional and European non-traditional markets

Source: Own research

Figure 66: Achievement of merger benefits

5.5 Case study B: CGU merges with Norwich Union (2000)

5.5.1 Motivation for the transaction

5.5.1.1 Market environment

CGU merged with NU in a period of increasing consolidation of the European and UK primary insurance markets.[419] The largest insurers were forerunners of the increasing concentration[420] in the UK life and non-life primary insurance market between 1993 and 2004: The 5-firm concentration ratios rose by roughly 20 percentage points, whilst the 10-firm and 15-firm concentration ratios increased notably only in the life insurance sector. A similar development is observed across Euro-12 countries, where the rising concentration was mostly driven by the 5 largest market participants, who increased their market share by 15 percentage points between 1993 and 2004. Figure 67 presents the respective evidence.

M&A was a major driver for the observed primary insurance market concentration in the UK and Europe. Momentum in the European insurance M&A market picked up in the early and mid 1990s, reaching its peak between 1997 and 1999, see Figure 68. CGU and NU merged in the first year of a downturn of the M&A market in the European primary and reinsurance industry: The overall M&A volume decreased from its peak at USD 51.6 bn in 1999 (27 deals) to USD 41.6 bn in 2000 (15 deals), and declined almost steadily for the successive four years. Transaction activity in the life insurance sector, which dominated the business of both insurers and was the strategic direction of the combined en-

419 The European Commission (2007, pp. 39) discusses prominence of primary insurers on a country level. However, Swiss Re (2000) argues that "European insurers", covering several European countries, are gaining importance in the primary markets. Thus, concentration is examined for CGU and NU's home market, the UK, but also for Europe.

420 This section discusses market concentration following the methodology applied in section 2.3.1. The concentration of the global reinsurance market is measured by concentration ratios, defined as "the percentages of total industry output [...] which a given number of large firms account for", see OECD (1993). The total industry output is defined as net reinsurance premiums written, as provided by Standard & Poor's (1995-1999).

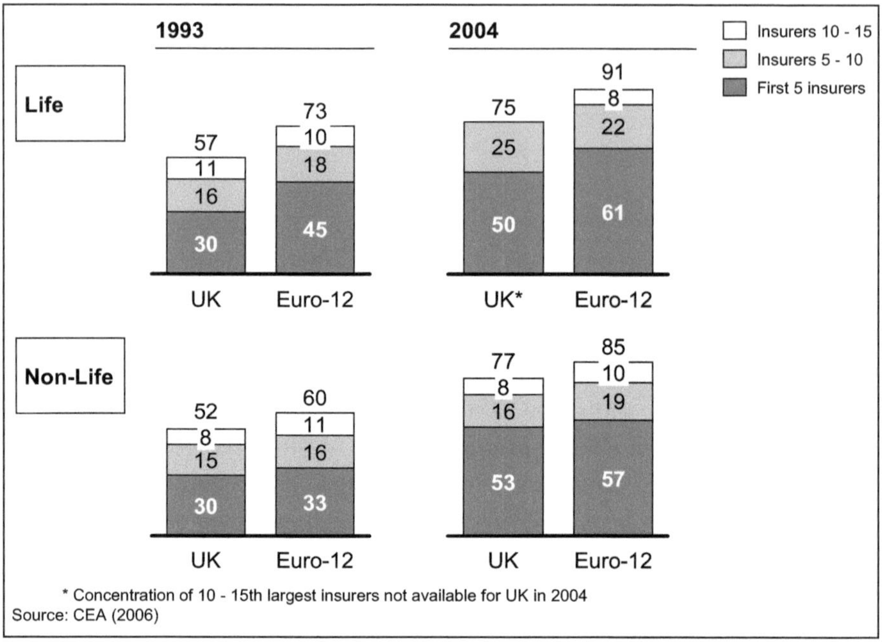

Figure 67: Development of UK and European primary insurance market concentration

tity,[421] was also slowing down. Most transactions (10 deals) and the highest total transaction volume (USD 32.6 bn) were recorded in 1999, but numbers and volumes of transactions were declining thereafter.

The M&A momentum in the primary life insurance market was driven by fundamental factors in underwriting markets, urging the industry to seek value creation by M&A. Firstly, a significant profitability gap between top and worst performing life carriers opened in the late 1990s. The development of return on reserves of major European life insurers presented in Figure 69 shows their median increased almost steadily until 1998. However, Standard & Poor's (4 August 1998) prediction that the European Union's move towards a single market

421 Compare sections 5.5.1.3.

		1990	91	92	93	94	95	96	97	98	99	2000	01	02	03	04	2005	Total
Transaction volume USD billions	Other - Other	0.0	0.0	0.0	0.0	0.5	0.5	6.0	0.7	3.7	8.7	0.3	2.3	2.1	0.6	0.0	7.8	**33.1**
	Other - Life	0.9	0.0	0.1	0.2	1.2	1.5	1.8	21.7	0.6	8.5	2.9	2.7	0.4	0.3	0.0	0.4	**43.2**
	Life - Other	3.1	0.4	0.0	0.0	0.0	0.0	1.2	5.4	0.5	1.7	0.0	0.3	2.8	0.1	0.8	0.0	**16.3**
	Life - Life	1.0	0.2	0.8	2.7	3.3	3.4	17.7	17.9	21.2	32.6	38.3	3.7	0.9	4.3	1.6	11.1	**160.7**
	Total	**5.0**	**0.6**	**0.9**	**2.9**	**4.9**	**5.3**	**26.7**	**45.7**	**25.9**	**51.6**	**41.6**	**9.0**	**6.2**	**5.4**	**2.3**	**19.3**	**253.3**
Average transaction volume USD billions	Other - Other	n/a	n/a	n/a	n/a	0.5	0.2	3.0	0.3	0.6	1.7	0.2	1.1	1.1	0.3	n/a	7.8	**16.8**
	Other - Life	0.5	n/a	0.1	0.1	1.2	0.4	0.4	3.6	0.2	1.1	0.6	0.7	0.4	0.2	n/a	0.2	**9.5**
	Life - Other	3.1	0.4	n/a	n/a	n/a	n/a	0.4	2.7	0.5	0.4	n/a	0.3	1.4	0.1	0.4	n/a	**9.7**
	Life - Life	0.3	0.2	0.4	1.3	0.6	0.8	3.0	1.5	2.1	3.3	4.8	0.6	0.5	0.7	0.8	2.2	**23.1**
	Total	**0.8**	**0.3**	**0.3**	**0.7**	**0.6**	**0.5**	**1.7**	**2.1**	**1.3**	**1.9**	**2.8**	**0.7**	**0.9**	**0.5**	**0.6**	**2.4**	**59.1**

* Based on long-term data sample of event study in this thesis

Source: Thomson Financial SDC platinum, Dealogic M&A database, press research

Figure 68: Development of M&A transactions* between 1990 and 2005

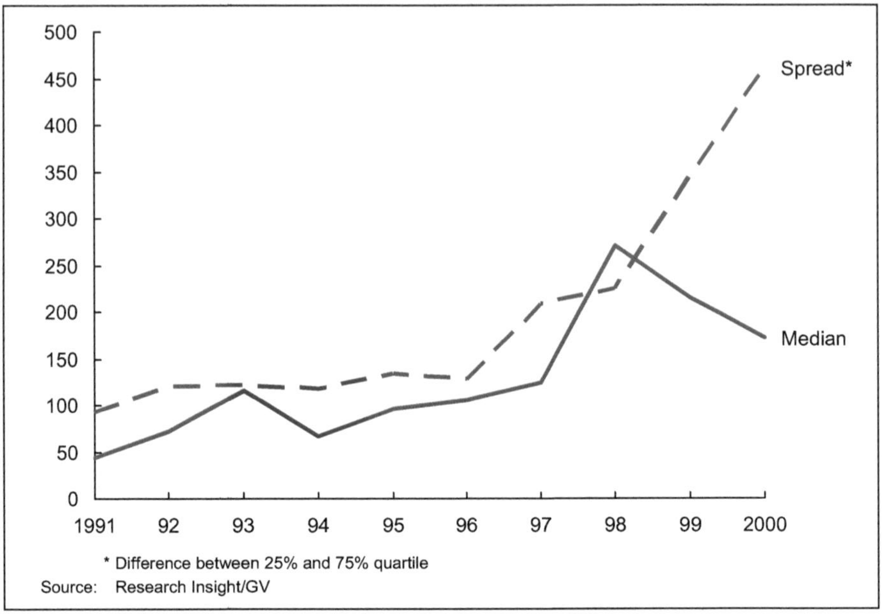

Figure 69: Development of return on reserves of major European life insurers (bp)

in financial services would reduce barriers for competition and lead to greater returns for policyholders and shareholders of life insurers realized only for few players in the industry: The median return on reserves fell sharply by 100 bp after 1998, but the profitability spread[422] opened strongly from roughly 220 bp in 1998 to 460 bp in 2000.

This loss of profitability of the life insurance industry may be partially attributed to the constant decline of interest rates in the UK and Europe from 1995 onwards, because life insurers were heavily invested in fixed income assets[423], and these assets had significantly shorter duration than the respective insurance liabilities. Depending on a life company's specific asset allocation in this period

422 Defined as the difference between the 75% quantile and the 25% quantile.

423 CEA (2006) reports for 1998 that in average, European life insurers allocate 39% of their assets to fixed income instruments, and invest 36% of their assets in equity.

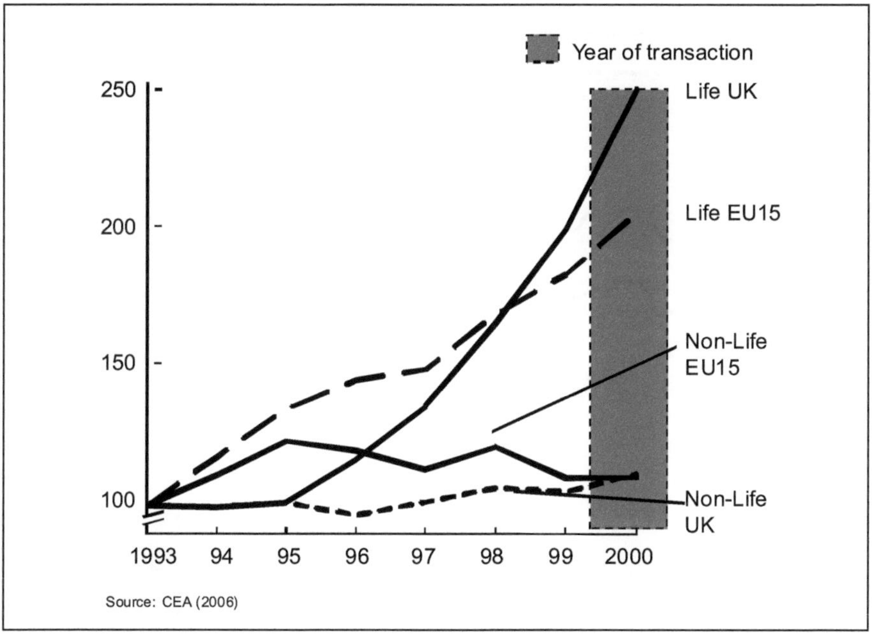

Figure 70: Development of life and non-life premiums (indexed 1.1.1993 = 100)

of time,[424] favorable equity markets may have contributed to the compensation for losses in the fixed income portfolio. Figures 71 and 72 present the development of relevant capital market indices.

Secondly, premiums grew only in the life primary insurance market. For the non-life market, CEA (2006) reports stagnating UK and EU-15 premiums since 1993 until the year of the transaction. In contrast, life primary markets achieved a CAGR of 13.9% in the UK and 10.7% across EU-15 countries in this period, see Figure 70. Investors preferred life insurance carriers to non-life carriers since an ageing population and progressing privatization of pensions markets promised

424 Company specific asset allocations are likely to differ significantly from the European average, e.g. for regulatory reasons: German life insurers' equity holdings are limited to 25% of their segregated funds.

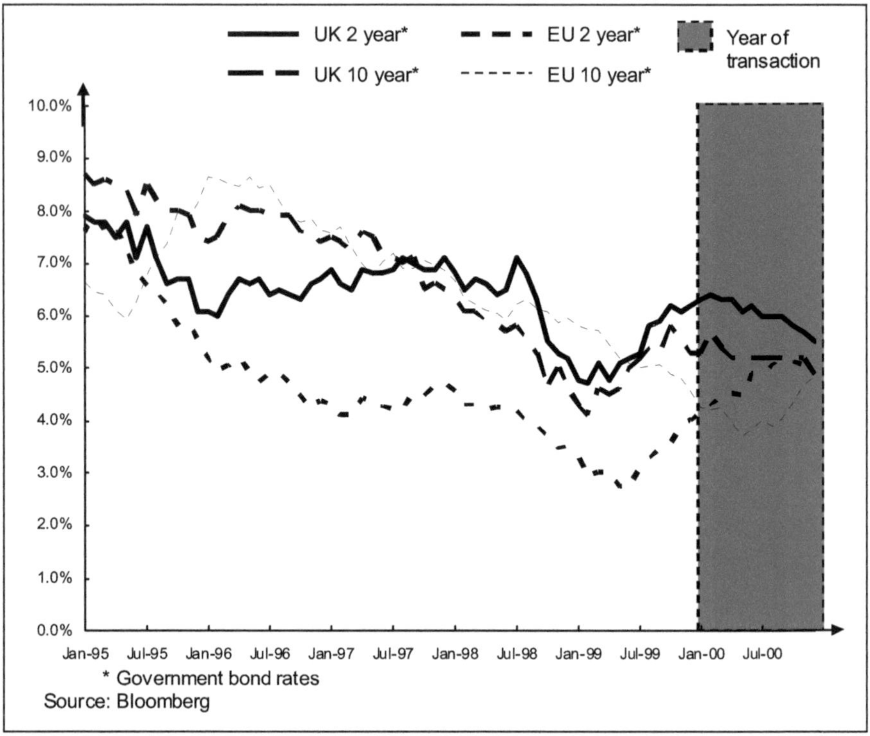

Figure 71: Development of UK and European fixed income rates

continuation of this growth trend for the foreseeable future.[425] Thirdly, solvency margins were threatened to deteriorate. Although increasing profits until 1998 lead to a comfortable capitalization of European insurers,[426] competition for market share in a stagnating non-life industry, and strong exposure of life insurers to unfavorable fixed income markets lead to an increasing spread in profit-

425 Standard & Poor's (4 August 1998). However, Life insurers were most prone to regulatory changes, such as France's introduction of a 7.5% tax on life products with terms of eight years and more on 1 January 1998 (Standard & Poor's, 4 August 1998). However, multi-national life insurers could diversify well against these legal risks due to their limited geographical scope. At the same time, reinsurance and primary non-life insurers showed strong volatility and future uncertainty of profits due to increasing natural catastrophes (compare section 5.4.1.1.).

426 Especially large German players were assumed to carry significant available capital (Standard & Poor's, 4 August 1998).

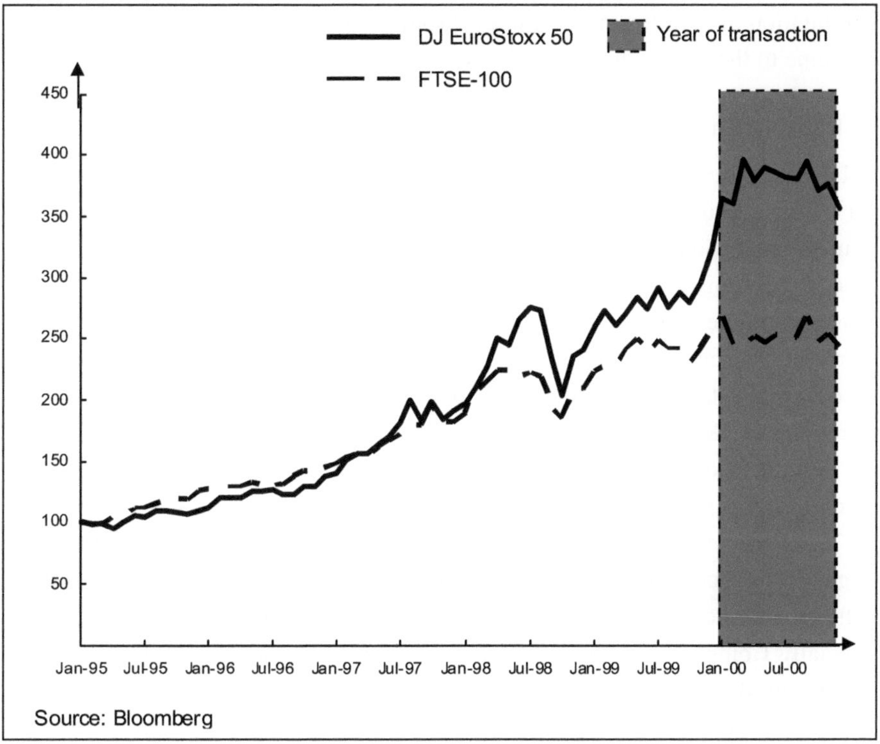

Figure 72: Development of equity market TRS (indexed 1.1.1995 = 100)

ability. At the same time, transparency for investors was increasing and they accordingly raised their dividend expectations.

Life insurers utilized M&A as a strategic tool to improve their profitability and their capital base, but also to secure their share in a growing market, especially against non-life insurers extending their outreach into the attractive life segment.[427] The discussions in the following sections illustrate that the transactions partners NU and especially CGU were also hit by the difficult market environment, and that a combination of both enterprises, in conjunction with a

427 Sources for profitability improvements (e.g., cost synergies, risk diversification) and growth (market power, revenue economies of scale) by M&A are systematized in section 2.3.2. and discussed specifically for the merger between CGU and NU in section 5.5.1.4.

reorientation of their business strategy, promised to mitigate most pressing issues and came to the advantage especially of NU's top management.

5.5.1.2 The transaction partners: CGU

CGU was created by two mergers between three insurance companies: Commercial Union, Hand-in-hand, and General Accident. Commercial Union was founded on 28 September 1861 by London merchants after a devastating fire in London warehouses resulted in insurance companies to announce premium increases. Commercial Union quickly expanded geographically, opening its first branch in December of the same year in Germany, and swiftly extended its product coverage, starting life operations only one year later in 1862, and Marine operations in 1863. Established in 1696, Hand-in-hand was the world's oldest fire insurance company, founded in London as a mutual society. In 1905, Commercial Union merged with Hand-in-hand. General Accident was founded in 1885 in Perth, Scotland, as a P&C insurance company, underwriting liability, burglary, fire, accident and motor insurance. In 1998, Commercial Union merged with General Accident, and changed its name to CGU. Figure73 illustrates that especially Commercial Union, but also General Accident gained significant experience in M&A transactions in their long standing history.

In the years prior to their merger, CGU was a dominant player in the UK primary insurance market, see Figure 74. In 1999, CGU held a market share of 4.7% in the UK life market, making it the third largest life insurer in terms of new business sales, and 6.3% in the UK non-life market, making it the second largest non-life insurer.[428] The European premium income outside of the UK was roughly as large as CGU's domestic business, see Figure 75.[429]

CGU may have decided to pursue an M&A strategy for three reasons. Firstly, a decomposition of CGU's market valuation into its drivers earnings and

428 CGU (1999).

429 The dominance of worldwide non-life activities is driven by CGU's U.S. subsidiary with a total premium income of USD 4.2 bn. This subsidiary was to be sold according to the merger plan of CGU and NU.

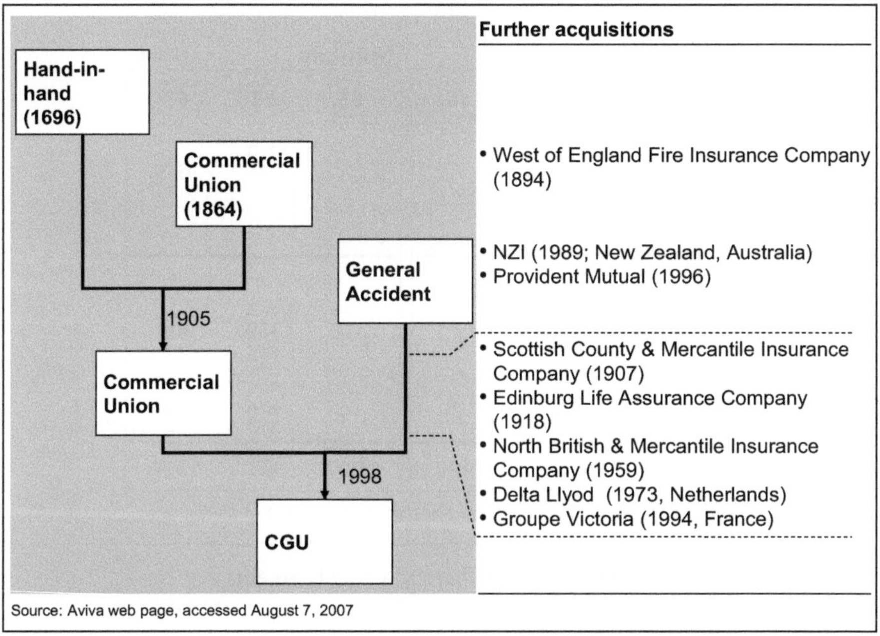

Figure 73: Major mergers and acquisitions in the history of CGU

growth[430] shows that 20% of its value can be attributed to growth expectations. The implied growth rate of 1.2% per annum[431] ranges at average premium growth rates in the UK and European non-life market, but well below the average premium growth rates of the respective life insurance markets, making the latter segment an attractive growth opportunity. However, CGU's prospects for future profitability and growth were endangered due to the rapid concentration of its home market between 1997 and 1999: In this period of time, all 12 recorded acquisitions of UK insurers[432] targeted life carriers, and 11 of these transactions

430 Computed as 3-year average of after tax earnings / (cost of equity x market value). Cost of equity calculated with 5% risk premium, risk free rate as average of 10 year UK government bond rates, and beta based on 3-year covariance with MSCI world index.

431 Computed as (combined market value x cost of equity – combined earnings) / (combined market value + combined earnings) as of 3 January 2000 based on previous year's earnings.

432 Based on long-term deal sample, see section 4.2, excluding the acquisitions of CGU (General Accident in 1998) and NU (London & Edinburgh Insurance Group Ltd in 1998).

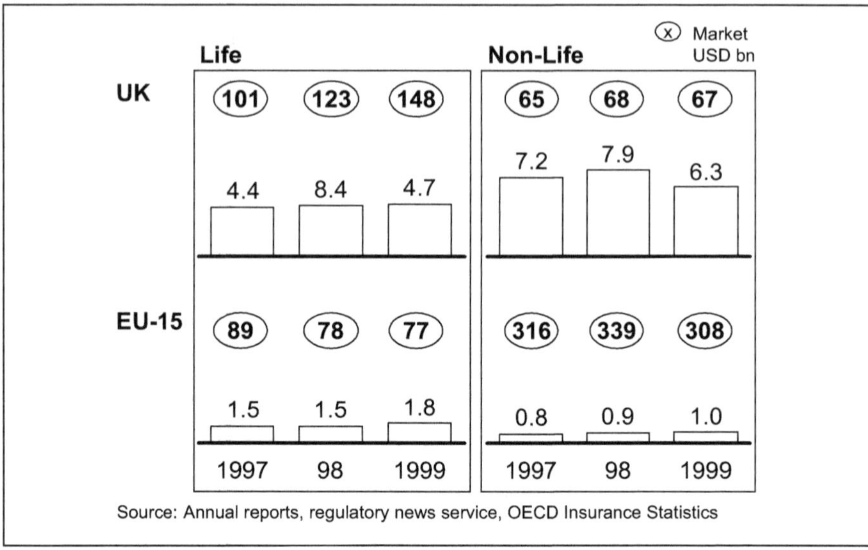

Figure 74: Development of market share of CGU (percent)

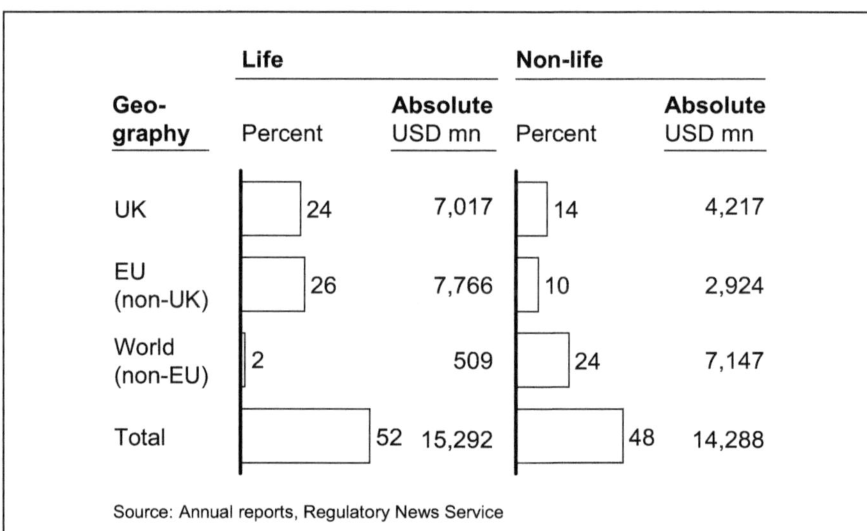

Figure 75: Business mix of CGU by geography (1999)

Table 51: Financial performance of CGU (1995–1999)

CGU	Unit	1995	1996	1997	1998	1999
Size						
Earnings	USD mn	679.8	601.8	593.0	870.8	784.0
Premiums	USD bn	13.2	12.5	13.5	27.4	27.1
Reserves	USD bn	70.4	77.1	82.4	150.3	157.0
Assets	USD bn	83.9	91.6	98.2	177.5	188.1
Shareholders' Equity	USD bn	6.9	7.3	7.9	16.0	16.3
Solvency						
Equity ratio	%	8.2%	8.0%	8.0%	9.0%	8.6%
Equity reserves ratio	%	9.8%	9.5%	9.5%	10.7%	10.4%
Operating leverage	times x	1.9	1.7	1.7	1.7	1.7
Reserves leverage	times x	57.2	86.4	91.0	111.5	127.7
Reserves ratio	times x	5.3	6.2	6.1	5.5	5.8
Profitability						
Return on reserves	bp	174.8	115.8	109.9	89.7	78.3
Return on equity	%	17.8%	12.2%	11.5%	8.4%	7.6%
Return on premiums	%	9.3%	7.1%	6.7%	4.9%	4.5%
Combined ratio	%	107.7%	117.9%	120.5%	132.9%	137.9%
Loss ratio	%	102.0%	93.3%	97.2%	103.1%	130.1%
Expense ratio	%	5.7%	24.7%	23.3%	29.8%	7.7%
Growth						
Growth of earnings	%	24.8%	-11.5%	-1.5%	46.8%	-10.0%
Growth of premiums	%	25.6%	-5.0%	8.3%	102.3%	-1.2%
Growth of reserves	%	22.0%	9.5%	6.8%	82.5%	4.5%
Growth of assets	%	20.4%	9.2%	7.2%	80.7%	6.0%
Growth of equity	%	31.2%	6.3%	6.9%	103.9%	1.6%

were carried out by British insurers.[433] Capital markets reflected concerns regarding future growth, valuing CGU with a P/E ratio of 16.2 compared to the life insurance industry average of 22.7. Thus, increasing dominance and growth prospects in the life insurance sector through a strategic combination with another insurer with a strong UK life franchise was both an opportunity but also a necessity for CGU given the market environment in the late 1990s.

Secondly, CGU's profitability declined notably on an absolute basis (see Table 51) and compared to its industry peers (see Table 52). Its return on reserves fell from 79 bp above the market median in 1995 to 137 bp below market

433 On a European level (including Norway and Switzerland), 27 out of 45 acquisitions in this period of time targeted life companies.

Table 52: Market adjusted financial performance of CGU (1995–1999)

CGU (market adj.*)	**Unit**	**1995**	**1996**	**1997**	**1998**	**1999**
Size						
Earnings	x times market	10.5	5.8	2.2	5.3	2.6
Premiums	x times market	6.2	5.0	3.1	5.8	5.0
Reserves	x times market	4.8	5.8	3.9	6.9	10.0
Assets	x times market	4.1	4.0	3.2	6.1	4.2
Shareholders' Equity	x times market	10.4	8.7	4.1	9.1	7.1
Solvency						
Equity ratio	Δ%pts to market	4.1%	3.4%	2.9%	4.5%	2.6%
Equity reserves ratio	Δ%pts to market	4.2%	4.0%	0.0%	2.0%	-0.8%
Operating leverage	Δtimes x to market	-1.5	-0.8	-0.5	-0.7	-0.2
Reserves leverage	Δtimes x to market	-42.5	0.0	11.1	74.6	81.2
Reserves ratio	Δtimes x to market	-2.4	0.0	0.6	-0.2	-0.1
Profitability						
Return on reserves	Δbp to market	79.2	10.5	-14.2	-180.7	-137.0
Return on equity	Δ%pts to market	-0.1%	-5.1%	-9.3%	-17.1%	-16.0%
Return on premiums	Δ%pts to market	-2.4%	2.4%	-0.4%	-7.4%	-4.9%
Combined ratio	Δ%pts to market	-26.8%	-21.0%	-29.1%	-20.8%	-7.9%
Loss ratio	Δ%pts to market	-4.9%	-21.0%	-28.5%	-31.6%	-4.3%
Expense ratio	Δ%pts to market	-21.9%	0.0%	-0.5%	10.9%	-3.6%
Growth						
Growth of earnings	Δ%pts to market	34.9%	-71.4%	-159.6%	84.8%	-91.5%
Growth of premiums	Δ%pts to market	62.0%	-22.8%	-64.3%	94.3%	-17.8%
Growth of reserves	Δ%pts to market	14.8%	19.6%	-51.1%	77.9%	32.5%
Growth of assets	Δ%pts to market	11.7%	-1.4%	-25.0%	84.4%	-46.7%
Growth of equity	Δ%pts to market	43.2%	-21.3%	-117.4%	111.7%	-29.2%

* Median of EU-15 peers.

level in 1999, and its return on equity and return on premiums already lied below market level in 1995 and dropped further. Investors penalized CGU for its lack of profitability: CGU was devalued to an average market value of 1.3 times its book value in 1999 (implying an return on equity of 8.0%), whereas its industry peers were valued at 3.1 times their book (return on equity of 13.4%). This low market valuation posed a threat for CGU management to fall prey to major European groups seeking to strengthen their UK presence. CGU's (still) healthy capitalization further increased its attractiveness as a takeover candidate.[434] Thirdly, CGU may have hoped to improve its profitability, e.g., through realization of cost synergies.

434 The increase of reserves leverage between 1995 and 1999 was driven by growing reserves, not declining earnings.

Based on improved profitability and anew growth fantasies, CGU hoped to regain investors' confidence to lift its market valuation back to industry level or above. Conversely, NU represented an attractive target for CGU as it was a similarly large insurer in their home markets with a strong focus on UK business and a powerful brand in life insurance. The next section presents an overview on NU and its strategic rationale for the negotiated merger with CGU.

5.5.1.3 The transaction partners: Norwich Union

NU was established in Norwich in 1797 by Thomas Bignold, a wine merchant and banker. The mutual insurance company started as a provider of fire insurance for houses, stock, and merchandise, and operated its own fire brigade. Eleven years later, in 1808, Mr. Bignold founded Norwich Union Life Insurance Society, after a particularly severe winter claimed many lives. NU was less active in M&A than CGU. It acquired Amicable Society in 1866, Norwich & London Accident Insurance Association in 1908, Scottish & National Insurance Company in 1959, and London & Edinburgh in 1998.

NU held a strong position in the UK life and non-life market with a market share of 4.1% and 6.3% in 1999, respectively. However, it lost 0.7 percentage points of market share in a growing UK life market (21.1% CAGR between 1997 and 1999). In the stagnating non-life market, NU gained 1.9 percentage points of market share in the same period of time. NU's and CGU's combined market position was strong in both markets with a life market share of 8.8%, and non-life market share of 12.6% in the UK in 1999, see Figure 76. However, NU added little to the market power of CGU on a European level, since 81% of its gross premiums were written in the UK. On an overall level, the merger with NU was designed to strengthen the life focus of the combined entity, since life business dominated 2/3 of NU's gross premiums, and the divestment of CGU's U.S. non-life activities (total premium income of USD 4.2 bn in 1999) as proposed in the merger plan would result in 61% of the combined premiums to come from life operations.

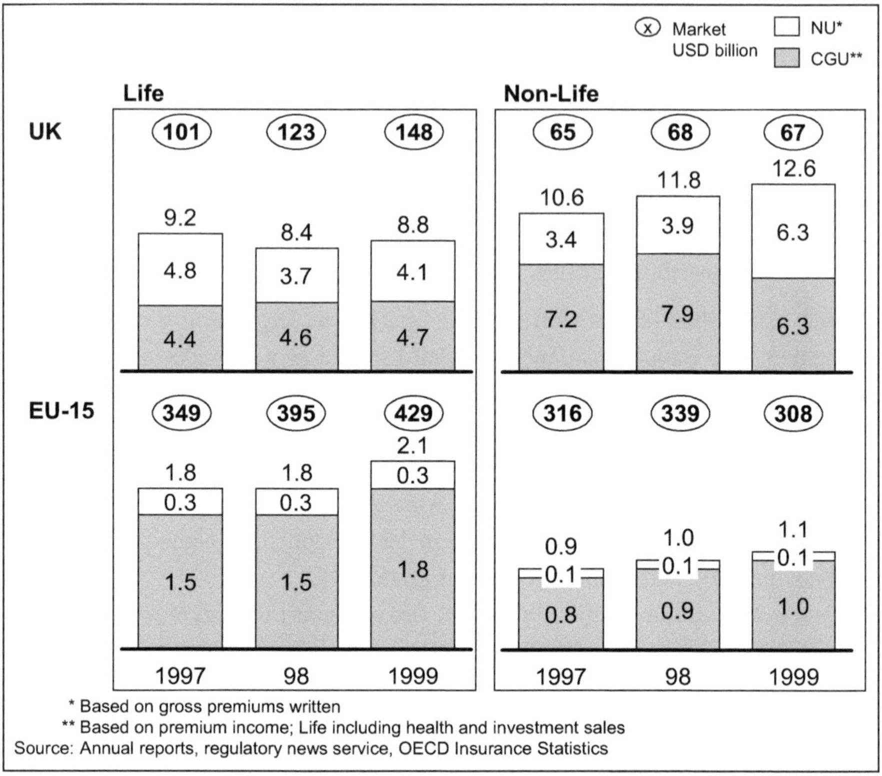

Figure 76: Development of market share of CGU and NU (percent)

In the three years prior to the merger, NU achieved solid financial results. Its capital base was strong with an equity ratio of above 9% between 1997 and 1999, see Table 53, and its leverage even improved further compared to the market median, see Table 54.

However, investors did not appreciate the fact that NU was additionally slightly more profitable than its industry peers based on most measures: Its return on equity as implied by average M/B and P/E ratios in 1999 was 8.8%, and thus considerably lower than the implied return on equity of 13.4% for its industry peers. Since investors doubted NU's growth perspectives (P/E ratio of 16.2

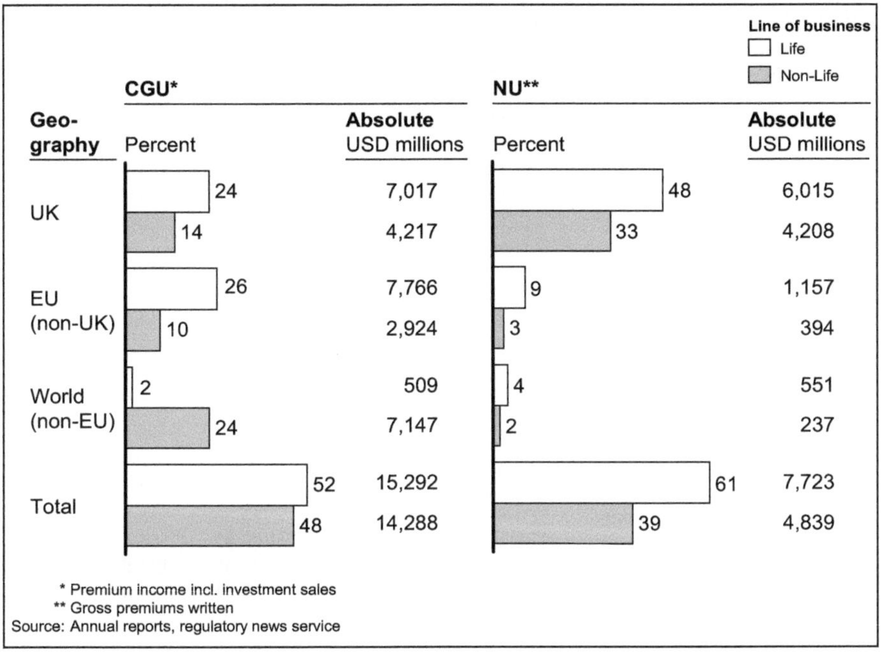

Figure 77: Complementarity of business mix by geography and lines of businesses (1999)

compared to market P/E ratio of 22.7), the life insurer was valued at merely 1.4 times its book value in 1999, whereas the life insurance market achieved an average M/B ratio of 3.1. The relatively low market valuation made NU vulnerable to hostile takeover bids in these times of strong M&A market momentum, especially by large foreign groups who seek to strengthen specifically their UK operations. Thus, the agreement of NU's top management to merge the company with CGU was to a lesser extent driven by operative performance issues,[435] but mostly welcome as an opportunity to renew growth prospects and a defensive strategy to prevent hostile bids and to secure their position and power. The next section reviews the transaction motives of both transaction partners and summarizes potential benefits along the framework laid out in section 2.3.2.1.

435 NU and their investors may benefit from the merger since the market power of both companies may allow the combined entity to outgrow the market again.

Table 53: Financial Performance of NU (1997–1999)

Norwich Union	Unit	1997	1998	1999
Size				
Earnings	USD mn	427.2	953.0	866.2
Premiums	USD bn	5.3	9.3	11.1
Reserves	USD bn	55.6	65.9	66.5
Assets	USD bn	86.9	100.4	107.0
Shareholders' Equity	USD bn	8.5	9.7	9.8
Solvency				
Equity ratio	%	9.8%	9.6%	9.2%
Equity reserves ratio	%	15.3%	14.6%	14.8%
Operating leverage	times x	0.6	1.0	1.1
Reserves leverage	times x	73.8	36.8	44.9
Reserves ratio	times x	10.6	7.1	6.0
Profitability				
Return on reserves	bp	135.6	271.8	222.8
Return on equity	%	8.9%	18.6%	15.1%
Return on premiums	%	14.3%	19.3%	13.3%
Combined ratio	%	164.2%	175.8%	166.4%
Loss ratio	%	158.7%	170.3%	161.5%
Expense ratio	%	5.5%	5.5%	4.9%
Growth				
Growth of earnings	%		123.0%	-9.1%
Growth of premiums	%		76.6%	19.9%
Growth of reserves	%		18.4%	0.9%
Growth of assets	%		15.4%	6.6%
Growth of equity	%		13.3%	1.8%

5.5.1.4 Benefits of the transaction

Robert Scott, Group Chief Executive of CGU, stated as main reasons for the transaction in an interview with BBC, that a merger of both companies would improve their market position, products, and capabilities to the customers in an environment of worldwide rapidly changing financial services.[436] The overall objective for the merger was to become leader in the UK as a core market, and one of the leaders in the European financial services industry.[437] But even more importantly, the merger served as a catalyst to transform both organizations fun-

436 Agence France Presse (21 February 2000b).
437 Regulatory News Service (21 February 2000).

Table 54: Market adjusted financial Performance of NU (1997–1999)

Norwich Union (market adj.*)	**Unit**	**1997**	**1998**	**1999**
Size				
Earnings	x times market	1.6	5.8	2.9
Premiums	x times market	1.2	2.0	2.0
Reserves	x times market	2.7	3.0	4.2
Assets	x times market	2.9	3.4	2.4
Shareholders' Equity	x times market	4.5	5.5	4.3
Solvency				
Equity ratio	Δ%pts to market	4.7%	5.1%	3.1%
Equity reserves ratio	Δ%pts to market	5.8%	6.0%	3.6%
Operating leverage	Δtimes x to market	-1.6	-1.5	-0.7
Reserves leverage	Δtimes x to market	-6.2	-0.1	-1.6
Reserves ratio	Δtimes x to market	5.1	1.4	0.1
Profitability				
Return on reserves	Δbp to market	11.4	1.4	7.5
Return on equity	Δ%pts to market	-12.0%	-7.0%	-8.5%
Return on premiums	Δ%pts to market	7.3%	6.9%	3.9%
Combined ratio	Δ%pts to market	14.6%	22.1%	20.7%
Loss ratio	Δ%pts to market	33.0%	35.5%	27.1%
Expense ratio	Δ%pts to market	-18.4%	-13.4%	-6.4%
Growth				
Growth of earnings	Δ%pts to market		161.1%	-90.6%
Growth of premiums	Δ%pts to market		68.6%	3.3%
Growth of reserves	Δ%pts to market		13.9%	28.9%
Growth of assets	Δ%pts to market		19.1%	-46.1%
Growth of equity	Δ%pts to market		21.1%	-28.9%

* Median of EU-15 peers.

damentally: NU was to become an important player in the league of Europe's top 5 insurers, and CGU would shift and sharpen its strategy from profitability orientation to aggressive portfolio management of its country subsidiaries with a focus on the attractively growing life markets, see Figure 78. In the following, these transaction partners' motives are discussed in the context of drivers and hurdles for M&A as identified in section 2.3.2.

Value creating motives. The long-term event study results in section 4.4.2.2 indicate that transactions in the peak of an M&A cycle create less value than those in the bottom phase. CGU and NU announced their merger in the downturn

	Profitability	Active portfolio management with focus on life
Overarching	• Become more competitive and profitable • Have depth in selected markets • Meet stringent financial targets	• Build top 5 position in each chosen market from leading domestic position • Withdraw where leading position or superior returns unattainable
Life	• Continue expansion of life and savings business from strong UK position	• Grow long-term savings business aggressively and profitably
Asset Management	• Continue to produce a consistently high performance record • Increase the proportion of external business • Strengthen coordination of fund management operations around the world	• Continue to build a world-class asset management business
Non-life	• Continue to focus on general insurance segments where CGU has particular strengths	• Have a focused approach to personal and small commercial lines general insurance with a focus on disciplined underwriting and efficient claims handling

Source: CGU (1998), Regulatory News Service (21 February 2000)

Figure 78: Strategic shift of CGU along with NU merger

the nature of phase of the market, and only one year prior to the beginning of the bottom phase.[438] From this perspective, the transaction timing was chosen well.

Profitability. CGU was under pressure to improve its performance, as it was less profitable than its industry peers by all examined measures. CGU may have assumed to benefit from *economies of scope* through underwriting or investment management skill transfer, because NU operated more profitable than its industry peers by most measures. Due to these merger benefits, retention of senior management is a crucial determinant of post-merger integration success. The realization of these economies of scope shall be tested through examining pre- and post-transaction profitability measures: If return on reserves and return on eq-

438 See section 4.2.3 for identification of the respective phases.

uity[439] increase relative to the market, and the combined entity achieves to maintain or even extend its market share, underwriting and investment efficiency and effectiveness are advancing. Further on, management estimated substantial *economies of scale* mainly from integration of UK insurance operations. For UK life, it rather imprecisely stated that projected unit costs would fall as a result of improved sales and significant cost reductions. For UK non-life, it assumed that sources for lower unit costs would be synergies in claims management, product purchasing, reinsurance cover, and electronic distribution channels. They originally estimated to realize cost savings of GBP 250 mn (corresponding to 21% of 1999 aggregated net administrative operating expenses) within 18 months after completion of the merger and one-off restructuring cost of GBP 350 mn. In order to meet these explicit targets, it is thus imperative for post-merger integration that restructuring of operations, e.g., redefinition of processes, decision on location and organization of central functions and systems, and streamlining of the IT, is planned well and tackled immediately. The realization of economies of scale is assessed by comparing planned cost savings with realized cost savings in 2002, the first year in which full merger benefits were to be reflected in the combined entity's annual results.[440]

Growth. Further on, management believed that value would be created from the increased *market power* of the combined entity as it would become UK's largest insurer, its second-largest writer of new life and pensions business, its second-largest fund manager, and Europe's fifth-biggest insurance player.[441] More specifically, the merger plan announced revenue growth in the companies' life business from an enhanced market profile, a larger share of the long-term savings market and further acquisitions especially in Europe,[442] and in asset management through a focus on UK and European retail markets under the Morley Brand. Analysts additionally believed that the combined entity may be able to realize

439 Return on premiums is not examined because denominator is strongly dependent on new business mix between single and recurring premium contracts.

440 The first case study compared pre- and post-transaction underwriting efficiency, measured by the expense ratio. This approach cannot be applied in this case study, because reliable operating expense data is unavailable.

441 Reactions (1 March 2000).

442 Acquisitions beyond Europe were to focus on markets such as South East Asia, India, and China (Dow Jones Newswire, 21 February 2000).

significant *revenue economies of scope* through the merger from cross-selling, e.g. from combination of its two diverse client bases in the Australian market.[443] Post-merger integration thus needs to quickly integrate brands, channels, channel support and products in order to bring hypothesized advantages of a combination of both businesses to the market. Further on, post-merger integration must drive extension to other markets through organic growth, M&A, distribution partnerships or joint ventures in order to achieve the planned strategic focus on the life segment and on markets where the combined entity could become a top 5 player. Realization of market power and revenue economies of scope would be indicated by an increase in the combined entity's premium market share, if profitability remains at the same level or improves compared to the market median.

Solvency. CGU may benefit from the merger, since the insurers available capital base is worse than that of its industry peers, while NU's capitalization ranges above market level. This *strengthening of capitalization* is assessed by comparing pre- and post-transaction solvency measures. From NU's perspective, geographical diversification associated with the merger results in *risk reduction.*[444] The effect of risk reduction cannot be tracked based on available financial performance measures, since required risk computations (e.g., based on internal models) are unavailable.

Other (non-value generating) motives. CGU and NU may hope that by entering the league of European insurance giants as their new number five, they will "join the hunters, rather than the hunted".[445] Thus, *empire building* is most definitely a further motive for management to proceed with the merger. In this respect, especially NU management benefits from the merger: An otherwise soon to be expected takeover by a large European insurer would most likely result in a significant loss of power for NU top management since they would probably be offered executive positions only on a country level. The merger with CGU promised NU's chairman and CEO the position of Deputies in the new organization immediately, with a fixed succession scheme as part of the plan of merger.

443 Australian Associated Press (22 February 2000).

444 The increased industry focus of the combined entity on the life segment, especially after exiting U.S. non-life business, may still result in a net risk reduction, as non-life business is considered more volatile than life business.

445 Financial Times (21 February 2000).

In summary, several value generating and non-value generating drivers can be identified for the merger between CGU and NU. Due to the nature of the targeted merger benefits, post-merger integration needs to well be prepared and quickly executed in order to retain senior management, realize operative cost savings, and realign distribution. But most importantly, both insurers needed to assure that the implicit organizational transformation would be pursued without compromises. The following section illustrates that these preconditions for the realization of merger benefits were achieved to a high degree because the transaction was negotiated privately between both transaction partners, thus freeing up significant capacity for a detailed preparation and early launch of post-merger integration. As a secondary effect, top management had more time to ensure smooth development of the post-announcement transaction process until completion of the transaction.

5.5.2 Conduct of the transaction

5.5.2.1 Transaction process and strategy

In the year prior to the announcement of the merger, NU was frequently involved in M&A rumors, fuelled by top management statements that they were considering M&A.[446] On 20 May 1999, the bank Lloyds TSB publicly announced their interest in NU,[447] and on 4 August 1999, NatWest Bank said it wanted to acquire the life insurer. However, Mr. Harvey, CEO of NU, insisted that a merger with a bank brought no advantages, and that NU remained interested in acquisitions itself.[448] Although proving his point by announcing the acquisition of Royal London Insurance's non-life business on 11 August 1999,[449] takeover talks between NatWest Bank and NU's competitor Legal & General in early September,

446 E.g., Mr. Harvey, the chief executive of NU, said on 3 March 1999 that the insurer would be keen on acquisitions given that they added value for shareholders (Financial Times, 3 March 1999).

447 The Independent (20 May 1999). As a consequence, NU's share price rose by 4.7%, and Lloyd TSB's share price went up by 3.4%.

448 The Guardian (4 August 1999). Analysts' supported Mr. Harvey's view that NU would rather be an acquirer than a target, as NU's share price contained no premium for a takeover (The Indepenedent – London, 4 August 1999).

449 The Evening Standard (11 August 1999).

and Generali's bid for INA caused NU's shares to jump again amid speculation it could be the next life insurer to be targeted by either a British bank or a European insurer.[450,451]

Although still in the process of post-merger integration with General Accident, M&A rumors surrounded CGU as well, but the insurer was rather seen as the acquirer than the target, supported by top management statements that the insurer "would be predator rather than prey in industry consolidation across Europe".[452] In early 1999, speculations persisted that CGU would be interested in fully acquiring Hibernian Group, an Irish non-life insurer, of which it already owned around 28 percent.[453] On 2 June 1999, CGU announced takeover talks of its wholly-owned Dutch subsidiary Delta Lloyd with Dutch insurer Nuts Ohra.[454] On 5 August 1999, Royal & Sun Alliance Insurance countered speculations that it was a potential target for CGU.[455]

However, rumors of a transaction between CGU and NU were only leaked to markets on 18 February 2000, immediately following Board approval of the merger plan after week-long talks.[456] The course of the transaction until completion of the merger, Figure 79 presents an overview, and during post-merger integration shows that the private and exclusive negotiation as opposed to an open auction came as a great advantage to the insurers. Firstly, integration could be prepared in great detail and launched immediately after shareholders' approval. Secondly, a bidding contest was avoided, which could have led large European insurance groups to offer NU shareholders more attractive transaction terms than CGU, e.g., a higher takeover premium and cash components to the consideration. Such a takeover was against personal interests of NU management as they would

450 Reuters News (3 September 1999).
451 Reuters News (14 September 1999).
452 The Herald (12 August 1999). On 11 November 1999, Peter Foster, CFO of CGU, re-emphasized Mr. Scotts statements, saying that the firm wants to continue to grow its life and savings business, possibly through more acquisitions (The Asian Wall Street Journal, 11 November 1999).
453 The transaction was announced on 4 November 1999.
454 Reuters News (2 June 1999). Agreement on the acquisition was reached on 30 September 1999 (CGU, 30 September 1999).
455 Reuters News (5 August 1999).
456 Reuters News (20 February 2000a). Information on the negotiations is not published.

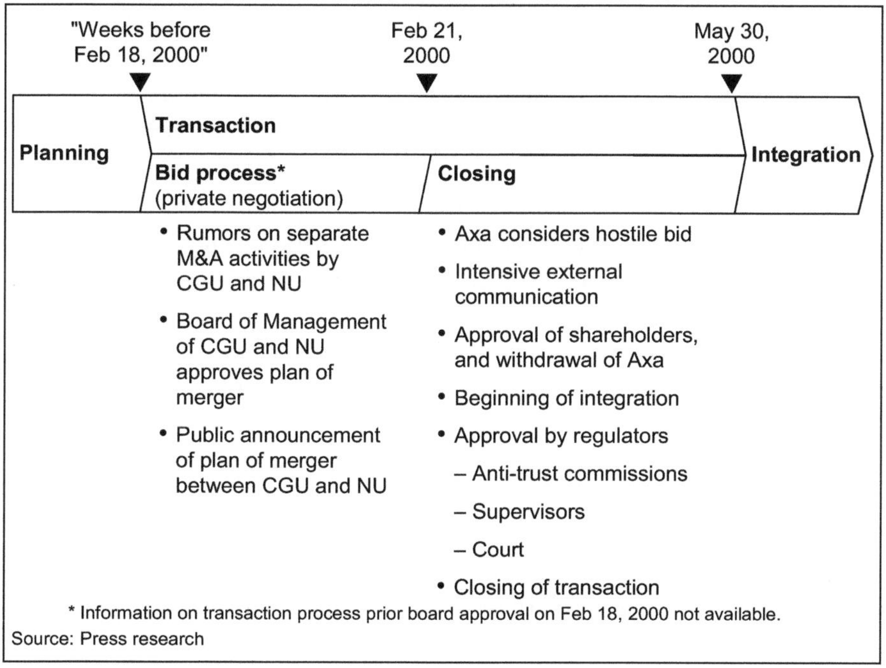

Figure 79: Overview of the transaction process

have most likely lost power. Thirdly, top management had more time to focus on external communication to solicit merger approval, which was uncertain due to unattractive conditions for NU shareholders and the danger of a merger break-up by French insurer Axa, as if additionally burdened with integration planning.

The official merger announcement on 21 February 2000 rendered leaked information on the planned merger more precisely, e.g., correcting cost savings to GBP 250 mn to be achieved after 18 months after completion, half of which would be realized through 5,000 jobs being cut[457] in asset management, public

457 Agence France-Presse (21 February 2000b). Information leaked prior to official announcement stated that CGU and NU aimed at GBP 200 mn cost savings and 4,000 jobs cut within 3 years. This came as a shock to CGU employees, since CGU had already shed 5,000 staff over the previous two years as a consequence of the merger between General Accident and Commercial Union. George Paul, chairman of NU, apologized that "the staff who work for our companies had to learn about it this way."

relations, IT and technical divisions, with the remainder expected to come from integrating computer networks, selling property and other sources.[458] At that time, investment banks were known to be working out proposals to Axa and Allianz on a "bearhug" combined bid for CGU and NU.[459] Mr. Scott dismissed speculations that a foreign hostile bid may break-up the planned transaction, and predicted closing of the transaction for early June[460]. However, on 1 March 2000, Axa was reported to consider breaking up CGU's merger with NU with a counterbid for either company. It was believed that both boards would not reject an offer comprising a major cash element,[461] and that NU is the more likely target.[462] Axa had to withdraw its counter bid after CGU's and NU's top management succeeded in soliciting institutional investors' support for the merger[463] by 15 March 2000.[464]

Obtaining merger approval of stakeholders turned out hard work for the CEOs of CGU and NU. Their initial external communication focused on the strategic rationale of the merger, but shareholders criticized that there was no cash element comprised in the merger, and that CGU as the larger transaction partner refused to pay a premium.[465] Further on, policyholders were worried on the surplus distribution from with-profit funds of both companies, and the broad public expressed its anger at the careless communication of planned job cuts.[466] CGU and NU swiftly switched to a double tracked communication strategy and decided to sweeten conditions for shareholders of NU. Firstly, they continued an

458 Associated Press Newswires (21 February 2000).

459 Financial Times (22 Febraury 2000b).

460 Agence France-Presse (21 February 2000b). Surprisingly, a spokesman of NU told a newspaper that a third party could disrupt the transaction (Associated Press, 21 February 2000).

461 The Independent – London (1 March 2000).

462 Evening News – Scotland (1 March 2000). Although Mark Wood, the chief executive of Sun Life & Provincial Holdings, Axa's British subsidiary, commented the report as "speculation" (Reuters, 1 March 2000), he added that if Axa would make a transaction, it would rather target a life company (The Times, 2 March 2000). Axa's shares fell by 1.4% and CGU's and NU's shares rose by 2% at the same time.

463 Reuters News (15 March 2000).

464 Axa's chairman told a news conference on annual results that the merger between CGU and NU "will go ahead without outside intervention" (Agence France-Presse, 16 March 2000).

465 Financial Times (26 February 2000b).

466 A British union asked the London Stock Exchange to investigate whether information leaks prior to the merger announcement violated the stock exchange's takeover code, see Reuters News (22 February 2000a).

extensive road show for institutional investors stressing the strategic rationale of the merger, after which Mr. Harvey told a news conference in Dublin on 15 March 2000 that "the basic reaction from institutions is that they see undeniable commercial value in this merger. They are indicating they will vote for it."[467] Secondly, the insurers appealed to British patriotism through extensive communication to the British public in popular media. On 27 February 2000, Mr. Scott gave a presentation to tabloid press, arguing that "France, Germany, Italy and Switzerland all have massive insurance groups that are winning customers across the globe, including from Britain. We must have the same here".[468] On 24 March 2000, only one week prior to shareholders' voting on the merger plan, Mr. Scott and Mr. Harvey countered a last-minute campaign of a rebel NU shareholder[469] by wrapping themselves into the Union Jack, asking investors for their support to create a British insurance giant.[470] Thirdly, Mr. Harvey announced on 5 March 2000, that NU shareholders would receive an extra dividend conditional upon completion of the merger.[471] Clearly, as top management was less tied-up in preparation of post-merger integration activities than it would have been the case in an open auction, their communication was not only well prepared, but they also reacted flexibly to feedback from their stakeholders, and were able to invest a significant amount of time personally.

The communication effort paid. On 31 March 2000, shareholders of both companies approved the merger,[472] allowing the companies to begin implementation of major integration measures. On 22 May 2000, the UK court sanctioned the scheme of arrangement relating to the proposed merger, after all outstanding regulatory and antitrust approvals had been received.[473] The merger became

467 Reuters News (15 March 2000).
468 The Mail on Sunday (27 February 2000).
469 Investors Chronicle (24 March 2000).
470 The Times (25 March 2000) quotes Mr. Scott asking "Do people want to see a British company that can compete on the level of the big European insurers or not? That is what this is about."
471 The Mail on Sunday (5 March 2000).
472 NU reported an approval ratio of more than 91%, based on counting of 83% of shareholders' votes, and CGU announced approval of its shareholders without releasing further details. With their votes, shareholders also agreed to the planned job cuts (Associated Press Newswires, 31 March 2000).
473 Regulatory News Service (22 May 2000). The European Commission approved the merger on 14 April 2000 (Agence France-Presse, 14 April 2000). The New Zealand antitrust commission approved the merger on 9 May 2000 (New Zealand Press Association, 9 May 2000). The

effective on 30 May 2000. Shares of NU were delisted,[474] new shares of the combined entity CGNU[475] were distributed to NU shareholders and to be included in the FTSE life assurance index.[476]

5.5.2.2 Structure of the transaction

The transaction was structured as a nil-premium all-share merger: CGU and NU proposed to issue 48 new CGNU shares for every 100 NU shares to NU shareholders.[477] Following the merger, CGU and NU shareholders held 58.5% and 41.5% of CGNU, respectively. CGU remained the listed holding company of the combined group, and was renamed to CGNU. In addition, CGU shareholders received a final dividend of 23.75 pence per share,[478] and NU shareholders were entitled for a final dividend of 9.35 pence per share in respect of the year ended 31 December 1999.

CGU's offer valued NU at USD 14.4 bn corresponding to a market-to-book ratio of 1.59 on the effective day 30 May 2000, which is low compared to the prevailing market average of 2.60, but in line with other acquisitions of UK life insurers in that period of time: Axa bought Guardian Royal Exchange PLC on 1 February 1999 at 1.22 times book value,[479] and The Royal London Mutual Insurance Society acquired United Assurance Group PLC for GBP 1.5 bn in cash[480] corresponding to 1.42 times book value on 22 February 2000.[481] However, the latter deal came at a very high premium of 56% compared to the closing price on 18 February 2000, and was structured as an all cash acquisition.

Polish Supervisory over Pension Funds allowed NU to keep shareholdings in its Polish pension fund for a period of up to six months following the completion of the merger (Regulatory News Service, 11 May 2000), although exceeding a combined market share of 33% (Interfax Poland Business Service, 22 February 2000).

474 Reuters News (15 May 2000).

475 Regulatory News Service (22 May 2000).

476 CGU was listed on the FTSE non-life insurance index, but Norwich Union on the higher-rated FTSE life assurance index.

477 Regulatory News Service (21 February 2000). The actual takeover premium for NU shareholders was -3.6% at announcement (+2.7% for CGU shareholders), and +0.2% at effective date (–0.1% for CGU shareholders) excluding dividend top-up.

478 The new CGNU shares issued to NU shareholders did not carry the right to receive CGU's 1999 final dividend.

479 Dow Jones Business News (1 February 1999).

480 Associated Press Newswires (22 February 2000).

481 Dow Jones Business News (22 February 2000).

The deal consideration was thus heavily criticized by NU shareholders and analysts. An analyst estimated a 30-40% chance of a deal breakup if the hostile bidder would be willing to pay a cash component.[482] Another analyst criticized that CGU as the larger partner doesn't pay a premium, thus putting the deal at risk.[483] Consequently, as laid out in section 5.5.2.1, CGU and NU top management had to invest heavily into investor communication and to promise a 30% increase of dividends for NU shareholders conditional upon completion of the merger in order to gain their approval for the merger against Axa's counter bid.

5.5.2.3 Post-merger integration

Since the merger was privately negotiated (not auctioned), post-merger integration could be neatly planned and launched early in the transaction process, both most likely well ahead of the announcement of the transaction. First concrete integration measures were announced immediately after shareholder approval, supporting the hypothesis that integration teams were already operating successfully in the background. The post-merger integration activities can be separated into three work streams: Retention and integration of staff, realignment of lines of business and distribution, and integration of operations, see the overview presented in Figure 80.

The first work stream, *retention and integration of staff*, began with the *integration of the top management team* immediately after shareholder approval. Already on 6 April 2000, shortly after having received shareholder approval on 31 March 2000, CGU and NU cemented the merger by appointing key positions across the group. Former NU executives were appointed to head CGNU's non-life and life business, despite the fact that NU was smaller than CGU in terms of premiums.[484] Directors of the new company could only be appointed on the effective date of the merger, and former CGU staff initially assumed the lead but

482 Financial Times (22 February 2000b).
483 Daily Mail (22 February 2000).
484 Reuters News (6 April 2000).

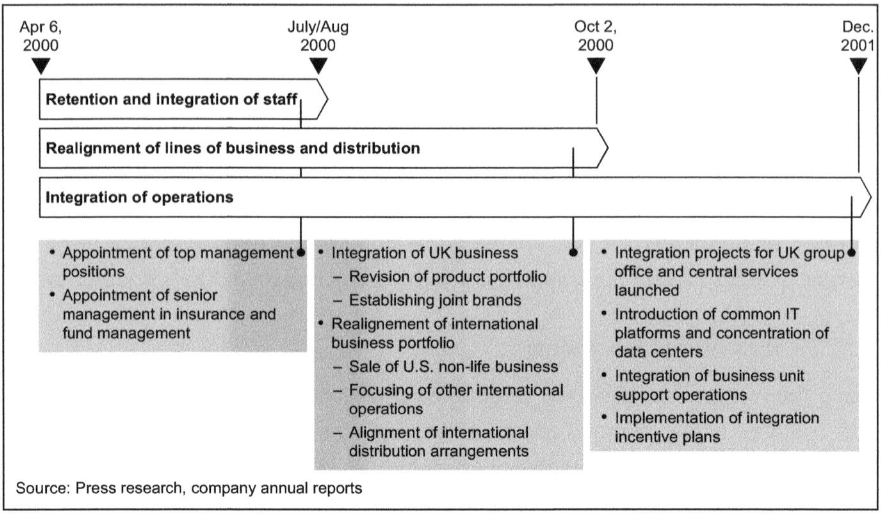

Figure 80: Overview of the post-merger integration process

a fixed replacement plan for former NU staff was put in place.[485] Beginning one week after appointment of the top management, the board members communicated further appointments across the group to ensure *retention of their senior management team*, such as staffing of the UK life office,[486] UK non-life office,[487] and the combined asset management business. The loss of few key employees, former CGU staff, in the latter unit became public in the beginning of June after they were beaten to top jobs by NU fund managers.[488] Later, more NU managers were to secure high-profile position in the combined asset management arm,[489]

485 The former chairman of CGU, Mr. Gyllenhammar, took over as Chairman of CGNU, and his counterpart of NU, Mr. Paul, was appointed Deputy Chairman. CGU's Group Chief Executive Director, Mr. Scott, became CGNU Group Chief Executive Director. Mr. Harvey, his NU counterpart, took the role of Deputy and succeeded Mr. Scott on 24 April 2001 (Regulatory News Service, 24 January 2001).

486 Four former CGU managers, and two former NU managers were selected (Money Marketing, 13 April 2000).

487 Insurance Brokers Monthly & Insurance Advisor (1 May 2000).

488 The Financial News (5 June 2000).

489 E.g., head of investment, head of property, head of pan-European and UK equities, centralized dealing desk, head of corporate research and quant analyst, head of strategy (The Financial News, 3 July 2000).

so that it can be assumed that CGNU top management factored risks and advantages of NU-biased promotions into their decisions.

The second work stream, *realignment of lines of business and distribution*, began with the *integration of UK insurance and fund management business.* CGNU consolidated advertising and creative accounts already in May 2000[490] to ensure a common branding for its UK non-life insurance and life insurance arm for its launch on 2 October 2000 under NU's brand.[491] By that date, sales forces should be fully trained on the integrated product portfolio. In order to simplify transition to the new products, CGNU decided to keep CGU's commercial lines and NU's personal lines, instead of pursuing a best-of-breed selection.[492,493] On the same date, CGU's and NU's Irish business were integrated under CGU's Hibernian brand.[494] Besides restructuring its UK and Irish operations, CGNU acted immediately to *realign its international business portfolio* according to the new strategic focus on the life insurance industry and on markets where it could achieve a top 5 position, see Figure 81 for an overview.

Already on the day of the merger announcement, a spokeswoman for CGU's U.S. operations confirmed that bidders are solicited for the U.S. non-life business,[495] and analysts assumed that CGU could realize up to USD 3 bn billion from the planned sale, but that potential buyers may be scarce.[496] CGNU's firm conviction of its strategy is reflected in its acceptance of a GBP 1,376 bn post tax loss on the sale of its U.S. non-life insurance operations to White Mountains Insurance Group for GBP 1.4 bn (USD 2.1 bn), announced on 25 September 2000. Further transactions followed soon to emphasize the strategic focus. Within one year after the announcement of the merger, a total of 11 deals were announced:

490 Marketing (18 May 2000).
491 Completion of integration was expected in June 2002. (Post Magazine, 8 June 2000).
492 Professional Broking (1 September 2000).
493 However, on 8 November 2000 the company stated the opposite, saying that its life and general businesses "now offer improved product ranges, reflecting the best of breed from the merged CGU and Norwich Union businesses", see Regulatory News Service (8 November 2000).
494 Regulatory News Service (8 November 2000).
495 Boston Herald (22 February 2000).
496 Reuters News (22 February 2000a).

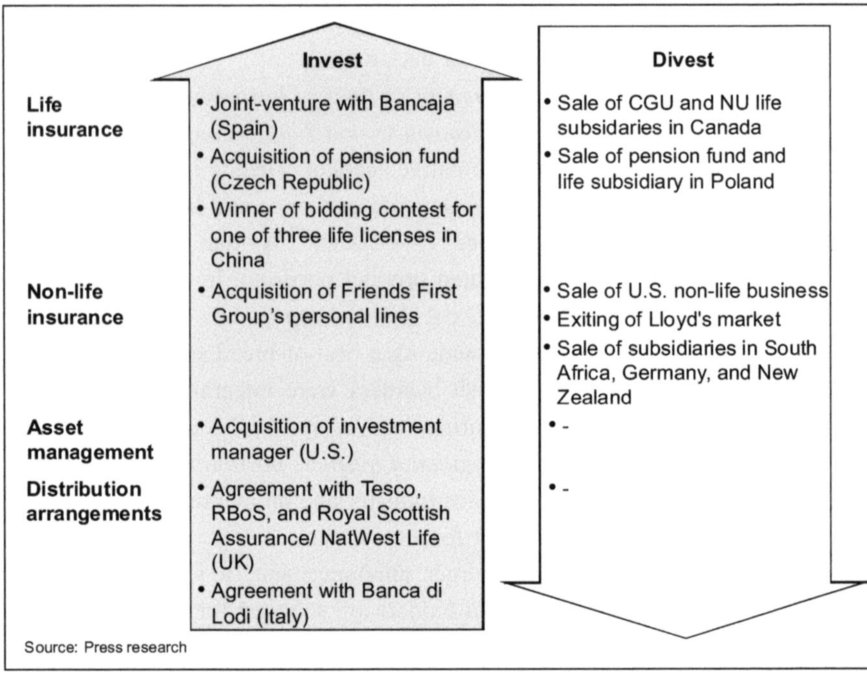

Figure 81: Realignment of CGNU's lines of business in the year after announcement of the merger

- 2 investments in the life insurance segment,[497] and 4 divestments in Canadian and Polish life insurance operations.[498] Additionally, CGNU won the

497 CGNU acquired a 50% stake in Bancaja's life insurance subsidiary on 19 May 2000 (CGNU, 19 May 2000). On 8 November 2000, CGNU announced to buy a 65% stake in Vseobecny vzajemny pensijni fond, Czech Republic's ninth-largest pension fund (Reuters News, 8 November 2000; Interfax Czech Republic Business News Service, 10 November 2000). CGNU further on joined the bidding contest for Equitable Life, a UK mutual insurer (Dow Jones International News, 1 September 2000), but pulled out (The Sunday Telegraph, 12 November 2000).

498 Manulife Financial, Canada's biggest insurance company, announced on 23 December 2000 to buy CGNU's Canadian life insurance operations for USD 93 mn (Financial Times, 23 December 2000). On 27 December 2000, CGNU announced the sale of Norwich Union Holdings Canada to American International Group for GBP 71mn (Financial Times, 27 December 2000). On 20 September 2000, Sampo Insurance Company, Finland's largest insurance group, announced that it acquires PTE Norwich Union S.A., the pensions provider, and Norwich Union Towarzystwo Ubezpieczen na Zycie S.A., the life insurance company.

bidding contest for one of three licenses granted by the Chinese government to sell life insurance in China.[499]

- 1 investment in non-life insurance,[500] but heavy divestments in non-life business besides sale of U.S. business operations through exiting Lloyd's market[501], and divesting in South African, German and New Zealand general markets.[502]

The strengthening of fund management proceeded at lower pace: NU's intended takeover of Gartmore, Royal Bank of Scotland's fund manager,[503] was outbid by Nationwide Mutual, a U.S. insurer.[504] However, on 15 November 2000, CGNU announced the acquisition of a medium-sized asset management company in the U.S.[505] Additionally, CGNU extended its international distribution arrangements at a fast pace by signing agreements with Tesco, Royal Bank of Scotland and NatWest in the UK,[506] and Banca Popolare di Lodi in Italy.[507]

499 Insurance Information Institute Database (10 November 2000).

500 Acquisition of Friends First Group's personal lines general business in Ireland through its subsidiary Hibernian Group, leading to a 26% market share (Regulatory News Service, 26 June 2000).

501 CGNU closed its entire global risk division (The Mail on Sunday, 6 August 2000), put its catastrophe and property syndicates into run-off (Post Magazine, 20 July 2000; Post Magazine, 24 August 2000), and sold its Lloyd's insurance market managing agency Marlborough Underwriting Agency to Berkshire Hathaway Group at undisclosed terms (Agence France-Presse, 1 November 2000).

502 CGNU sold its 51% shareholdings in CGU South Africa to Mutual & Federal Insurance Company on 30 June 2000 (Regulatory News Service, 30 June 2000). On 25 July 2000, CGNU had agreed to sell its German non-life insurance business to German insurer Gerling (Agence France-Presse, 25 July 2000). On 19 October 2000, CGNU announced to sell one of its two insurance business in New Zealand, State Insurance. (Financial Times, 27 October 2000).

503 Dow Jones International News (15 March 2000).

504 The Times (31 March 2000).

505 Reuters News (15 November 2000).

506 On 4 April 2000, CGNU announced a life and pensions alliance with Tesco Personal Finance, a joint venture between Tesco, a British supermarket group, and Royal Bank of Scotland. As part of the alliance, CGNU buys Tesco Personal Finance Life, Tesco's joint venture with Scottish Widows (Reuters News, 4 April 2000). On 26 April 2000, CGNU announced a distribution agreement with Royal Bank of Scotland, enabling it to sell through the bank's branches. Further on, CGNU agreed with Royal Scottish Assurance and NatWest Life to acquire 50% stakeholdings of the banks subsidiaries on 17 July 2000 (The Scotsman, 27 April 2000; Regulatory News Service, 17 July 2000).

507 Corriere della Sera (27 July 2000).

In the third work stream, *integration of operations*, CGNU setup integration projects for the UK group office and central service units early in the transaction process to ensure that benefits from economies of scale through common service platforms, centralized facilities management and IT infrastructure are achieved for its UK businesses.[508] Already on 20 April 2000, CGU and NU announced centralization of their UK locations. life insurance functions were to reside in York, non-life functions to operate from Norwich, and group corporate functions to be based in London.[509] In July, the front office structures of UK fund management were reportedly integrated.[510] In August, the integration of business unit support infrastructures was mostly complete.[511] In February 2002,[512] CGNU announced that the integration process was completed, and operations of CGU and Norwich Union were successfully merged by the end of 2001, including consolidation of UK data centers in Norwich, and movement of non-life operational platforms to a common system.[513] An *integration incentive plan* conditional upon fulfillment of integration targets was put in place,[514] and CGNU raised its original estimate of annualized pre-tax cost savings of GBP 250 mn and integration cost of GBP 350 mn to savings of GBP 275 mn and integration cost (to be fully included in annual results in 2002) of GBP 425 mn (to be fully accounted for in 2001).[515] The ramp-up of planned and achieved cost savings and integration cost as reported by CGNU is presented in Figure 82.

508 Regulatory News Service (8 November 2000).
509 Money Marketing (20 April 2000).
510 Regulatory News Service (2 August 2000).
511 Regulatory News Service (2 August 2001).
512 Regulatory News Service (27 February 2001).
513 Regulatory News Service (2 August 2001).
514 Regulatory News Service (27 February 2001). As a consequence, GBP 49 mn bonus payments for staff of certain business units and senior management were included in 2001 accounts (CGNU, 2000 and 2001).
515 Regulatory News Service (2 August 2000).

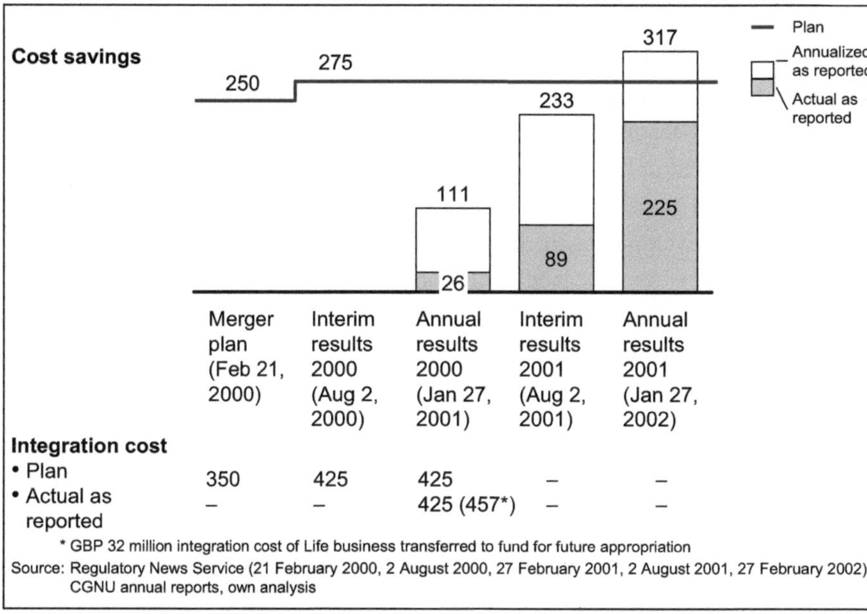

Figure 82: Reported planned and realized cost savings and integration cost (GBP mn)

5.5.3 Value creation by the transaction

5.5.3.1 Capital market reactions

The merger announcement sparked off considerable momentum in the UK M&A market.[516] Still, analysts mostly disapproved the deal, saying that the strategic rationale is unclear and that there is a 30-40% change of a break up if hostile bidders would offer cash component,[517,518] whereas major European insurers

516 On 22 February 2000, The Royal London Mutual Insurance Society announced to acquire United Assurance Group PLC for GBP 1.5 bn (Associated Press, 22 February 2000). Five days later, Royal & Sun Alliance said to solicit a buyer willing to pay more than GBP 6 bn (USD 10 bn) for its business (Reuters News, 27 February 2000). On 28 February 2000, Prudential, the British insurance company, was considering a bid of as much as GBP 4 bn (USD 6.4 bn), for its rival Equitable Life Assurance Society (The New York Times, 28 February 2000).

517 The Independent (21 February 2000).

518 Financial Times (22 February 2000b).

such as Allianz, Axa, Aegon, Generali, Fortis, ING or Zurich Financial were considered potential buyers of NU.[519] Amongst the few positive assessments, a Scottish fund manager appreciated that "all-share offers are not ideal but here are two management teams trying to realize shareholder value",[520] and an analyst considered the deal to be sensible, but remarked that previous insurance mergers haven't delivered value.[521]

The TRS development in the short-term after the announcement reflected analysts' criticism. As they labeled the deal "defensive" and "unexciting",[522,523] CGU's and NU's shares dropped by –7.3% and –12.5% during the first two trading days after board approval (life insurance market –3.8%), see Figure 83.

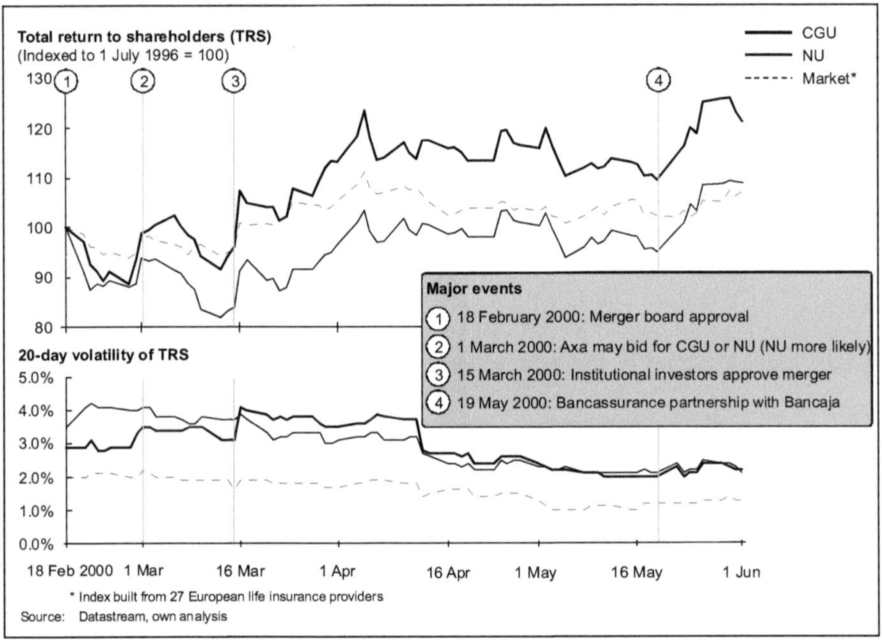

Figure 83: Short-term capital market reactions to events in transaction process

519 Reuters News (21 February 2000a).
520 Financial Times (22 February 2000a).
521 Reuters News (21 February 2000b).
522 The Times (23 February 2000).
523 Reuters News (21 February 2000b).

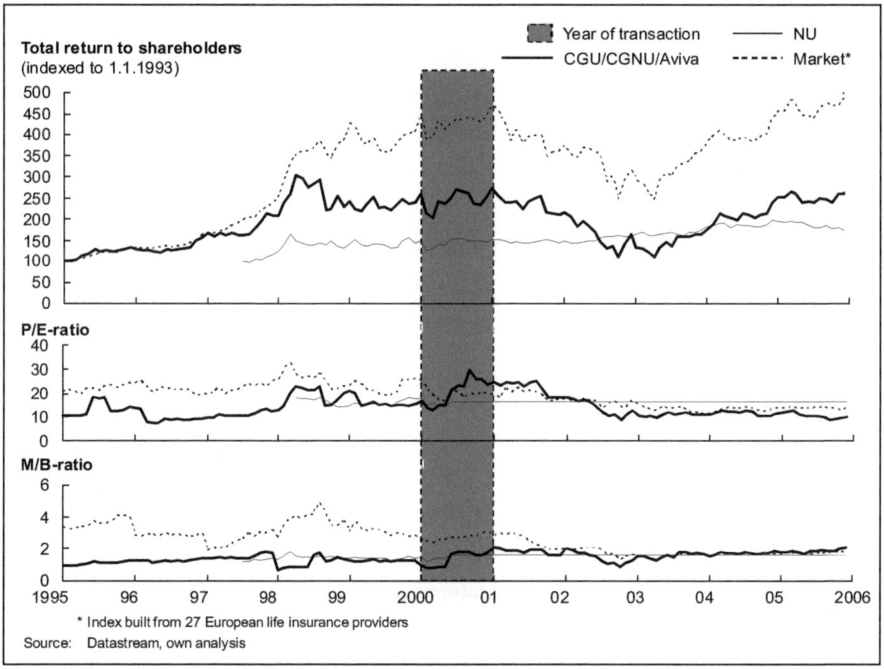

Figure 84: Long-term capital market reactions to merger announcement

Share prices of both transactions partners briefly rose by 5.4% and 6.0% (life insurance market 3.3%) on the day Axa publicly announced its possible hostile counter bid. Only after CGU and NU reported on 15 March 2000 that institutional investors approved the merger and Axa withdrew its plans to break up the transaction, share prices of both companies began to follow the generally positive trend of the life insurance market.

In the long run, the combined entities TRS developed quite similar to the life insurance market, see Figure 84. Thus, CGNU was not able to close the stock market performance gap to the life insurance market that opened in 1998 and widened until 2000.[524] Further on, after a history of below market level market-

524 CGU and NU increased their TRS index by 25.3% and 23.8% between 1.1.1998 and 3.1.2000, whilst the life insurance market index increased by 78.6% in the same period of time.

to-book valuation of CGU and NU,[525] CGNU's market-to-book ratio converged back to market level in 2002 and thereafter,[526] but at the same time its P/E ratios dropped below market level,[527] implying that investors began to appreciate the earnings level of CGNU, but (still) doubted their growth.

5.5.3.2 Event study results

Figure 85 presents the results of the analyses of short and long-term value creation in Chapter 4 for CGU's merger with NU. Capital markets reacted positively in the event window [–20; +20] days around announcement of the merger. The

Short-term*	
Value generation	USD 698 mn
CER	5.6%
CAR acquirer	7.7%
CAR target	2.7%

Long-term	
Value generation	USD 4.2 bn
BAHR 1 year	-12.1%
BAHR 2 years	31.4%
BAHR 3 years	25.1%

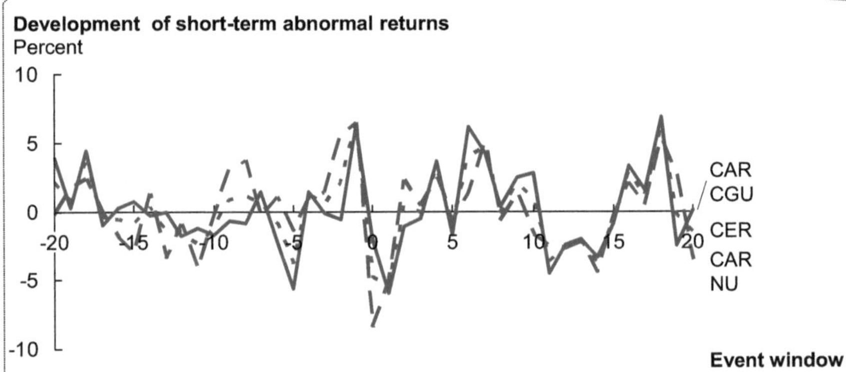

* Event window [-20; +20] trading days
Source: Own research

Figure 85: Event study results for CGU's merger with NU

525 E.g., on 1 January 1998, the M/B-ratio of the life insurance industry was 2.6, the one of CGU was 0.7, and the one of NU was 1.34.

526 E.g., on 1 January 2002, the M/B ratio of the life insurance industry and CGNU was 2.0.

527 E.g., from M/B-ratios of the life insurance industry and CGNU of 17.7 and 18.3 on 1 January 2002 to 15.1 and 10.3 on 1 January 2003, respectively.

combined entity achieved an abnormal return of 5.6% (corresponding to the 66% quantile of CERs of all transactions), and CARs of CGU (7.7%) and NU (2.7%) turned out positive as well. However, abnormal returns shortly after announcement are strongly negative, e.g., with –8.2% for the combined entity in the event window [0; +5] days. In the long run, the merger created value of USD 4.2 bn, with a 3-year BAHR of 25.1% (corresponding to the 82% quantile of all transactions). Thus, the hypothesis that the transaction timing was chosen well cannot be rejected.[528]

5.5.3.3 Impact on financial performance

Table 55 and Table 56 present the absolute and market adjusted financial performance of CGNU/Aviva[529] three years before the merger[530] until the third year of full realization of operative merger benefits.[531] Between 2001 and 2004, CGNU/Aviva increased its size in terms of premiums, reserves and assets by more than 50%. Its overall profitability decreased by most measures, but less so than profitability of its industry peers.[532] CGNU's/Aviva's return on reserves dropped from an average of 129 bp between 1997 and 1999 to 61 bp between 2002 and 2004, but its performance differential to the market improved but remained worse than the market median: The 3-year average improved from –74 bp (1997 to 1999) to –43 bp (2002 to 2004). At the same time, CGNU/Aviva achieved higher growth than the market in terms of premiums and assets (9 percentage points above market growth in 2002 to 2004), and the market share of

528 It could be argued that a merger announcement during the peak of the M&A cycle could have led to a hostile breakup of the merger, whereas the potential benefits of the eventual transaction may have been smaller or the final acquirer may have destroyed value through overbidding for NU. Since the merger was announced during the downturn of the M&A cycle, decreasing market momentum may have allowed potential hostile bidders to abstain from transaction proposals with doubtful rationale or at excessive considerations.

529 Shareholders of CGNU agreed on the 2002 general annual meeting to change CGNU's name to AVIVA, thus consolidating more than 50 trading names under one brand in order to increase awareness and earn marketing synergies (CGNU, 1 July 2002). For commercial reasons five of the strongest brands will not change.

530 Based on a pro-forma aggregation of financial performance measures.

531 Cost synergies were to be fully reflected in 2002 results (Regulatory News Service, 2 August 2000).

532 Its return on equity improved due to worsening capitalization.

Table 55: Financial performance of CGNU/Aviva before and after the merger

CGNU/Aviva*	Unit	1997	1998	1999	2000	2001	2002	2003	2004
Size									
Earnings	USD mn	1,020.3	1,823.7	1,650.3	-2,640.7	47.3	-891.4	1,730.5	2,117.4
Premiums	USD bn	18.8	36.7	38.2	42.8	39.7	45.2	51.1	59.1
Reserves	USD bn	138.0	216.2	223.5	202.7	187.6	207.7	255.2	293.5
Assets	USD bn	185.2	277.9	295.2	288.8	274.0	297.7	373.7	446.1
Shareholders' Equity	USD bn	16.4	25.7	26.1	21.2	18.2	16.8	13.2	17.8
Solvency									
Equity ratio	%	9.2%	9.2%	8.8%	7.4%	6.7%	5.6%	3.5%	4.0%
Equity reserves ratio	%	11.9%	11.9%	11.7%	10.5%	9.7%	8.1%	5.2%	6.0%
Operating leverage	times x	1.1	1.4	1.5	2.0	2.2	2.7	3.9	3.3
Reserves leverage	times x	83.2	68.9	82.4	-112.5	254.7	-176.5	85.0	82.0
Reserves ratio	times x	7.3	5.9	5.8	4.7	4.7	4.6	5.0	5.0
Profitability									
Return on reserves	bp	120.2	145.2	121.3	-88.9	39.3	-56.7	117.6	121.9
Return on equity	%	10.1%	12.2%	10.4%	-8.5%	4.0%	-7.0%	22.8%	20.2%
Return on premiums	%	8.8%	8.6%	7.1%	-4.2%	1.9%	-2.6%	5.9%	6.1%
Combined ratio	%	132.7%	143.7%	146.2%	101.8%	93.2%	80.2%	133.6%	129.3%
Loss ratio	%	114.4%	120.1%	139.3%	94.9%	88.1%	75.9%	128.9%	121.6%
Expense ratio	%	18.3%	23.6%	6.9%	6.9%	5.1%	4.3%	4.7%	7.6%
Growth									
Growth of earnings	%	0.0%	78.7%	-9.5%	-436.8%	-101.8%	-1985.3%	-294.1%	22.4%
Growth of premiums	%	0.0%	95.1%	4.2%	57.9%	-7.1%	13.7%	13.2%	15.6%
Growth of reserves	%	0.0%	56.7%	3.4%	29.1%	-7.5%	10.7%	22.9%	15.0%
Growth of assets	%	0.0%	50.1%	6.2%	53.5%	-5.1%	8.7%	25.5%	19.4%
Growth of equity	%	0.0%	56.7%	1.7%	30.5%	-14.2%	-8.0%	-21.3%	34.6%

* Pro forma aggregation of CGU and NU financial performance measures.

Table 56: Market adjusted financial performance of CGNU/Aviva before and after the merger

CGNU/Aviva* (market adj.**)	**Unit**	**1997**	**1998**	**1999**	**2000**	**2001**	**2002**	**2003**	**2004**
Size									
Earnings	x times market	3.8	11.0	5.5	-15.1	0.6	-28.0	7.3	8.4
Premiums	x times market	4.3	7.8	7.0	13.5	6.0	7.1	7.9	7.9
Reserves	x times market	6.6	9.9	14.2	14.9	11.0	8.6	8.9	9.6
Assets	x times market	6.1	9.5	6.6	10.1	6.2	4.8	7.9	8.6
Shareholders' Equity	x times market	8.6	14.6	11.4	10.6	9.1	8.4	6.0	7.6
Solvency									
Equity ratio	Δ%pts to market	4.1%	4.7%	2.8%	1.2%	0.3%	0.2%	-1.2%	-0.9%
Equity reserves ratio	Δ%pts to market	2.3%	3.2%	0.5%	-1.1%	-1.6%	-1.9%	-4.4%	-3.0%
Operating leverage	Δtimes x to market	-1.1	-1.0	-0.4	-0.5	-0.1	-0.1	0.4	0.0
Reserves leverage	Δtimes x to market	3.2	32.0	35.9	-167.8	211.7	-185.4	18.9	27.0
Reserves ratio	Δtimes x to market	1.8	0.2	0.0	-0.2	-0.9	-1.5	-0.7	-0.6
Profitability									
Return on reserves	Δbp to market	-3.9	-125.3	-94.0	-261.3	-8.9	-69.7	-19.8	-38.6
Return on equity	Δ%pts to market	-10.7%	-13.3%	-13.2%	-30.3%	-1.6%	-11.4%	7.2%	1.3%
Return on premiums	Δ%pts to market	1.8%	-3.8%	-2.3%	-13.2%	-1.1%	-3.9%	-0.6%	-0.8%
Combined ratio	Δ%pts to market	-16.8%	-9.9%	0.5%	1.9%	-6.9%	-4.7%	-9.8%	-3.3%
Loss ratio	Δ%pts to market	-11.3%	-14.6%	4.9%	2.5%	-1.9%	-1.5%	-2.6%	-2.9%
Expense ratio	Δ%pts to market	-5.5%	4.7%	-4.4%	-0.6%	-5.0%	-3.1%	-7.1%	-0.4%
Growth									
Growth of earnings	Δ%pts to market	0.0%	116.8%	-91.1%	-395.1%	-44.2%	-1928.2%	-934.8%	15.3%
Growth of premiums	Δ%pts to market	0.0%	87.1%	-12.5%	99.7%	-114.9%	17.9%	10.7%	-0.4%
Growth of reserves	Δ%pts to market	0.0%	52.1%	31.4%	43.1%	-33.3%	-30.1%	4.0%	8.4%
Growth of assets	Δ%pts to market	0.0%	53.7%	-46.5%	89.2%	-59.0%	-31.2%	48.8%	9.3%
Growth of equity	Δ%pts to market	0.0%	64.5%	-29.1%	43.0%	-13.6%	-7.6%	-31.1%	27.1%

* Pro forma aggregation of CGU and NU financial performance measures.

** Median of EU-15 peers.

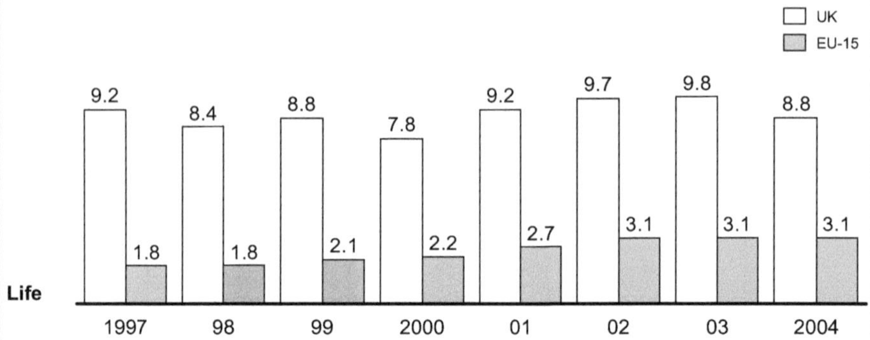

Non-life								
• UK	10.6	11.8	12.6	11.5	10.3	9.4	8.4	8.8
• EU-15	0.9	1.0	1.1	1.4	1.0	0.9	0.8	0.7

Source: OECD Insurance Statistics, Annual reports

Figure 86: Development of the market share of the combined entity (percent)

the combined entity increased steadily after the merger in the UK and European life insurance segment, see Figure 86.[533] The strategic shift from a multi-line insurer to a life insurer is further emphasized by increasing share of life premiums to total premium of the combined entity, see Figure 87. Thus, realization of *market power* and *revenue economies of scope* from skill transfer and cross-selling cannot be rejected.

However, an analysis of realized cost savings indicates that *economies of scale* may not have been realized as planned. Due to hypothesized sources of these cost savings,[534] the effect should largely be reflected in a reduction of unit costs[535] based on net administrative operating expenses before one-off restructur-

533 The declining market share in non-life insurance reflects CGNU's announced shift in strategic focus to life insurance and according divestments in non-life business in the U.S. and other geographies.

534 According to the merger plan (Regulatory News Service, 21 February 2000), estimated sources of cost savings were staff 48%, property 6%, IT 19%, and other 27%.

535 According to the merger plan (Regulatory News Service, 21 February 2000), economies of scale should reflect in a reduction of unit costs, not absolute costs.

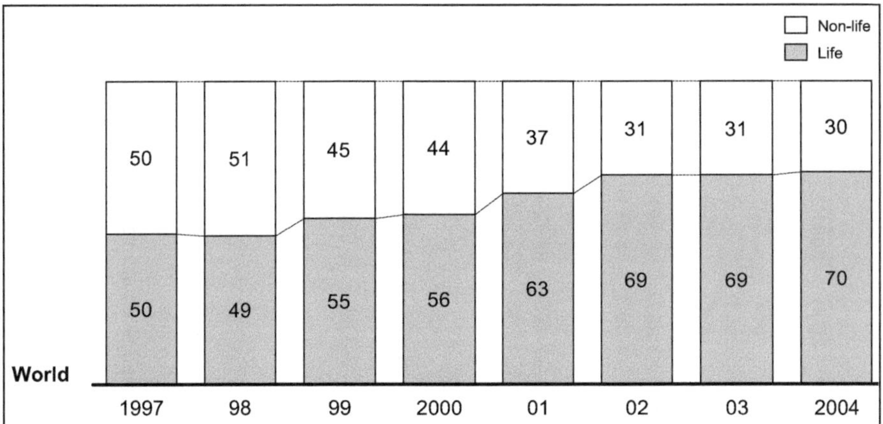

	1997	98	99	2000	01	02	03	2004
• UK	58	56	61	64	64	64	63	62
• EU-15	42	44	39	36	36	36	37	38

Source: Company annual reports

Figure 87: Development of premium share of the combined entity (percent)

ing cost. Full cost savings were to be visible in 2002 results.[536] Table 57 presents a computation of unit costs based on net earned premiums and reserves, and respective cost savings in 2002 normalized on level of business in 1999. Although CGNU states in its 2001 annual result filings that GBP 317 mn of cost savings were realized,[537] the presented analyses provide only support for cost savings ranging between GBP 47 mn and GBP 113 mn at the maximum.[538]

Further on, Aviva did not achieve to *strengthen its capitalization*. Its equity ratio and equity reserves ratio worsened notably. E.g., its 3-year average equity ratio declined from 9.1% between 1997 and 1999 (3.9 percentage points better than the industry) to 4.4% between 2002 and 2004 (0.6 percentage points below the industry). A series of rating downgrades beginning at the end of 2002, see Figure 88, provides further support for these observations.

536 CGNU (27 February 2002).
537 CGNU (27 February 2002).
538 It shall be noted that utilization of different bases for unit cost computation may yield different results.

Table 57: Analysis of realized cost savings

Financial indicators	Unit	1999**	2000	2001**	2002
Net administrative operating expenses*					
Administrative (long-term account)	GBP mn	475	482	701	737
- Thereof one-time effect introduction of EUR	GBP mn	9	11	0	0
Administrative (general account)	GBP mn	719	886	590	483
- Thereof one-time effect introduction of EUR	GBP mn	6	7	0	0
Total	GBP mn	1,194	1,368	1,291	1,220
Total before effect introduction of EUR	GBP mn	1,179	1,350	1,291	1,220
Bases for unit costs					
Net earned premiums	GBP mn	25,101	27,470	27,720	27,062
Reserves - Traditional business	GBP mn	109,438	121,348	121,629	125,304
Reserves - Total	GBP mn	135,802	149,306	150,870	155,179
Unit costs* **					
Net earned premiums	-	0.0470	0.0491	0.0466	0.0451
Reserves - Traditional business	-	0.0108	0.0111	0.0106	0.0097
Reserves - Total	-	0.0087	0.0090	0.0086	0.0079
Normalized cost savings******					
Net earned premiums	GBP mn	47			
Reserves - Traditional business	GBP mn	113			
Reserves - Total	GBP mn	111			

* Without integration costs and financial services compensation scheme levy.

** Restated figures.

*** Total admin. operating expenses before introduction of EUR divided by respective balance sheet position.

**** (unit costs 1999 - unit costs 2002) * respective balance sheet position.

Source: CGNU/Aviva annual reports (2000 - 2002).

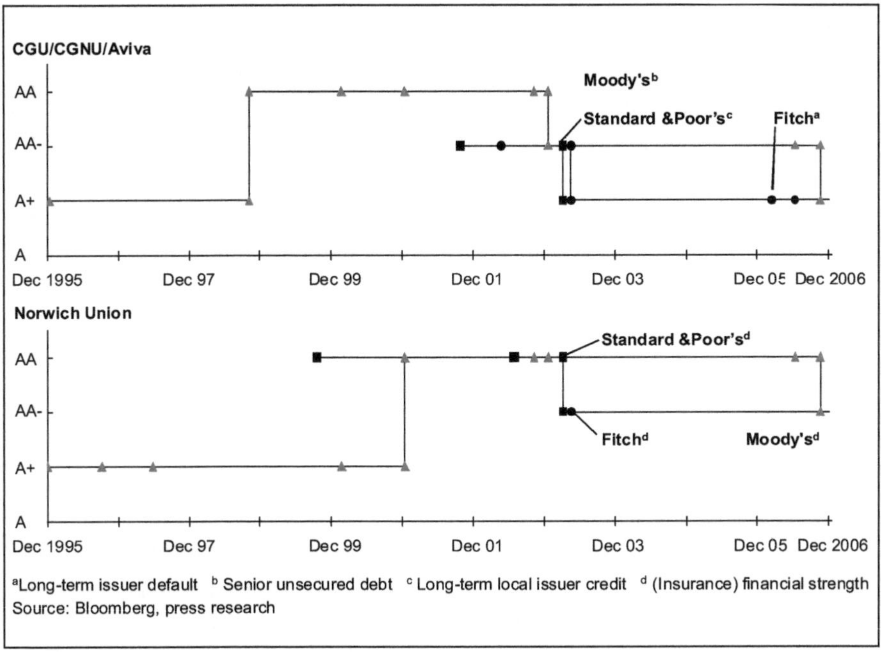

Figure 88: Development of CGU and NU ratings

5.5.4 Conclusion

This section analyzed CGU's merger with NU in February 2000. This transaction is chosen for three reasons. Firstly, the merger was announced during the downturn of the M&A market, thus capturing a different phase of the market cycle than the Munich Re's acquisition of American Re. Secondly, among other transactions also fulfilling this criterion, the examined merger carried the largest relative transaction volume with 71%, thus supporting visibility of M&A effects in capital market reactions and financial performance measures. Thirdly, the transaction built the nucleus for the highly successful UK life insurer Aviva.

Motivation, conduct and value creation

In the 1990s, European insurance industry giants drove an intense process of market concentration, and it was not before 2000 for the European insurance M&A market to enter a downturn phase. In contrast to non-life business, life insurance premiums showed healthy growth, a trend which was likely to continue. However, life insurers' results were under pressure especially from falling interest rates, leading to a widening profitability gap between top and worst performing carriers. As a consequence, life insurers sought M&A to improve their profitability and their capital base, but also to strengthen their footprint in the growing segment.

The public company CGU was the outcome of the mergers of Commercial Union (established 1861) with Hand-in-hand (established in 1696) in 1905, and Commercial Union with General Accident (established in 1885) in 1998. In 1999, CGU was Britain's third largest life insurer and second largest non-life insurer with a roughly equal global premium share of both business lines. CGU decided to pursue M&A primarily because it sought to increase participation in the attractive life insurance markets through a transformational strategic shift. NU with its strong life franchise in CGU's home market promised a good basis from where to rejuvenate international expansion in the life segment.

NU was established in 1797 as a mutual insurance company, and converted and floated not before 1997. In 1999, NU was similarly strongly positioned in the UK compared to CGU with a market share of 4.1% and 6.3% in the life and non-life market, respectively. Further on, it achieved solid financial results with above market capitalization, and slightly higher profitability. However, capital markets valued NU notably below the market average, doubting its current earnings level and its ability to grow earnings. As a consequence, NU was frequently involved in rumors of a potential takeover by large European insurers in the year before the transaction, threatening its management to lose its position and influence. The merger with NU promised its management to secure their power due to a fixed succession scheme in the merger plan, giving rise to the non-value generating M&A motive of *empire building*. Further on, value could be created based on *economies of scale* from integrating UK operations, *revenue economies of scope* through skill transfer and cross-selling, increase in *market power*, and *strengthening of capitalization.* Over and above, the merger was designed to serve as a catalyst for a major organizational transformation.

On 21 February 2000, CGU and NU announced that both boards approved the companies plan to merge after week long negotiations. The fact that the merger was privately negotiated (not auctioned) allowed the transaction partners to prepare integration in detail, to begin with integration immediately after shareholders' approval, to avoid a bidding contest which could have led to a foreign insurance group breaking up the merger, and to free up capacity for external communication. Due to the extensive communication effort, top management of CGU and NU gained shareholder approval, despite the fact that the nil-premium all-share structure of the merger was rather unattractive for NU investors, urging Axa to withdraw its plan of a potential counter bid. First concrete post-merger integration measures became apparent already few days after shareholder approval. CGU and NU announced integrated top management positions and appointments of senior staff in the respective departments, and thus achieved retention of most key staff as a prerequisite for realization of economies of scope through skill transfer. Further on, CGU and NU proceeded right after announcement with the realignment of their UK and international lines of business and distribution. The U.S. non-life insurance operations were sold in September 2000, UK insurance and fund management functions and products were integrated by October 2000, and a total of 4 investments and 8 divestments were carried out across all business segments to further push organizational transformation towards the new strategic focus. Lastly, CGNU achieved to integrate operations quickly, as the new location strategy was announced already in April 2000, most business unit support functions integrated by August 2000, and full integration completed by the end of 2001. The realization of planned merger benefits and determinants of failure and success are discussed in the following. Figure 89 presents an overview.

	Planned merger benefits	Achieved results	Root causes (under-) achievement
Motives that create value	• Value creation by avoiding transaction in the M&A peak	• Notable value created	• „Inexpensive“ deal (nil-premium, all-share), but might have led to breakup in peak phase of M&A cycle • Extensive external communication
• **Profitability**	• Economies of scale through cost synergies	• Cost savings realized but probably less than planned and reported	• Negotiated merger allowed detailed planning and early launch of integration of operations
• **Growth**	• Further organic growth through – Market power increase especially in UK life market – Revenue economies of scope through cross-selling	• Market share in life increased while improving profitability compared to the market	• Retention and integration of key staff • Realignment of international businesses and distribution arrangements
• **Solvency**	• Strengthening of capitalization • (Risk reduction for NU through global diversification)	• Solvency dropped below market level, rating down-grades followed	• Growth without capacity increase
Other motives	• Empire building	• Position as leading European insurer (top 5) strengthened	• –

* U.S. traditional and European non-traditional markets

Source: Own research

Figure 89: Achievement of planned merger benefits

Realization of merger benefits

Value: Although analysts disapproved the deal shortly after its announcement, the transaction created value in the short-term with a CER of 5.6% in the event window [–20; +20] (corresponding to a value creation of USD 0.7 bn) and in the long-term with a BAHR of 25.1% over three years (corresponding to a value creation of USD 4.2 bn).

Profitability: Profitability of CGNU improved, but remained below the market median: The average market adjusted return on reserves increased from –111 bp (1997 to 1999) to –43 bp (2002 to 2004). However, planned *economies of scale* were most likely only partly realized. Against a first target of GBP 250 mn, revised to GBP 275 mn at announcement of 2000 interim results, the company reported to have achieved annualized cost savings of GBP 317 mn in 2001. A unit cost analysis however yields a maximum normalized cost saving of GBP 113 mn.

Growth: Revenue *economies of scope* or *market power* effects were realized. The market share of the combined entity remained at 8.8% (1999 and 2004) in the UK life insurance market, but increased from 2.1% (1999) to 3.1% (2004) in the European life insurance market, while overall profitability improved compared to CGNU's industry peers.

Solvency: CGNU's capitalization deteriorated, as its average equity ratio dropped from 3.3 percentage points above market (1997 to 1999) to 0.6 percentage points (2002 to 2004) below the market median. Further on, Aviva suffered from a series of rating downgrades after the end of 2002, providing additional evidence that *strengthening of capitalization* was not realized.

Identification of process-related determinants of value creation

Three major determinants of value creation relating to the conduct of the transaction can be identified from the conduct of the transaction. Firstly, the merger was *negotiated privately (not auctioned)*, which allowed management to plan integration in detail, launch integration early, and free up top management capacity to actively steer the post-announcement transaction and integration process.

Prior event study research on the comparative benefits and pitfalls of negotiations vs. auctions in the context of M&A obtains mixed results:

- Dasgupta and Hansen (2007, p. 33) summarize results of empirical research on short-term value creation by auctioned vs. negotiated transactions that "auctions tend to yield great results [i.e. abnormal returns] for targets but [...] competition in the auction tends to ensure that gains to bidders are at best minimal".
- Roll (1986) attributes this inferiority of bidder gains in auctions to overbidding, following the notion of the winner's curse in auction theory.[539]
- However, Boone and Mulherin (2007) do not detect significant differences between short-term wealth effects for shareholders depending on whether transactions are negotiated or auctioned on their sample of 400 transactions between major U.S. corporations.[540]

It shall be noted that the reviewed prior research does not actually test the presented hypotheses that private negotiation leads to detailed planning and early launch of integration, which in turn increases success[541] of the transaction. The presented event studies focus on short-term value creation after announcement, whereas superior value extraction by smooth integration are likely to become apparent only in the mid to long-term after announcement.[542] Further on, they test the joint hypothesis of existence and realization of value creation potentials in their transaction sample. By doing that, these studies do not separate out effects of further possible determinants of success related to the decision to either auction or negotiate a transaction. Consequently, the above hypothesis cannot be rejected, but is also not confirmed by prior research.

---

539 Bulow and Klemperer (1996) provide support for Roll's (1986) hypothesis in their theoretical research by concluding that under reasonable assumptions in their transaction model, a firm should always put up itself for an auction if it is contacted by a bidder in private and if at least one further serious bidder exists.

540 Analyzed event windows are [–1; +1], [–20; +20], and [–63; +126] days around announcement. A long-term study is not conducted.

541 I.e. degree of realization of existing value potentials.

542 Assuming that investors are unlikely to anticipate superiority of negotiations vs. auctions in transactions already around announcement.

The second determinant of success during the conduct of the transaction is the *extensive external communication* in order to gain shareholders' approval, and to ensure transparency on the progress of integration. Heldenberg et al. (2006) identify several key characteristics of successful financial communication to external stakeholders in their case study of three Belgian bank mergers. The growing demand for information should be satisfied with temporary structures, drawing on the full set of means of communication. Rapid reaction to information requests is important to avoid diffusion of misleading information to volatile financial markets. Further on, the general manager needs to assume an active role in communication to raise the level of importance and ensure unified messages. Toole and Herget (2005, p. 362) emphasize the difficulty to communicate optimally to all stakeholders at the same time, and agree with Heldenbergh et al. (2006) that communication should be timely and frequent.[543]

Thirdly, the transaction partners achieved to aggressively drive integration of CGU's and NU's staff and operations at high pace, while pursuing realignment of their business according to the new strategic direction. Toole and Herget (2005, p. 361) identify "*maintaining business continuity and generating momentum during the integration stage* [as] the single most important factor in the ultimate success of the transaction". Further on, they argue that integration success increases with speed of integration, because uncertainty is avoided and synergies are achieved earlier. Gerds (2006) points out that overly fast paced integration processes endanger success of the integration, e.g., due to excessive demands to employees, only partial fulfillment of activities, the risk of wrong decisions, and difficulties to stay in full control of the complex process.

Summary

CGU and NU achieved most of the planned merger benefits due to integration excellence: Top management positions were integrated at a very early stage of the transaction process, key senior management was appointed and thus retained immediately thereafter, lines of business and distribution arrangements were realigned rapidly according to the new strategic orientation, and operations were integrated according to the timeline. As a consequence, most planned merger

543 Empirical research on the importance of external communication could not be identified.

benefits were achieved. Detailed integration planning already during the private merger negotiations enabled the rapid and successful implementation. Freed up capacity of top management was imperatively required to react flexibly to arising issues as the merger proceeded, such as hesitance of NU shareholders to approve the nil-premium all-share deal and Axa's hostile counterbid. In summary, the merger between CGU and NU catalyzed a transformational change of the transactions partners strategy, thus creating the nucleus for Aviva, one of Europe's most successful life insurers.

5.6 Summary

Event studies on value creation through M&A in the insurance conclude that completed transactions created value over a short and long-term horizon. However, the question especially of process-related determinants of success has not yet been answered satisfactory. Thus, recent research on value creation through M&A and its determinants turned to analyzing individual transactions in case studies, but insurance transactions have never been investigated before.

This research analyzes two prominent transactions. Munich Re's acquisition of American Re in 1996 is chosen because it presents the largest reinsurance transaction by European acquirers between 1990 and 2005. Further on, it is one of the most heavily criticized transactions in the same period of time, causing Munich Re severe issues with its business portfolio, operative performance, and valuation on the capital market. CGU's merger with Norwich Union in 2000 is selected since it enabled a fundamental transformation of both large but undervalued insurers and built the nucleus for Aviva, one of the most successful life insurers in Europe, which dominates the UK life market and aggressively manages it portfolio of country businesses.

The specific objectives of the case study analyses presented in this research are twofold: Firstly, occurrence of drivers and hurdles for M&A shall be tested. Secondly, the influence of the transaction conduct ("process perspective") on value extraction shall be investigated. With respect to the former objective, both transactions were primarily driven by growth aspirations of the larger transaction partner. Benefits were assumed to come from an increase of market power, and revenue economies of scope through skill transfer in product development and cross-selling of products. CGNU clearly realized these benefits as its market share and profitability increased, but the realization in the case of Munich Re can be doubted at best. The secondary motive for the two examined transactions was a lack of profitability of the larger transaction partner, which was speculating on improvement through M&A from two sources. Firstly, underwriting effectiveness was assumed to improve due to economies of scope from skill transfer. Munich Re did not achieve this. Secondly, cost synergies in operations were believed to exist due to economies of scale. CGNU achieved to reduce unit costs, but most likely failed to meet its initial cost savings targets. Further motives for M&A, assumed benefits through M&A, and the respective degree of achievement in the two case studies are summarized in Figure 90.

The results of the case studies with respect to the second objective, identification of process-related determinants of value creation, are summarized in Figure 91. Munich Re acted hasty in the pre-acquisition process, seeking for early exclusivity in the transaction process, and did not carry out a proper actuarial appraisal of American Re's book. During the post-acquisition process, Munich Re lost experienced top management, failed to gain control on underwriting of risky liability lines, and did not achieve to properly communicate negligibility of relatd reserving issues externally. In the case of Aviva, as major success factors emerged private negotiation, allowing management to prepare the merger process in detail and to launch integration early, extensive external communication to gain shareholders' approval and to convince markets of integration success, and aggressive implementation of integration plans while retaining top management and maintaining business continuity. Sections 5.4.4 and 5.5.4 discuss these factors in detail in the context of prior research.

The findings emphasize the importance of process-related determinants for the realization of value creation potential from a transaction. Certainly, further case study research on the matter is required. An enlarged case study repository would provide a better empirical basis for conclusions, and would allow to build a more comprehensive model of value creation through insurance M&A.

Average degree of achievement ● Full ○ Null

	Motives of Munich Re and American Re	Motives of CGU and Norwich Union	Merger benefits and obstacles
Motives that create value	• M&A market for reinsurers in upswing (especially U.S.)	• M&A market for primary insurers in downturn	◐ Value creation by avoiding transaction in M&A peak
• **Profitability**	• MR underwriting less effective than AR underwriting	• CGU less profitable than NU and life insurance market	◐ Economies of scope (skill tran-sfer pri-marily for underwriting effectiveness) ◐ Economies of scale through cost synergies
• **Growth**	• MR's valuation strongly based on growth • MR's market share declining, AR's market share constant	• Life market growing at higher rate than CGU's valuation implied growth rate • NU's market share declining in growing UK life market • NU's market share increasing in stagnating UK nonlife market	Further organic growth through ◕ – Market power increase ◕ – Revenue economies of scope (cross-selling, skill transfer new products) (?) – Revenue economies of scale ("flight to quality")
• **Solvency**	• MR capitalized worse than market, AR better • MR is European player, AR has North American focus	• CGU capitalized worse than NU • CGU is European player, NU has UK focus	○ Strengthening of capitalization ○ Risk reduction (diversification, less risky products)
Other motives	• Acquisition of German re-insurers by U.S. reinsurers	• CGU and NU may become takeover target (for non-UK insurer)	◕ Empire building

Source: Own research

Figure 90: Overview of motives, expected benefits, and degree of achievement of these benefits in the presented case studies

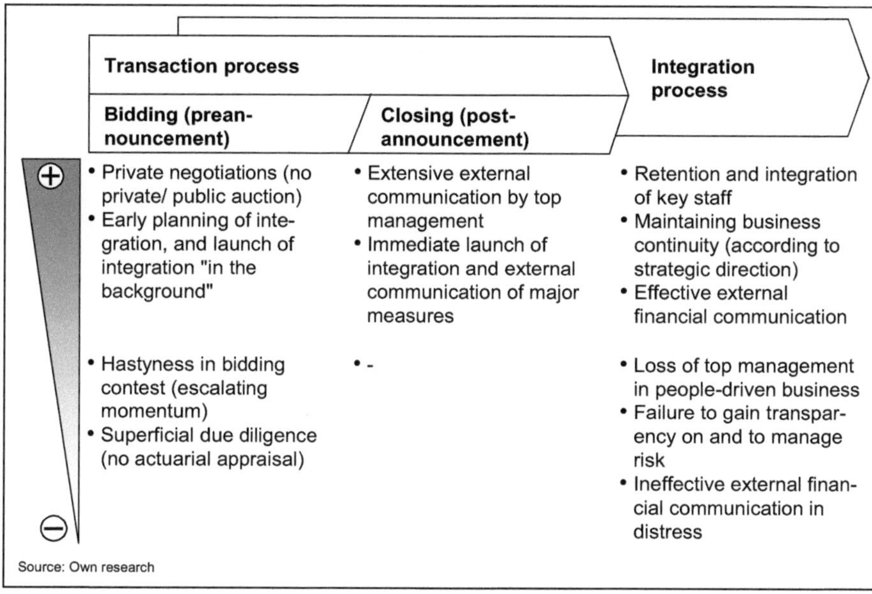

Figure 91: Overview process-related determinants of value creation in the presented case studies

6 Conclusion

The European insurance sector went through a radical transformation since the 1990s, causing a strong pickup especially in cross-border M&A activity after introduction of the Third Generation Insurance Directives in 1992. After reaching its peak in 1999, the European insurance M&A market calmed down for several consecutive years, but gained momentum again in 2005. Therefore, this study analyzes the three research questions:

- Is this pickup in M&A momentum merely a blip in the market, or does it mark the entry into the next cycle of transactions in the European insurance market? (section 2)
- Does M&A in the European insurance industry create value, and what are major determinants of its success? (methodology in section 3, analyses in section 4)
- How does value creation materialize in individual transactions, and how does the conduct of the transaction influence extraction of potential benefits? (section 5)

The analyses show that the current rise in M&A activity is likely to continue, thus marking the entry into a new cycle of transactions in the European insurance industry. The fundamental drivers for further consolidation resemble those motives identified for the M&A cycle between 1990 and 2005, e.g., necessity of insurers to withstand margin pressure by increasing market power and reaping economies of scale and scope, utilizing currently high free cash flow for funding, and reduction of hurdles due to further harmonization of jurisdictions. However, since antitrust concerns of the European Commission are likely due to an already high level of primary insurance market concentration, further M&A may again strongly involve cross-border transactions, possibly even in combination with prior disengagement of acquirers in their local markets.

In the light of these findings, stakeholders of insurance M&A will appreciate the fact that European insurance transactions in the previous M&A cycle created value in the average on a short-term horizon (highest significant CER of 2.06% in [–10; +10] based on sample size $N = 54$), and that these results may hold for future transactions due to the resemblance of underlying motives and types of expected benefits. Nevertheless, insurers should pursue further inorganic growth with particular caution, since these past transactions did not create value in the average on a longer term horizon (insignificant BAHR of –6.6% on a 3-year horizon based on sample size $N = 158$, and insignificant CTAR of –0.4% per month based on sample size $N = 157$). Obviously, some insurers achieved to create notable value through their transactions (see e.g., case study of CGU merging with Norwich Union in 2000 further below), raising the question which factors influence value creation. An analysis of major hypothesized determinants yields the following results:

- In the short-term, industry or geographical diversification created value compared to full focus strategies, but in the long-term, only full focus or full diversification strategies created value.
- In the short-term, transactions in the peak phase of the M&A market were rewarded by investors compared to transactions during the bottom, but in the long-term, transactions in the bottom phase proved superior.
- In the short-term, value creation decreased with speed of acquirer growth, but in the long-term, faster growing acquirers generated more value than slower growing acquirers.
- In the short- and the long-term, medium experienced acquirers destroyed value compared to inexperienced and most experienced acquirers.

These results are relevant for regulators, management and shareholders. Regulators need to carefully choose timing and scope of their decisions to harmonize jurisdictions in order to limit irrational transaction decisions in overheated M&A markets. Management of insurers should align their investor communication with their transaction timing and strategy: In the bottom phase of the M&A market cycle, communication should emphasize strategic rationale and resulting value added for investors, whereas potential benefits from economies of scale and increased market power should be highlighted in fully focused transactions. In addition, strongly growing insurers could use their momentum to cement their success through further inorganic growth. Conversely, shareholders of insurers should more carefully assess transactions announced in periods of high M&A activity and more thoroughly evaluate benefits of focused transactions.

Certainly, these empirical analyses provide a solid perspective on the average transaction and its major determinants of success, but they do not account for detailed specifics of individual transactions. Therefore, the two transactions Munich Re acquires American Re (1996), and CGU merges with Norwich Union (2000) to form Aviva are analyzed to provide further insights into root causes for the success or failure of individual transactions, especially with respect to aspects related to the conduct of a transaction. Both transactions were primarily driven by growth aspirations of the larger transaction partners, which speculated on increasing market power, and revenue economies of scope through skill transfer in product development and cross-selling of products. The secondary motive in both transactions was the larger transaction partner's ambition to improve its profitability from economies of scope and cost synergies. In addition, top management teams sought to secure their power through empire building especially in the case of the CGU/NU merger.

Munich Re destroyed value in the long-term, as it acted hasty in the bidding contest, and failed to have an independent actuarial appraisal of the risky business lines carried out, although indications of top-line orientation of underwriting and resulting portfolio issues at American Re were recognizable from published financial data. Clearly, potentially risky portfolios should be assessed by actuaries during due diligence, or transaction terms should be linked to the outcome of such an assessment in the near future. Further on, Munich implemented integration measures quite late, lost key staff of American Re, failed to gain transparency and control risk in American Re underwriting, and ineffectively communicated Munich Re's actual situation to external stakeholders when reserving issues appeared. The result was disastrous, as Munich Re destroyed USD 20.8 bn value in the first three years after transaction announcement. In contrast, CGU and NU achieved to transform their business entirely through the merger. Private negotiations allowed a detailed planning of integration, early launch integration "in the background", and freed up top management capacity for steering of the merger process. Further on, CGU and NU achieved to retain and integrate key staff, to realign their business according to the new strategic direction through a massive firework of investments and divestments, and to effectively communicate the progress of integration to external stakeholders. The merger created USD 4.2 bn value in the three years following its announcement.

Future research could extend the presented empirical analyses and case studies. In particular, further event studies should compare value creation by transactions of the observed new wave of transactions in the European insurance M&A market with the findings of this study as soon as sufficient data becomes available. These analyses are important to assess whether results are indeed comparable, to provide further evidence for or modify the above conclusions, and to examine the rationale for possibly occurring differences. Further on, the reasons for observed differences in value creation between geographies[544] and sub-industries within financial services[545] should be examined. If they were caused by structural differences, governments or regulators should assess whether factors preventing value creating M&A should be tackled in future legislation. Otherwise, financial service providers should share "M&A best practice" across sub-industries in order to improve value creation in their sector. Additionally, case study research should be pursued further. A growing repository of transaction cases would provide a better empirical basis to cover all types of structurally different transactions, and to derive conclusions from the observations despite random fluctuations in otherwise equal transactions. Based on the extended empirical analyses and case study research, a more comprehensive model for value creation through M&A could be built to better capture determinants of successfully identifying value potential, extracting value through proper conduct, and negotiating adequate terms of transactions.

544 Boubakri et al. (2006) observe strong positive value creation in U.S. insurance M&A, but this study detects insignificant negative value creation in European insurance M&A.

545 Empirical studies of M&A in the financial services industry frequently doubt value creation, in particular in the banking industry, see overviews in Beitel and Schiereck (2003), and Pilloff and Santomero (1998).

7 Appendix

7.1 Event Study – Additional details on short-term analyses

Table 58: Descriptive statistics for metric and polytomous variables

Metric variables

Statistics	***CER****	***CAR Acquirer****	***CAR Target****	***LNSIZE***	***GROWTH***	***LNRELVOLUME***
Mean	1.1%	-0.6%	12.1%	8.9781	1.3072	-1.8792
St.dev.	5.2%	5.4%	20.8%	1.5536	0.3803	1.7021
Min	-8.9%	-17.1%	-9.8%	4.6958	0.3193	-5.7228
Max	17.0%	20.9%	91.4%	11.6487	3.8566	1.2295
N	54	54	54	54	54	54

Polytomuous variables

Cat.	***TIMING***	Freq.	***STRATEGY***	Freq.	**EXPERIENCE**	Freq.
0**	Bottom	11	National/within-industry	11	No experience	25
1	Upswing	7	National/cross-industry	7	Little experience	2
2	Peak	30	Cross-border EU/within-industry	10	Extensive experience	12
3	Downturn	6	Cross-border EU/cross-industry	4	Most experience	15
4			Cross-border world/within-industry	10		
5			Cross-border world/cross-industry	12		
N	total	54	total	54	total	54

Cat.	***ACQREGION***	Freq.	***TARREGION***	Freq.	***ACQINDUSTRY***	Freq.	***TARINDUSTRY***	Freq.
0**	EU-15	44	EU-15	30	P&C	8	P&C	9
1	EU-25	0	EU-25	0	Life	36	Life	30
2	Swiss	10	Swiss	1	Re	9	Re	0
3	Norway	0	Norway	1	Agents/Brokers	1	Agents/Brokers	3
4	World	0	World	22	Other	0	Other	12
N	total	54	total	54	total	54	total	54

* Event window [-5; +5].

** Reference category.

Table 59: Results of robustness tests of short-term multivariate regression model

	CER (Full model)			**CER** (Weaker multicoll.)			**CER** (Reduced)		
Model specification	DF	sig DF		DF	sig DF		DF	sig DF	
Ramsey Reset	0.0279	97.3%		2.1109	13.7%		0.0228	97.7%	
Normality of residuals	Z	asy sig		Z	asy sig		Z	asy sig	
K-S	0.5882	88.0%		0.7713	59.1%		0.7226	67.3%	
Model fit	R-square	Adj. R-square		R-square	Adj. R-square		R-square	Adj. R-square	
R-square	0.6686	0.4145		0.6058	0.4030		0.5400	0.4459	
Model significance	Coeff.	F/t	VIF	Coeff.	F/t	VIF	Coeff.	F/t	VIF
Entire model		2.6313 ***			2.9877 ***			5.7387 ****	0.0
(Constant)	0.0610	0.7823		-0.0426	-0.7066		-0.0683	-3.9555 ****	0.0
STRATEGY1	-0.0144	-0.5953	2.2						
STRATEGY2	0.0479	1.9539 *	3.1						
STRATEGY3	0.0671	1.7142 *	3.6						
STRATEGY4	0.0646	2.2481 **	4.2						
STRATEGY5	0.0446	1.7624 *	3.8						
TIMING1	0.1126	4.1876 ****	2.8	0.0955	3.8945 ****	2.3	0.0899	4.6490 ****	1.5
TIMING2	0.0526	2.6292 **	3.4	0.0433	2.4360 **	2.6	0.0336	2.3792 **	1.8
TIMING3	0.0605	2.4905 **	2.0	0.0548	2.3738 **	1.8	0.0534	2.6443 **	1.4
ACQREGION2	-0.0223	-1.0837	2.2						
ACQINDUSTRY1	0.0128	0.6250	3.2	0.0181	0.9369	2.7			
ACQINDUSTRY2	-0.0148	-0.5119	3.9	-0.0009	-0.0328	3.2			
ACQINDUSTRY3	0.0233	0.4583	1.6	0.0243	0.4990	1.4			
EXPERIENCE1	-0.0663	-1.4705	2.5	-0.0858	-1.9397 *	2.3			
EXPERIENCE2	-0.0003	-0.0146	2.4	-0.0149	-0.8208	1.9			
EXPERIENCE3	0.0335	1.1316	6.0	-0.0064	-0.3098	2.8			
LNSIZE	-0.0150	-1.6740	6.4	-0.0038	-0.5141	4.3			
GROWTH	-0.0250	-1.2676	1.9	-0.0092	-0.5386	1.4			
TARREGION2	0.0521	0.7705	2.8	0.0076	0.1278	2.1	-0.0574	-1.3834	1.1
TARREGION3	0.1382	2.5827 **	1.8	0.1796	3.7841 ****	1.4	0.1716	4.0809 ****	1.2
TARREGION4				0.0199	1.3548	1.7	0.0201	1.7818 *	1.1
TARINDUSTRY1	0.0344	1.6601	3.6	0.0519	2.8227 ***	2.8	0.0461	2.8907 ***	2.2
TARINDUSTRY3	0.0059	0.1977	1.6	0.0129	0.4364	1.5	0.0173	0.6393	1.4
TARINDUSTRY4	0.0101	0.3913	3.9	0.0307	1.3695	2.9	0.0266	1.4481	2.1
LNRELVOLUME	0.0010	0.1824	3.2	-0.0027	-0.5168	2.6			

DF: Change in F-statistic between initial and extended regression model according to Ramsey Reset test.
sig DF: Significance of change in F-statistic DF. Z: Kolmogorov-Smirnov Z-statistic.
asy sig: Asymptotic significance of Z-statistic Z. F/t: F-statistic for entire model, t-statistics for coefficients.
VIF: Variance Inflation Factors for coefficients.
*-**** Statistically significant at 10%, 5%, 1% or 0.1% level according to t-test

Table 60: Significance of CERs in national transactions

Event window	CER%		Sign of CERs		Dodd-Warner		Boehmer		Generalized Sign		Wilcoxon Signed Rank	
	mean	**median**	Pos	Neg	Statistic	p-value	Statistic	p-value	Statistic	p-value	Statistic	p-value
[-20; +0]	-0.26%	1.70%	10	8	-0.1662	86.8%	-1.5420	12.3%	0.8096	41.8%	0.6315	52.8%
[-10; +0]	0.12%	0.63%	10	8	0.8609	38.9%	-0.9101	36.3%	0.8096	41.8%	0.4573	64.7%
[-5; +0]	0.90%	-0.90%	8	10	2.5205	1.2%	0.2831	77.7%	-0.1362	89.2%	0.2831	77.7%
[-2; +0]	1.11%	0.01%	9	9	3.9604	0.0%	0.7652	44.4%	0.3367	73.6%	0.6315	52.8%
[-1; +0]	1.53%	0.16%	9	9	5.5509	0.0%	1.6103	10.7%	0.3367	73.6%	0.9363	34.9%
[+0; +0]	0.95%	0.43%	10	8	6.1929	0.0%	1.1323	25.7%	0.8096	41.8%	0.6750	50.0%
[+0; +1]	-0.08%	-0.77%	8	10	2.4669	1.4%	-0.4522	65.1%	-0.1362	89.2%	0.0218	98.3%
[+0; +2]	-0.33%	-1.11%	8	10	1.6569	9.8%	-0.5940	55.3%	-0.1362	89.2%	-0.0218	98.3%
[+0; +5]	-0.33%	-3.98%	8	10	1.3718	17.0%	0.0557	95.6%	-0.1362	89.2%	-0.1960	84.5%
[+0; +10]	2.14%	1.66%	12	6	3.1708	0.2%	2.2382	2.5%	1.7554	7.9%	1.3718	17.0%
[+0; +20]	2.73%	1.34%	11	7	2.7437	0.6%	1.8514	6.4%	1.2825	20.0%	1.7638	7.8%
[-1; +1]	0.50%	-2.62%	6	12	2.9710	0.3%	0.2918	77.0%	-1.0820	27.9%	0.0218	98.3%
[-2; +2]	-0.16%	-2.04%	7	11	1.5816	11.4%	-0.3738	70.9%	-0.6091	54.2%	0.2395	81.1%
[-5; +5]	-0.38%	-1.69%	8	10	1.0074	31.4%	-0.0912	92.7%	-0.1362	89.2%	-0.5008	61.6%
[-10; +10]	1.32%	1.88%	11	7	1.5665	11.7%	0.7142	47.5%	1.2825	20.0%	0.8928	37.2%
[-20; +20]	1.52%	3.67%	10	8	0.8775	38.0%	0.0446	96.4%	0.8096	41.8%	1.1976	23.1%

Table 61: Significance of CERs in cross-border EU transactions

Event window	CER%		Sign of CERs		Dodd-Warner		Boehmer		Generalized Sign		Wilcoxon Signed Rank	
	mean	**median**	Pos	Neg	Statistic	p-value	Statistic	p-value	Statistic	p-value	Statistic	p-value
[-20; +0]	2.39%	3.11%	11	3	1.3208	18.7%	0.9828	32.6%	2.3336	2.0%	2.2286	2.6%
[-10; +0]	1.94%	1.78%	11	3	1.2943	19.6%	0.9408	34.7%	2.3336	2.0%	2.4169	1.6%
[-5; +0]	1.27%	1.00%	9	5	1.4028	16.1%	1.1362	25.6%	1.2631	20.7%	1.9775	4.8%
[-2; +0]	0.15%	0.01%	8	6	0.1533	87.8%	0.0786	93.7%	0.7279	46.7%	0.5964	55.1%
[-1; +0]	0.31%	0.10%	8	6	0.7324	46.4%	1.0144	31.0%	0.7279	46.7%	0.7847	43.3%
[+0; +0]	-0.13%	0.08%	7	7	-0.0138	98.9%	-0.0124	99.0%	0.1927	84.7%	0.4708	63.8%
[+0; +1]	0.95%	0.06%	8	6	0.9934	32.1%	0.5128	60.8%	0.7279	46.7%	0.6592	51.0%
[+0; +2]	0.53%	-0.27%	6	8	0.0789	93.7%	-0.5098	61.0%	-0.3425	73.2%	-0.1569	87.5%
[+0; +5]	0.81%	0.43%	8	6	0.2249	82.2%	-0.1384	89.0%	0.7279	46.7%	0.7219	47.0%
[+0; +10]	2.35%	1.36%	8	6	1.1264	26.0%	0.9768	32.9%	0.7279	46.7%	1.8519	6.4%
[+0; +20]	2.19%	0.83%	8	6	0.7840	43.3%	0.6165	53.8%	0.7279	46.7%	1.4125	15.8%
[-1; +1]	1.40%	0.47%	7	7	1.4171	15.6%	1.2541	21.0%	0.1927	84.7%	1.7891	7.4%
[-2; +2]	0.81%	-0.14%	7	7	0.1861	85.2%	-0.3285	74.3%	0.1927	84.7%	0.5336	59.4%
[-5; +5]	2.21%	2.15%	8	6	1.2063	22.8%	0.7407	45.9%	0.7279	46.7%	2.0402	4.1%
[-10; +10]	4.42%	2.83%	9	5	1.7550	7.9%	1.3906	16.4%	1.2631	20.7%	2.4797	1.3%
[-20; +20]	4.71%	5.25%	8	6	1.5085	13.1%	1.1465	25.2%	0.7279	46.7%	2.0402	4.1%

Table 62: Significance of CERs in cross-border world transactions

Event window	CER%		Sign of CERs		Dodd-Warner		Boehmer		Generalized Sign		Wilcoxon Signed Rank	
	mean	**median**	Pos	Neg	Statistic	p-value	Statistic	p-value	Statistic	p-value	Statistic	p-value
[-20; +0]	1.31%	0.25%	11	11	0.8724	38.3%	0.8415	40.0%	0.3266	74.4%	1.0551	29.1%
[-10; +0]	1.65%	2.66%	13	9	1.5269	12.7%	2.0419	4.1%	1.1814	23.7%	1.9317	5.3%
[-5; +0]	1.46%	1.86%	15	7	1.6677	9.5%	2.2388	2.5%	2.0363	4.2%	2.5486	1.1%
[-2; +0]	0.77%	1.00%	12	10	1.2090	22.7%	0.9186	35.8%	0.7540	45.1%	1.9966	4.6%
[-1; +0]	0.63%	0.17%	12	10	1.1774	23.9%	0.6686	50.4%	0.7540	45.1%	1.4447	14.9%
[+0; +0]	0.81%	0.05%	11	11	2.2073	2.7%	1.6458	10.0%	0.3266	74.4%	1.0551	29.1%
[+0; +1]	1.03%	0.19%	14	8	2.0588	4.0%	1.9150	5.5%	1.6089	10.8%	1.6071	10.8%
[+0; +2]	0.93%	0.21%	12	10	1.5911	11.2%	1.4523	14.6%	0.7540	45.1%	1.5097	13.1%
[+0; +5]	0.88%	-0.55%	10	12	0.9538	34.0%	0.8747	38.2%	-0.1009	92.0%	0.8928	37.2%
[+0; +10]	0.32%	0.40%	12	10	0.2769	78.2%	-0.0614	95.1%	0.7540	45.1%	0.6006	54.8%
[+0; +20]	-0.60%	-0.99%	10	12	-0.0017	99.9%	-0.3615	71.8%	-0.1009	92.0%	-0.1136	91.0%
[-1; +1]	0.84%	0.68%	15	7	1.3679	17.1%	1.1593	24.6%	2.0363	4.2%	1.8343	6.7%
[-2; +2]	0.90%	0.33%	13	9	1.1818	23.7%	1.1004	27.1%	1.1814	23.7%	1.8343	6.7%
[-5; +5]	1.53%	0.52%	14	8	1.2706	20.4%	1.8032	7.1%	1.6089	10.8%	2.1265	3.3%
[-10; +10]	1.16%	1.97%	13	9	0.8238	41.0%	1.0742	28.3%	1.1814	23.7%	1.1850	23.6%
[-20; +20]	-0.10%	-2.12%	8	14	0.2784	78.1%	0.0865	93.1%	-0.9557	33.9%	-0.0812	93.5%

Table 63: Significance of CERs in within-industry transactions

Event window	CER%		Sign of CERs		Dodd-Warner		Boehmer		Generalized Sign		Wilcoxon Signed Rank	
	mean	**median**	Pos	Neg	Statistic	p-value	Statistic	p-value	Statistic	p-value	Statistic	p-value
[-20; +0]	2.83%	2.80%	23	8	2.5292	1.1%	2.3212	2.0%	3.0269	0.2%	3.1844	0.1%
[-10; +0]	2.12%	2.52%	24	7	2.7356	0.6%	2.4133	1.6%	3.3868	0.1%	2.8317	0.5%
[-5; +0]	1.29%	1.35%	19	12	2.5328	1.1%	1.9588	5.0%	1.5876	11.2%	1.8911	5.9%
[-2; +0]	0.91%	0.68%	20	11	2.2034	2.8%	1.2831	19.9%	1.9474	5.1%	1.5187	12.9%
[-1; +0]	0.99%	0.24%	18	13	2.7656	0.6%	1.6485	9.9%	1.2278	22.0%	1.3424	17.9%
[+0; +0]	0.35%	-0.12%	15	16	1.9334	5.3%	0.6403	52.2%	0.1483	88.2%	0.3037	76.1%
[+0; +1]	0.81%	0.07%	18	13	1.9378	5.3%	0.8160	41.4%	1.2278	22.0%	0.9700	33.2%
[+0; +2]	0.92%	0.30%	18	13	1.6227	10.5%	0.6976	48.5%	1.2278	22.0%	1.2052	22.8%
[+0; +5]	0.96%	0.53%	17	14	1.0774	28.1%	0.3814	70.3%	0.8679	38.5%	0.7545	45.1%
[+0; +10]	1.62%	0.98%	16	15	1.6146	10.6%	1.1348	25.6%	0.5081	61.1%	1.2640	20.6%
[+0; +20]	1.26%	1.13%	18	13	0.9947	32.0%	0.5090	61.1%	1.2278	22.0%	1.2640	20.6%
[-1; +1]	1.44%	1.20%	19	12	2.7241	0.6%	1.6426	10.0%	1.5876	11.2%	1.6951	9.0%
[-2; +2]	1.48%	1.57%	20	11	2.0991	3.6%	1.2479	21.2%	1.9474	5.1%	2.0282	4.3%
[-5; +5]	1.90%	1.00%	19	12	2.0833	3.7%	1.5353	12.5%	1.5876	11.2%	2.2046	2.7%
[-10; +10]	3.39%	2.69%	23	8	2.7265	0.6%	2.4282	1.5%	3.0269	0.2%	2.7141	0.7%
[-20; +20]	3.74%	3.84%	18	13	2.2200	2.6%	1.9255	5.4%	1.2278	22.0%	2.4790	1.3%

Table 64: Significance of CERs in cross-industry transactions

Event window	CER%		Sign of CERs		Dodd-Warner		Boehmer		Generalized Sign		Wilcoxon Signed Rank	
	mean	median	Pos	Neg	Statistic	p-value	Statistic	p-value	Statistic	p-value	Statistic	p-value
[-20; +0]	-1.30%	-0.24%	9	14	-1.1996	23.0%	-2.6450	0.8%	-0.6594	51.0%	-0.6235	53.3%
[-10; +0]	0.00%	-1.19%	10	13	0.0889	92.9%	-1.2223	22.2%	-0.2410	81.0%	0.2281	82.0%
[-5; +0]	1.13%	0.35%	13	10	2.0148	4.4%	0.3990	69.0%	1.0142	31.1%	1.4143	15.7%
[-2; +0]	0.48%	-0.41%	9	14	2.2475	2.5%	-0.3434	73.1%	-0.6594	51.0%	0.2889	77.3%
[-1; +0]	0.65%	-0.04%	11	12	3.4227	0.1%	0.5509	58.2%	0.1774	85.9%	0.5931	55.3%
[+0; +0]	0.96%	0.12%	13	10	5.3820	0.0%	1.4590	14.5%	1.0142	31.1%	1.3535	17.6%
[+0; +1]	0.41%	0.04%	12	11	2.7212	0.7%	0.0982	92.2%	0.5958	55.1%	0.2585	79.6%
[+0; +2]	-0.28%	-0.28%	8	15	1.1996	23.0%	-1.2239	22.1%	-1.0778	28.1%	-0.9277	35.4%
[+0; +5]	-0.22%	-0.76%	9	14	1.0711	28.4%	-0.5689	56.9%	-0.6594	51.0%	-0.6843	49.4%
[+0; +10]	1.22%	1.30%	16	7	2.0801	3.8%	1.1900	23.4%	2.2693	2.3%	1.8401	6.6%
[+0; +20]	1.19%	-0.09%	11	12	1.8824	6.0%	1.2893	19.7%	0.1774	85.9%	0.5627	57.4%
[-1; +1]	0.10%	-0.39%	9	14	1.9093	5.6%	-0.3124	75.5%	-0.6594	51.0%	-0.5323	59.5%
[-2; +2]	-0.76%	-1.06%	7	16	0.2632	79.2%	-1.8665	6.2%	-1.4961	13.5%	-1.3839	16.6%
[-5; +5]	-0.05%	-0.01%	11	12	0.6564	51.2%	-0.5653	57.2%	0.1774	85.9%	-0.0152	98.8%
[-10; +10]	0.26%	-0.40%	10	13	0.3953	69.3%	-0.3417	73.3%	-0.2410	81.0%	0.2585	79.6%
[-20; +20]	-1.07%	-2.54%	8	15	-0.3519	72.5%	-1.1981	23.1%	-1.0778	28.1%	-0.6539	51.3%

Table 65: Significance of CERs in bottom phase of M&A cycle

Event window	CER%		Sign of CERs		Dodd-Warner		Boehmer		Generalized Sign		Wilcoxon Signed Rank	
	mean	**median**	Pos	Neg	Statistic	p-value	Statistic	p-value	Statistic	p-value	Statistic	p-value
[-20; +0]	-2.97%	-0.14%	5	6	-1.0815	27.9%	-1.1316	25.8%	-0.1160	90.8%	-0.4001	68.9%
[-10; +0]	-2.62%	-1.63%	5	6	-1.1666	24.3%	-1.3672	17.2%	-0.1160	90.8%	-0.7557	45.0%
[-5; +0]	-0.61%	-0.76%	4	7	-0.2294	81.9%	-0.2491	80.3%	-0.7199	47.2%	-0.4001	68.9%
[-2; +0]	-0.46%	-0.17%	4	7	-0.5678	57.0%	-0.6088	54.3%	-0.7199	47.2%	-0.4001	68.9%
[-1; +0]	-0.36%	0.11%	7	4	-0.6334	52.6%	-0.6650	50.6%	1.0920	27.5%	0.3112	75.6%
[+0; +0]	-0.63%	-0.36%	4	7	-1.2942	19.6%	-1.3923	16.4%	-0.7199	47.2%	-0.8447	39.8%
[+0; +1]	-1.60%	-1.71%	2	9	-2.3223	2.0%	-1.9676	4.9%	-1.9279	5.4%	-1.5559	12.0%
[+0; +2]	-2.42%	-1.27%	3	8	-2.8816	0.4%	-2.3899	1.7%	-1.3239	18.6%	-1.4670	14.2%
[+0; +5]	-3.13%	-3.06%	1	10	-2.8583	0.4%	-3.5255	0.0%	-2.5318	1.1%	-2.3561	1.8%
[+0; +10]	-1.27%	0.63%	6	5	-0.7606	44.7%	-1.0664	28.6%	0.4880	62.6%	-0.4890	62.5%
[+0; +20]	-1.47%	1.34%	6	5	-0.4945	62.1%	-0.5523	58.1%	0.4880	62.6%	-0.4001	68.9%
[-1; +1]	-1.33%	-0.92%	4	7	-1.6660	9.6%	-1.3457	17.8%	-0.7199	47.2%	-1.2892	19.7%
[-2; +2]	-2.25%	-1.06%	4	7	-2.0931	3.6%	-1.7001	8.9%	-0.7199	47.2%	-0.7557	45.0%
[-5; +5]	-3.10%	-1.97%	2	9	-1.8902	5.9%	-2.3680	1.8%	-1.9279	5.4%	-1.5559	12.0%
[-10; +10]	-3.26%	-1.25%	3	8	-1.1124	26.6%	-1.4575	14.5%	-1.3239	18.6%	-1.0225	30.7%
[-20; +20]	-3.80%	-3.11%	4	7	-0.9258	35.5%	-0.9877	32.3%	-0.7199	47.2%	-0.8447	39.8%

Table 66: Significance of CERs in peak phase of M&A cycle

Event window	CER%		Sign of CERs		Dodd-Warner		Boehmer		Generalized Sign		Wilcoxon Signed Rank	
	mean	median	Pos	Neg	Statistic	p-value	Statistic	p-value	Statistic	p-value	Statistic	p-value
[-20; +0]	1.31%	1.52%	17	13	0.7803	43.5%	0.4747	63.5%	1.1216	26.2%	1.9231	5.4%
[-10; +0]	1.39%	1.07%	18	12	1.1261	26.0%	0.8487	39.6%	1.4877	13.7%	2.0260	4.3%
[-5; +0]	0.66%	0.90%	17	13	0.8551	39.3%	0.8161	41.4%	1.1216	26.2%	1.4912	13.6%
[-2; +0]	-0.05%	-0.04%	15	15	-0.3064	75.9%	-0.7195	47.2%	0.3895	69.7%	0.2777	78.1%
[-1; +0]	0.20%	-0.09%	12	18	0.3914	69.6%	0.2823	77.8%	-0.7087	47.9%	0.2777	78.1%
[+0; +0]	0.12%	0.14%	16	14	0.3949	69.3%	0.2345	81.5%	0.7556	45.0%	0.6273	53.0%
[+0; +1]	0.75%	0.11%	19	11	1.3129	18.9%	0.9048	36.6%	1.8538	6.4%	1.4089	15.9%
[+0; +2]	0.48%	-0.11%	14	16	0.6123	54.0%	0.1454	88.4%	0.0234	98.1%	0.1954	84.5%
[+0; +5]	0.44%	0.21%	16	14	0.4201	67.4%	0.4417	65.9%	0.7556	45.0%	0.3188	75.0%
[+0; +10]	0.71%	0.40%	16	14	0.4612	64.5%	0.4755	63.4%	0.7556	45.0%	0.9564	33.9%
[+0; +20]	0.63%	-0.06%	15	15	0.3611	71.8%	0.2282	81.9%	0.3895	69.7%	0.7302	46.5%
[-1; +1]	0.83%	-0.08%	15	15	1.1636	24.5%	0.8339	40.4%	0.3895	69.7%	0.9153	36.0%
[-2; +2]	0.31%	-0.51%	13	17	0.0604	95.2%	-0.5496	58.3%	-0.3426	73.2%	0.2571	79.7%
[-5; +5]	0.97%	0.71%	18	12	0.8227	41.1%	0.8582	39.1%	1.4877	13.7%	1.5735	11.6%
[-10; +10]	1.98%	2.24%	20	10	1.0627	28.8%	0.9072	36.4%	2.2199	2.6%	1.7997	7.2%
[-20; +20]	1.81%	-1.25%	13	17	0.7552	45.0%	0.4665	64.1%	-0.3426	73.2%	1.0798	28.0%

Table 67: Significance of CERs in transactions of 14 fastest growing acquirers

Event window	CER%		Sign of CERs		Dodd-Warner		Boehmer		Generalized Sign		Wilcoxon Signed Rank	
	mean	median	Pos	Neg	Statistic	p-value	Statistic	p-value	Statistic	p-value	Statistic	p-value
[-20; +0]	-2.16%	-2.67%	5	9	-0.9522	34.1%	-3.0103	0.3%	-0.6478	51.7%	-1.0986	27.2%
[-10; +0]	0.23%	-0.49%	7	7	0.4690	63.9%	-1.7870	7.4%	0.4283	66.8%	0.5964	55.1%
[-5; +0]	1.38%	1.47%	9	5	1.9393	5.2%	-0.6716	50.2%	1.5043	13.3%	1.8519	6.4%
[-2; +0]	0.72%	-0.26%	6	8	1.8315	6.7%	-1.3468	17.8%	-0.1098	91.3%	0.6592	51.0%
[-1; +0]	1.26%	-0.06%	6	8	3.1507	0.2%	-0.1311	89.6%	-0.1098	91.3%	0.8475	39.7%
[+0; +0]	1.87%	0.25%	8	6	5.7855	0.0%	1.5965	11.0%	0.9663	33.4%	1.5380	12.4%
[+0; +1]	2.11%	0.30%	10	4	4.5224	0.0%	1.5398	12.4%	2.0423	4.1%	1.9775	4.8%
[+0; +2]	1.56%	0.36%	8	6	2.7915	0.5%	0.0952	92.4%	0.9663	33.4%	1.2241	22.1%
[+0; +5]	1.85%	0.61%	8	6	2.4590	1.4%	0.5990	54.9%	0.9663	33.4%	1.1614	24.5%
[+0; +10]	1.95%	1.21%	8	6	1.9319	5.3%	0.8782	38.0%	0.9663	33.4%	1.2869	19.8%
[+0; +20]	0.74%	-1.23%	5	9	1.0718	28.4%	-0.1497	88.1%	-0.6478	51.7%	-0.0314	97.5%
[-1; +1]	1.50%	-0.17%	6	8	2.9248	0.3%	0.2284	81.9%	-0.1098	91.3%	1.0358	30.0%
[-2; +2]	0.41%	-0.87%	5	9	0.9936	32.0%	-1.6834	9.2%	-0.6478	51.7%	0.1569	87.5%
[-5; +5]	1.35%	0.15%	7	7	1.5040	13.3%	-0.5350	59.3%	0.4283	66.8%	1.0358	30.0%
[-10; +10]	0.31%	-0.11%	7	7	0.4752	63.5%	-1.0062	31.4%	0.4283	66.8%	0.2825	77.8%
[-20; +20]	-3.28%	-4.76%	2	12	-0.8179	41.3%	-2.5109	1.2%	-2.2618	2.4%	-1.4752	14.0%

Table 68: Significance of CERs in transactions of 26 medium growing acquirers

Event window	CER%		Sign of CERs		Dodd-Warner		Boehmer		Generalized Sign		Wilcoxon Signed Rank	
	mean	median	Pos	Neg	Statistic	p-value	Statistic	p-value	Statistic	p-value	Statistic	p-value
[-20; +0]	2.45%	2.39%	17	9	1.7411	8.2%	1.0512	29.3%	1.8654	6.2%	2.2985	2.2%
[-10; +0]	2.11%	2.53%	19	7	2.3809	1.7%	1.5845	11.3%	2.6512	0.8%	2.3493	1.9%
[-5; +0]	1.65%	0.64%	14	12	2.6562	0.8%	1.4611	14.4%	0.6868	49.2%	1.6890	9.1%
[-2; +0]	1.15%	0.52%	16	10	2.8295	0.5%	1.3022	19.3%	1.4725	14.1%	1.4350	15.1%
[-1; +0]	1.27%	0.18%	16	10	3.9068	0.0%	2.0898	3.7%	1.4725	14.1%	1.6128	10.7%
[+0; +0]	0.67%	0.05%	13	13	3.7616	0.0%	0.9890	32.3%	0.2939	76.9%	0.6984	48.5%
[+0; +1]	0.86%	-0.05%	13	13	2.5218	1.2%	0.6170	53.7%	0.2939	76.9%	0.2159	82.9%
[+0; +2]	0.81%	0.08%	13	13	1.9370	5.3%	0.4159	67.8%	0.2939	76.9%	0.8000	42.4%
[+0; +5]	0.74%	-0.31%	13	13	1.1279	25.9%	-0.0753	94.0%	0.2939	76.9%	0.3175	75.1%
[+0; +10]	1.80%	1.36%	15	11	2.0865	3.7%	1.4342	15.2%	1.0796	28.0%	1.4350	15.1%
[+0; +20]	1.48%	0.83%	14	12	1.4532	14.6%	0.8161	41.4%	0.6868	49.2%	0.9524	34.1%
[-1; +1]	1.47%	0.68%	15	11	3.0772	0.2%	1.6391	10.1%	1.0796	28.0%	1.2064	22.8%
[-2; +2]	1.29%	1.30%	15	11	2.0099	4.4%	0.8885	37.4%	1.0796	28.0%	1.7144	8.6%
[-5; +5]	1.72%	1.59%	16	10	1.6605	9.7%	0.7253	46.8%	1.4725	14.1%	1.8921	5.8%
[-10; +10]	3.23%	2.75%	17	9	2.4124	1.6%	1.9690	4.9%	1.8654	6.2%	2.1461	3.2%
[-20; +20]	3.26%	3.67%	14	12	1.6986	8.9%	1.1819	23.7%	0.6868	49.2%	1.9175	5.5%

Table 69: Significance of CERs in transactions of 14 slowest growing acquirers

Event window	CER%		Sign of CERs		Dodd-Warner		Boehmer		Generalized Sign		Wilcoxon Signed Rank	
	mean	**median**	Pos	Neg	Statistic	p-value	Statistic	p-value	Statistic	p-value	Statistic	p-value
[-20; +0]	1.73%	2.36%	10	4	0.8054	42.1%	1.2812	20.0%	1.7612	7.8%	2.2913	2.2%
[-10; +0]	0.55%	1.12%	8	6	0.4709	63.8%	1.1087	26.8%	0.6912	48.9%	0.9103	36.3%
[-5; +0]	0.28%	1.45%	9	5	0.7924	42.8%	1.7487	8.0%	1.2262	22.0%	0.7847	43.3%
[-2; +0]	-0.06%	0.75%	7	7	0.4720	63.7%	0.6226	53.4%	0.1562	87.6%	1.1614	24.5%
[-1; +0]	-0.36%	0.06%	7	7	0.0276	97.8%	0.0043	99.7%	0.1562	87.6%	0.1569	87.5%
[+0; +0]	-0.76%	0.00%	7	7	-1.1365	25.6%	-0.8317	40.6%	0.1562	87.6%	-0.2197	82.6%
[+0; +1]	-1.26%	0.10%	7	7	-1.5875	11.2%	-1.2130	22.5%	0.1562	87.6%	-0.0942	92.5%
[+0; +2]	-1.48%	-0.14%	5	9	-1.4789	13.9%	-1.2211	22.2%	-0.9138	36.1%	-0.7219	47.0%
[+0; +5]	-1.46%	-0.97%	5	9	-1.0201	30.8%	-1.0083	31.3%	-0.9138	36.1%	-0.8475	39.7%
[+0; +10]	0.32%	0.54%	9	5	0.2934	76.9%	0.6572	51.1%	1.2262	22.0%	1.3497	17.7%
[+0; +20]	1.26%	2.23%	10	4	0.8408	40.0%	1.5548	12.0%	1.7612	7.8%	1.6636	9.6%
[-1; +1]	-0.86%	0.00%	7	7	-0.6175	53.7%	-0.5067	61.2%	0.1562	87.6%	-0.4708	63.8%
[-2; +2]	-0.78%	-0.06%	7	7	-0.2717	78.6%	-0.0917	92.7%	0.1562	87.6%	-0.1569	87.5%
[-5; +5]	-0.42%	0.01%	7	7	0.1745	86.2%	0.7976	42.5%	0.1562	87.6%	0.1569	87.5%
[-10; +10]	1.62%	2.28%	9	5	0.8012	42.3%	1.4595	14.4%	1.2262	22.0%	1.7264	8.4%
[-20; +20]	3.75%	4.94%	10	4	1.3556	17.5%	2.1596	3.1%	1.7612	7.8%	2.5424	1.1%

Table 70: Significance of CERs of acquirers with no transaction experience

	CER%		Sign of CERs		Dodd-Warner		Boehmer		Generalized Sign		Wilcoxon Signed Rank	
Event window	**mean**	**median**	Pos	Neg	Statistic	p-value	Statistic	p-value	Statistic	p-value	Statistic	p-value
[-20; +0]	0.42%	0.23%	13	12	0.3630	71.7%	-0.9511	34.2%	0.6052	54.5%	0.6727	50.1%
[-10; +0]	0.61%	0.44%	14	11	1.2423	21.4%	-0.4126	68.0%	1.0065	31.4%	0.8610	38.9%
[-5; +0]	1.35%	0.73%	15	10	2.9898	0.3%	0.8455	39.8%	1.4078	15.9%	1.4530	14.6%
[-2; +0]	1.05%	-0.01%	12	13	3.6427	0.0%	0.5379	59.1%	0.2039	83.8%	0.6189	53.6%
[-1; +0]	1.40%	0.23%	16	9	5.4336	0.0%	1.9596	5.0%	1.8091	7.0%	1.4799	13.9%
[+0; +0]	1.17%	0.10%	13	12	6.7350	0.0%	1.5058	13.2%	0.6052	54.5%	0.7265	46.8%
[+0; +1]	1.37%	0.15%	13	12	4.7289	0.0%	1.0460	29.6%	0.6052	54.5%	0.6189	53.6%
[+0; +2]	0.84%	-0.13%	11	14	2.7276	0.6%	-0.1750	86.1%	-0.1974	84.3%	0.4574	64.7%
[+0; +5]	1.26%	-0.76%	12	13	2.4821	1.3%	0.4357	66.3%	0.2039	83.8%	0.5112	60.9%
[+0; +10]	1.91%	1.30%	15	10	2.7925	0.5%	1.5115	13.1%	1.4078	15.9%	1.2377	21.6%
[+0; +20]	2.04%	0.70%	13	12	2.4985	1.2%	1.4738	14.1%	0.6052	54.5%	1.0494	29.4%
[-1; +1]	1.60%	0.31%	14	11	4.4092	0.0%	1.5847	11.3%	1.0065	31.4%	0.9417	34.6%
[-2; +2]	0.72%	0.05%	13	12	1.9225	5.5%	-0.3923	69.5%	0.6052	54.5%	0.6189	53.6%
[-5; +5]	1.44%	0.70%	14	11	2.0106	4.4%	0.4922	62.3%	1.0065	31.4%	1.1839	23.6%
[-10; +10]	1.35%	1.32%	14	11	1.4505	14.7%	0.4667	64.1%	1.0065	31.4%	0.8610	38.9%
[-20; +20]	1.28%	-1.69%	12	13	0.9961	31.9%	0.1389	89.0%	0.2039	83.8%	0.7265	46.8%

Table 71: Significance of CERs of acquirers with extensive transaction experience

	CER%		Sign of CERs		Dodd-Warner		Boehmer		Generalized Sign		Wilcoxon Signed Rank	
Event window	**mean**	**median**	Pos	Neg	Statistic	p-value	Statistic	p-value	Statistic	p-value	Statistic	p-value
[-20; +0]	0.84%	1.86%	9	3	0.2801	77.9%	0.1087	91.3%	1.8839	6.0%	1.6474	9.9%
[-10; +0]	1.90%	2.34%	9	3	1.2403	21.5%	1.4255	15.4%	1.8839	6.0%	2.1181	3.4%
[-5; +0]	1.20%	1.10%	7	5	1.1027	27.0%	0.9974	31.9%	0.7281	46.7%	1.6474	9.9%
[-2; +0]	0.94%	0.53%	8	4	1.2237	22.1%	1.0740	28.3%	1.3060	19.2%	1.6474	9.9%
[-1; +0]	0.56%	-0.20%	6	6	0.8374	40.2%	0.5674	57.0%	0.1503	88.1%	0.7060	48.0%
[+0; +0]	-0.44%	-0.16%	5	7	-0.5698	56.9%	-0.2636	79.2%	-0.4276	66.9%	0.0000	100.0%
[+0; +1]	-0.68%	-0.18%	5	7	-0.8659	38.7%	-0.5463	58.5%	-0.4276	66.9%	-0.2353	81.4%
[+0; +2]	-0.38%	0.04%	6	6	-0.2024	84.0%	-0.0093	99.3%	0.1503	88.1%	0.3138	75.4%
[+0; +5]	-0.47%	0.43%	8	4	-0.3880	69.8%	-0.2547	79.9%	1.3060	19.2%	0.6276	53.0%
[+0; +10]	1.60%	1.12%	8	4	1.0693	28.5%	1.1991	23.1%	1.3060	19.2%	1.9612	5.0%
[+0; +20]	1.52%	1.07%	7	5	0.6695	50.3%	0.4554	64.9%	0.7281	46.7%	1.5689	11.7%
[-1; +1]	0.33%	-0.54%	5	7	0.3057	76.0%	0.1694	86.5%	-0.4276	66.9%	0.7060	48.0%
[-2; +2]	1.00%	1.32%	7	5	1.0459	29.6%	0.9426	34.6%	0.7281	46.7%	1.6474	9.9%
[-5; +5]	1.18%	0.86%	7	5	0.6997	48.4%	0.6280	53.0%	0.7281	46.7%	1.6474	9.9%
[-10; +10]	3.95%	4.56%	9	3	1.7959	7.3%	1.9570	5.0%	1.8839	6.0%	2.7456	0.6%
[-20; +20]	2.80%	4.66%	7	5	0.7686	44.2%	0.4449	65.6%	0.7281	46.7%	1.8827	6.0%

Table 72: Significance of CERs of acquirers with most transaction experience

Event window	CER%		Sign of CERs		Dodd-Warner		Boehmer		Generalized Sign		Wilcoxon Signed Rank	
	mean	**median**	Pos	Neg	Statistic	p-value	Statistic	p-value	Statistic	p-value	Statistic	p-value
[-20; +0]	1.77%	1.65%	8	7	1.1816	23.7%	0.8995	36.8%	0.5385	59.0%	1.7891	7.4%
[-10; +0]	1.57%	1.87%	9	6	1.2062	22.8%	1.1853	23.6%	1.0562	29.1%	1.8459	6.5%
[-5; +0]	1.60%	2.25%	10	5	1.5698	11.6%	1.6697	9.5%	1.5739	11.6%	2.4138	1.6%
[-2; +0]	0.80%	0.44%	9	6	0.8081	41.9%	0.6693	50.3%	1.0562	29.1%	1.7891	7.4%
[-1; +0]	0.73%	-0.05%	7	8	1.0021	31.6%	0.8366	40.3%	0.0207	98.3%	1.2779	20.1%
[+0; +0]	0.97%	0.31%	9	6	1.9330	5.3%	1.8723	6.1%	1.0562	29.1%	1.9595	5.0%
[+0; +1]	0.99%	0.38%	11	4	1.3720	17.0%	1.3295	18.4%	2.0917	3.6%	2.1299	3.3%
[+0; +2]	0.74%	0.23%	9	6	0.8325	40.5%	0.8060	42.0%	1.0562	29.1%	1.3915	16.4%
[+0; +5]	0.69%	-0.40%	6	9	0.5398	58.9%	0.4298	66.7%	-0.4970	61.9%	0.5964	55.1%
[+0; +10]	1.00%	0.35%	8	7	0.4657	64.1%	0.4184	67.6%	0.5385	59.0%	1.2779	20.1%
[+0; +20]	-0.39%	-0.64%	7	8	-0.1387	89.0%	-0.2914	77.1%	0.0207	98.3%	-0.0284	97.7%
[-1; +1]	0.75%	1.16%	9	6	0.8225	41.1%	0.6876	49.2%	1.0562	29.1%	1.6187	10.6%
[-2; +2]	0.57%	-0.25%	7	8	0.4063	68.4%	0.3054	76.0%	0.0207	98.3%	0.9371	34.9%
[-5; +5]	1.32%	0.72%	9	6	0.9752	32.9%	0.9861	32.4%	1.0562	29.1%	1.5619	11.8%
[-10; +10]	1.59%	0.18%	8	7	0.7882	43.1%	0.7521	45.2%	0.5385	59.0%	1.1643	24.4%
[-20; +20]	0.41%	-1.55%	5	10	0.4445	65.7%	0.1428	88.6%	-1.0148	31.0%	0.2556	79.8%

7.2 Event Study – Additional details on long-term analyses

Table 73: Descriptive statistics for metric variables

Statistics	*BAHR**	*LNSIZE*	*GROWTH*	*LNRELVOLUME*
Mean	-6.6%	8.5095	1.2836	-2.1693
St.dev.	75.6%	1.6172	0.4751	1.6956
Min	-246.2%	4.6958	0.3193	-5.7228
Max	284.6%	11.6487	3.8566	1.2295
N	158	158	158	158

Cat.	*TIMING*	Freq.	*STRATEGY*	Freq.	*EXPERIENCE*	Freq.
0*	Bottom	11	National/within-industry	36	No experience	67**
1	Upswing	7	National/cross-industry	18	Little experience	5
2	Peak	30	Cross-border EU/within-industry	29	Extensive experience	33
3	Downturn	6	Cross-border EU/cross-industry	19	Most experience	42
4			Cross-border world/within-industry	25		
5			Cross-border world/cross-industry	31		
N	total	54	total	158	total	147**

Cat.	*ACQREGION*	Freq.	*TARREGION*	Freq.	*ACQINDUSTRY*	Freq.	*TARINDUSTRY*	Freq.
0*	EU-15	125	EU-15	94	P&C	15	P&C	30
1	Other EU-25	0	Other EU-25	2	Life	116	Life	90
2	Swiss	32	Swiss	4	Re	26	Re	0
3	Norway	1	Norway	2	Agents/Brokers	1	Agents/Brokers	9
4	World	0	World	56	Other	0	Other	29
N	total	158	total	158	total	158	total	158

* 3-year horizon.
** Reference category.
*** 1st quartile overrepresented due to large amount of acquirers with no transaction in last three years.
**** Only transactions after 31.12.1992 allocated due to lack of transaction history.

7.3 Case Study A – Additional details on Munich Re and American Re

Table 74: Supervisory Board and Management Board of Munich Re in 1995

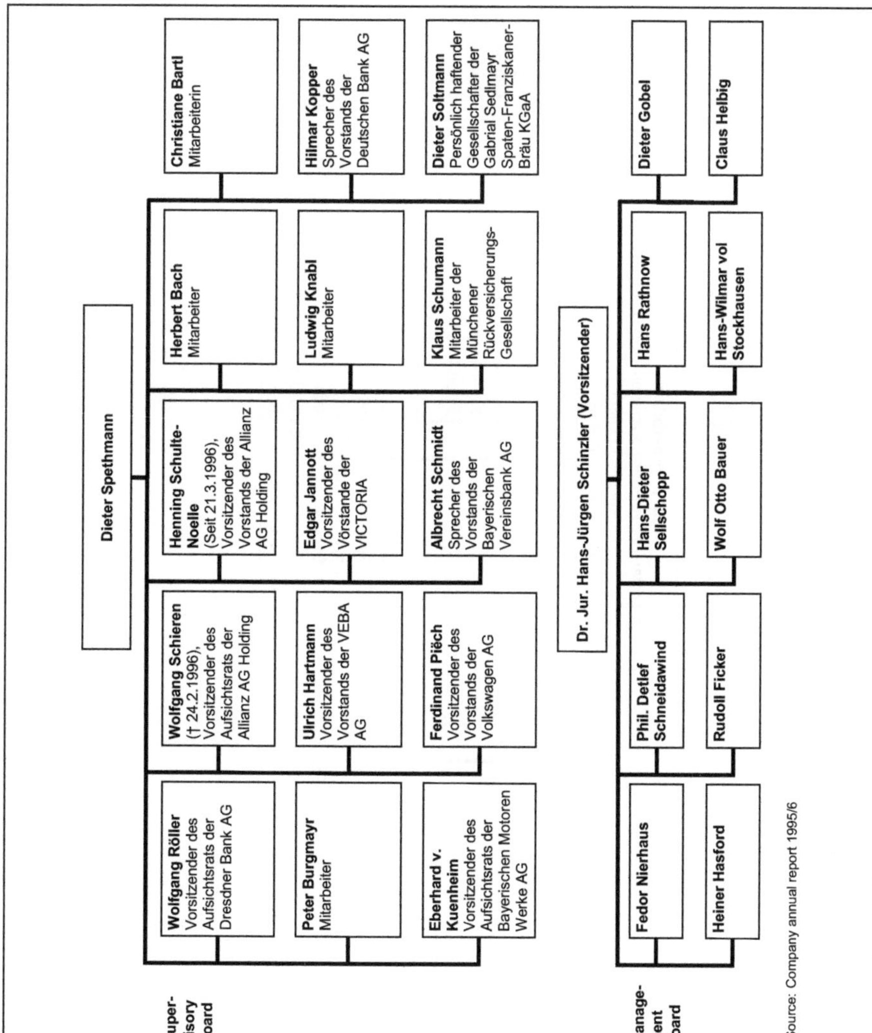

Source: Company annual report 1995/6

Table 75: Board of Directors of American Re in 1995

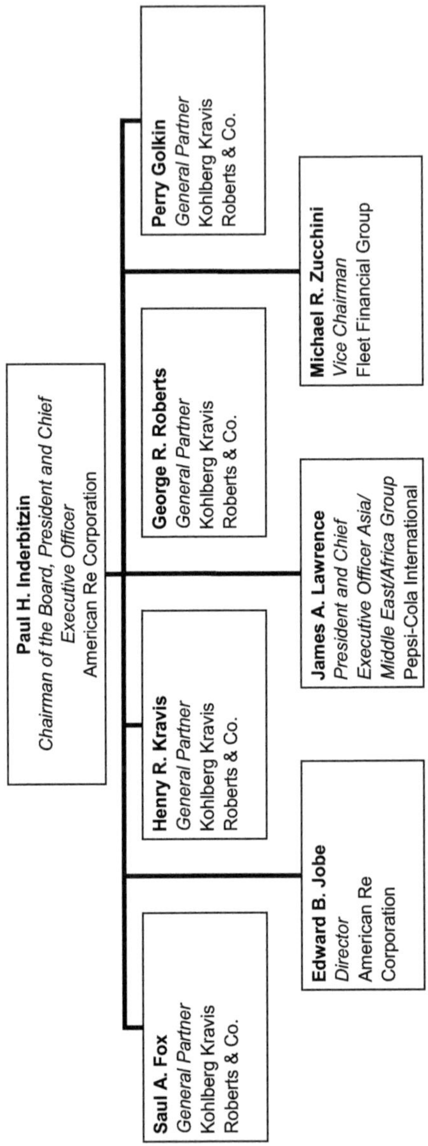

Source: Company annual report 1995

Table 76: Senior management of American Re in 1995

Paul H. Inderbitzin
Chairman, President and Chief Executive Officer,
American Re Corporation,
American Re-Insurance Company

Mahmoud M. Abdallah *President, International Operations* American Re-Insurance Company *President* Am-Re-Brokers, Inc	**Albert J. Beer** *Senior Vice President, Branch Operations Domestic Insurance Company Operations* American Re-insurance Company	**Robert K. Burgess** *Senior Vice President, General Counsel and Secretary* American Re Corporation American Re-Insurance Company	**Mary R. Hennessey** *Senior Vice President, Chief Actuary* American Re-Insurance Company *President,* American Re Services Inc.	**Robert E. Humes** *Senior Vice President, Human Resources* American Re-Insurance Company
Michael A. Jones *Senior Vice President and Senior Corporate Underwriting Officer Corporate Underwriting* American Re-insurance Company	**James R. Kroner** *Senior Vice President, and Treasurer* American Re-Corporation American Re-Insurance Company	**Kenneth J. Lestrange** *Senior Vice President,* American Re-Insurance Company *President* Am-Re-Managers, Inc.	**Edward J. Noonan** *President, Domestic Insurance Company Operations* American Re-Insurance Company	**Harold S. Swann** *Senior Vice President,* American Re-Insurance Company
Robert W. Trainer *Senior Vice President, Marketing Domestic Insurance Company Operations* American Re-Insurance Company	**David W. Tritton** *Senior Vice President, Claims* American Re-Insurance Company	**Thomas H. Walker, Jr** *Senior Vice President, Investor Relations and Corporate Communications* American Re-Insurance Company	**James R. Fisher** *Senior Vice President, Chief Financial and Accounting Officer* American Re Corporation American Re-Insurance Company *President, Financial products* American Re-Insurance Company	

Source: Company annual report 1995

Table 77: Financial performance of American Re before and after acquisition by Munich Re

AMERICAN RE	Unit	1991	1992	1993	1994	1995	1996	1997	1998	1999	2000
Size											
Earnings	USD mn	158.1	94.8	98.4	97.5	-87.6	111.7	221.4	226.0	-101.0	-64.4
Premiums	USD bn	0.9	1.0	1.2	1.5	1.5	1.8	2.5	2.4	2.9	3.2
Reserves	USD bn	2.1	4.1	4.3	4.7	5.6	8.5	8.7	8.6	9.6	10.1
Assets	USD bn	3.8	5.5	5.4	6.7	7.8	8.4	13.3	13.5	14.3	14.9
Shareholders' Equity	USD bn	1.0	0.4	0.8	0.8	0.8	1.0	2.6	2.9	2.5	2.4
Solvency											
Equity ratio	%	25.3%	7.0%	14.7%	11.8%	10.8%	11.5%	19.5%	21.1%	17.4%	16.2%
Equity reserves ratio	%	46.8%	9.5%	18.4%	16.8%	15.0%	11.4%	29.6%	33.1%	25.9%	24.1%
Operating leverage	times x	1.0	2.5	1.6	1.9	1.8	1.9	1.0	0.8	1.2	1.3
Reserves leverage	times x	10.2	34.5	30.0	39.0	-35.4	36.7	39.0	26.8	-53.9	-101.8
Reserves ratio	times x	2.2	4.2	3.5	3.2	3.7	4.7	3.5	3.6	3.3	3.1
Profitability											
Return on reserves	bp	983.0	289.8	333.2	256.6	-282.4	272.8	256.7	373.2	-185.6	-98.2
Return on equity	%	21.0%	30.7%	18.1%	15.3%	-18.8%	24.0%	8.7%	11.3%	-7.2%	-4.1%
Return on premiums	%	21.8%	12.3%	11.5%	8.3%	-10.4%	12.9%	9.0%	13.3%	-6.1%	-3.0%
Combined ratio	%	100.4%	103.3%	96.0%	99.2%	117.1%	94.7%	102.8%	103.3%	120.4%	117.4%
Loss ratio	%	72.9%	69.9%	63.8%	69.2%	87.5%	65.0%	69.0%	69.6%	90.7%	86.8%
Expense ratio	%	27.5%	33.4%	32.3%	30.1%	29.6%	29.7%	33.7%	33.8%	29.7%	30.6%
Net investment result ratio	%	23.7%	21.5%	13.2%	12.9%	14.5%	13.8%	17.2%	17.3%	14.2%	14.3%
Net investment yield	%	5.8%	3.8%	3.0%	2.8%	2.8%	3.0%	3.2%	3.1%	2.9%	3.1%
Growth											
Growth of earnings	%	4.5%	-40.1%	3.8%	-0.9%	-189.8%	-227.5%	98.2%	2.1%	-144.7%	-36.2%
Growth of premiums	%	11.8%	3.6%	29.7%	16.9%	4.8%	17.4%	38.4%	-2.7%	21.0%	10.7%
Growth of reserves	%	-1.0%	98.0%	5.8%	8.8%	20.1%	51.0%	2.5%	-1.4%	11.4%	4.9%
Growth of assets	%	1.8%	44.3%	-1.2%	22.9%	17.0%	7.5%	58.1%	1.9%	5.4%	4.7%
Growth of equity	%	10.0%	-60.0%	106.4%	-1.0%	7.3%	14.4%	166.8%	10.3%	-12.8%	-2.8%

Table 78: Market adjusted financial performance of American Re before and after acquisition by Munich Re

AMERICAN RE (market adj.)	**Unit**	**1991**	**1992**	**1993**	**1994**	**1995**	**1996**	**1997**	**1998**	**1999**	**2000**
Size											
Earnings	x times market	1.8	1.5	1.7	1.5	-1.6	2.0	4.0	6.0	-2.3	-1.1
Premiums	x times market	0.4	0.5	0.4	0.5	0.5	1.0	2.3	2.4	1.8	1.5
Reserves	x times market	0.3	0.5	0.5	0.5	0.7	2.1	2.6	2.4	1.8	1.6
Assets	x times market	0.4	0.5	0.4	0.5	0.9	1.4	2.7	2.7	2.0	1.6
Shareholders' Equity	x times market	0.9	0.3	0.6	0.5	1.0	1.1	4.1	4.7	3.0	2.0
Solvency											
Equity ratio	Δ%pts to market	15.9%	-2.5%	4.5%	1.6%	0.3%	-1.1%	1.7%	4.6%	2.8%	-1.0%
Equity reserves ratio	Δ%pts to market	35.3%	-1.4%	6.4%	4.6%	2.0%	-4.5%	1.9%	8.1%	5.1%	-2.8%
Operating leverage	Δtimes x to marke	-1.9	0.3	-0.9	-0.4	-0.5	-0.3	-0.6	-0.7	-0.4	0.2
Reserves leverage	Δtimes x to marke	-54.3	-46.5	-41.1	-23.8	-85.2	-15.7	11.5	-15.5	-99.8	-159.0
Reserves ratio	Δtimes x to marke	-0.7	0.8	0.3	0.1	0.8	1.9	0.9	0.5	-0.3	0.1
Profitability											
Return on reserves	Δbp to market	828.8	166.6	195.4	97.2	-472.8	81.6	-28.2	166.2	-381.7	-270.7
Return on equity	Δ%pts to market	6.9%	19.6%	5.0%	1.8%	-34.1%	10.5%	-7.0%	-0.6%	-16.1%	-13.5%
Return on premiums	Δ%pts to market	17.4%	8.0%	7.1%	3.3%	-16.6%	6.7%	-1.2%	6.7%	-11.2%	-8.2%
Combined ratio	Δ%pts to market	-5.3%	2.7%	1.1%	9.9%	25.6%	-1.5%	13.4%	13.7%	28.6%	25.0%
Loss ratio	Δ%pts to market	-5.4%	-4.1%	-6.2%	3.0%	18.5%	-7.5%	1.4%	-0.5%	17.4%	13.7%
Expense ratio	Δ%pts to market	0.2%	6.8%	7.3%	6.9%	7.2%	6.0%	12.0%	14.2%	11.2%	11.3%
Net investment result ratio	Δ%pts to market	2.3%	-3.7%	-11.8%	-9.9%	-7.0%	-9.6%	-4.4%	-3.4%	-1.0%	-6.6%
Net investment yield	Δ%pts to market	-0.8%	-2.0%	-3.3%	-2.8%	-3.2%	-3.2%	-2.1%	-1.3%	0.8%	0.7%
Growth											
Growth of earnings	Δ%pts to market	n/a*	-9.8%	8.1%	-11.4%	-173.8%	-228.1%	99.2%	33.9%	-159.7%	-71.3%
Growth of premiums	Δ%pts to market	110.8%	-1.4%	-5.4%	9.8%	1.9%	12.9%	28.3%	-6.0%	0.0%	-3.8%
Growth of reserves	Δ%pts to market	-6.0%	75.4%	-13.6%	1.6%	16.5%	45.5%	-13.4%	-10.9%	-19.2%	-2.4%
Growth of assets	Δ%pts to market	-2.6%	22.6%	-19.8%	14.7%	17.1%	-1.8%	38.5%	-8.7%	-24.4%	-3.2%
Growth of equity	Δ%pts to market	n/a*	-72.0%	91.1%	-8.5%	48.0%	14.9%	192.2%	15.6%	-48.8%	-47.4%

* Market figures not available for 1990.

Table 79: Mapping of rating classes

Rating agency	**Rating classes**						
Standard & Poor's, Fitch	AAA	AA+	AA	AA-	A+	A	A-
Moody's	Aaa	Aa1	Aa2	Aa3	A1	A2	A3
A.M. Best	A++	A+	A(+)	A	A(-)	A-	

Source: Rating agencies, own research

8 References

Acharya, S., 1993. Value of Latent Information: Alternative Event Study Methods. Journal of Finance 48 (1).

Achleitner, A.-K., 1999. Handbuch Investment Banking. Gabler, Wiesbaden.

Actuarial Standards Board, 1991. Actuarial Appraisals. Actuarial Standard of Practice 19.

Agence France-Presse, 1 November 2000. CGNU to sell Marlborough Underwriting Agency.

Agence France-Presse, 14 April 2000. EU Commission approves merger of insurers Norwich Union and CGU.

Agence France-Presse, 16 March 2000. Axa indicates it will not counterbid for CGU or Norwich Union.

Agence France-Presse, 21 February 2000b. CGU, Norwich merge to form biggest British insurer.

Agence France-Presse, 25 July 2000. British CGNU sells German general insurance business.

AISAM, 2006a. Comments from the mutual insurance sector to the European Commission regarding the future priorities for the Action Plan on the Modernisation of Company Law and Corporate Governance. Association Internationale des Sociétés d'Assurance Mutuelle.

AISAM, 2006b. Governance of Mutual Insurance Companies: the current state of legislation. Association Internationale des Sociétés d'Assurance Mutuelle.

AISAM, 2007. Mutual insurance in figures. Association Internationale des Sociétés d'Assurance Mutuelle.

Akhigbe, A., and Madura, J., 2001. Intra-Industry Signals Resulting from Insurance Company Mergers. Journal of Risk and Insurance Volume 68, Number 3, 489-505.

Amel, D., Barnes, C., Panetta, F., and Salleo, C., 2003. Consolidation and efficiency in the financial sector: a review of international evidence. CEIS Research Paper No. 20.

Anderson, R. I., Ennsfellner, K. C., and Lewis, D., 2004. Production Efficiency in the Austrian Insurance Industry: A Bayesian Examination. Journal of Risk and Insurance 71 (1).

Associated Press Newswires, 21 February 2000. 5,000 jobs to go in planned British insurance merger.

Associated Press Newswires, 22 February 2000. Royal London buying United Assurance for dlrs 2.4 billion.

Associated Press Newswires, 31 March 2000. CGU, Norwich Shareholders OK Deal.

Associated Press, 21 February 2000. Insurance companies merge to form largest in Britain.

Australian Associated Press, 22 February 2000. Unions fear Norwich-CGU merger will cost hundreds of jobs.

Backhaus, K., Erichson, B., Plinke, W., and Weiber, R., 2006. Multivariate Analysemethoden – Eine anwendungsorientierte Einführung. Springer Book, Berlin, Germany.

Barber, B. M., and Lyon, J. D., 1997. Detecting long-run abnormal stock returns: The empirical power and specification of test statistics. Journal of Financial Economics 43, 341-372.

BarNiv, R., and J. Hathorn, 1997. The Merger or Insolvency Alternative in the Insurance Industry:. The Journal of Risk and Insurance 64 (1), 89-113.

Barry, T., and Walsh, P., 2000. Demutualisation – Combining North American and European Requirements. Society of Actuaries in Ireland.

Beckmann, R., Eppendorfer, C., and Neimke, M., 2002. Financial integration within the European Union: Towards a single market for insurance.

Beitel, P., 2002. Akquisitionen und Zusammenschlüsse europäischer Banken. Deutscher Universitäts-Verlag.

Beitel, P., and Schiereck, D., 2003. Zum Erfolg von Akquisitionen und Zusammenschlüssen zwischen Banken: eine Bestandsaufnahme der empirischen Forschung. Österreichisches Bankarchiv 51, 501-515.

Berens, W. et al., 1998. Unternehmensakquisitionen. Due Diligence bei Unternehmensakquisitionen. In Berens, W. and Brauner, H. (eds.), Schäffer-Poeschel, Ulm.

Berger, A. N., and Humphrey, D., 1992. The Megamergers in Banking and the Use of Cost Efficiency as an Antitrust Device. Journal of Financial Economics, Antitrust Bulletin 50, 187-229.

Berger, A. N., Cummins, J. D., Weiss, M. A., and Zi, H., 2000a. Conglomeration Versus Strategic Focus: Evidence from the Insurance Industry. Journal of Financial Intermediation 9, 323-362.

Berger, A. N., De Young, R., and Udell, G. F., 2000b. Efficiency Barriers to the Consolidation of the European Financial Services Industry. European Financial Management 7 (1), 117.

Berger, A. N., Demsetz, R. S., and Strahan, P. E., 1999. The consolidation of the Financial services industry: Causes, consequences, and implications for the future. Journal of Banking and Finance 23, 135-194.

Bestwire, 14 August 1996. A.M. Best Puts American Re, Munich Re Under Review.

Bestwire, 15 November 2001. Munich Re to Give American Re a $1 Billion Boost.

Bestwire, 7 July 1997. Munich Re U.S. Business Merged into American Re.

BIS, 2001. Report on consolidation in the financial sector. Bank for International Settlements, Group of Ten, Basle, Switzerland.

Black, B. S., 1989. Bidder Overpayment in Takeovers. Stanford Law Review 41, 597-660.

Bloomberg Business News, 15 August 1996. Reinsurer Munich Re agrees to buy American Re.

Boehmer, E., Masumeci, J., Poulsen, A. B., 1991. Event-study methodology under conditions of event-induced variance. Journal of Financial Economics 30, 253-272.

Boone, L. A., and Mulherin, J. H., 2007. How are Firms Sold?. The Journal of Finance 62 (2), 847-875.

Bosch, K., 1998. Statistik-Taschenbuch. Oldenbourg, München/Wien.

Boston Herald, 22 February 2000. CGU put on block as part of $12B deal.

Boubakri, N., Dionne, G., and Triki, T., 2006. Consolidation and value creation in the insurance industry: The role of governance.

Bradley, M., Desai, A., and Kim, E. H., 1983. The Rationale behind Interfirm Tender Offers, Information or Synergy?. Journal of Financial Economics 11, 183-206.

Brav, A., and Gompers, P. A., 1997. Myth or reality? The long-run underperformance of initial public offerings: Evidence from venture and nonventure capital-backed companies. Journal of Finance 52, 1791-1821.

Brav, A., Géczy, C., and Gompers, P. A., 1995. Underperformance of seasoned equity offerings revisited. Working paper, Harvard University.

Brown, S. and Warner, J. B., 1985. Using daily stock returns: The case of event studies. Journal of Financial Economics 14, 3-31.

Bulow, J., and Klemperer, P., 1996. Auctions Versus Negotiations. The American Economic Review 86 (1), 180-194.

Buono, A. F., and Bowditch, J. L., 1985. When cultures collide: the anatomy of a merger. Human Relations 38 (5), 477-500.

Business Wire, 14 August 1996. Despite Denials, Munich Re to buy American Re.

Business Wire, 15 March 1997. Edward Noonan Succeeds Paul Inderbitzin as CEO of American Re.

Business Wire, 17 November 2003. American Re Closes the Sale of Becher + Carlson Risk Management, Inc.

Business Wire, 2 November 1998. American Re and Munich Re Launch Powerful New Force in the Strategic Management of Risk: Munich American RiskPartners.

Business Wire, 20 October 2003. American Re Announces the Sale of Becher + Carlson Risk Management, Inc.

Business Wire, 21 November 1996. American Re Corporation Stockholders Approve Acquisition By Munich Re.

Business Wire, 5 August 1996. American Re Considering Strategic Alternatives.

Business Wire, 5 February 1997. American Re Makes Senior Management Appointments, Including Several Executives from Munich American Re.

Cable, J., and Holland, K., 1999b. Modeling normal returns in event studies: A model selection approach and pilot study. The European Journal of Finance 5, 331-334.

Cable, J., and Holland, K., 2000. Robust vs. OLS estimation of the market model: Implications for event studies. Economics Letters 69, 385-391.

Calomiris, 1999. Gauging the Efficiency of Bank Consolidation during a Merger Wave. Journal of Banking and Finance 23, 615-621.

Calomiris, C., and Karceski, J., 1998. Is the Bank Merger Waev of the 1990s Efficient? Lessons Learned from Nine Case Studies. The AEI Press, Washington, D. C.

Carhart, M., 1997. On Persistence in Mutual Fund Performance. Journal of Finance 52 (1).

CEA, 2006. European Insurance in Figures. CEA Statistics No 24.

CGNU, 19 May 2000. CGU & Bancaja forge alliance in Spain.

CGNU, 1 July 2002. CGNU becomes AVIVA.

CGU, 1998. Annual Report.

CGU, 1999. Annual Report.

Chamberlain, S. L., and Tennyson, S., 1998. Capital Shocks and Merger Activity in the Property-Liability Insurance Industry. The Journal of Risk and Insurance 65 (4), 563-595.

Chandler, A. D. jr., 1990. Scale and Scope: the Dynamics of Industrial Capitalism. Harvard University Press, Cambridge/Massachusetts.

Chatterjee, S., and Price, B., 1991. Regression Diagnostics. Wiley & Sons, New York.

Chen, Z., and Knez, P. J., 1995. Measurement of Market Integration and Arbitrage. The Review of Financial Studies 8 (2), 287-325.

Core, J. E., 2001. A review of the empirical disclosure literature: discussion. Journal of Accounting and Economics 31 (1-3), 441-456.

Corrado, C.J., 1989. A non parametric test for abnormal security price perforamance in event studies. Journal of Financial Economics 23, 385-395.

Corriere della Sera, 27 July 2000. CGNU of the UK forges closer ties with Popolare di Lodi.

Coutts, J. A., Mills, T. C., and Roberts, J., 1994. The Market Model and The Event Study Method: A Synthesis of the Econometric Criticism. International Review of Financial Analysis 3, 149-171.

Cowan, A. R. and Sergeant, A. M. A., 1996. Trading Frequency and Event Study Test Specification. Journal of Banking and Finance 20, 1731-1757.

Cowan, A. R., 1992. Nonparametric Event Study Tests. Review of Accounting 2, 343-358.

Cummins, J. D., and Rubio-Misas, M., 2006. Deregulation, Consolidation, and Efficiency: Evidence from the Spanish Insurance Industry. Journal of Money, Credit, and Banking.

Cummins, J. D., and Weiss, M. A., 1993. Measuring Cost Efficiency in the Property-Liability Insurance Industry. Journal of Banking and Finance 17 (2-3), 463-482.

Cummins, J. D., and Weiss, M. A., 2000. The Global Market for Reinsurance – Consolidation Capacity and Efficiency. Brookings-Wharton Papers on Financial Services, 159-220.

Cummins, J. D., and Weiss, M. A., 2004. Consolidation in the European Insurance Industry: Do Mergers and Acquisitions Create Value for Shareholders? The Brookings/Wharton Conference papers.

Cummins, J. D., and Xie, X., 2005. Efficiency and Value Creation in Acquisitions and Divestitures: Evidence from the US Property-Liability Insurance Industry. Working Paper.

Cummins, J. D., and Zi, H., 1998. Comparison of Frontier Efficiency Methods: An Application to the U.S. Life Insurance Industry. Journal of Productivity Analysis 10 (2), 131-152.

Cummins, J. D., Tennyson, S., and Weiss, M. A., 1998. Efficiency Scale Economies and Consolidation in the US Life Insurance Industry. Working paper.

Cummins, J. D., Weiss, M. A., and Xie, X., 2006. Market Concentration, Vertical Integration and Bancassurance: Consolidation and the "Insurance Middleman". ARIA Annual Meeting 2006, Washington, D.C.

Cyree, K. B., and DeGennaro, R. P., 2002. A Generalized Method for Detecting Abnormal Returns and Changes in Systematic Risk. Review of Quantitative Finance and Accounting 19 (4), 399-416.

Daily Mail, 22 February 2000. Failure to pay premium could scupper CGU deal.

Dasgupta, S., and Hansen, R. G., 2006. Auctions in Corporate Finance. Working paper.

Datta, D. K., 1991. Organizational fit and acquisition performance: effects of post-acquisition integration. Strategic Management Journal 12, 281-297.

Diven, D. L., 1984. Organizational planning: neglected factor in mergers and acquisition strategy. Managerial Planning July-August, 4-12.

Dodd, P. and Warner, J. B., 1983. On corporate governance: A study of proxy contests. Journal of Financial Economics 11, 401-438.

Dombrow, J., Rodriguez, M., and Sirmans, C. F., 2000. A Complete Nonparametric Event Study Approach. Review of Quantitative Finance and Accounting 14, 4.

Donni, O., and Fecher, F., 1997. Efficiency and Productivity of the Insurance Industry in the OECD countries. Geneva Papers on Risk and Insurance 22 (85), 523-535.

Dow Jones Business News, 1 February 1999. France's AXA Offers $5.67 Billion For U.K.'s Guardian Royal Exchange.

Dow Jones Business News, 22 February 2000. Royal London Offers $2.4 Billion To Buy U.K. Insurer United Assurance.

Dow Jones International News, 1 July 1996. National Re: General Re Seen Most Likely to Buy Co.

Dow Jones International News, 1 September 2000. CGNU A Potential Bidder For U.K. Equitable Life – Source.

Dow Jones International News, 15 March 2000. UK's CGU-Norwich Interested In Gartmore.

Dow Jones International News, 23 April 2007. Allianz Conversion Into SE Saved Co Up To EUR1B -Report.

Dow Jones International News, 4 September 1996. Germany's Munich Re To See American Re Profits By 1998.

Dow Jones International News, 6 August 2004. Munich Re CEO: Ergo Unit May Earn Cost of Cap Already 04.

Dow Jones News Service, 14 August 1996a. Munich Re/Amer Re Pact: Sees Close By Year End.

Dow Jones News Service, 14 August 1996b. Munich Re, American Re: Munich Re Could Fall Further.

Dow Jones Newswire, 21 February 2000. CGU/Norwich New Group To Take GBP350 Million Charge For Cost Savings.

Dow Jones-VWD Unternehmen Deutschland, 15 February 2005. Münchener Rück: Weitere Reservenerhöhung für American Re möglich.

Easterbrook, F. H., and Fischel, D. R., 1991. The Economic Structure of Corporate Law. Harvard University Press, Cambridge/Massachusetts.

Ebert, M., 1998. Evaluation von Synergien bei Unternehmenszusammenschlüssen. Dr. Kovac Verlag, Hamburg.

Eisenhardt, K. M., 1989. Building Theories from Case Study Research. The Academy of Management Review 14 (4), 532-550.

European Central Bank (ECB), 2005. EU Banking Structure.

European Commission, 2007a. European Commission – Competition – Publications, press-releases and Commission decisions on individual cases. http://ec.europa.eu/comm/competition/mergers/cases/; accessed May 8, 2007.

European Commission, 2007b. Inquiry into the European business insurance sector pursuant to Article 17 of Regulation 1/2003 – Interim report.

European Council, 1973. First Council Directive 73/239/EEC of 24 July 1973 on the coordination of laws, regulations and administrative provisions relating to the taking-up and pursuit of the business of direct insurance other than life assurance. Official Journal L 228.

European Council, 1979. First Council Directive 79/267/EEC of 5 March 1979 on the coordination of laws, regulations and administrative provisions relating to the taking up and pursuit of the business of direct life assurance. Official Journal L 063.

European Council, 2002a. Directive 2002/13/EC of the European Parliament and of the Council amending Council Directive 73/239/EEC as regards the solvency margin requirements for non-life insurance undertakings. Official Journal of the European Communities L 77/17.

European Council, 2002b. Directive 2002/83/EC of the European Parliament and of the Council concerning life assurance. Official Journal of the European Communities L 345/1.

European Council, 2004. Council Regulation (EC) No 139/2004 of 20 January 2004 on the control of concentrations between undertakings (the EC Merger Regulation). Official Journal of the European Union.

Evening News – Scotland, 1 March 2000. Axa set to gatecrash GBP 17bn deal for merger.

Fama, E. F. and French, K. R., 1993. Common risk factors in returns on stocks and bonds. Journal of Financial Economics 33, 3-56.

Fecher, F., and Pestieau, P., 1993. Efficiency and Competition in O.E.C.D. Financial Services. The Measurement of Productive Efficiency: Techniques and Application, Harold O. Fried, Knox C. A. Lovell and Shelton S. Schmidt (eds).

Financial Times, 21 February 2000. Companies & Finance – UK – An attempt to become hunter not hunted.

Financial Times, 22 February 2000a. Wave of consolidation ready to break forth.

Financial Times, 22 February 2000b. Market cool on CGU-Norwich link.

Financial Times, 23 December 2000. Companies & Finance International – Manulife agrees deal.

Financial Times, 26 February 2000b. Companies & Finance – UK – Why the Bob and Richard merger show fell so very flat.

Financial Times, 27 December 2000. CGNU sells two Canadian units for GBP133m.

Financial Times, 27 October 2000. CGNU sells NZ's State Insurance.

Financial Times, 3 March 1999. Norwich Union lifts annuities provisions.

Floreani, A., and Rigamonti, S., 2001. Mergers and shareholders' wealth in the insurance industry. Working paper, Universita del S.Cuore.

Focarelli, D., 1992. Economie di Scala e Della Diversificazione Produttiva nel Settore Assicurativo. Rivista di Politica Economica 82 (4), 23-44.

Gaughan, P., 1999. Mergers, acquisitions, and corporate restructurings. Wiley & Sons, New York.

Gelb, D. S., and Zarowin, P., 2002. Corporate Disclosure Policy and the Informativeness of Stock Prices. Review of Accounting Studies 7, 33-52.

Gerds, J., 2006. Post Merger Integration: Unternehmenserfolg durch Integration excellence. Springer Book, Berlin, Germany.

Halpern, P., 1983. Corporate acquisitions: A theory of special cases? A review of event studies applied to acquisitions. Journal of Finance 37, 297-317.

Hamilton, J. D., 1989. A New Approach to the Economic Analysis of Nonstationary Time Series and the Business Cycle. Econometrica 57 (2), 357-384.

Hanweck, G. A., and Hogan, A. M. B., 1996. The Structure of the Property/Casualty Insurance Industry. Journal of Economics and Business 48 (2), 141-155.

Hayes, R. H., 1979. The human side of acquisitions. Management Review 68 (11), 41-46.

Heldenberg, A., Scoubeau, C., Arnone, L., and Croquet, M., 2006. The financial communication during a period of transition. Corporate Communications: An International Journal 11 (2), 174-188.

Higgins, E. J., and Peterson, D. R., 1998. The Power of One and Two Sample t-Statistics Given Event-Induced Variance Increases and Nonnormal Stock Returns: A Comparative Study. Quarterly Journal of Business and Economics Winter, 27-49.

ING, 2006. Insurance sector: The M&A dance begins. Wholesale Banking Equity Markets Sector update.

Insurance Brokers Monthly & Insurance Advisor, 1 May 2000. Appointment at CGU/ Norwich Union.

Insurance Information Institute Database, 10 November 2000. Skandia, CGNU, others cleared for insurance licenses in China.

Interfax Czech Republic Business News Service, 10 November 2000. British CGNU buys 65% of VVPF pension fund, MUS retains 35%.

Interfax Poland Business Service, 22 February 2000. Commercial Union and Norwich Union pension funds would take one third of market and regulator opposition if merged.

Investors Chronicle, 24 March 2000. News Analysis: Norwich Union Shareholder Hits Out At Proposed CGU Deal.

Jemison, D. B., and Sitkin, S. B., 1986. Corporate acquisitions: A process perspective. Academy of Management Review 11 (1), 145-163.

Jennings, E. H., 1971. An Empirical Analysis of Some Aspects of Common Stock Diversification. Journal of Financial and Quantitative Analysis, Papers and Proceedings 6, 797-815.

Jensen, M. C., 1986. Agency costs of free cash flow, corporate finance, and takeovers.. American Economic Review, Papers and Proceedings 76, 323-329.

Jensen, M. C., and Ruback, R. S., 1983. The market for corporate control. Journal of Financial Economics 11, 5-50.

Johnson, Norman J., 1978. Modified t tests and confidence intervals for asymmetrical populations. Journal of the American Statistical Association 73, 536-544.

Katrishen, F. A., and Scordis, N. A., 1998. Economies of Scale in Services: A Study of Multinational Insurers. Journal of International Business Studies 2, 305-324.

Kaye, G., 1991. Economies of Scale in U.K.: Life Insurance Companies: An Empirical Approach. Geneva Papers on Risk and Insurance 16 (60), 302-314.

Kiranand, S., 2004. Alternatives for Stock Market Integration Measurement: Investigation of Asian Stock Markets. Finance India 18 (1), 57-102.

Klumpes, P. J. M., 2006. Consolidation and effficiency in the major European insurance markets. Presentation at "Dynamics of Insurance Markets: Structure, Conduct, and Performance in the 21st Century".

Koch, P., and Weiss, W. (eds.), 1994. Gabler Versicherungslexikon. Gabler, Wiesbaden.

Kothari, S. P. and Jerold B. Warner, 2004. Econometrics of Event Studies. Handbook of Corporate Finance: Empirical Corporate Finance.

Larsen, Pia Veldt, 2006. Regression and analysis of variance. Lecture notes.

Leng, C.-C., and Meier, U. B., 2002. Analysis of Multi-National Underwriting Cycles in Property-Liability Insurance. Working draft.

Levy, H., and Sarnat, M., 1970. Diversification, Portfolio Analysis and the Uneasy Case of Conglomerate Mergers. Journal of Finance 25, 795-802.

Lloyd's List International, 17 August 1996. No hitch seen over American Re deal.

Lorenz, J.-T., 2006. European Banking-M&A – Die Kapitalmarktperspektive. Doctoral thesis at the European Business School, Oestrich-Winkel, Germany.

Loughran, T. and Ritter, J., 1995. The new issues puzzle. Journal of Finance 50, 23-52.

Lyon, J. D., Barber, B. M., and Tsai, C.-L., 1999. Improved Methods for Tests of Long-Run Abnormal Stock Returns. The Journal of Finance 1, 165-201.

Mahlberg, B. and Url, T., 2000. The Transition to the Single Market in the German Insurance Industry. Working paper.

Major, R., 2005. Runoffs, Insurance, & Reinsurance. Asia Insurance Review November.

March, J. G., and Shapira, Z., 1987. Managerial perspectives on risk and risk-taking. Management Science 33, 1404-1418.

Marketing, 18 May 2000. CGNU asks three to contest #20m creative account.

Marris, R., 1963. A Model of the "Managerial" Enterprise. Quarterly Journal of Economics 77, 185-209.

McKinsey & Company, 2005. Valuation – Measuring and Managing the Value of Companies. Wiley & Sons, New York 4th edition.

McKinsey & Company, 2006a. Performance 2006 – Schaden/Unfall.

McKinsey & Company, 2006b. Performance 2006 – Leben.

Money Marketing, 13 April 2000. News – Top posts are filled at mega firm CGNU.

Money Marketing, 20 April 2000. News – The merged group

Munich Re, 10 January 2002. Personnel changes at North American subsidiaries of the Munich Re Group. Press release.

Munich Re, 10 July 2002. Munich Re Group makes extensive provision for developments in the US / Very positive overall result nevertheless expected for first half year, thanks to large capital gains from transactions with Allianz and favourable trend in reinsurance business. Press release.

Munich Re, 14 August 1996. Munich Re acquires American Re. Press release.

Munich Re, 19 July 2005a. Line drawn under American Re's past. Press release.

Munich Re, 1996/1997. Annual report.

Munich Re, 2000. Annual report.

Munich Re, 2004. Annual report.

Munich Re, 27 May 2002. Munich Re Group generally optimistic again after "extreme year 2001"/Schinzler: "First-class insurance and reinsurance are scarce commodities; higher exposures and larger risks require further premium increases." / For the current year, the Group expects a bigger profit than in 2000, with substantial income from the sale of Allianz shares. Press release.

Munich Re, 30 September 2002. Realization of previously announced capital strengthening at American Re: Munic Re utilizing own resources to strengthen subsidiary's position in the positively developing US reinsurance market. Press release.

Munich Re, 8 November 2004. Profit of EUR 1.5 bn for the first nine months. Press release.

Munich Re, 9 May 2005. Business figures 1 January–March 2005. Press release.

Munich Re, April 2003. European Roadshow.

Mußhoff, J., 2007. Erfolgreiche M&A-Transaktionen in der europäischen Bankenindustrie. Doctoral thesis at the European Business School, Oestrich-Winkel, Germany.

National Post, 11 July 2002a. Munich Re injects another USD 2 bn into American Re.

National Post, 11 July 2002b. Munich Re faces credit downgrade: USD 2 bn payout to U.S. unit.

National Underwriter Property & Casualty-Risk & Benefits Management Edition, 19 August 1996. Munich Re bolsters foothold in the U.S.

New Zealand Press Assocation, 9 May 2000. Commission clears NZI and State merger.

OECD, 1993. Glossary of Industrial Organisation Economics and Competition Law, compiled by R. S. Khemani and D. M. Shapiro, commissioned by the Directorate for Financial, Fiscal and Enterprise Affairs.

OECD, 1998. Directive of the European Parliament and of the Council on the supplementary supervision of insurance undertakings in an insurance group.

OECD, 1999a. Cross-border trade in financial services: Economics and regulation.

OECD, 2000a. Mergers and acquisitions in the financial services sector.

OECD, 2000b. Insurance regulation and supervision in OECD countries.

OECD, 2001a. Insurance and solvency supervision: compilation of country reports.

OECD, 2007. OECD Insurance Statistics – online database. http://www.oecd.org/document/19/0,2340,en_2649_37411_37506643_1_1_1_37411,00.html; accessed May 8, 2007.

O'Neil, M. L., 1984. Evaluation of the Financial Condition of Insurance Companies – A Theoretical Approach. Casualty Actuarial Society Discussion Paper Program Casualty Actuarial Society – Arlington, Virginia, 124-159.

Pablo, A. L., Sitkin, S. B., and Jemison, D. B., 1996. Acquisition Decision-Making Processes: The Central Role of Risk. Journal of Management 22 (5), 723-746.

Pack, H., 2002. Due Diligence. Picot, G. (ed.): Handbuch Merger & Acquisitions, Schäffer-Poeschel, Stuttgart, 267-299.

Panzar, J. C., and Willig, R. C., 1981. Economies of Scope. American Economic Review, Papers and Proceedings 71, 268-272.

Paprottka, S., 1996. Unternehmenszusammenschlüsse, Synergiepotentiale und ihre Umsetzungsmöglichkeiten durch Integration. Gabler, Wiesbaden.

Pausenberger, E., 1993. Unternehmenszusammenschlüsse. Wittmann, W., (ed.): Handwörterbuch der Betriebswirtschaft, Schäffer-Poeschel, Stuttgart, Sp. 4436-4448.

Pentikäinen, T., 1967. On the Solvency of Insurance Companies. Astin Bulletin 4 (3), 236-247.

Perin, S., 1996. Synergien bei Unternehmensakquisitionen: empirische Untersuchung von Finanz-, Markt- und Leistungssynergien. Deutscher Universitäts-Verlag, Wiesbaden.

Picot, G., 1995. Kauf und Restrukturierung von Unternehmen. Beck-Verlag, München.

Picot, G., 2002. Wirtschaftliche und wirtschaftsrechtliche Parameter bei der Planung von Mergers & Acquisitions, in: Picot, Gerhard (eds.). Handbuch Merger & Acquisitions, 2nd edition, Schäffer-Poeschel, Stuttgart.

Pilloff, S. J., and Santomero, A. M., 1998. The Value Effects of Bank Mergers and Acquisitions. Mergers of Financial Institutions, Amihud, Y. and G. Miller, Norwell MA, Kluwer Academic Publishers, 59-78.

Post Magazine, 20 July 2000. CGNU forces 744 into run off.

Post Magazine, 22 August 1996. Munich Re buy may lower its ratings.

Post Magazine, 24 August 2000. CGNU faces turmoil as team resigns.

Post Magazine, 8 June 2000. CGNU names top team.

PR Newswire, 26 February 2004. Arthur J. Gallagher & Co. Increases Ownership of Risk Management Partners Ltd To 100%.

Preuschl, M., 1997. Unternehmensübernahmen als Instrument der Managementkontrolle? – Eine Analyse am Beispiel der USA. PhD thesis, Regensburg.

Professional Broking, 1 September 2000. CGU branches remain in new look Norwich Union.

PWC, 2006. Financial Services M&A – Review of and outlook for mergers and acquisitions in the European financial services market. PriceWaterhouseCoopers Industry Views.

Ramsey, J.B., 1969. Tests for Specification Errors in Classical Linear Least Squares Regression Analysis. Journal of the Royal Statistical Society B 32, 350-371.

Reactions, 1 March 2000. Merger creates top five European Insurance Group – #19bn CGU/NU merger to create UK's largest insurance group.

Reactions, 26 February 1996. Rate cuts begin to bite. Reactions Publishing Group 8.

Reactions, 31 August 1998. Munich Re announces plan to raise DM3.3bn in capital.

Reactions, 31 October 1996. News Feature – Munich Re – Now the 'S' Factor?

Regulatory News Service, 11 May 2000. Norwich Union PLC Polish Government Statement.

Regulatory News Service, 17 July 2000. Royal Bk Scot.Grp. CGNU Joint Venture.

Regulatory News Service, 2 August 2000. CGNU PLC Interim Results 2000 – Part 1.

Regulatory News Service, 2 August 2001. CGNU PLC CGNU Interim Results 2001.

Regulatory News Service, 21 February 2000. Norwich Union PLRC Re Merger.

Regulatory News Service, 22 May 2000. Norwich Union PLC Merger Update.

Regulatory News Service, 24 January 2001. CGNU PLC Re Directorate.

Regulatory News Service, 26 July 2000. CGNU PLC CGNU Bancassurance in Italy.

Regulatory News Service, 27 February 2001. REG-CGNU PLC 2001 Full year results.

Regulatory News Service, 30 June 2000. CGNU PLC CGNU Sale of Subsidiary.

Regulatory News Service, 8 November 2000. CGNU PLC 9 Months Results 2000-Part 1.

Reinsurance Association of America, 2004. Reinsurance Underwriting Review: 2004 Industry Results.

Reuters News, 10 July 2002. Munich Re see Q2 profit pre-exceptionals below Q1.

Reuters News, 11 November 1996. Munich Re sees Amer Re deal complete by end-Nov.

Reuters News, 14 August 1996a. Munich Re liquid assets to finance bulk of US buy.

Reuters News, 14 August 1996b. Cartel office says was informed of Munich Re deal.

Reuters News, 14 September 1999. Generali move restokes bid talk for Norwich.

Reuters News, 15 March 2000. Norwich chief says institutions back merger.

Reuters News, 15 May 2000. Norwich Union lists dates in CGU merger.

Reuters News, 15 November 2000. Interview-CGNU looking for U.S fund acquisition.

Reuters News, 18 December 1998. Muenchner Rueck up, Allianz down on share-swap.

Reuters News, 2 June 1999. CGU says its Dutch insurer in merger talks.

Reuters News, 20 February 2000. Britain's Norwich Union and CGU to merge – sources.

Reuters News, 21 February 2000b. FOCUS-CGU, Norwich merger gets cool reception.

Reuters News, 22 February 2000a. Union seeks press leak probe in UK insurance link.

Reuters News, 27 February 2000. Royal & Sun Alliance seeks buyer – paper.

Reuters News, 3 September 1999. Norwich Union jumps as bid talk intensifies.

Reuters News, 4 April 2000. CGU forms life venture with Tesco Finance.

Reuters News, 4 September 1996. Munich Re sees Amer Re merger hurting 97 earnings.

Reuters News, 5 August 1999. Royal & Sun says no plans for "jumbo" merger.

Reuters News, 6 April 2000. CGU, Norwich make key CGNU appointments.

Reuters News, 8 November 2000. CGNU to buy Czech pension fund from miner Mostecka.

Reuters, 1 March 2000. AXA weist Bericht über Interesse an Norwich zurück.

Reuters, 14 August 1996. Münchener Rück – Kein Paketzuschlag für KKR.

Review, 28 February 1997. American Re.

Rockel, W., Helten, E., Loy, H., and Ott, P., 2005. Versicherungsbilanzen. Schäffer-Poeschel, Stuttgart.

Roll, R., 1986. The hubris hypothesis of corporate takeovers. Journal of Business 59 (4), 197-216.

Romano, R., 1991. A Guide to Takeovers: Theory, Evidence and Regulation. Yale Law School Working Paper No. 138, Yale.

Rubin, H. W., 2000. Barron's Dictionary of Insurance Terms. Barron's Educational Series, Hauppauge New York.

Sautter, M. T., 1989. Strategische Analyse von Unternehmensakquisitionen. Peter Lang Verlag, Frankfurt am Main.

Schedule 14A Statement, 23 October 1996.

Select Federal Filings Newswires, 23 August 1996. American Rre 13D: Munich Re Has 63.9% Stake.

Select Federal Filings Newswires, 24 October 1996. American Re/Munich Re Deal Carries USD26M Term Fee.

Seth, A., 1990. Sources of Value Creation in Acquisitions: An Empirical Investigation. Strategic Management Journal 11, 431-446.

Settnik, U., 2006. Mergers & Acquisitions auf dem deutschen Versicherungsmarkt – Eine empirische Analyse. Deutscher Universitäts-Verlag.

Solibakke, P., 2002. Efficient estimated mean and volatility characteristics for the Nordic spot electricity power market. International Journal of Business 7(2), 17-35.

Standard & Poor's, 1994-2006. Global Reinsurance Highlights – 1994-2006 Editions. Standard & Poor's Ratings Services, London/New York, and Reactions Publishing Group, London.

Standard & Poor's, 2007a. Property/Casualty Insurance Criteria: Operational Analysis. Standard & Poor's Ratings Services, http://www2.standardandpoors.com/portal/site/sp/en/eu/page.article/2,1,5,0,1084804631707.html; accessed May 22, 2007.

Standard & Poor's, 2007b. Life Insurance Criteria: Operational Analysis. Standard & Poor's Ratings Services, http://www2.standardandpoors.com/portal/site/sp/en/us/page.article/2,1,5,0,1086103092844.html; accessed May 22, 2007.

Süddeutsche Zeitung, 14 July 2005. A.M. Best examines Munich Re Rating.

Swiss Re, 1999a. Life Insurance: Will the urge to merge continue? Sigma report 6.

Swiss Re, 2000. Europe in Focus: Non-Life Markets Undergoing Structural Change. Sigma report 3.

Swiss Re, 2003. Reinsurance – a systemic risk? Swiss Re Sigma 5.

The Asian Wall Street Journal, 11 November 1999. Insurer CGU of U.K. Posts Slight Decline In Its Operating Profit.

The Economist, 17 August 1996. Global Reinsurance.

The Evening Standard, 11 August 1999. Norwich in non-life buy.

The Financial News, 3 July 2000. Norwich loses equity heads to Morley.

The Financial News, 5 June 2000. Pipped at the post – Sanjana quits Morley.

The Financial Times, 23 February 2000. Companies & Finance – UK – From dull and marginal to centre stage.

The Geneva Association, 2004. Insurance and Finance – Research on Finance Issues in Insurance. Geneva Association Information Newsletter.

The Guardian, 4 August 1999. Norwich chief predicts 15% car insurance rise.

The Herald, 12 August 1999. CGU on lookout as profits advance.

The Independent – London, 1 March 2000. AXA considers gatecrashing CGNU merger.

The Independent – London, 4 August 1999. The Investment Column – Norwich Union.

The Independent, 20 May 1999. Norwich Union catches bid bug over Lloyds talk.

The Independent, 21 February 2000. #19bn merger of CGU and Norwich Union could trigger bids from rivals.

The Mail on Sunday, 27 February 2000. CGU boss fears turmoil if NU marriage fails.

The Mail on Sunday, 5 March 2000. Norwich Union plans big dividend bonanza.

The Mail on Sunday, 6 August 2000. Threat to 600 jobs in CGNU cutback.

The New York Times, 28 February 2000. Britain's Prudential Considers Bid for Rival.

The Scotsman, 27 April 2000. CGU wins RBS deal after support in takeover battle.

The Sunday Telegraph, 12 November 2000. City – CGNU quits the race for Equitable Life.

The Times, 2 March 2000. Sun Life leaves option open for rival NU bid – Takeover – Norwich Union.

The Times, 25 March 2000. Insurers call for UK champion.

The Times, 31 March 2000. Gartmore goes to US insurer.

Toole, J., and Herget, T., 2005. Insurance Industry Mergers & Acquisitions. Society of Actuaries, Schaumburg.

Towers Perrin Tillinghast, 2006. Solvency II The Pace Quickens.

Tremblay, F., 2006. Embedded Value Calculation for a Life Insurance Company. Actuarial Practice Forum of the Society of Actuaries October.

Tucker, J., 2007. Is Openness Penalized? Stock Returns around Earnings Warnings. Accounting Review July.

U.S. Department of Justice and the Federal Trade Commission , 1997. Horizontal Merger Guidelines. http://www.usdoj.gov/atr/public/guidelines/horiz_book/hmg1.html, accessed May 4, 2007.

Viswanathan, K. and Cummins, J. D., 2003. Ownership Structure Changes in the Insurance Industry: An Analysis of Demutualization . Journal of Risk & Insurance 70 (3), 401-437.

Wells, B. P, Cox, L. A., and Gaver, K. M., 1995. Free Cash Flow in the Life Insurance Industry. Journal of Risk and Insurance 62, 50-66.

Weston, J. F., Chung, K.S., and Siu, J.A., 1990. Takeovers, restructuring, and corporate governance. Upper Saddle River, New Jersey, Prentice Hall.

World Insurance Report, 16 June 1995. World Insurance Report. The Financial Times.

Yuengert, A. W., 1993. The Measurement of Efficiency in Life Insurance: Estimates of a Mixed Normal-Gamma Error Model. Journal of Banking and Finance 17 (2-3), 483-496.

Zeppetella, T., 2002. Allocation of Required Capital by Line of Business.

Zollo, M., and Singh, H., 2004. Deliberate Learning in Corporate Acquisitions: Post-Acquisition Strategies and Integration Capability in U.S. Bank Mergers. Strategic Management Journal 25, 1233-1256.

MIX
Papier aus verantwortungsvollen Quellen
Paper from responsible sources
FSC® C105338

If you have any concerns about our products,
you can contact us on
ProductSafety@springernature.com

In case Publisher is established outside the EU,
the EU authorized representative is:
Springer Nature Customer Service Center GmbH
Europaplatz 3, 69115 Heidelberg, Germany

Printed by Libri Plureos GmbH
in Hamburg, Germany